CLOCKWORK PLANET

VIII

STORY BY YUU KAMIYA & TSUBAKI HIMANA
MANGA BY KURO
CHARACTER DESIGN BY SINO

ClockWork Planet
CONTENTS

VIII

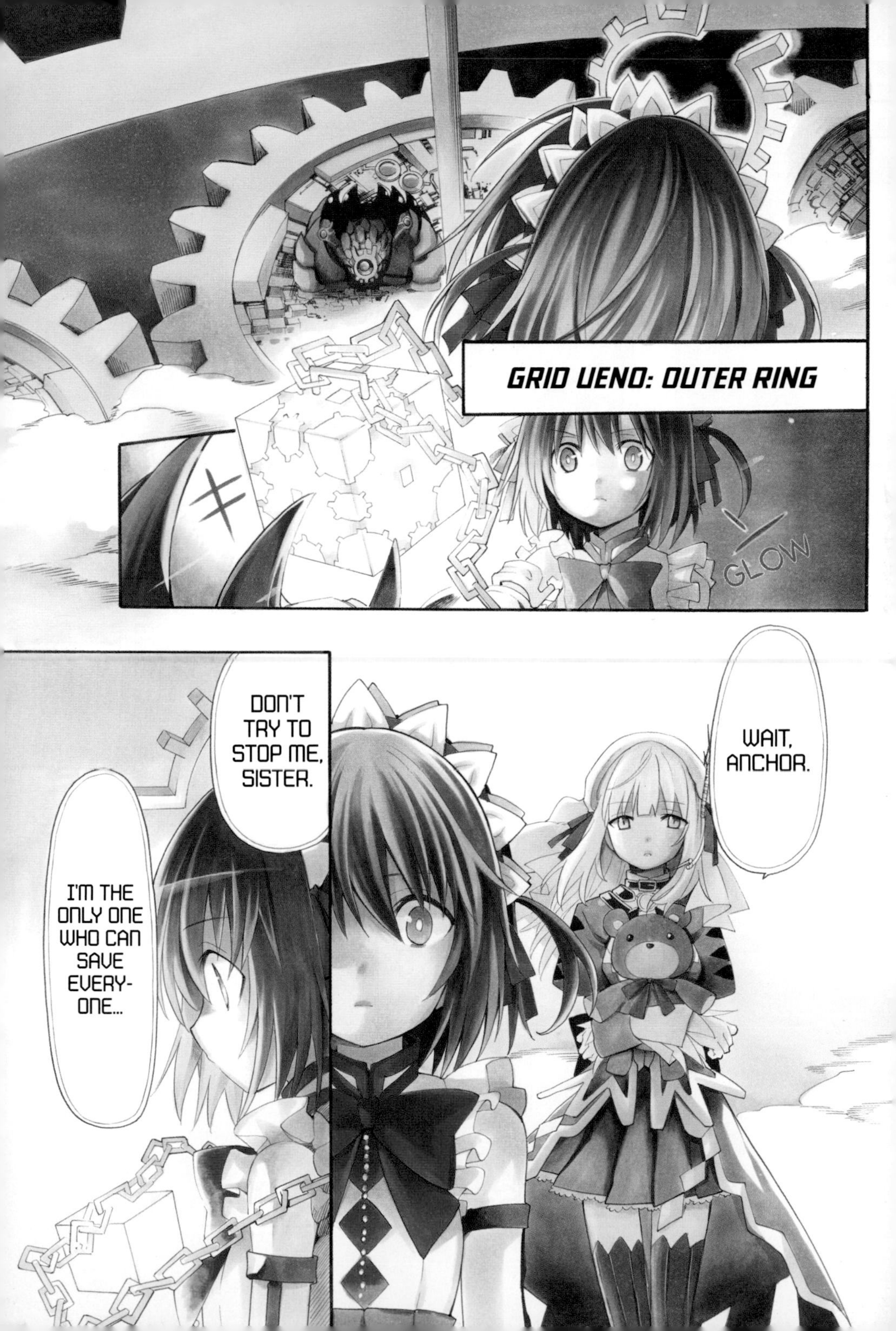
GRID UENO: OUTER RING
GLOW
WAIT, ANCHOR.
DON'T TRY TO STOP ME, SISTER.
I'M THE ONLY ONE WHO CAN SAVE EVERY-ONE...

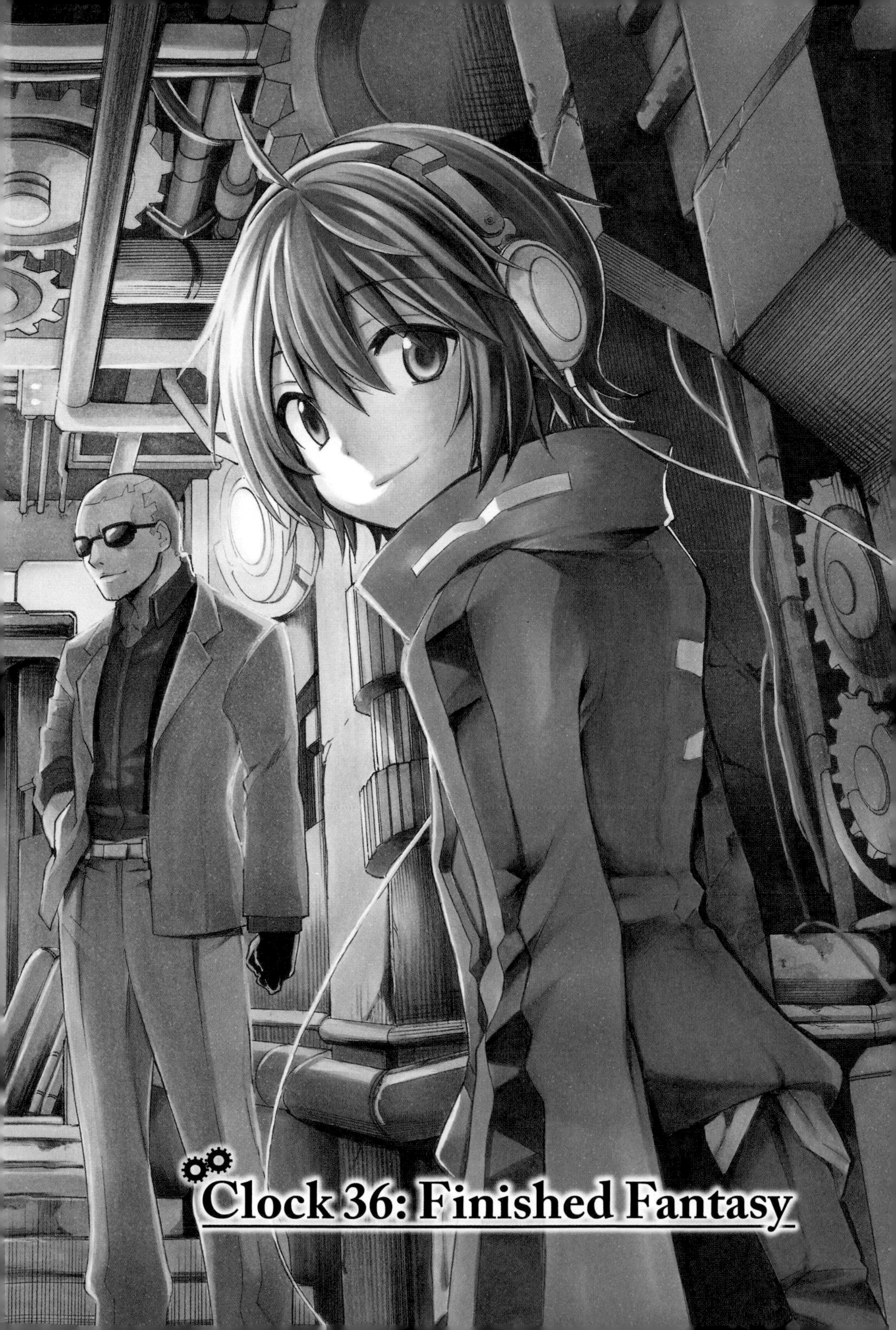
Clock 36: Finished Fantasy

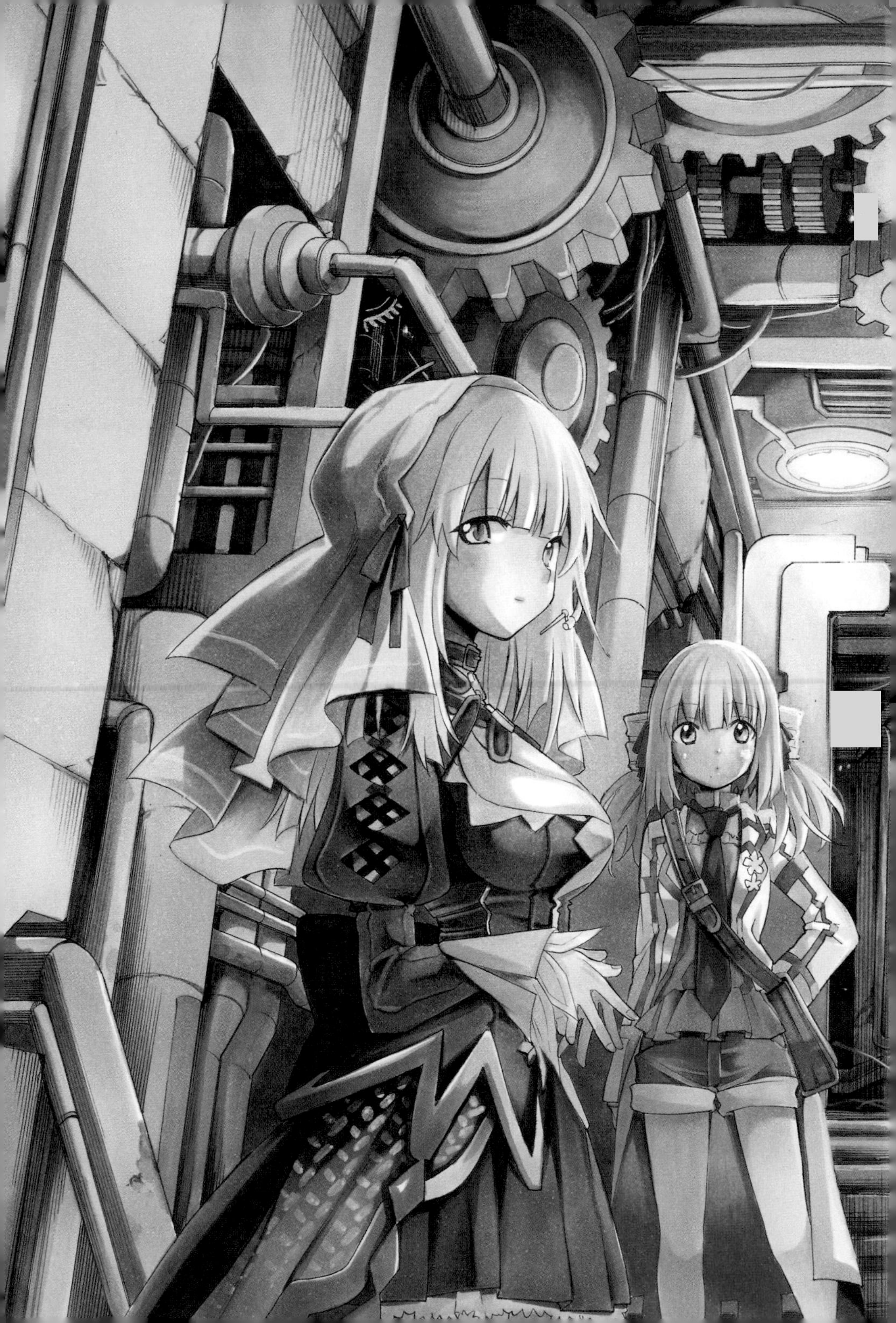

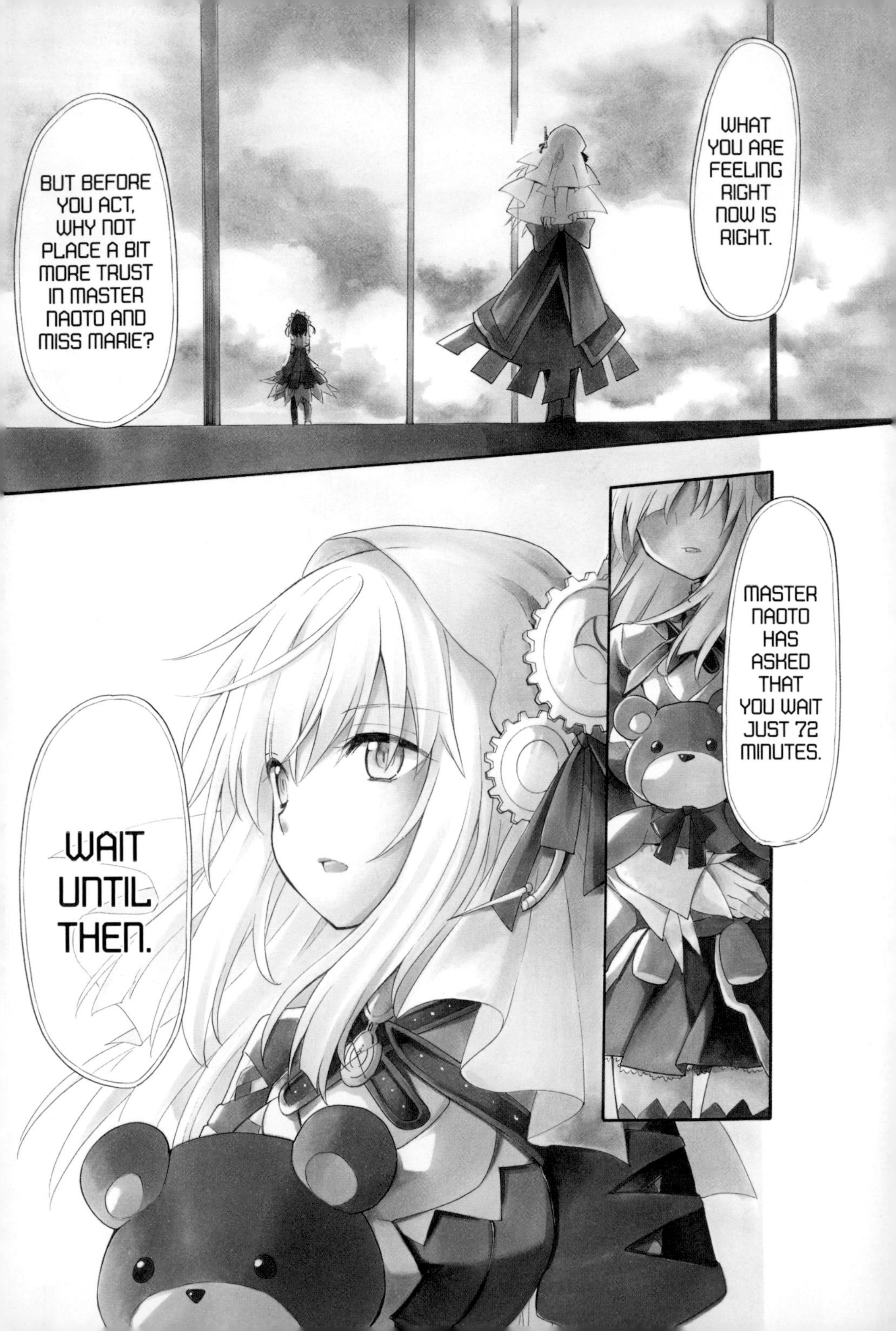
WHAT YOU ARE FEELING RIGHT NOW IS RIGHT.
BUT BEFORE YOU ACT, WHY NOT PLACE A BIT MORE TRUST IN MASTER NAOTO AND MISS MARIE?
MASTER NAOTO HAS ASKED THAT YOU WAIT JUST 72 MINUTES.
WAIT UNTIL THEN.

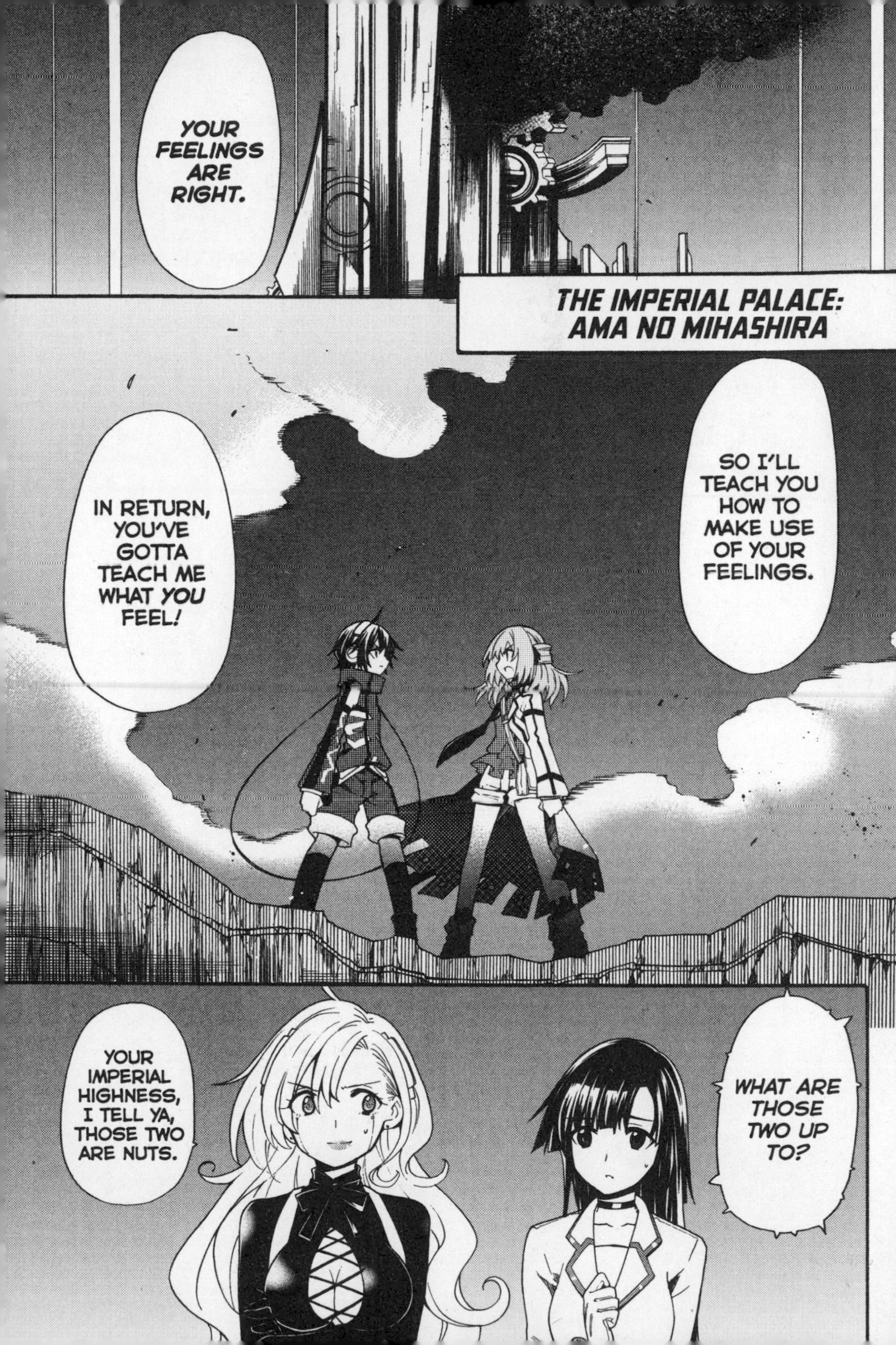
YOUR FEELINGS ARE RIGHT.
THE IMPERIAL PALACE: AMA NO MIHASHIRA
SO I'LL TEACH YOU HOW TO MAKE USE OF YOUR FEELINGS.
IN RETURN, YOU'VE GOTTA TEACH ME WHAT *YOU* FEEL!
WHAT ARE THOSE TWO UP TO?
YOUR IMPERIAL HIGHNESS, I TELL YA, THOSE TWO ARE NUTS.

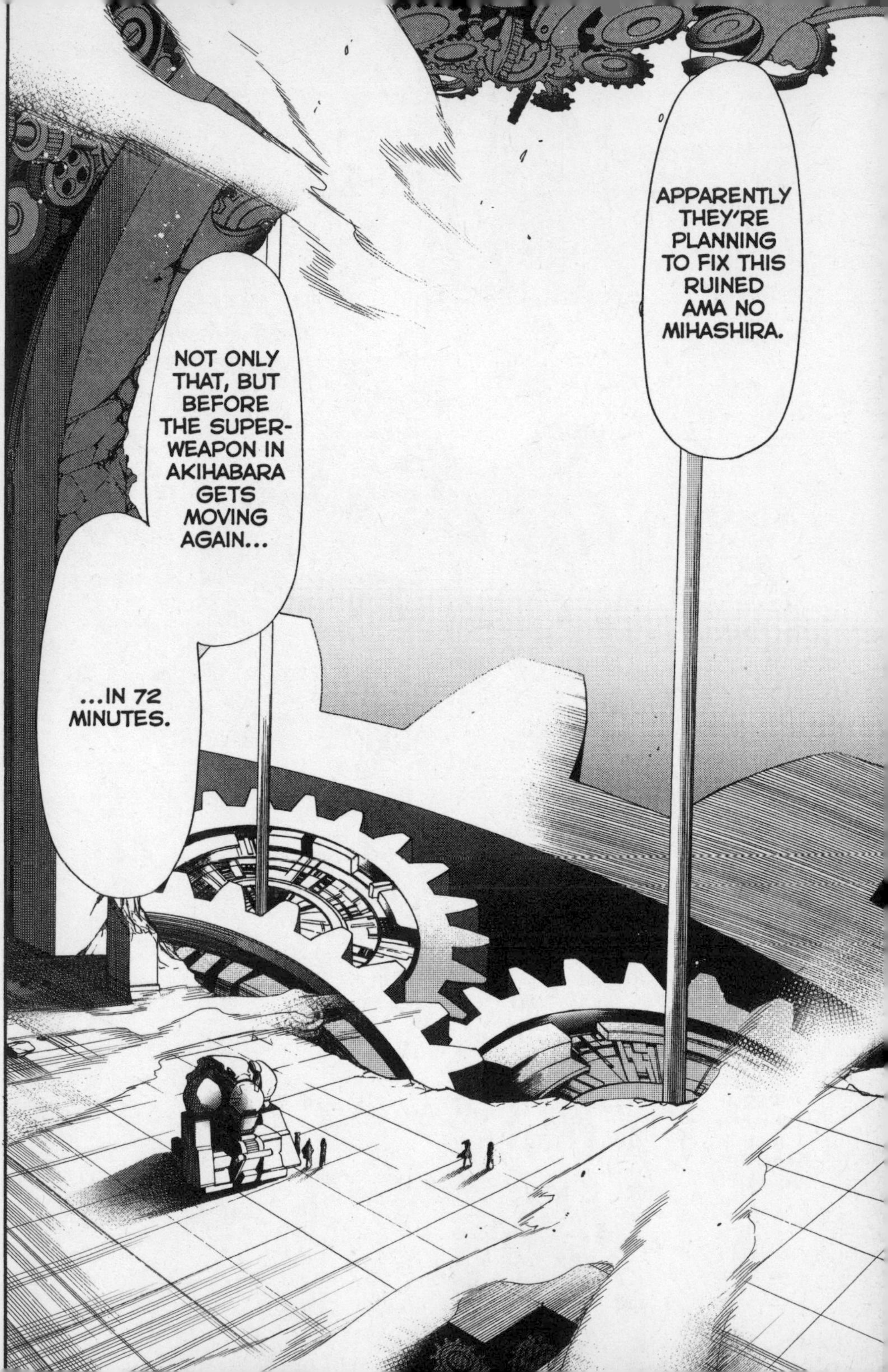
APPARENTLY THEY'RE PLANNING TO FIX THIS RUINED AMA NO MIHASHIRA.
NOT ONLY THAT, BUT BEFORE THE SUPER-WEAPON IN AKIHABARA GETS MOVING AGAIN...
...IN 72 MINUTES.

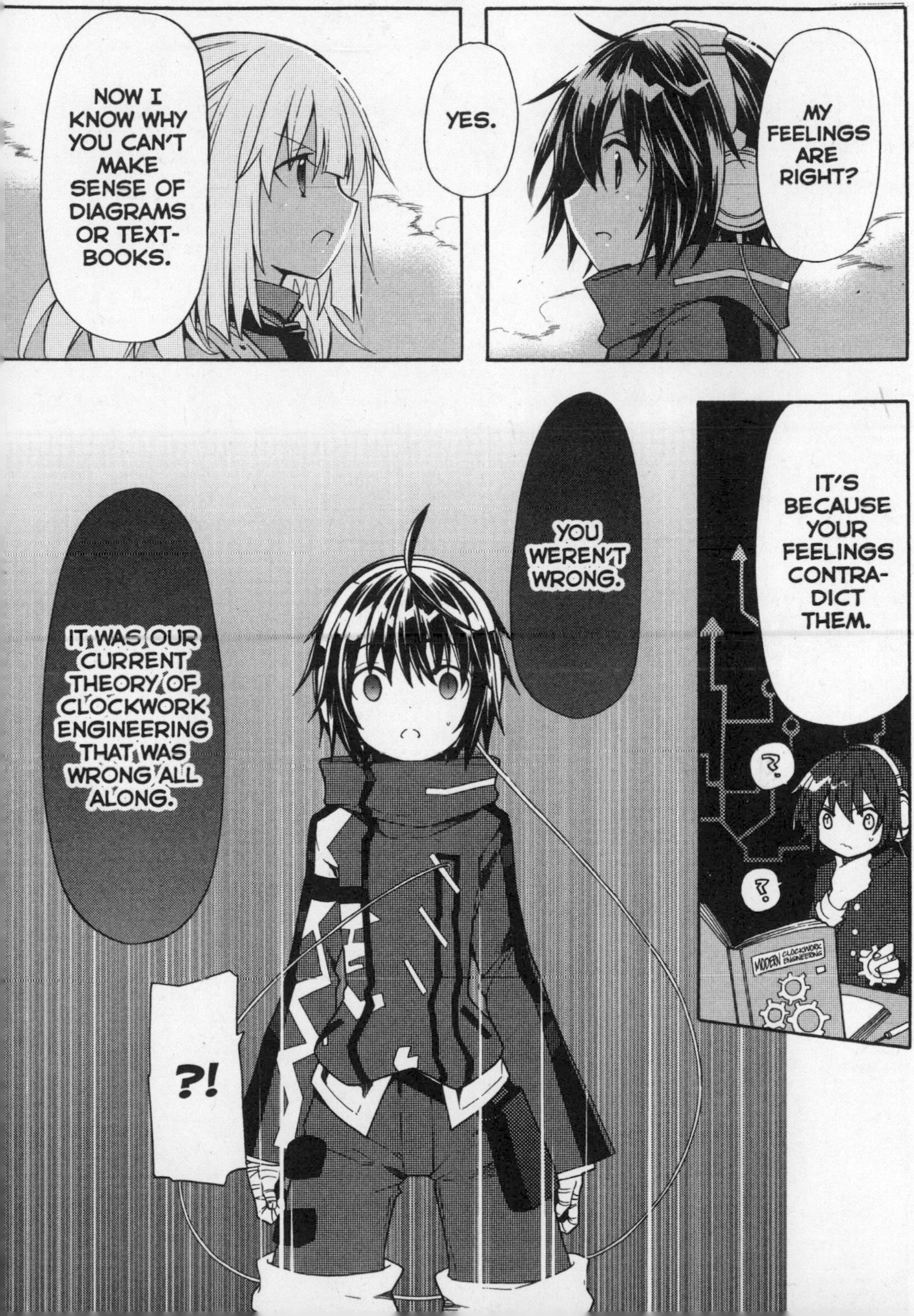
MY FEELINGS ARE RIGHT?
YES.
NOW I KNOW WHY YOU CAN'T MAKE SENSE OF DIAGRAMS OR TEXT-BOOKS.
IT'S BECAUSE YOUR FEELINGS CONTRA-DICT THEM.
?
?
MODERN CLOCKWORK ENGINEERING
YOU WEREN'T WRONG.
IT WAS OUR CURRENT THEORY OF CLOCKWORK ENGINEERING THAT WAS WRONG ALL ALONG.
?!

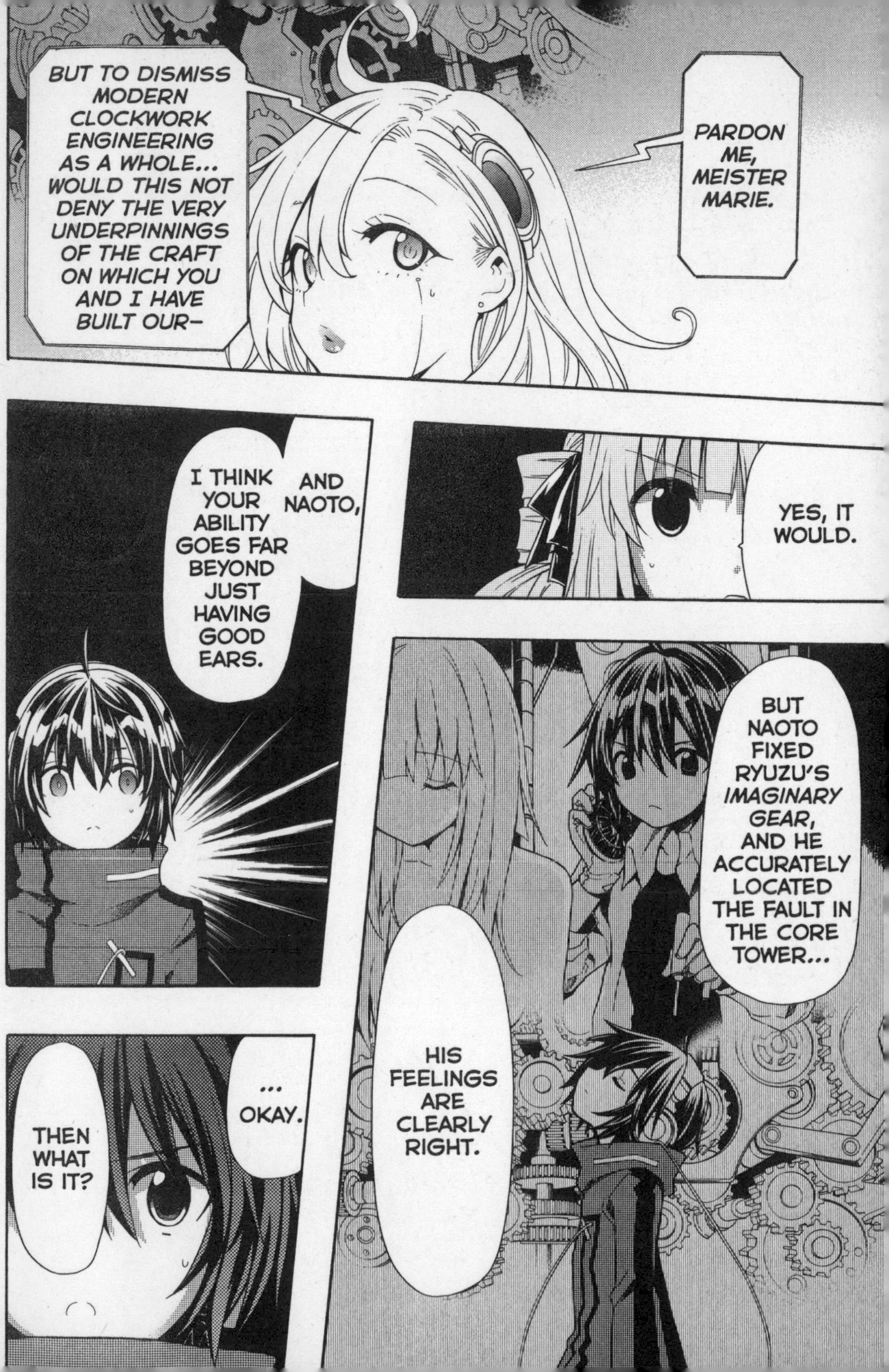
PARDON ME, MEISTER MARIE.
BUT TO DISMISS MODERN CLOCKWORK ENGINEERING AS A WHOLE... WOULD THIS NOT DENY THE VERY UNDERPINNINGS OF THE CRAFT ON WHICH YOU AND I HAVE BUILT OUR–
YES, IT WOULD.
AND NAOTO,
I THINK YOUR ABILITY GOES FAR BEYOND JUST HAVING GOOD EARS.
BUT NAOTO FIXED RYUZU'S *IMAGINARY GEAR,* AND HE ACCURATELY LOCATED THE FAULT IN THE CORE TOWER...
HIS FEELINGS ARE CLEARLY RIGHT.
...OKAY.
THEN WHAT IS IT?

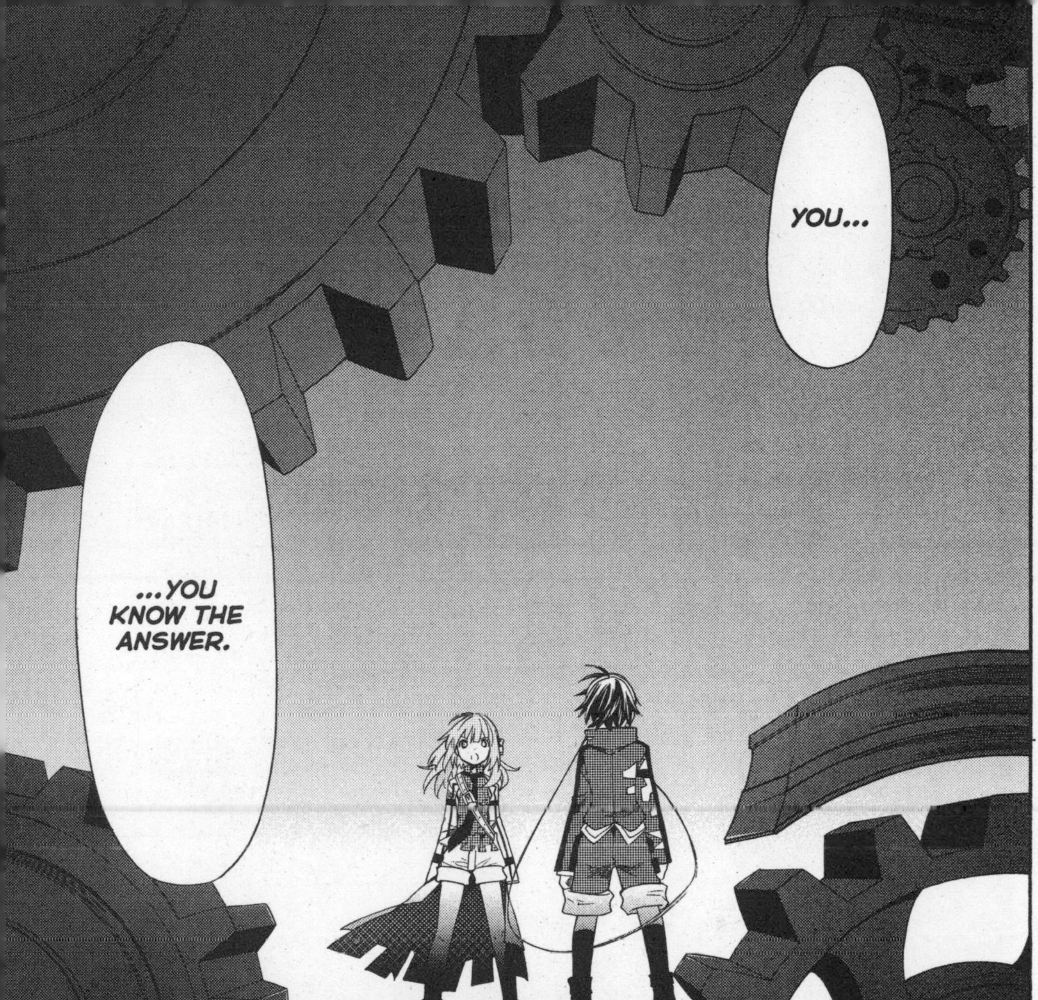
YOU...
...YOU KNOW THE ANSWER.

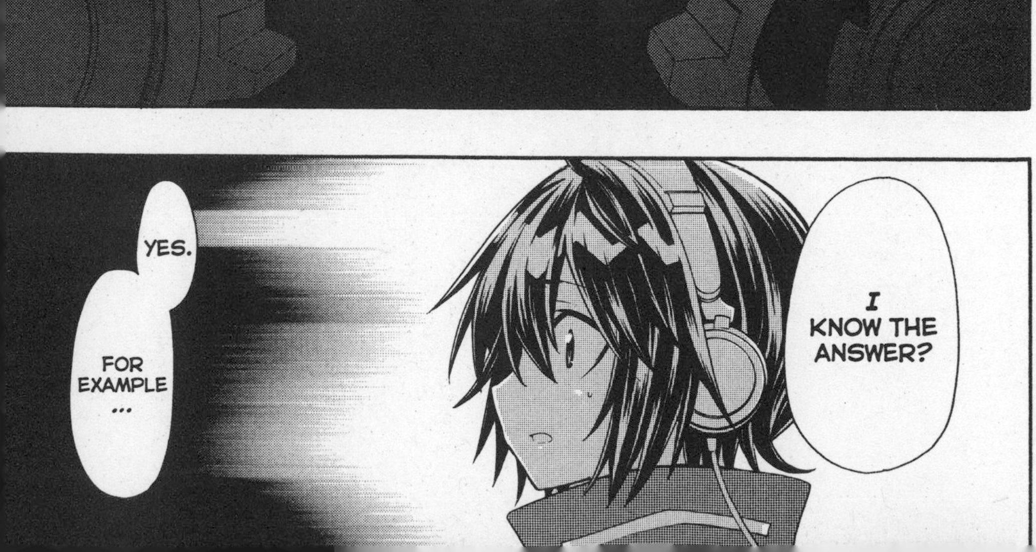
I KNOW THE ANSWER?
YES.
FOR EXAMPLE ...

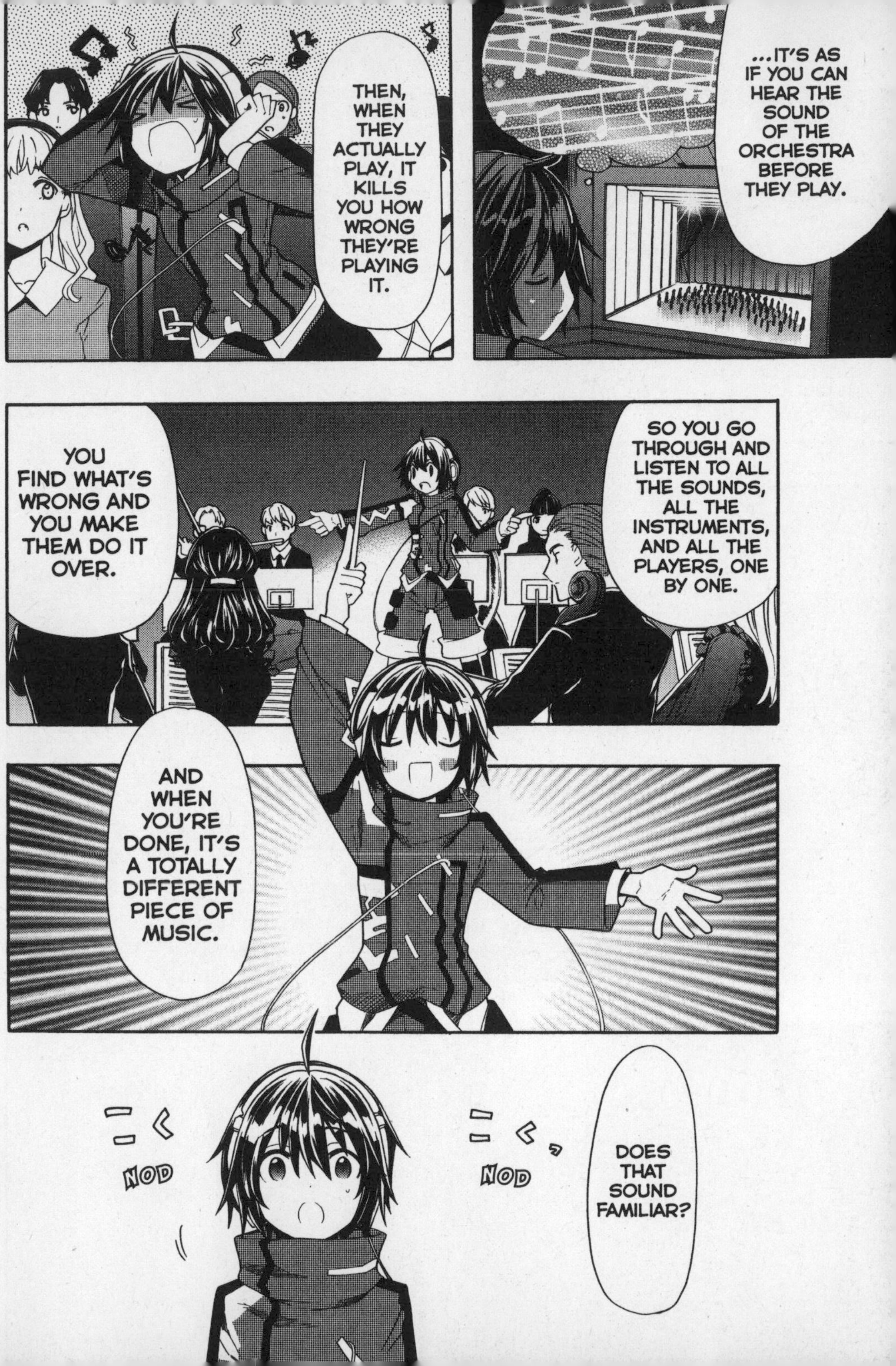
...IT'S AS IF YOU CAN HEAR THE SOUND OF THE ORCHESTRA BEFORE THEY PLAY.
THEN, WHEN THEY ACTUALLY PLAY, IT KILLS YOU HOW WRONG THEY'RE PLAYING IT.
SO YOU GO THROUGH AND LISTEN TO ALL THE SOUNDS, ALL THE INSTRUMENTS, AND ALL THE PLAYERS, ONE BY ONE.
YOU FIND WHAT'S WRONG AND YOU MAKE THEM DO IT OVER.
AND WHEN YOU'RE DONE, IT'S A TOTALLY DIFFERENT PIECE OF MUSIC.
DOES THAT SOUND FAMILIAR?
NOD
NOD

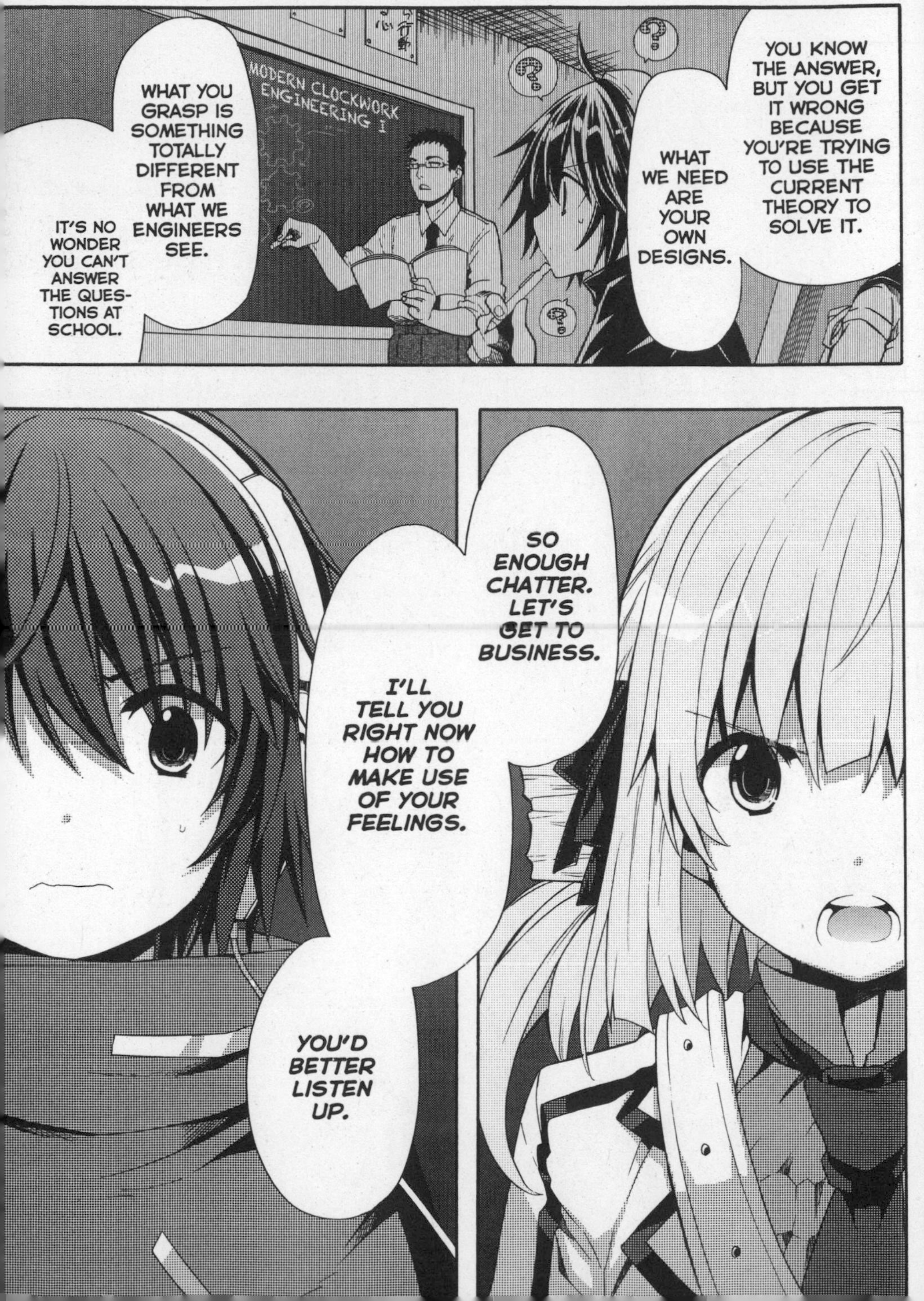
YOU KNOW THE ANSWER, BUT YOU GET IT WRONG BECAUSE YOU'RE TRYING TO USE THE CURRENT THEORY TO SOLVE IT.
WHAT WE NEED ARE YOUR OWN DESIGNS.
MODERN CLOCKWORK ENGINEERING I
WHAT YOU GRASP IS SOMETHING TOTALLY DIFFERENT FROM WHAT WE ENGINEERS SEE.
IT'S NO WONDER YOU CAN'T ANSWER THE QUESTIONS AT SCHOOL.
SO ENOUGH CHATTER. LET'S GET TO BUSINESS.
I'LL TELL YOU RIGHT NOW HOW TO MAKE USE OF YOUR FEELINGS.
YOU'D BETTER LISTEN UP.

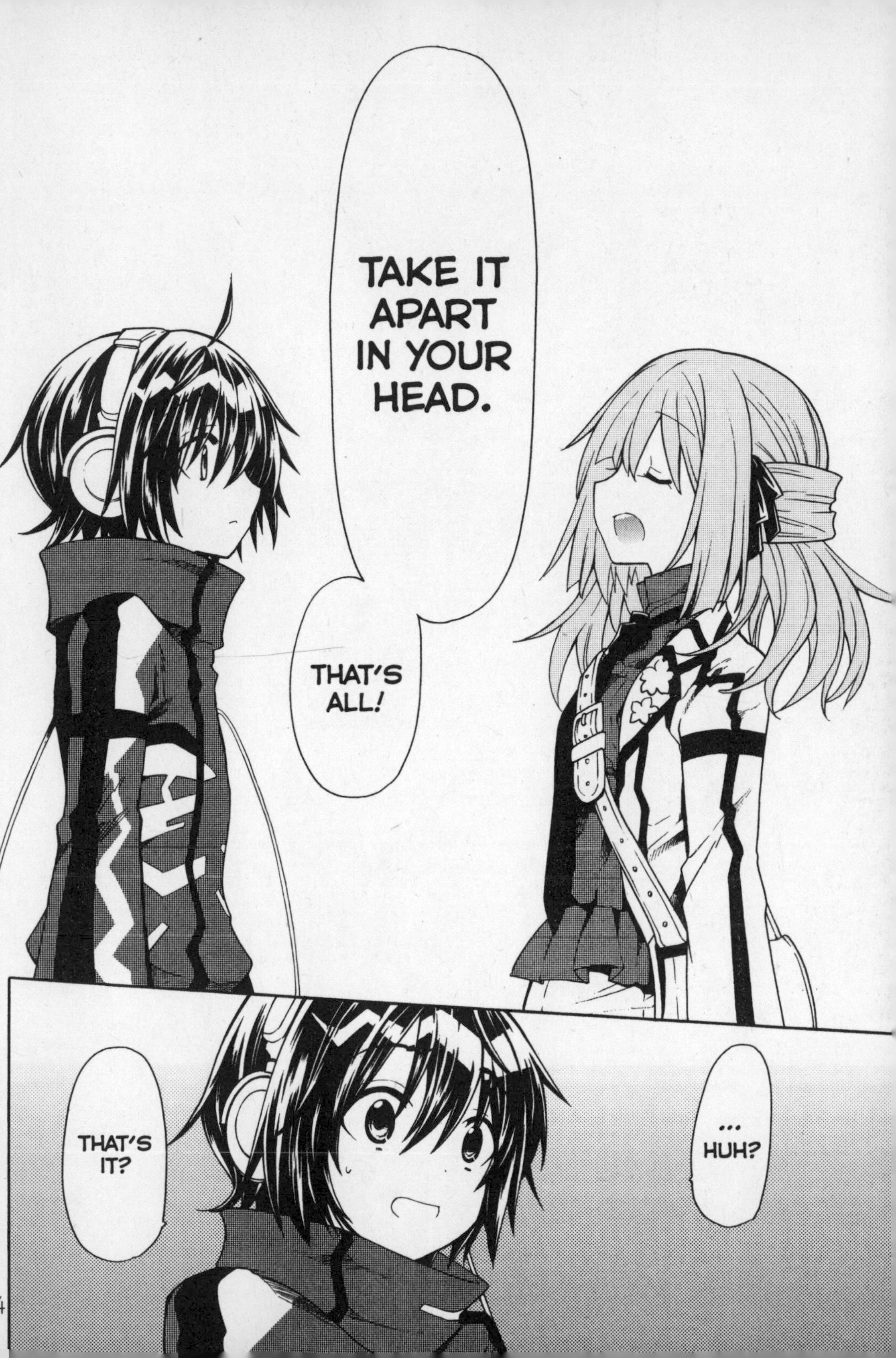
TAKE IT APART IN YOUR HEAD.
THAT'S ALL!
... HUH?
THAT'S IT?

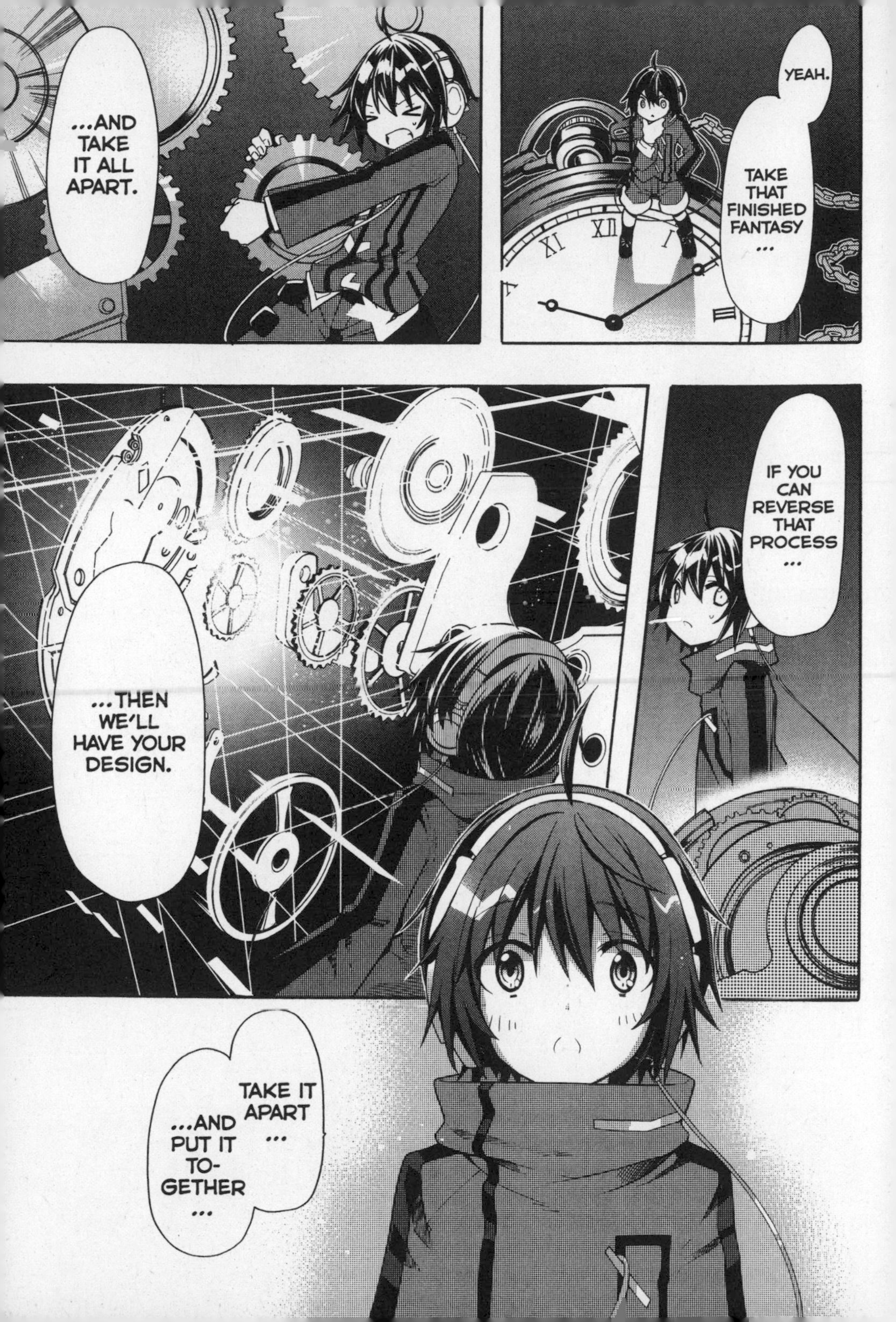
YEAH.
TAKE THAT FINISHED FANTASY ...
...AND TAKE IT ALL APART.
IF YOU CAN REVERSE THAT PROCESS ...
...THEN WE'LL HAVE YOUR DESIGN.
TAKE IT APART ...
...AND PUT IT TO-GETHER ...

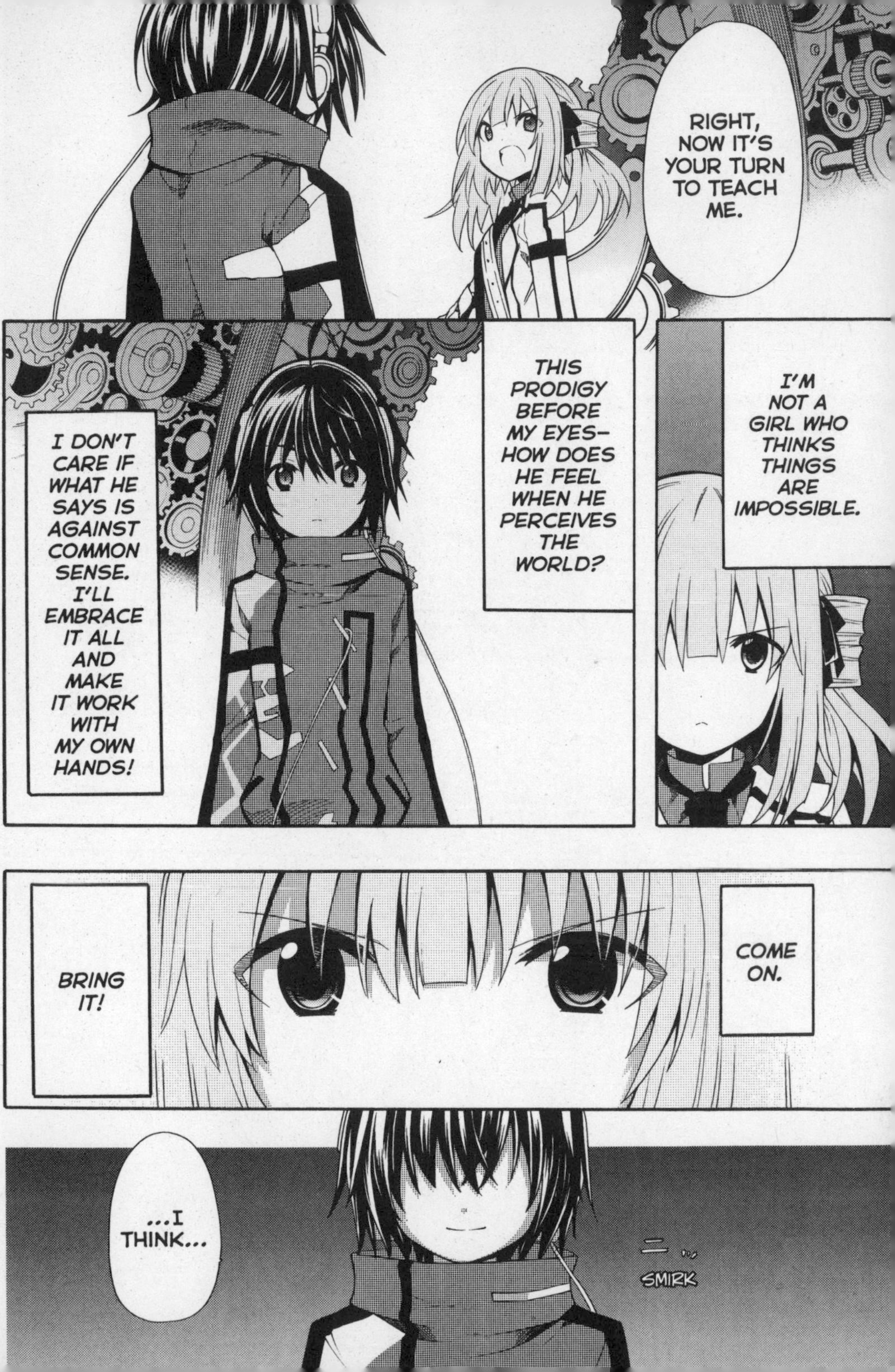
RIGHT, NOW IT'S YOUR TURN TO TEACH ME.
I'M NOT A GIRL WHO THINKS THINGS ARE IMPOSSIBLE.
THIS PRODIGY BEFORE MY EYES—HOW DOES HE FEEL WHEN HE PERCEIVES THE WORLD?
I DON'T CARE IF WHAT HE SAYS IS AGAINST COMMON SENSE. I'LL EMBRACE IT ALL AND MAKE IT WORK WITH MY OWN HANDS!
COME ON.
BRING IT!
...I THINK...
SMIRK

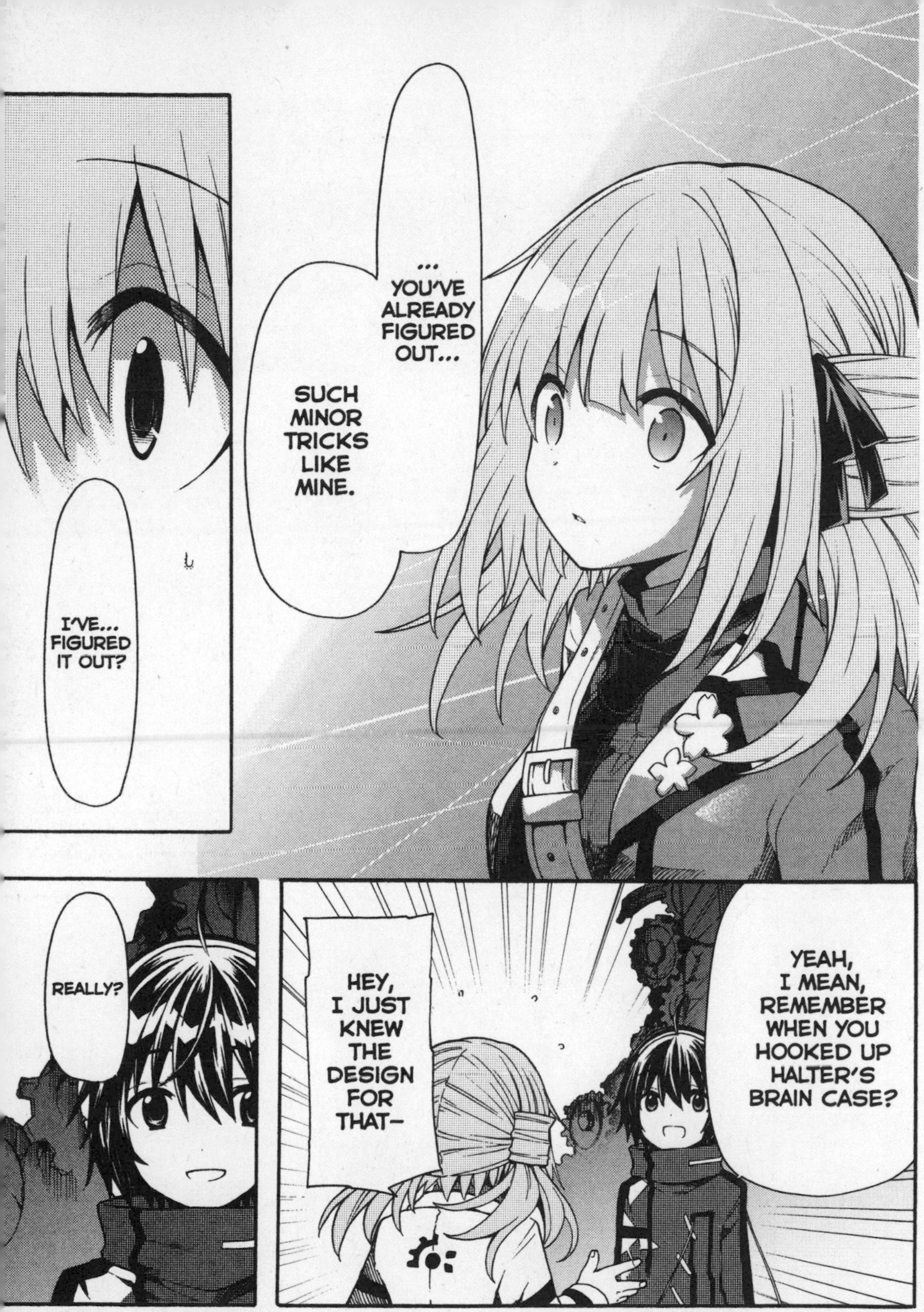
... YOU'VE ALREADY FIGURED OUT...
SUCH MINOR TRICKS LIKE MINE.
I'VE... FIGURED IT OUT?
YEAH, I MEAN, REMEMBER WHEN YOU HOOKED UP HALTER'S BRAIN CASE?
HEY, I JUST KNEW THE DESIGN FOR THAT-
REALLY?

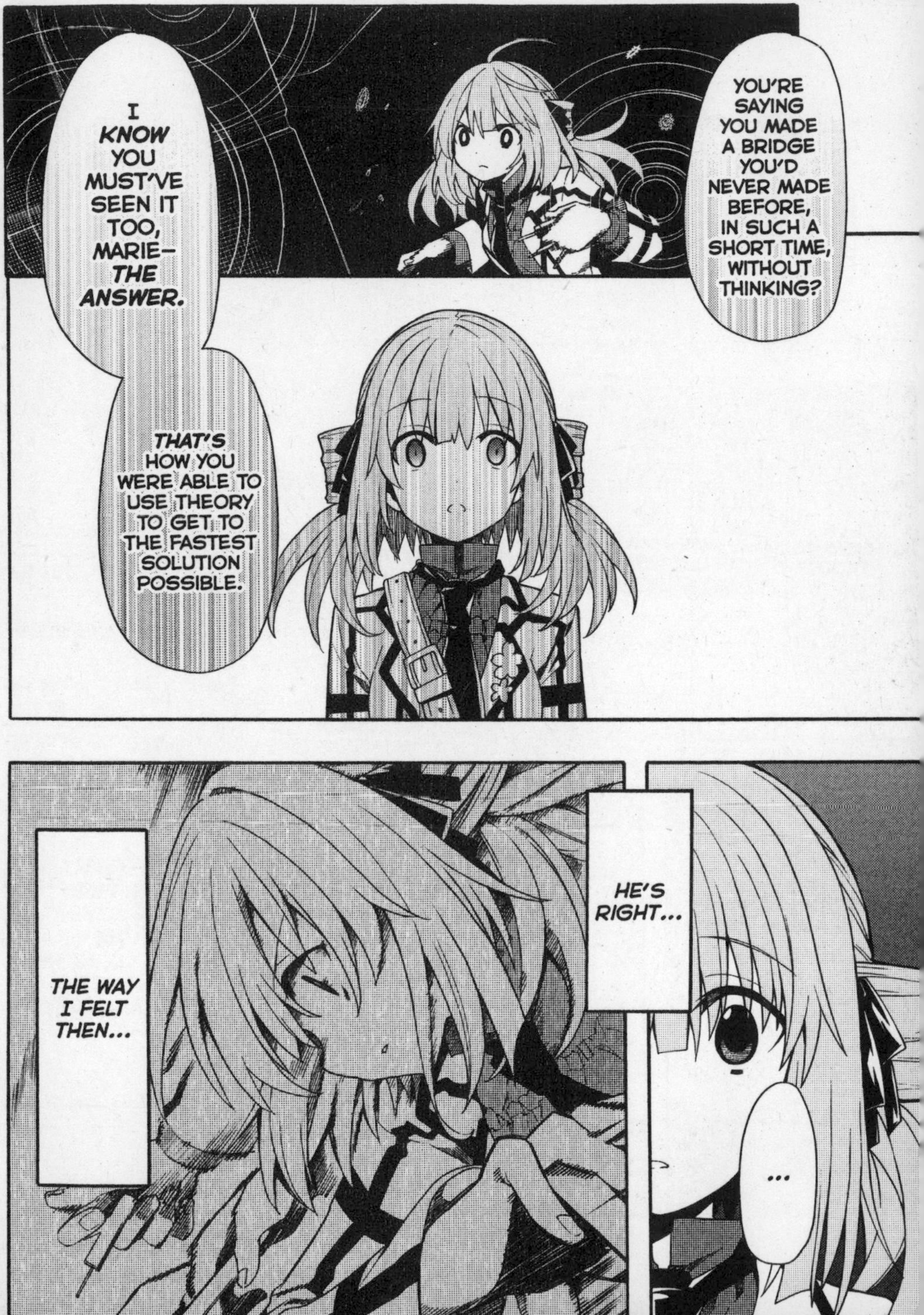
YOU'RE SAYING YOU MADE A BRIDGE YOU'D NEVER MADE BEFORE, IN SUCH A SHORT TIME, WITHOUT THINKING?
I KNOW YOU MUST'VE SEEN IT TOO, MARIE— THE ANSWER.
THAT'S HOW YOU WERE ABLE TO USE THEORY TO GET TO THE FASTEST SOLUTION POSSIBLE.
HE'S RIGHT...
...
THE WAY I FELT THEN...

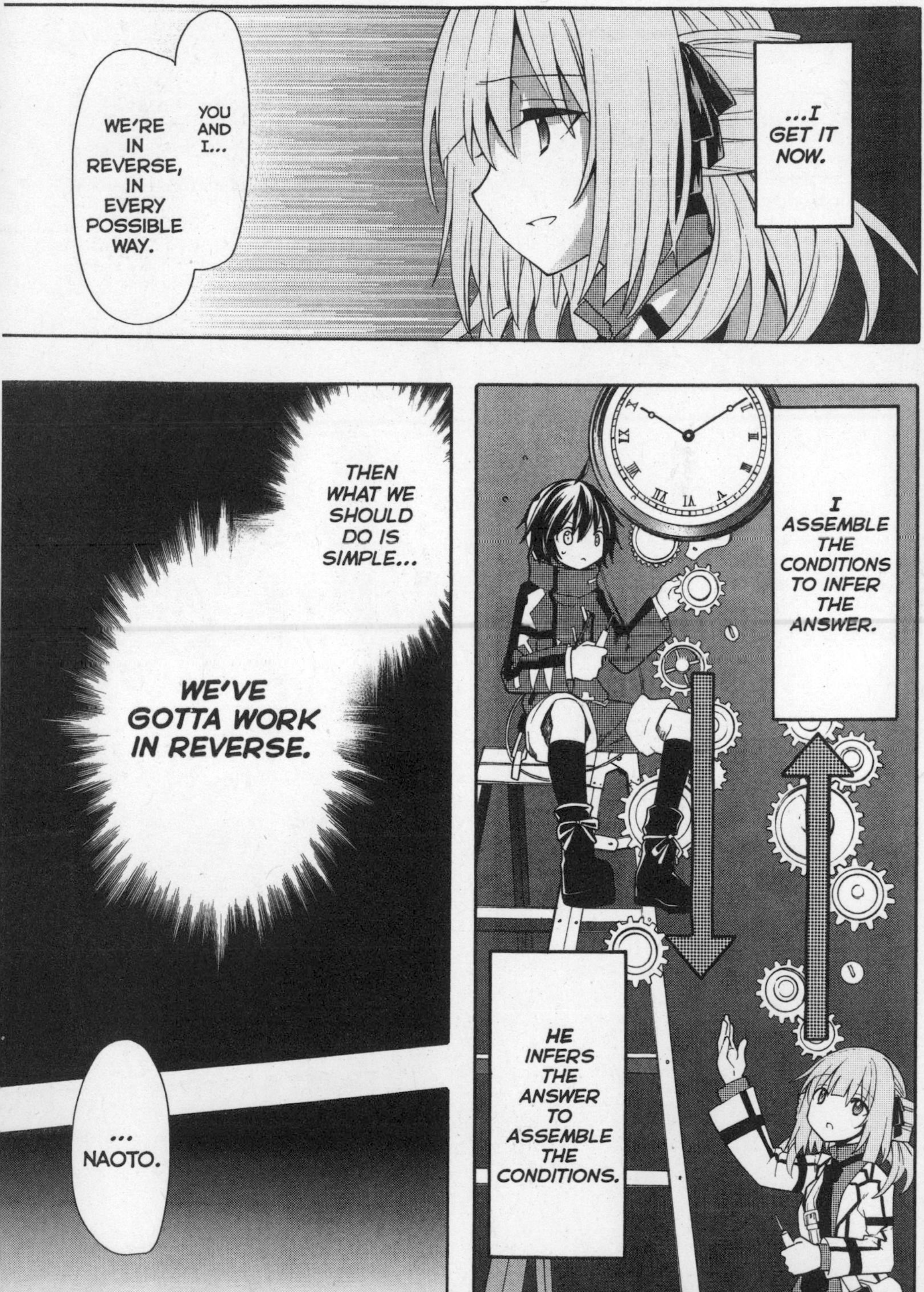

...I GET IT NOW.
YOU AND I...
WE'RE IN REVERSE, IN EVERY POSSIBLE WAY.
I ASSEMBLE THE CONDITIONS TO INFER THE ANSWER.
HE INFERS THE ANSWER TO ASSEMBLE THE CONDITIONS.
THEN WHAT WE SHOULD DO IS SIMPLE...
WE'VE GOTTA WORK IN REVERSE.
... NAOTO.

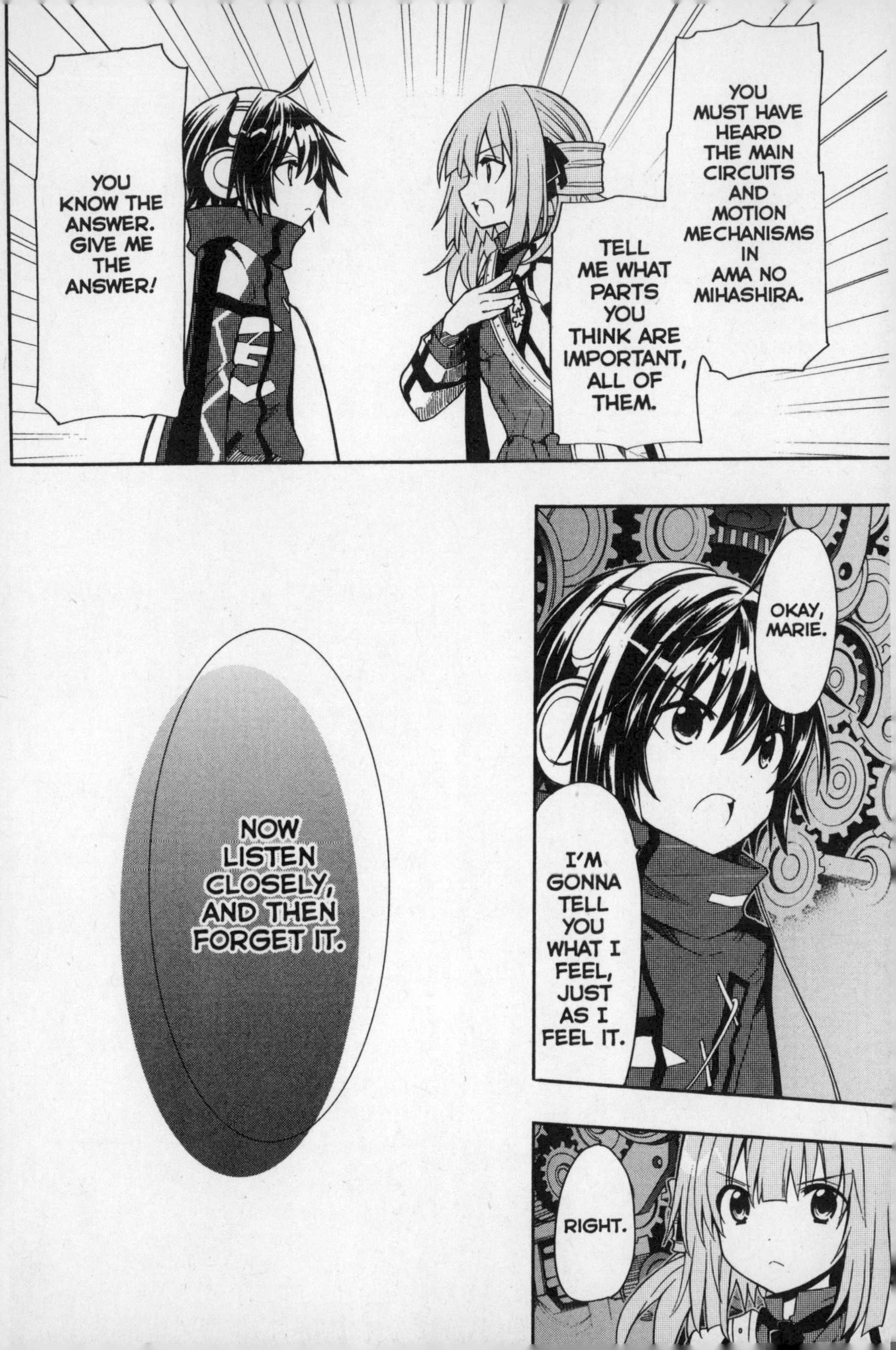
YOU MUST HAVE HEARD THE MAIN CIRCUITS AND MOTION MECHANISMS IN AMA NO MIHASHIRA.
TELL ME WHAT PARTS YOU THINK ARE IMPORTANT, ALL OF THEM.
YOU KNOW THE ANSWER. GIVE ME THE ANSWER!
OKAY, MARIE.
I'M GONNA TELL YOU WHAT I FEEL, JUST AS I FEEL IT.
RIGHT.
NOW LISTEN CLOSELY, AND THEN FORGET IT.

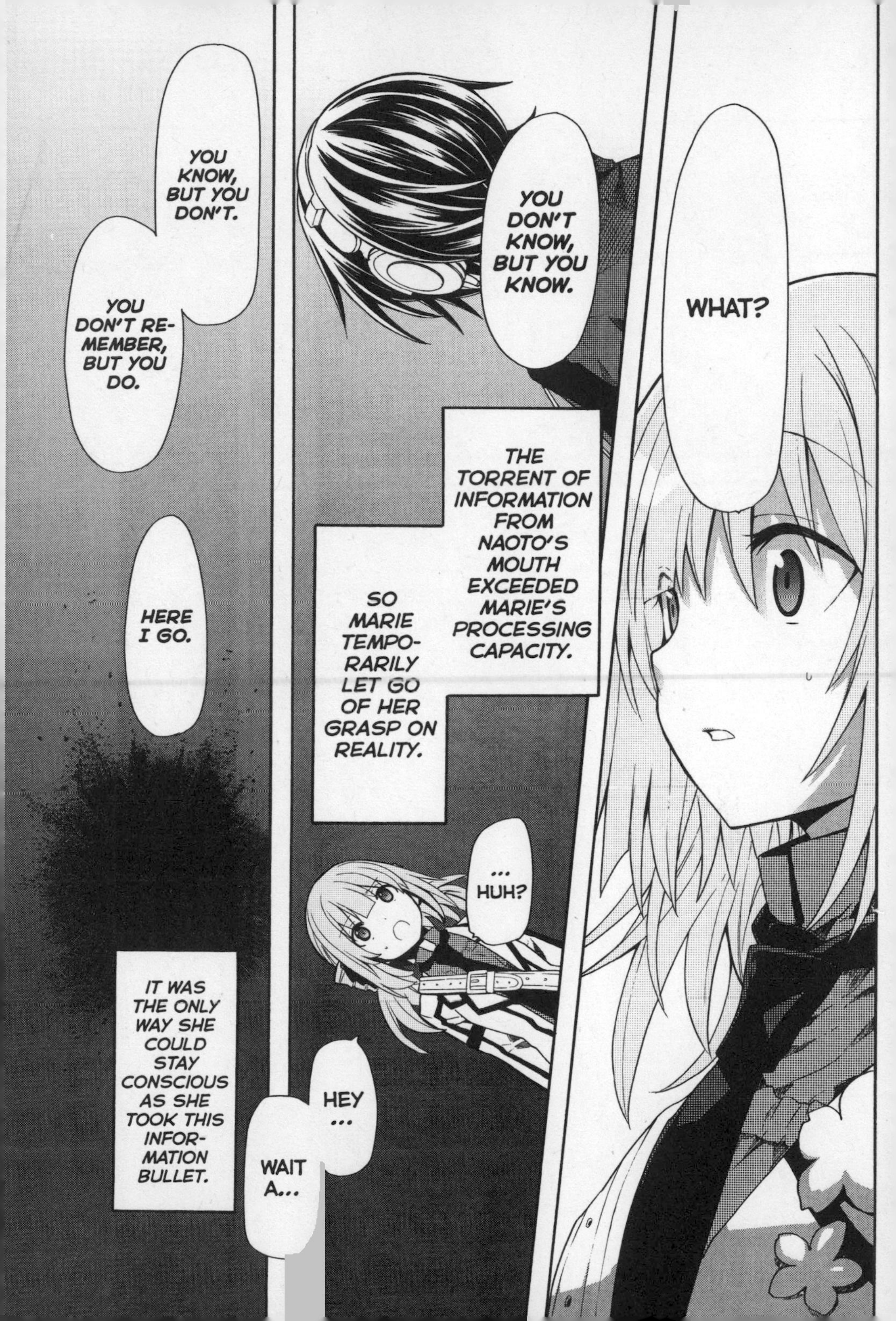
WHAT?
YOU DON'T KNOW, BUT YOU KNOW.
THE TORRENT OF INFORMATION FROM NAOTO'S MOUTH EXCEEDED MARIE'S PROCESSING CAPACITY.
SO MARIE TEMPORARILY LET GO OF HER GRASP ON REALITY.
... HUH?
HEY ...
WAIT A...
YOU KNOW, BUT YOU DON'T.
YOU DON'T REMEMBER, BUT YOU DO.
HERE I GO.
IT WAS THE ONLY WAY SHE COULD STAY CONSCIOUS AS SHE TOOK THIS INFORMATION BULLET.

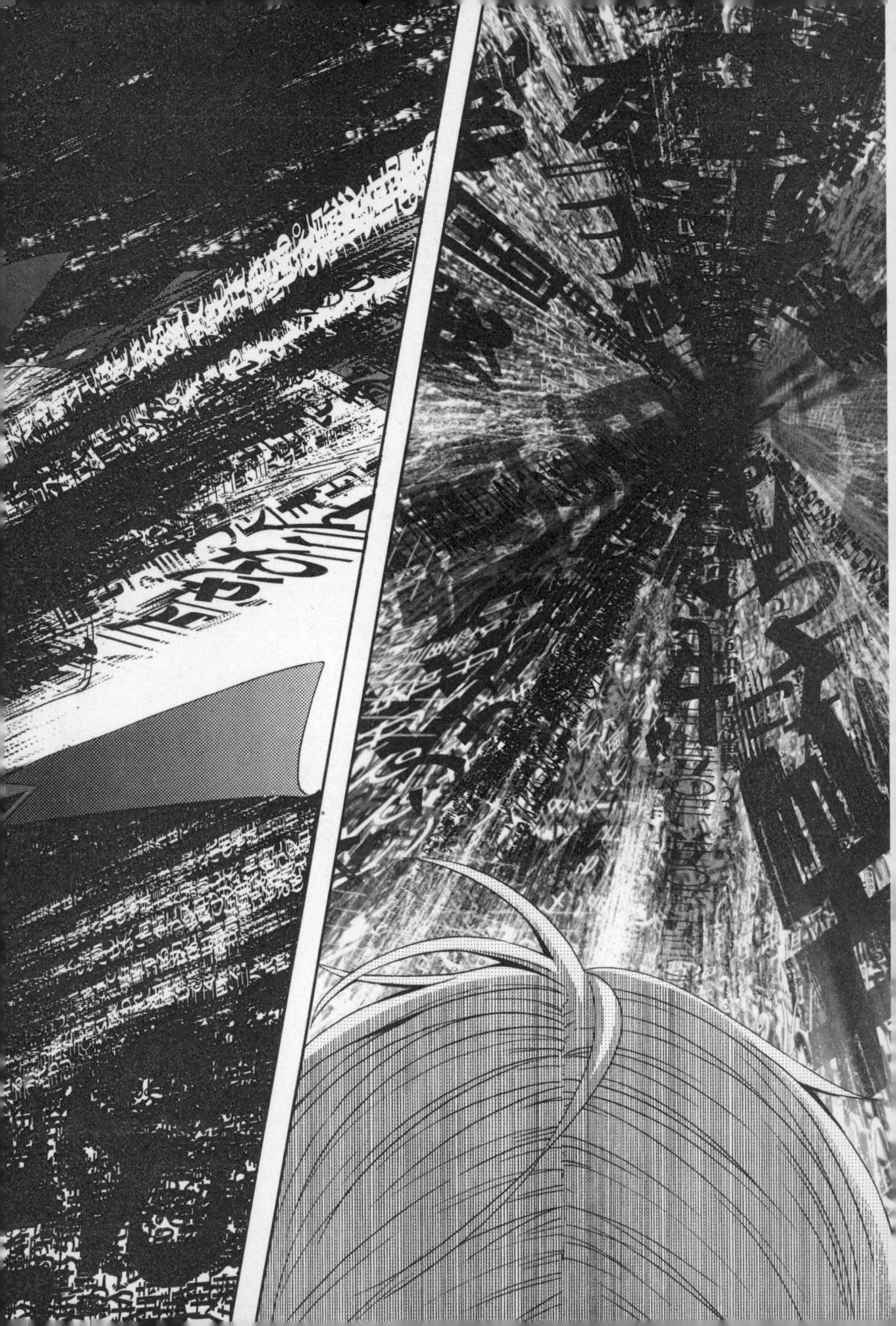

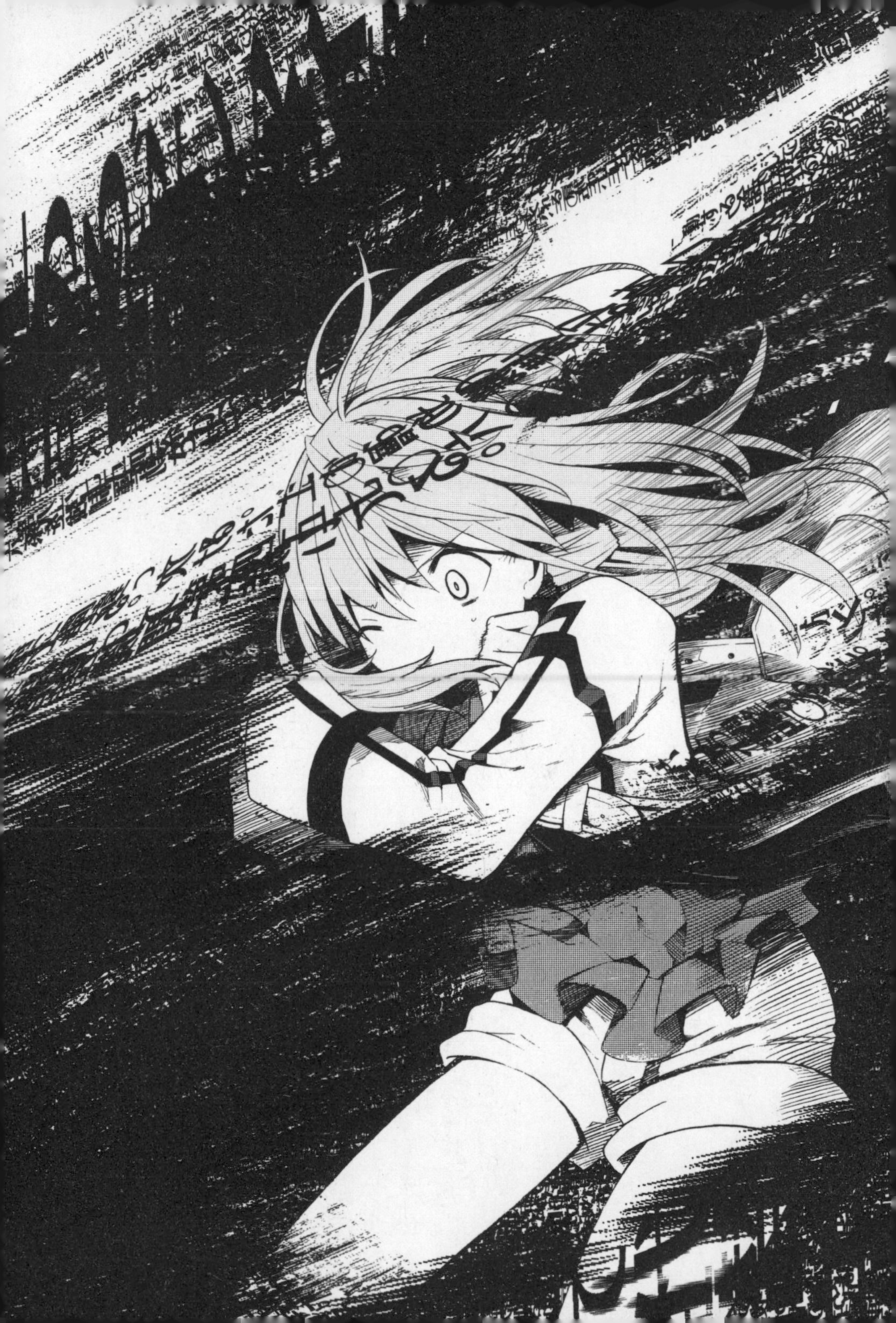

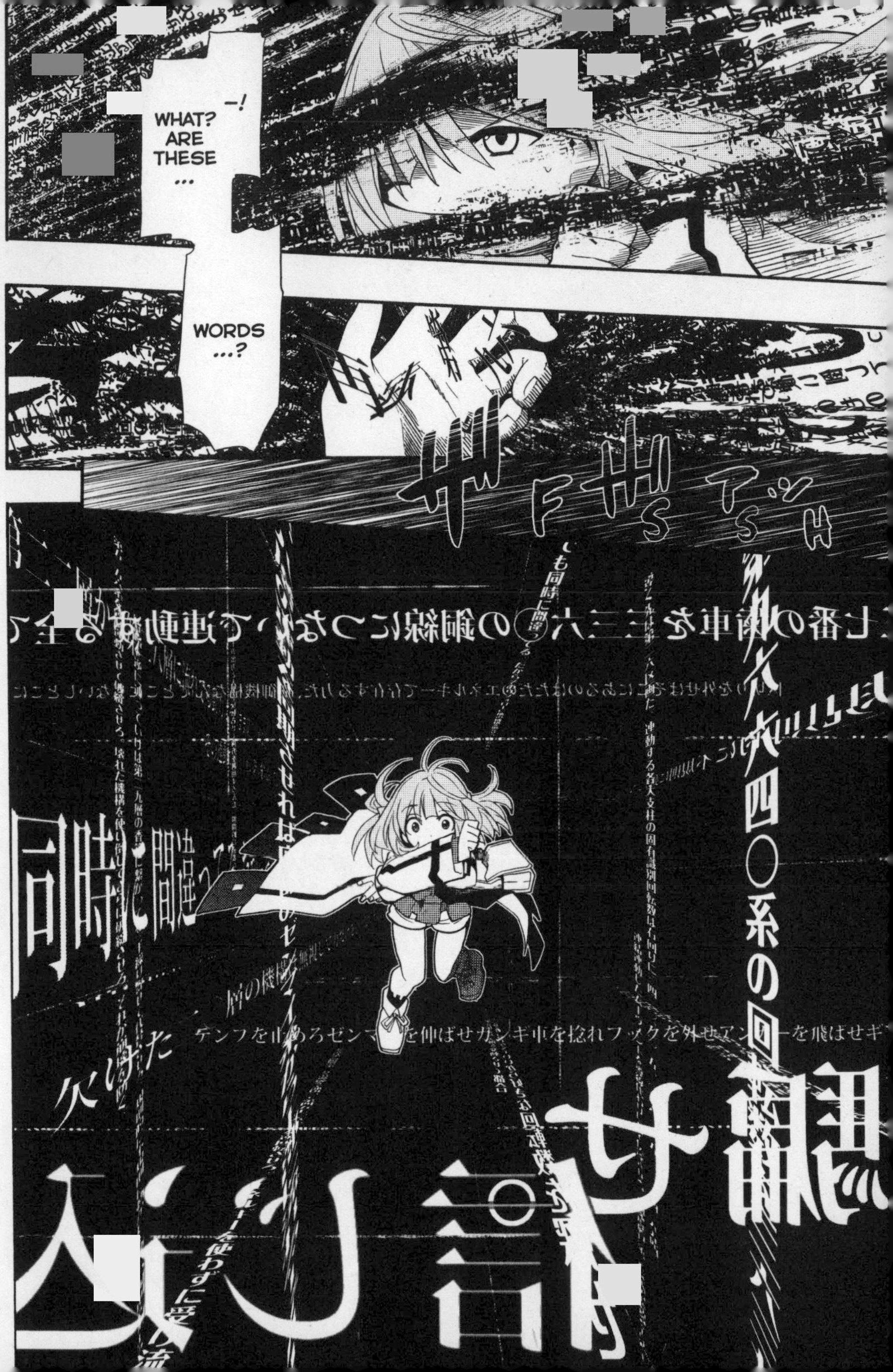
—!
WHAT? ARE THESE ...
WORDS ...?
FSSH

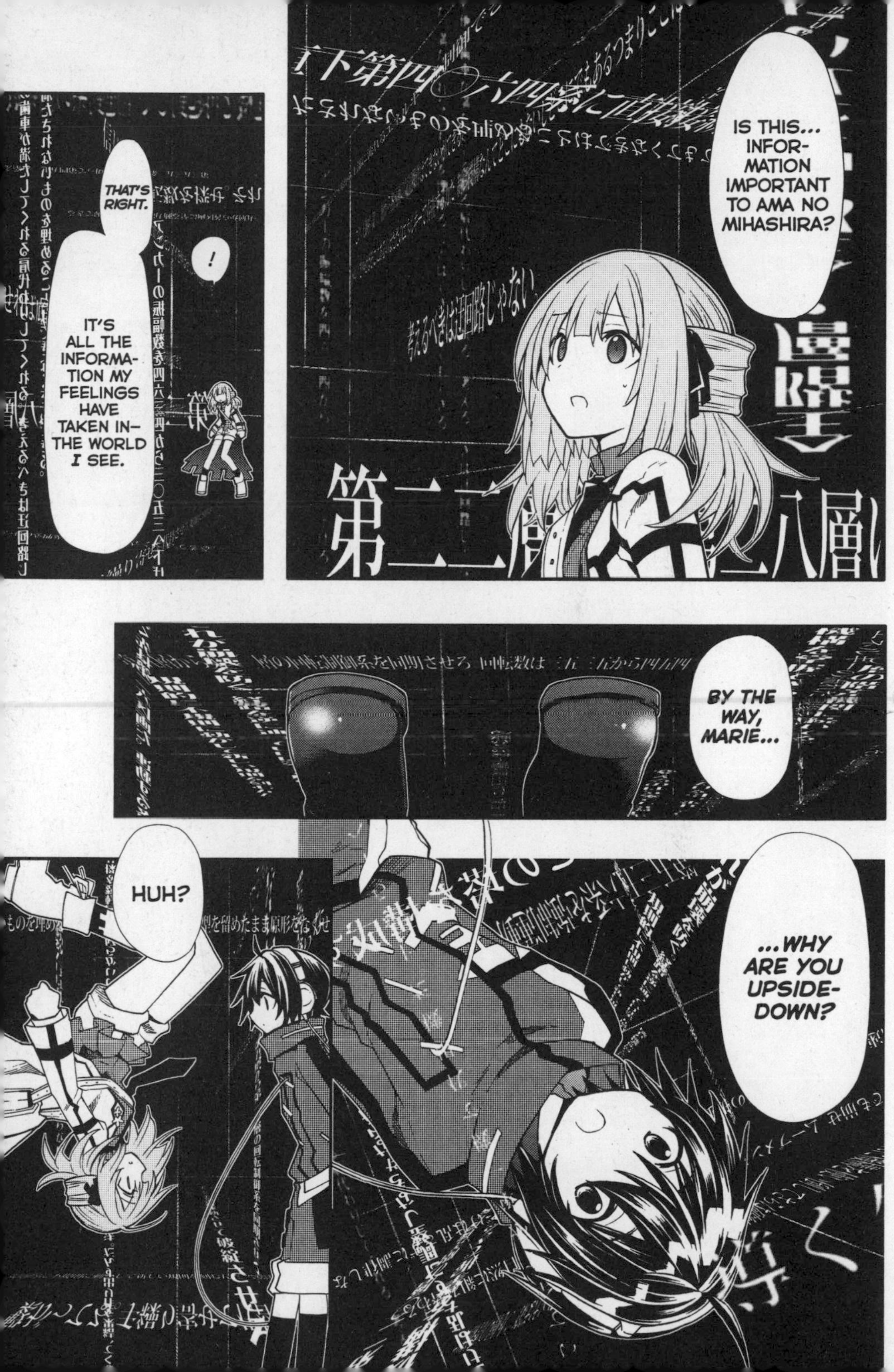
IS THIS... INFOR-MATION IMPORTANT TO AMA NO MIHASHIRA?
THAT'S RIGHT.
!
IT'S ALL THE INFORMA-TION MY FEELINGS HAVE TAKEN IN—THE WORLD I SEE.
BY THE WAY, MARIE...
...WHY ARE YOU UPSIDE-DOWN?
HUH?

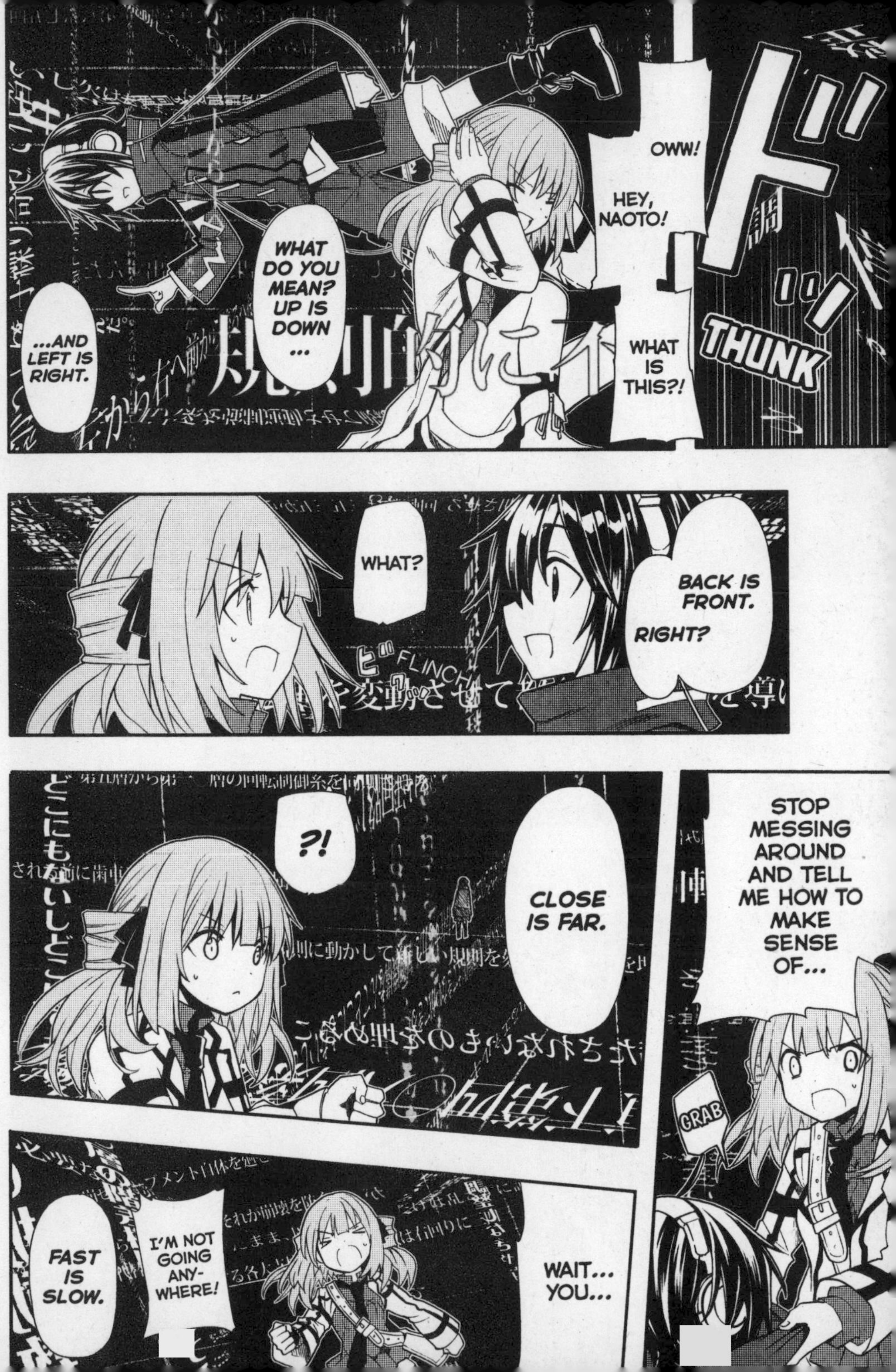
THUNK
OWW!
HEY, NAOTO!
WHAT IS THIS?!
WHAT DO YOU MEAN? UP IS DOWN ...
...AND LEFT IS RIGHT.
BACK IS FRONT.
RIGHT?
WHAT?
FLINCH
STOP MESSING AROUND AND TELL ME HOW TO MAKE SENSE OF...
GRAB
CLOSE IS FAR.
?!
WAIT... YOU...
I'M NOT GOING ANY-WHERE!
FAST IS SLOW.

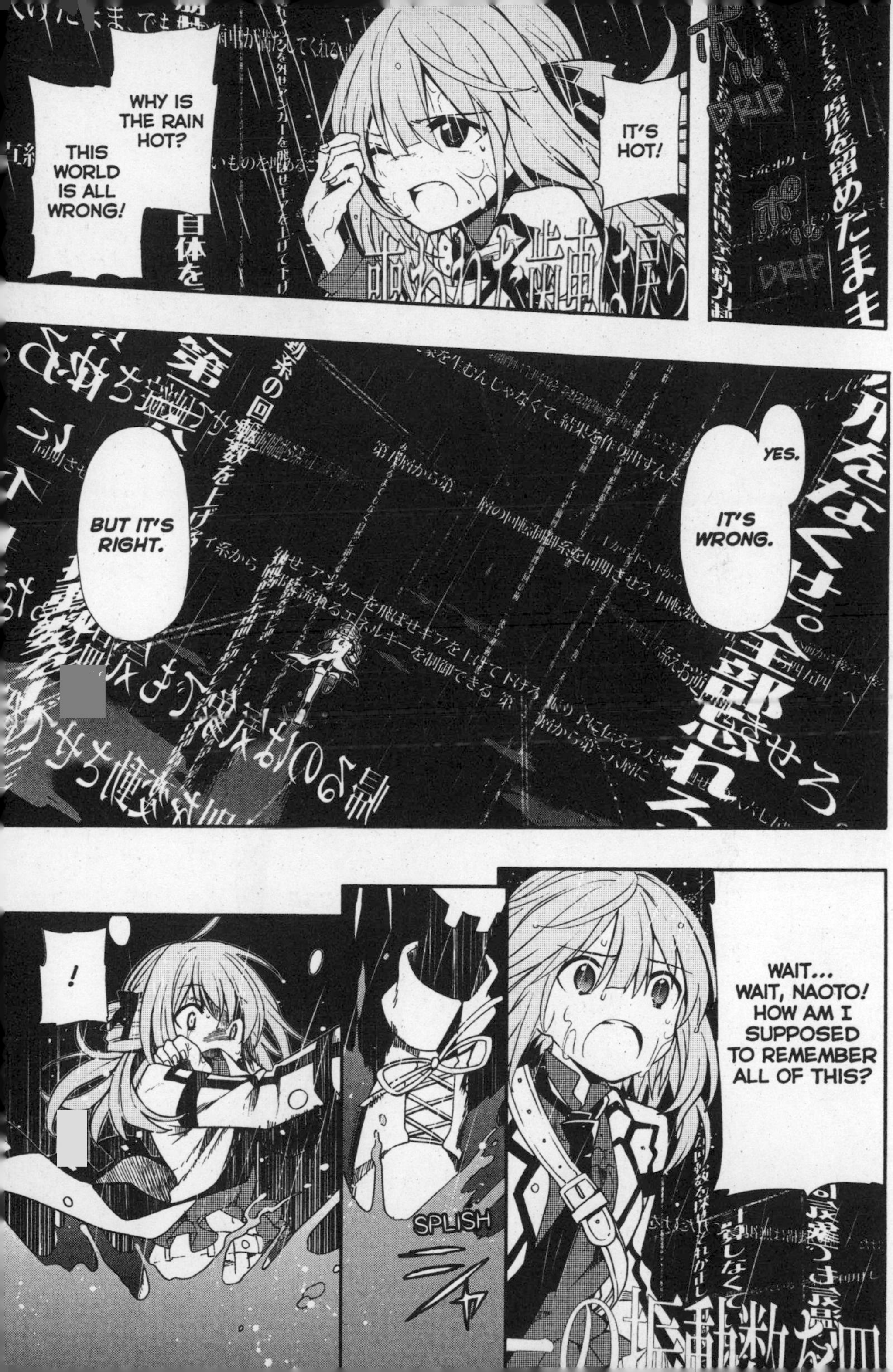
DRIP
DRIP
IT'S HOT!
WHY IS THE RAIN HOT?
THIS WORLD IS ALL WRONG!
YES.
IT'S WRONG.
BUT IT'S RIGHT.
WAIT... WAIT, NAOTO! HOW AM I SUPPOSED TO REMEMBER ALL OF THIS?
SPLISH
!

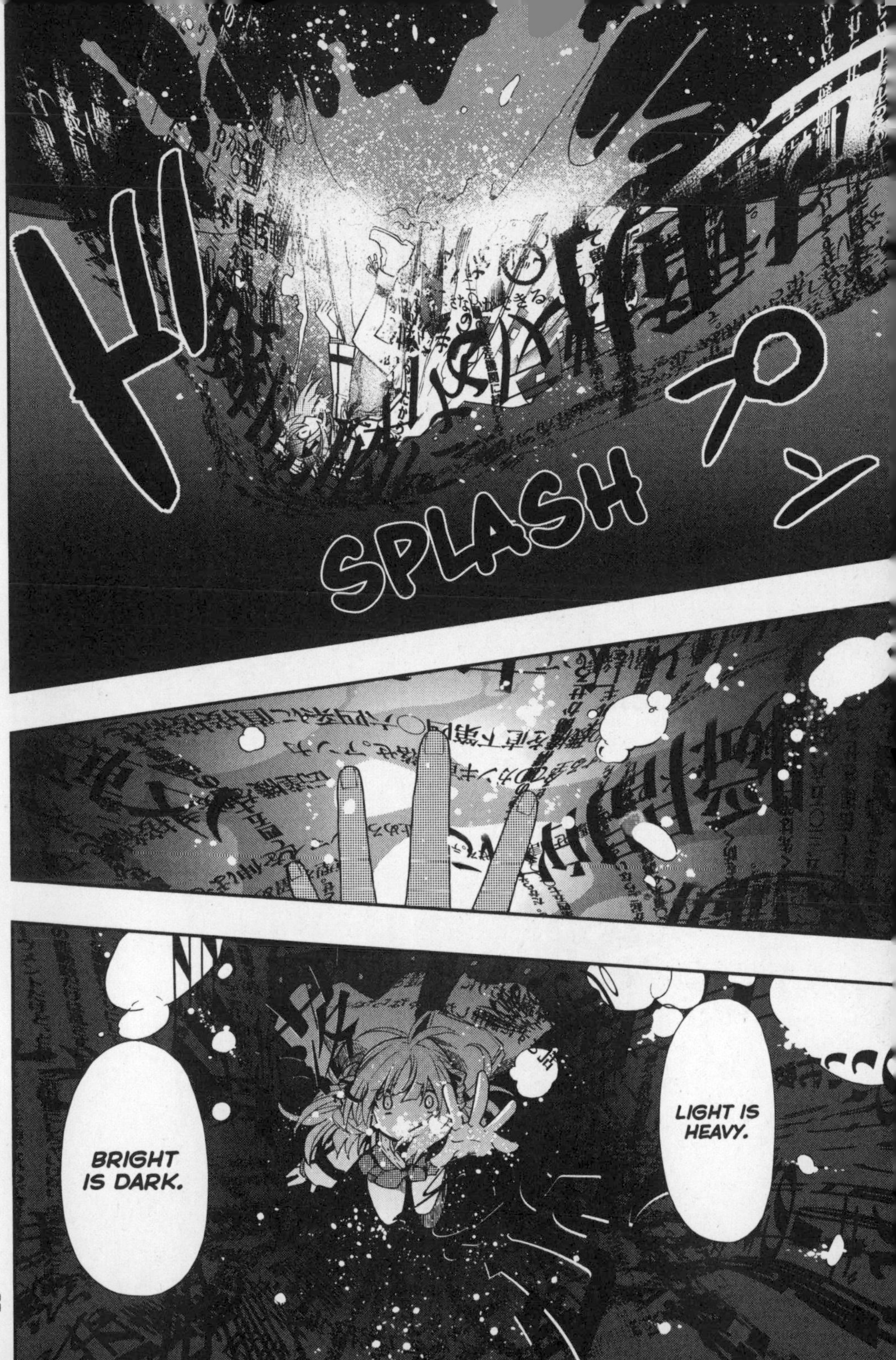
ドプン
SPLASH
LIGHT IS HEAVY.
BRIGHT IS DARK.

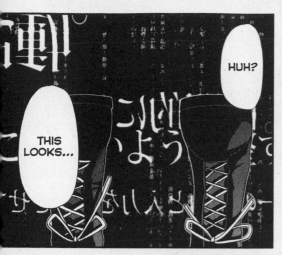

HUH?

THIS LOOKS...

FIRST IS LAST.

29

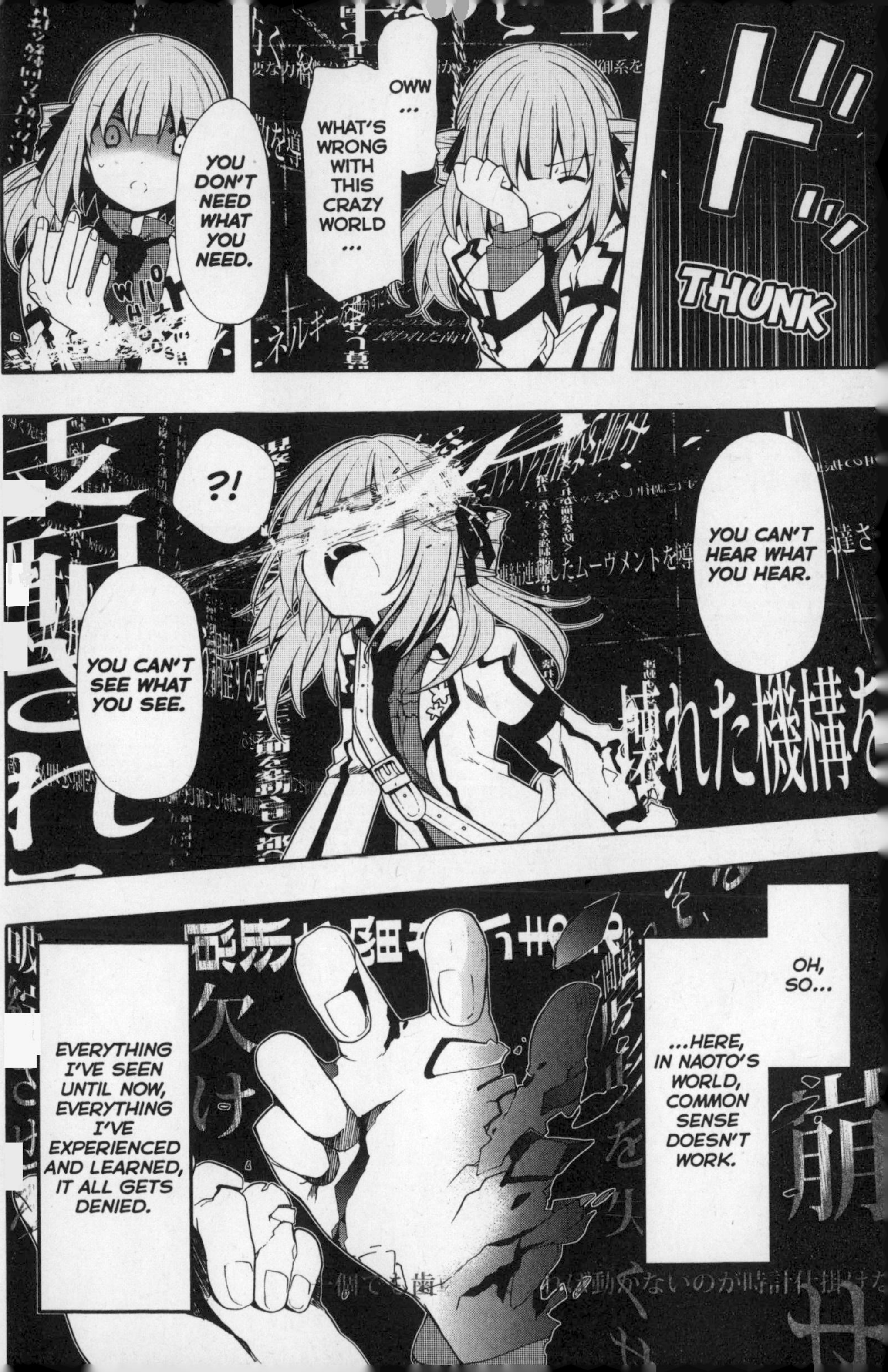
THUNK
OWW... WHAT'S WRONG WITH THIS CRAZY WORLD...
YOU DON'T NEED WHAT YOU NEED.
WHOOSH
YOU CAN'T HEAR WHAT YOU HEAR.
?!
YOU CAN'T SEE WHAT YOU SEE.
壊れた機構を
OH, SO...
...HERE, IN NAOTO'S WORLD, COMMON SENSE DOESN'T WORK.
EVERYTHING I'VE SEEN UNTIL NOW, EVERYTHING I'VE EXPERIENCED AND LEARNED, IT ALL GETS DENIED.

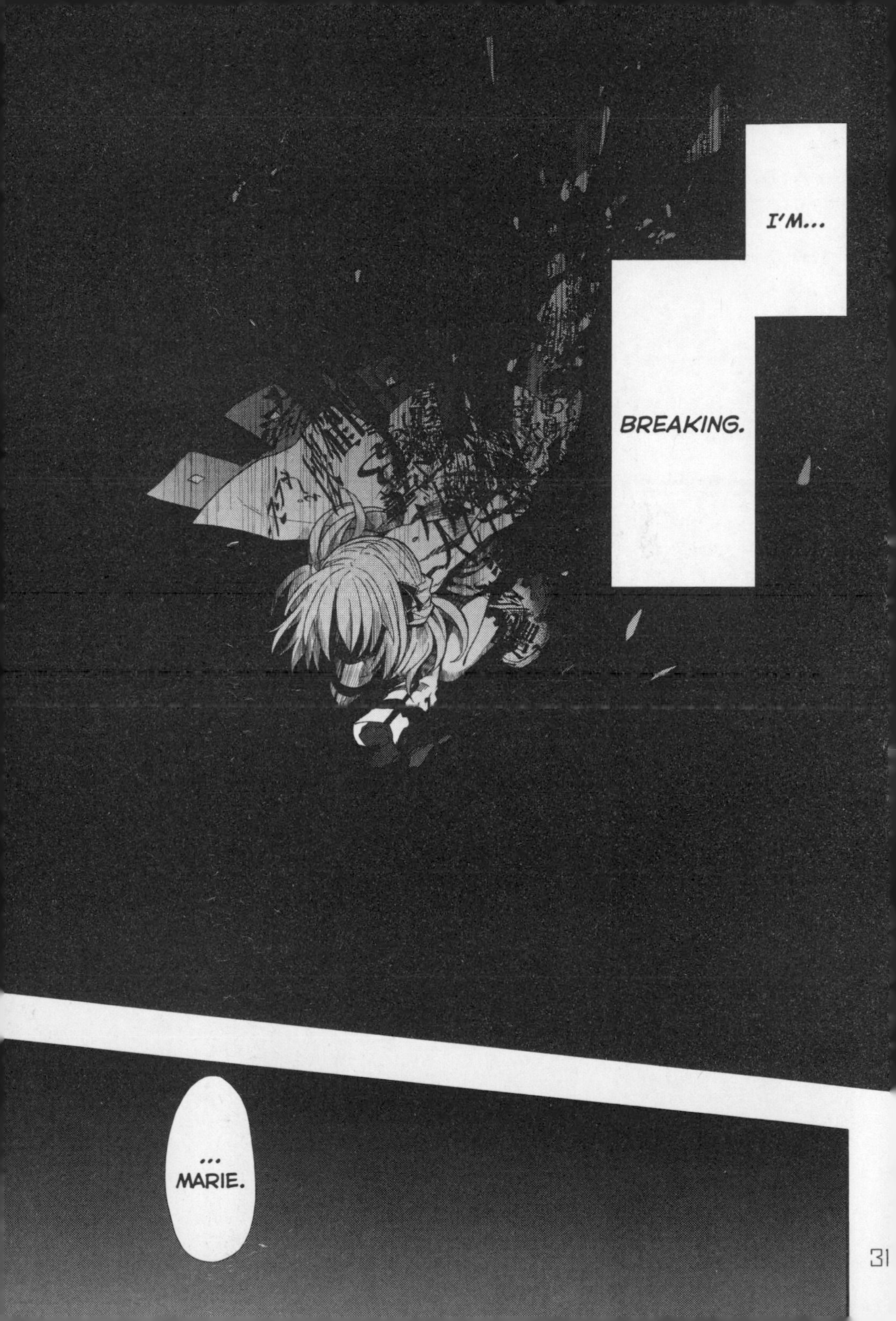
I'M...
BREAKING.
... MARIE.

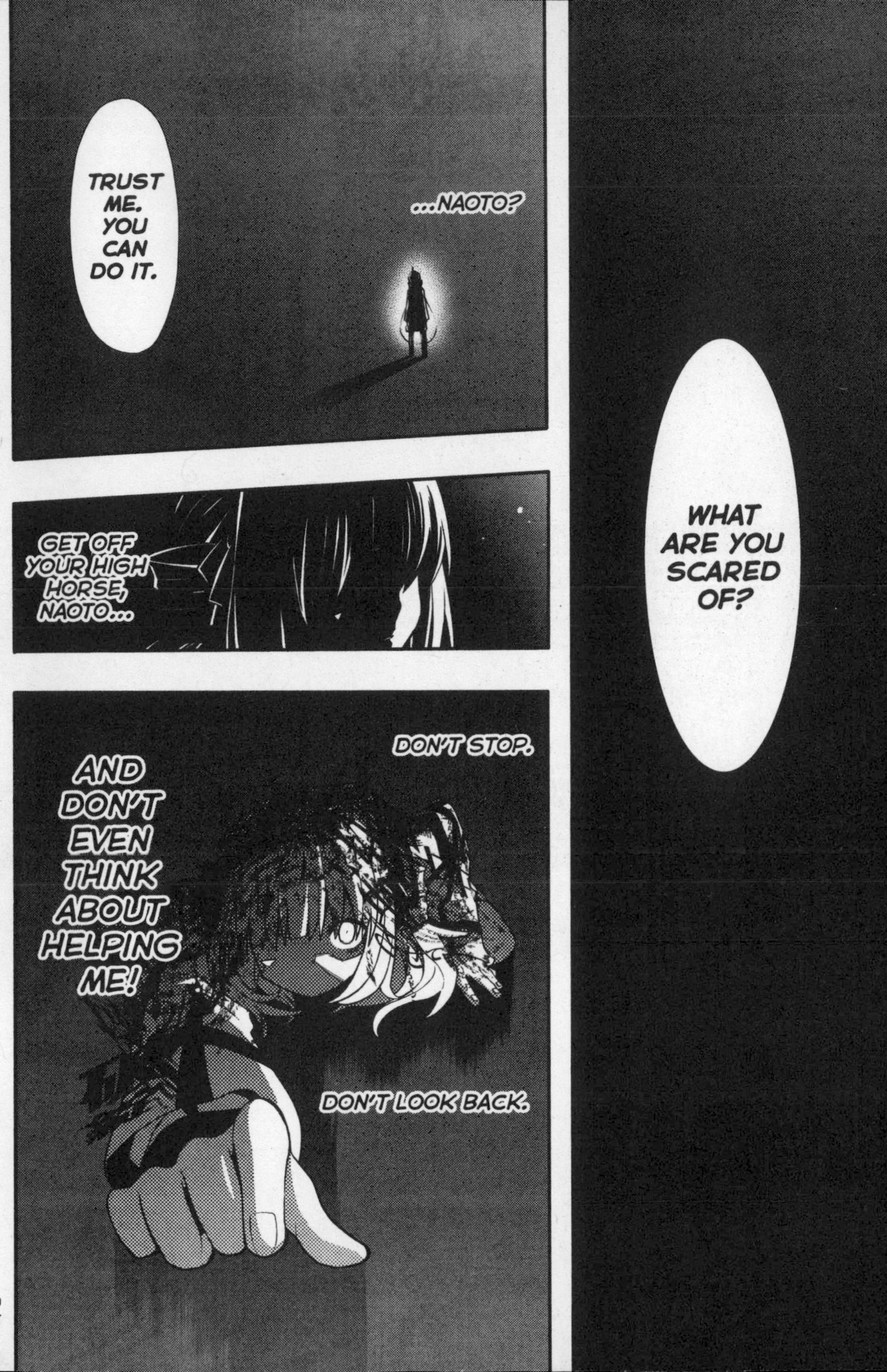

WHAT ARE YOU SCARED OF?
TRUST ME. YOU CAN DO IT.
...NAOTO?
GET OFF YOUR HIGH HORSE, NAOTO...
DON'T STOP.
AND DON'T EVEN THINK ABOUT HELPING ME!
DON'T LOOK BACK.

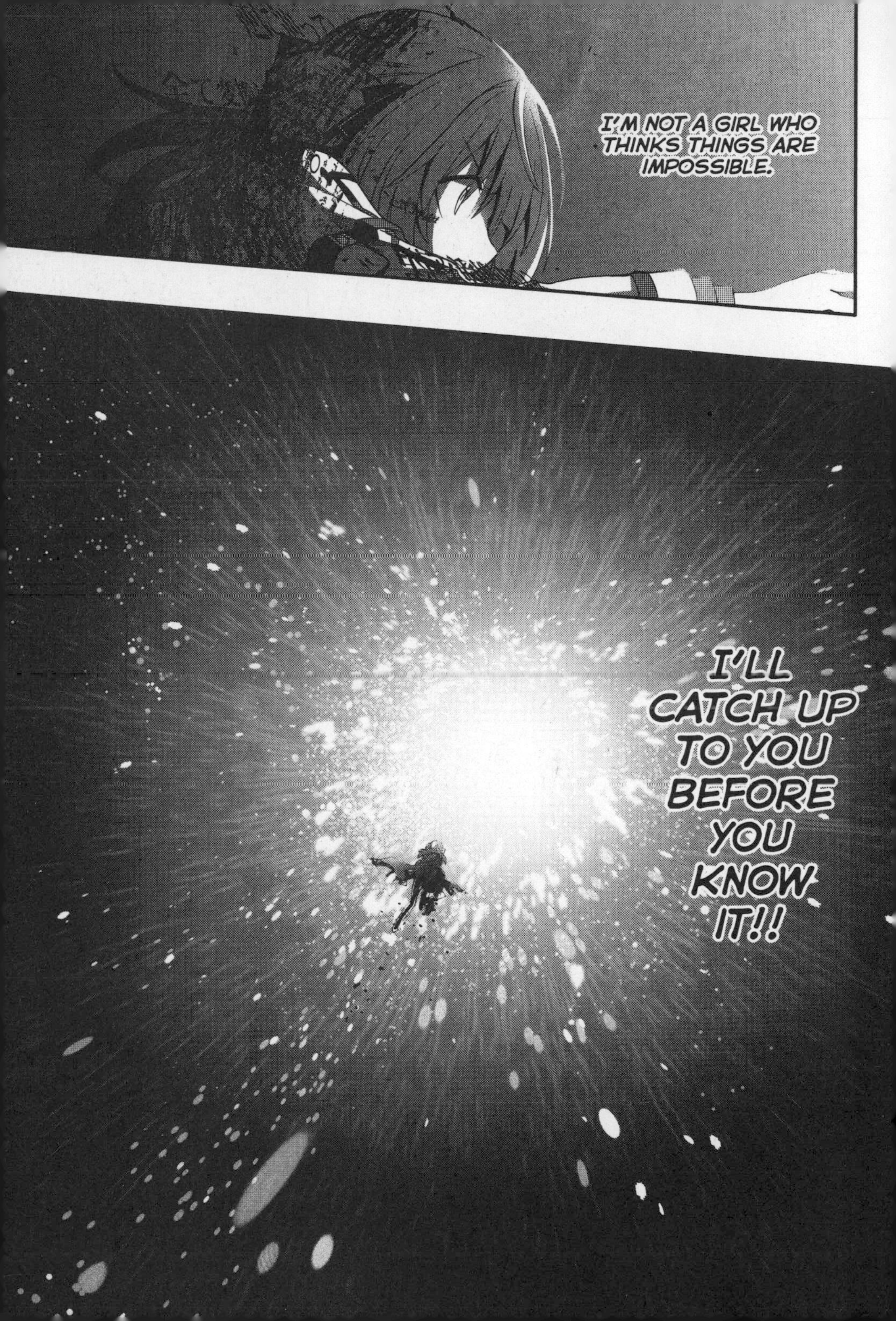
I'M NOT A GIRL WHO THINKS THINGS ARE IMPOSSIBLE.
I'LL CATCH UP TO YOU BEFORE YOU KNOW IT!!

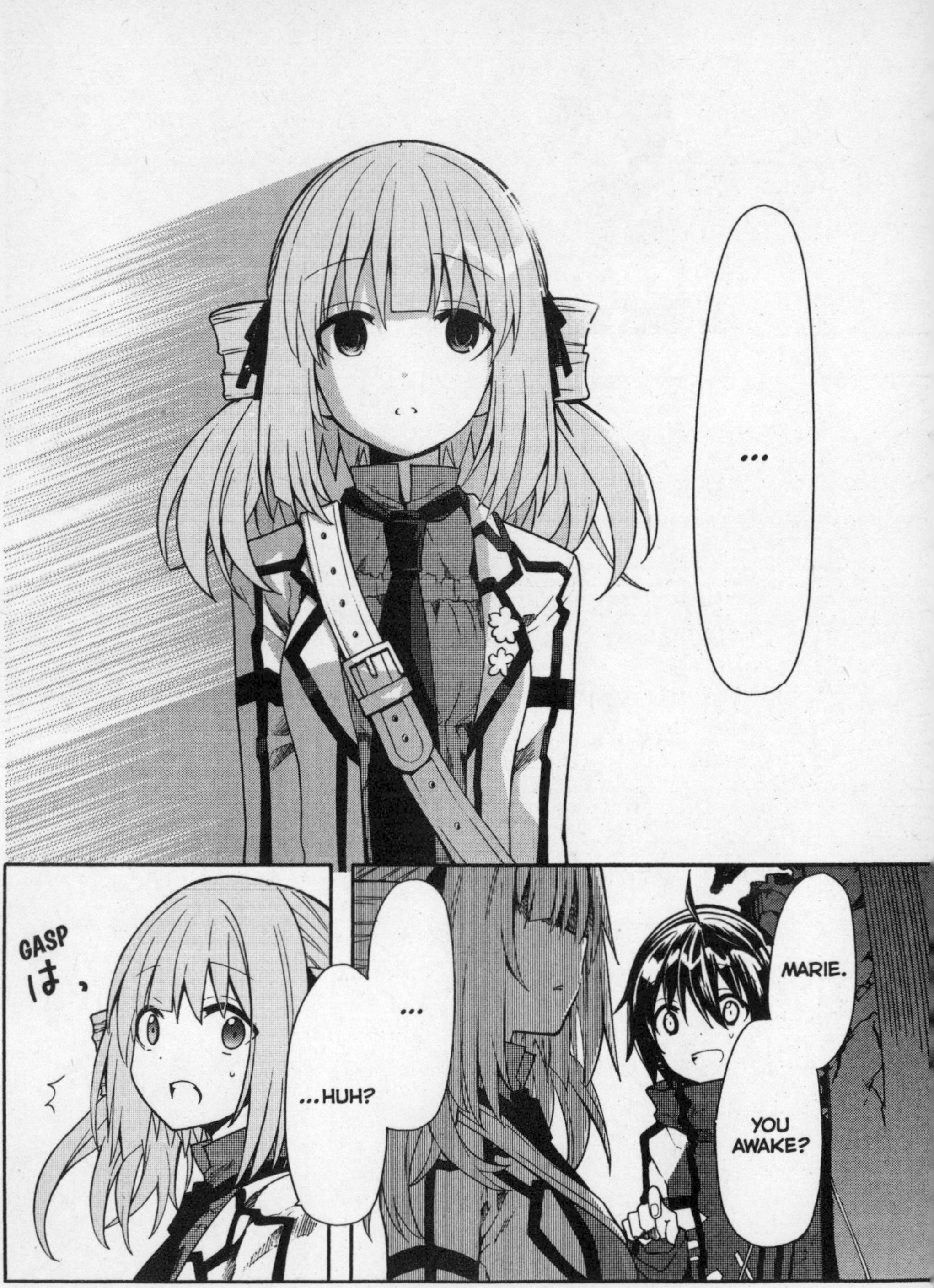
...
MARIE.
YOU AWAKE?
...
...HUH?
GASP
は、

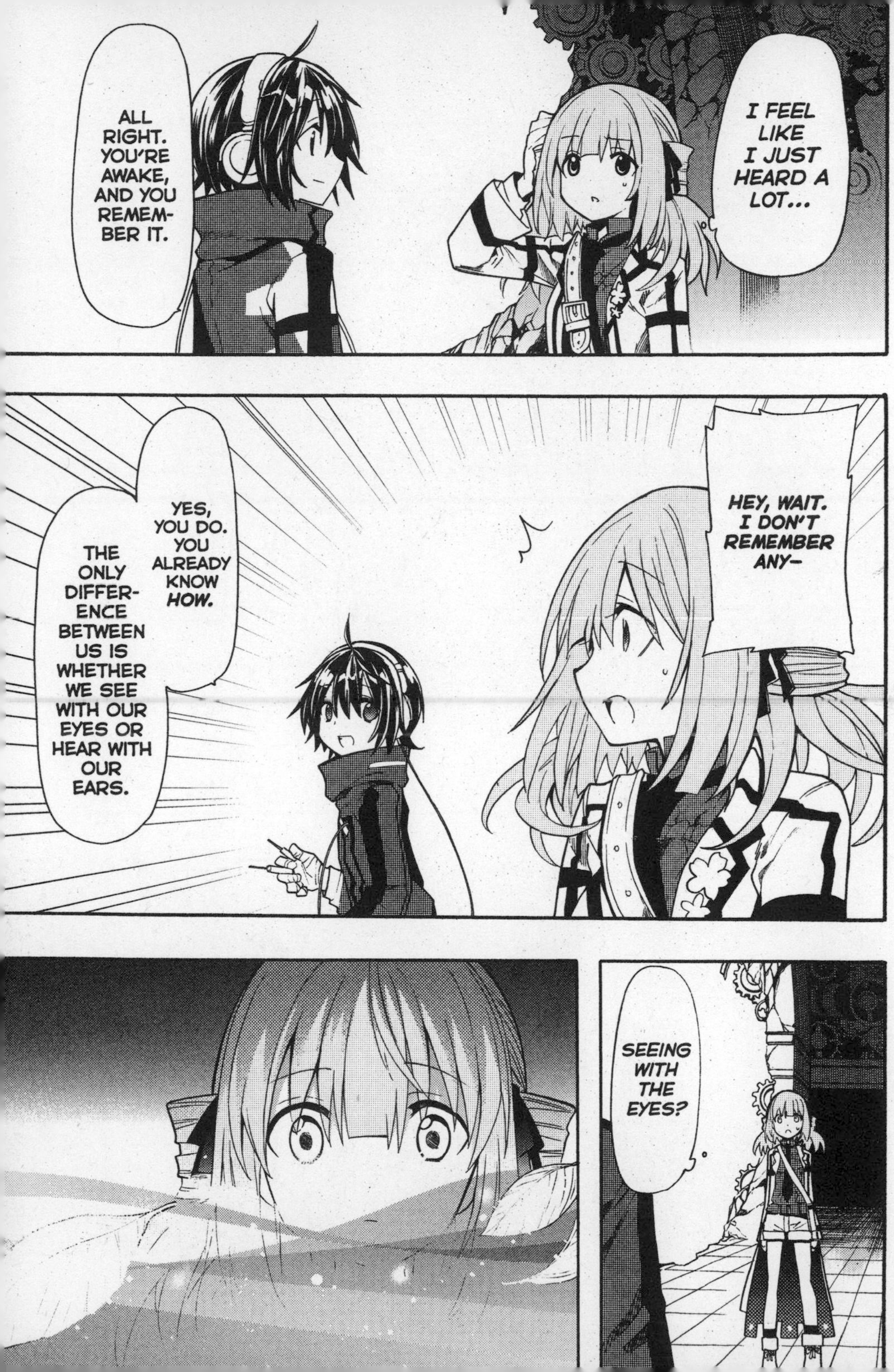
I FEEL LIKE I JUST HEARD A LOT...
ALL RIGHT. YOU'RE AWAKE, AND YOU REMEMBER IT.
HEY, WAIT. I DON'T REMEMBER ANY—
YES, YOU DO. YOU ALREADY KNOW *HOW.*
THE ONLY DIFFERENCE BETWEEN US IS WHETHER WE SEE WITH OUR EYES OR HEAR WITH OUR EARS.
SEEING WITH THE EYES?

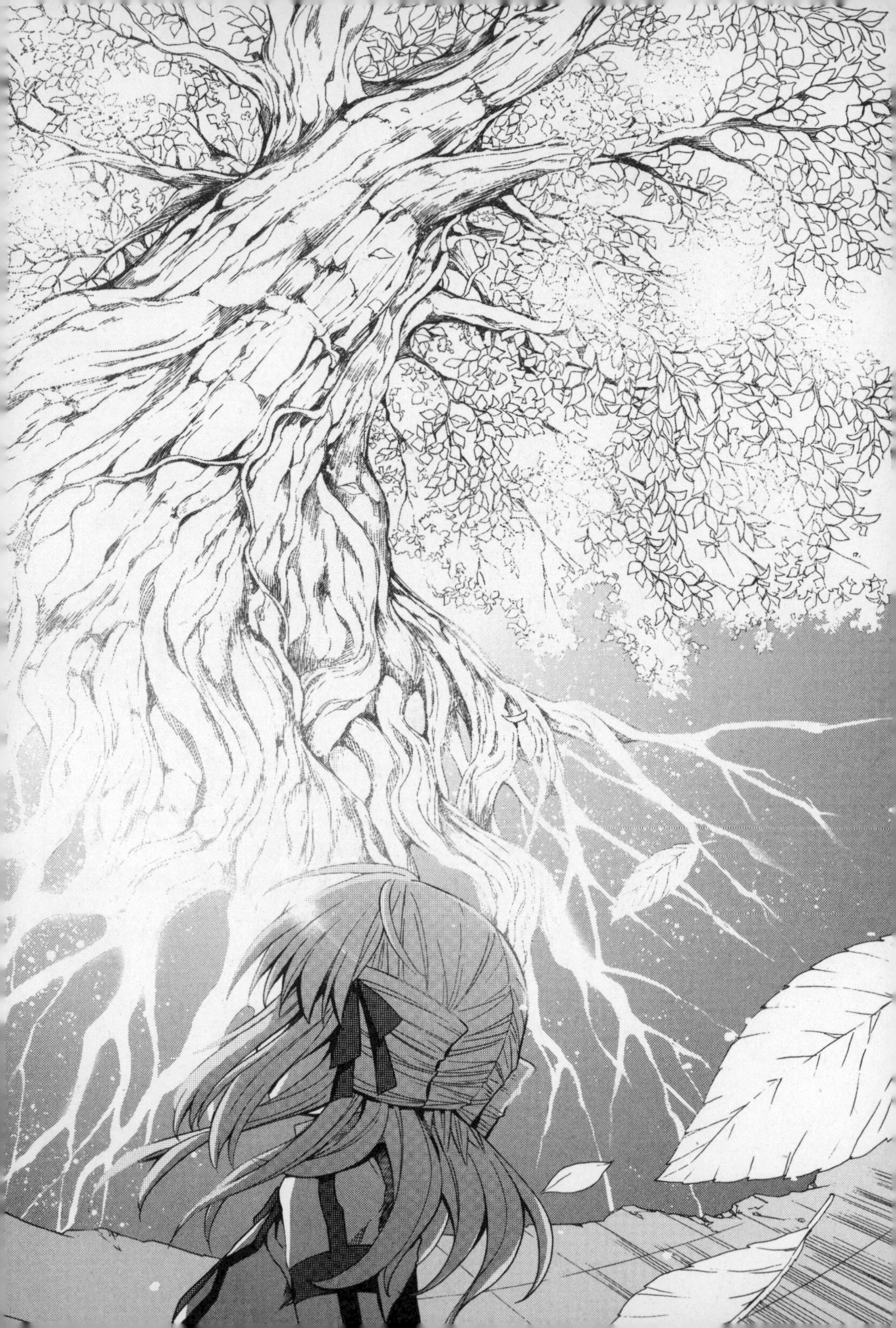

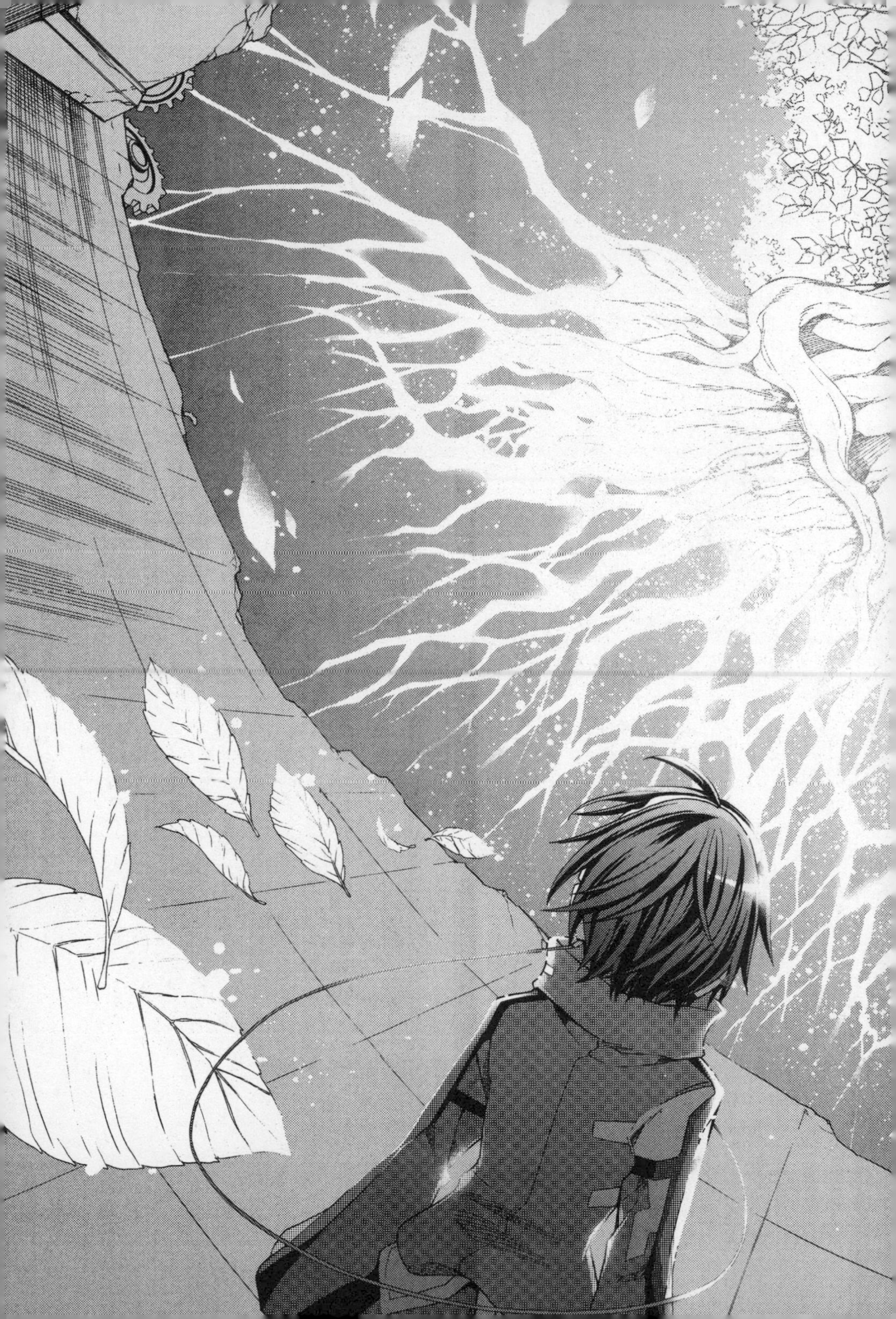

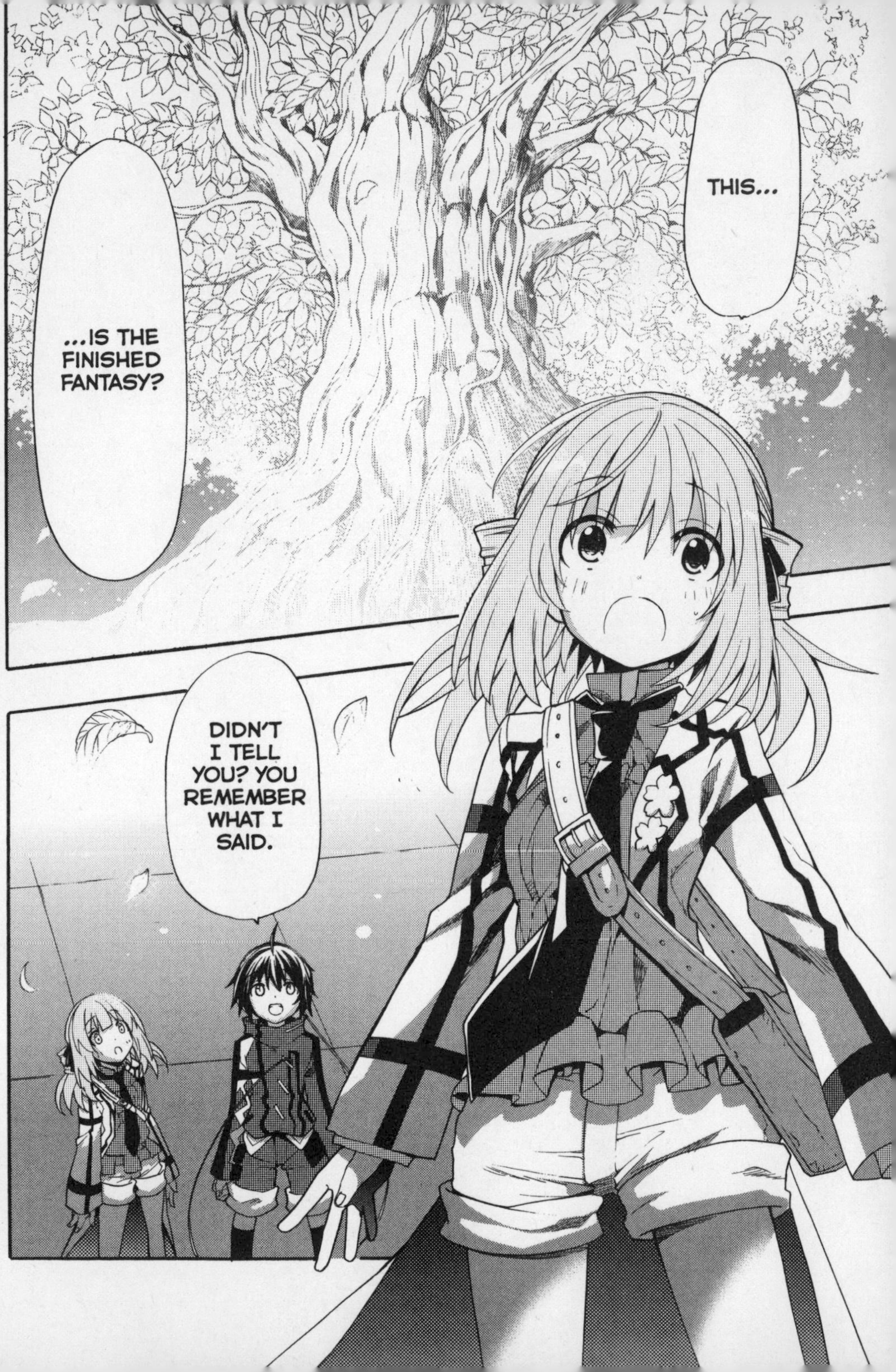
THIS...
...IS THE FINISHED FANTASY?
DIDN'T I TELL YOU? YOU REMEMBER WHAT I SAID.

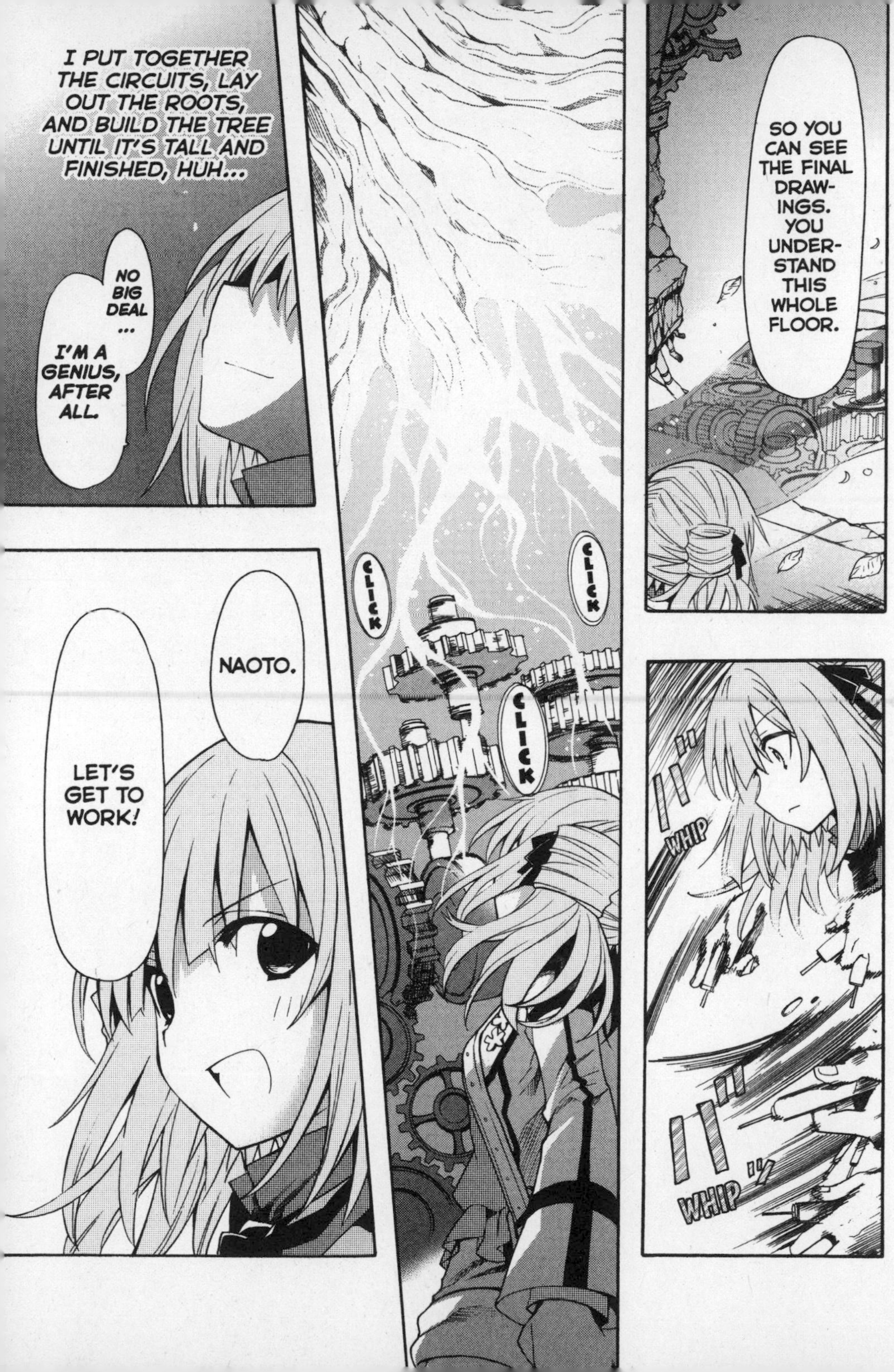
SO YOU CAN SEE THE FINAL DRAW-INGS. YOU UNDER-STAND THIS WHOLE FLOOR.
WHIP
WHIP
CLICK
CLICK
CLICK
I PUT TOGETHER THE CIRCUITS, LAY OUT THE ROOTS, AND BUILD THE TREE UNTIL IT'S TALL AND FINISHED, HUH...
NO BIG DEAL... I'M A GENIUS, AFTER ALL.
NAOTO.
LET'S GET TO WORK!

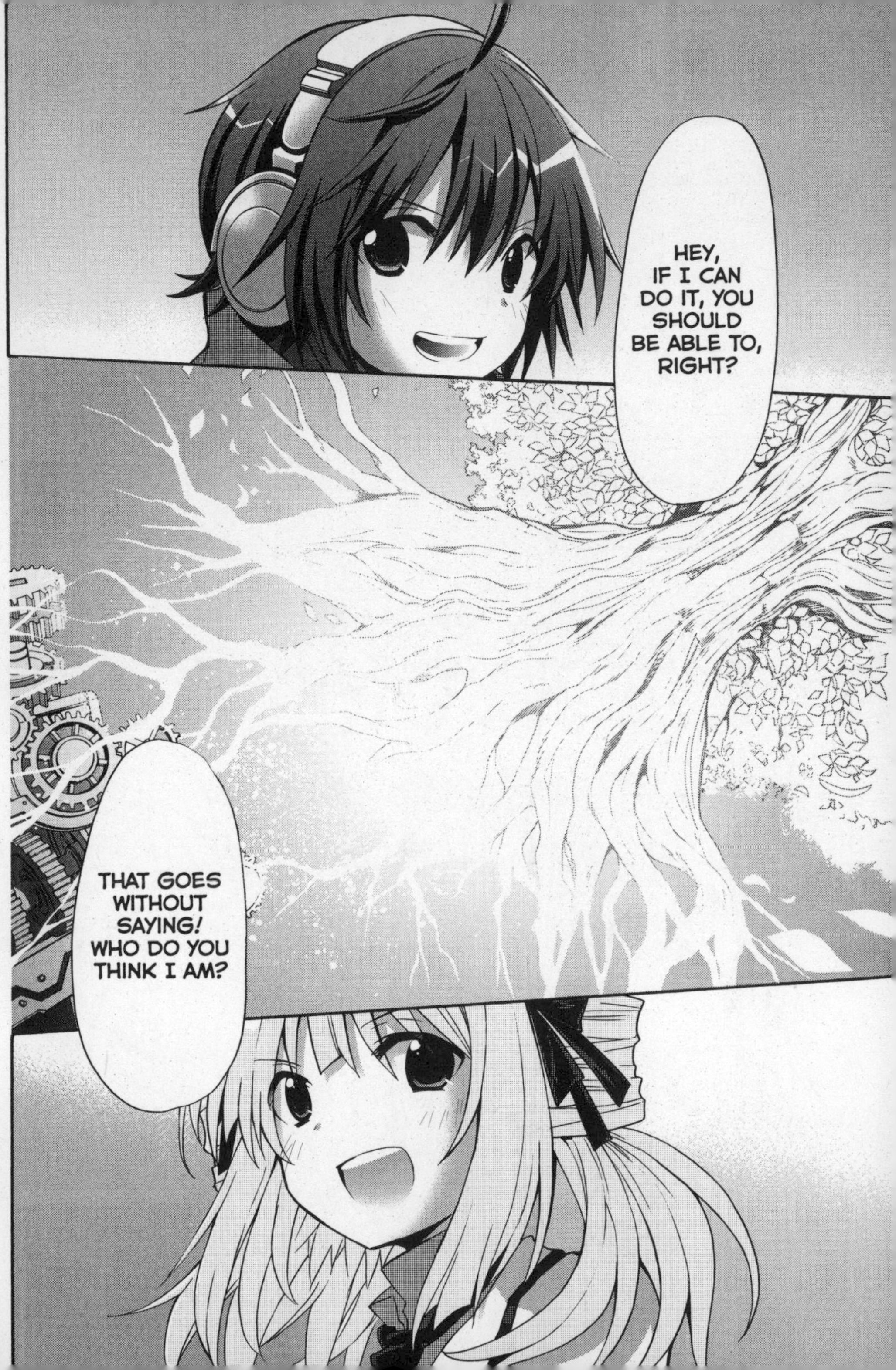
HEY, IF I CAN DO IT, YOU SHOULD BE ABLE TO, RIGHT?
THAT GOES WITHOUT SAYING! WHO DO YOU THINK I AM?

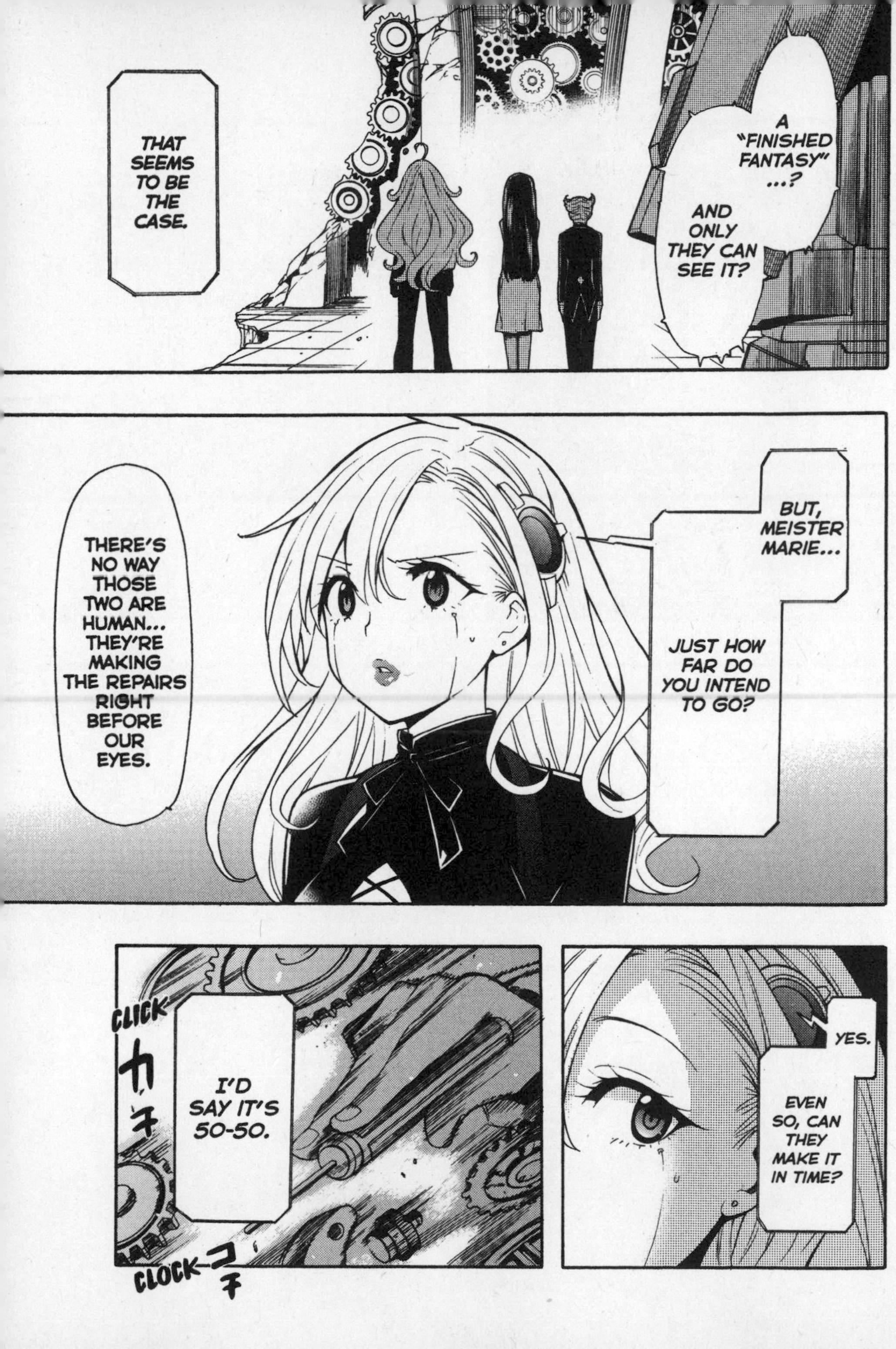
A "FINISHED FANTASY" ...?
AND ONLY THEY CAN SEE IT?
THAT SEEMS TO BE THE CASE.
BUT, MEISTER MARIE...
JUST HOW FAR DO YOU INTEND TO GO?
THERE'S NO WAY THOSE TWO ARE HUMAN... THEY'RE MAKING THE REPAIRS RIGHT BEFORE OUR EYES.
YES.
EVEN SO, CAN THEY MAKE IT IN TIME?
CLICK
カチ
I'D SAY IT'S 50-50.
CLOCK
コチ

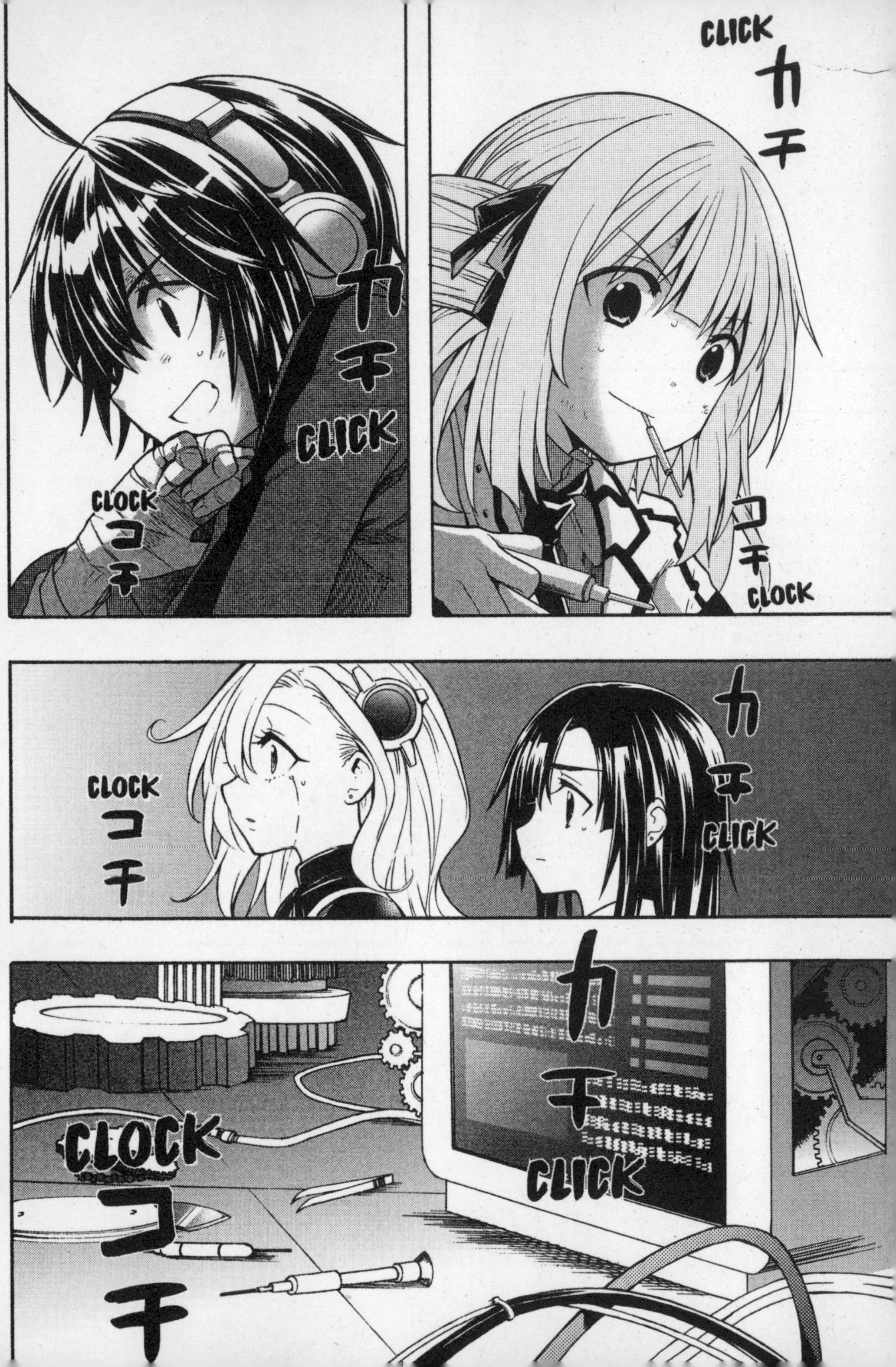
CLICK
カチ
コチ
CLOCK
カチ
CLICK
CLOCK
コチ
カチ
CLICK
CLOCK
コチ
カチ
CLICK
CLOCK
コチ

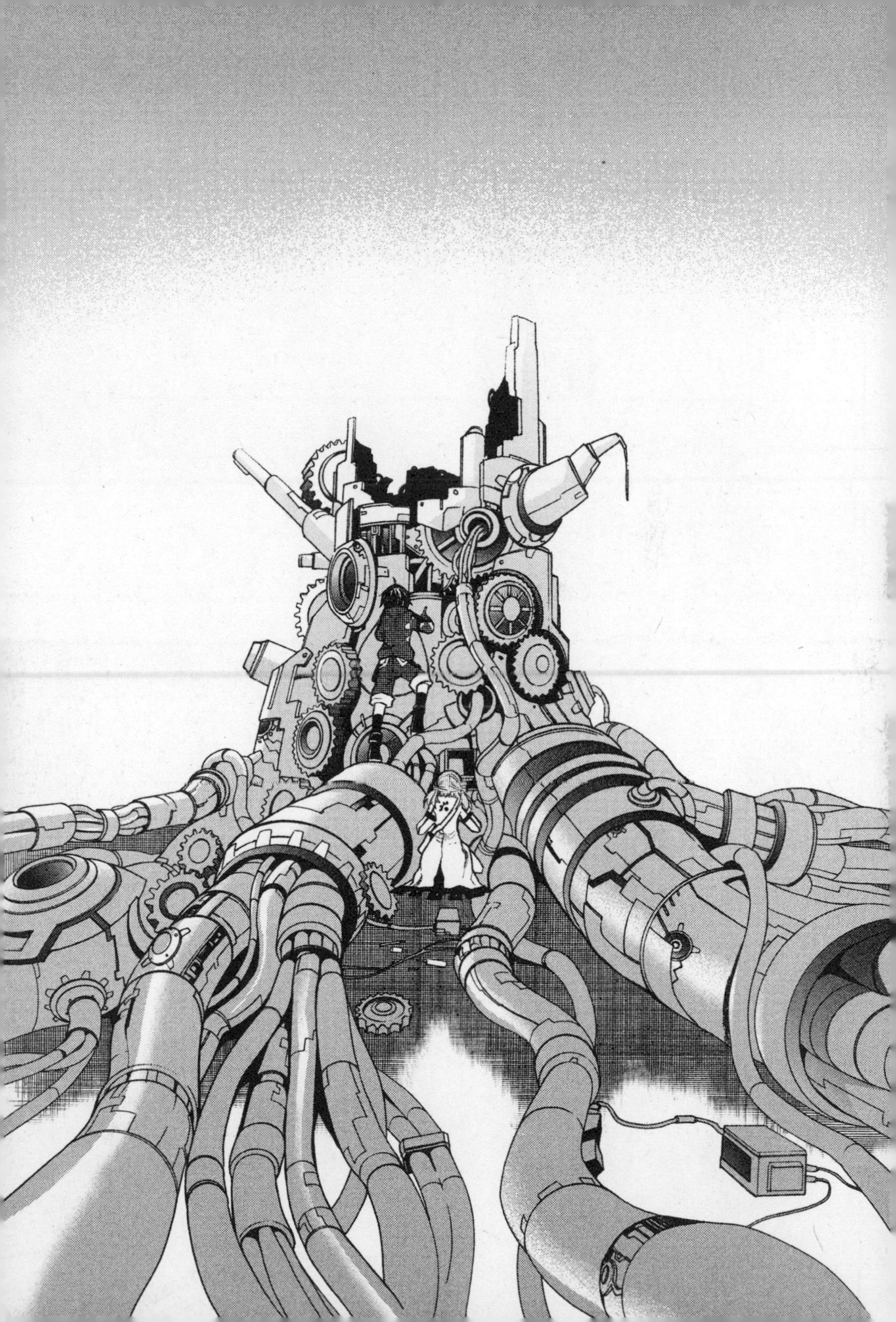

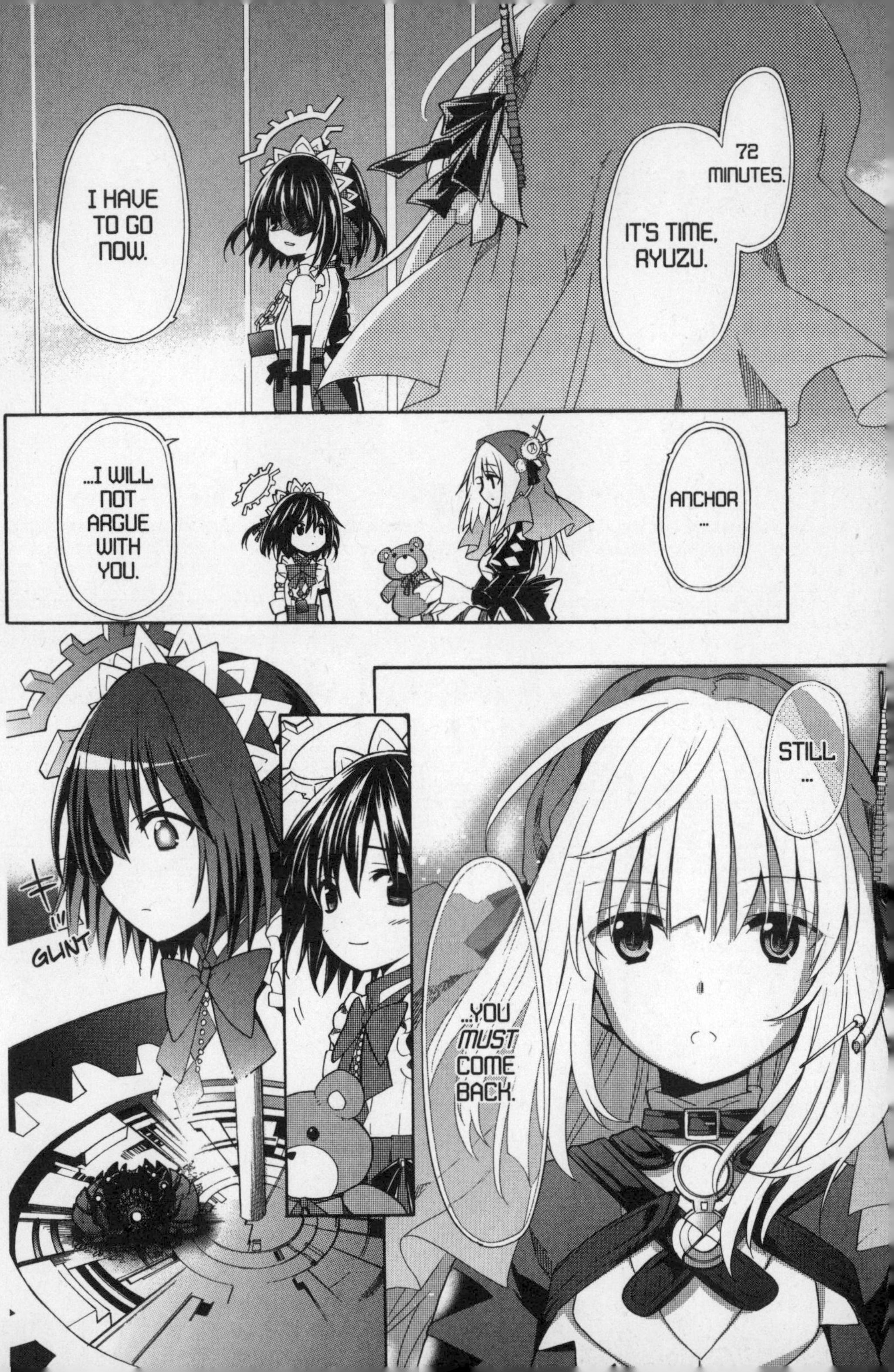
72 MINUTES.
IT'S TIME, RYUZU.
I HAVE TO GO NOW.
ANCHOR ...
...I WILL NOT ARGUE WITH YOU.
STILL ...
...YOU *MUST* COME BACK.
GLINT

Clockwork Planet

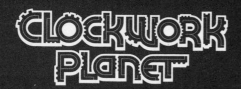

Clockwork Planet

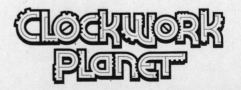

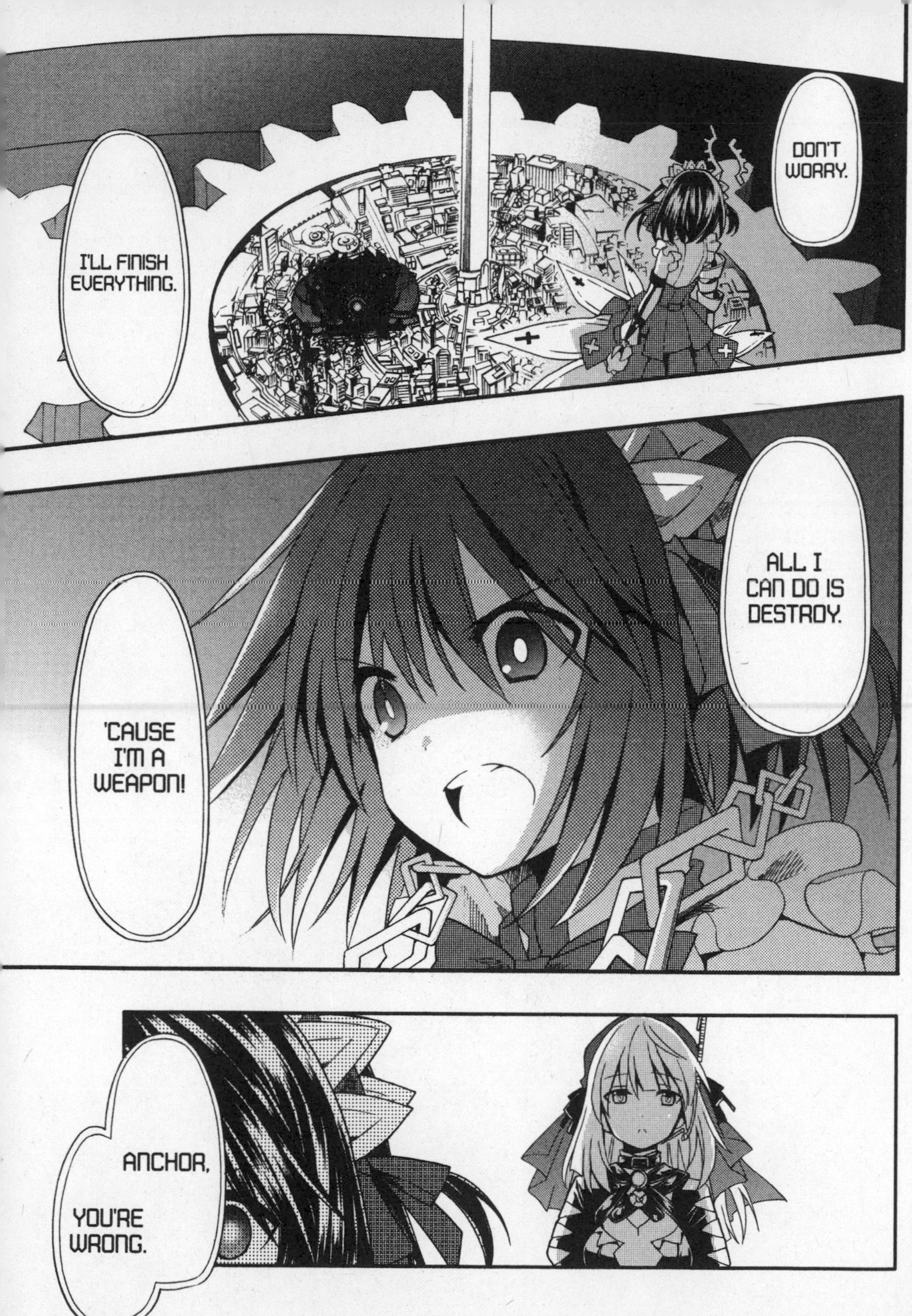
DON'T WORRY.
I'LL FINISH EVERYTHING.
ALL I CAN DO IS DESTROY.
'CAUSE I'M A WEAPON!
ANCHOR, YOU'RE WRONG.

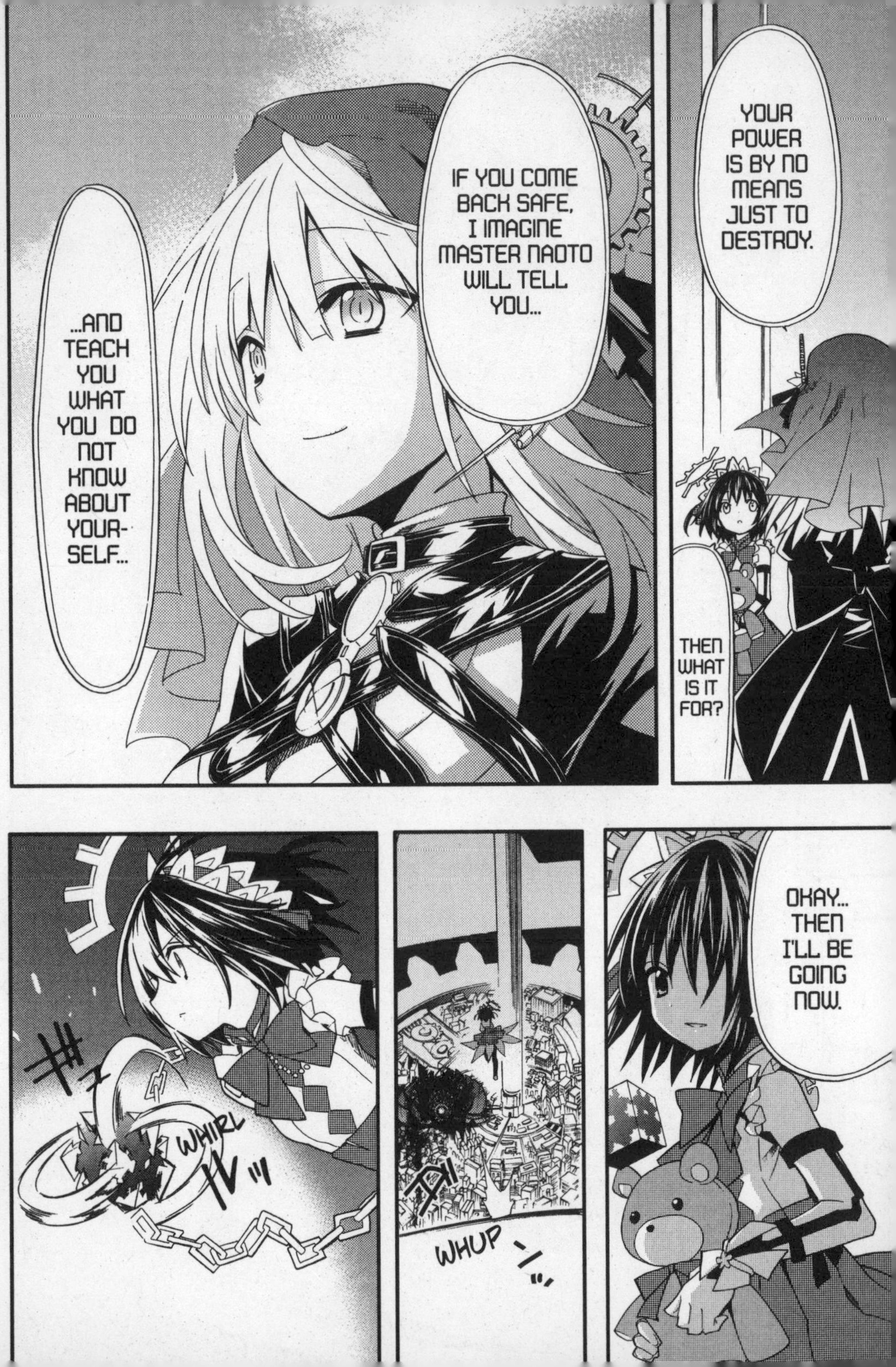
YOUR POWER IS BY NO MEANS JUST TO DESTROY.
THEN WHAT IS IT FOR?
IF YOU COME BACK SAFE, I IMAGINE MASTER NAOTO WILL TELL YOU...
...AND TEACH YOU WHAT YOU DO NOT KNOW ABOUT YOURSELF...
OKAY... THEN I'LL BE GOING NOW.
WHUP
WHIRL

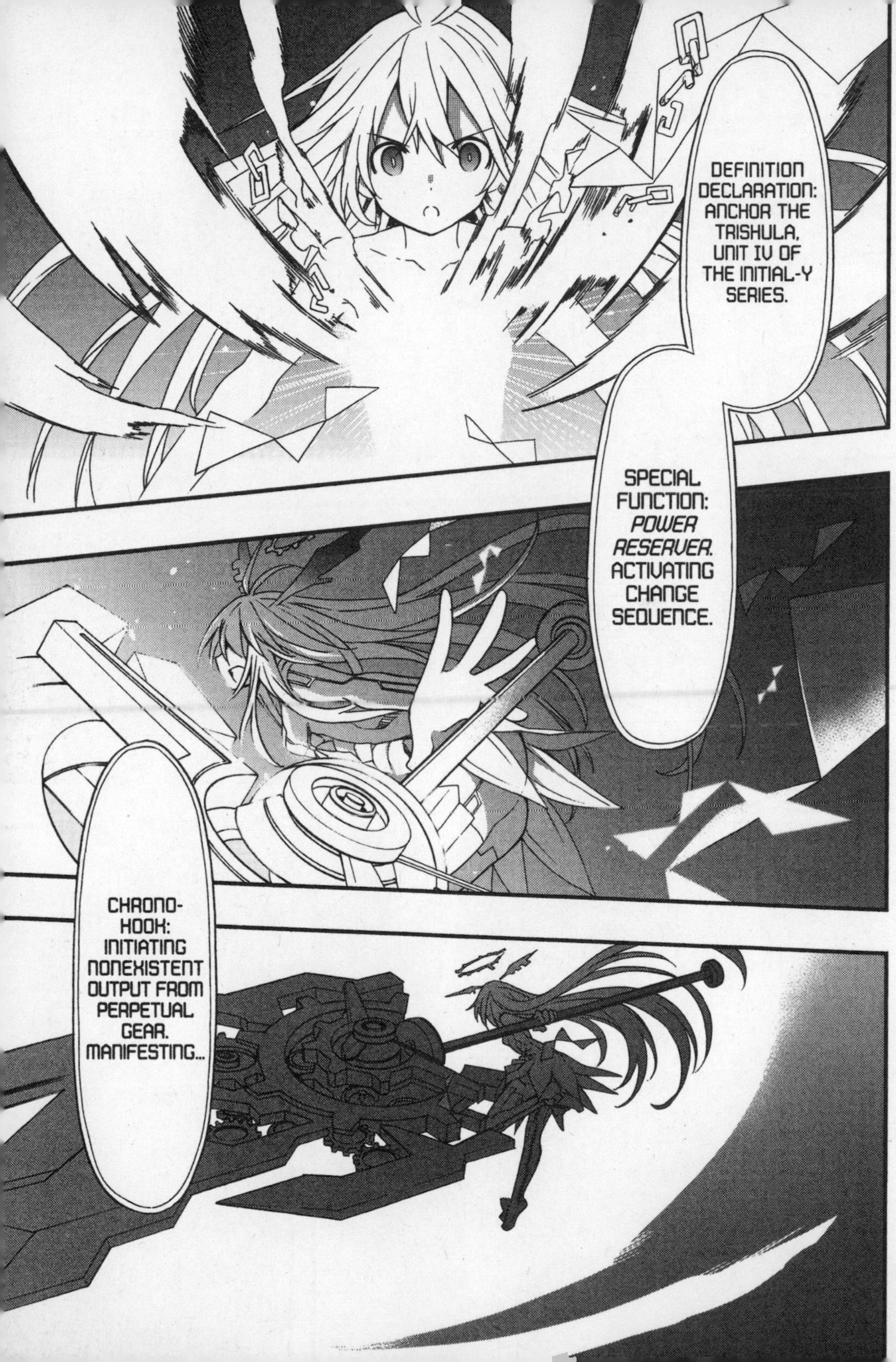
DEFINITION DECLARATION: ANCHOR THE TRISHULA, UNIT IV OF THE INITIAL-Y SERIES.
SPECIAL FUNCTION: *POWER RESERVER*. ACTIVATING CHANGE SEQUENCE.
CHRONO-HOOK: INITIATING NONEXISTENT OUTPUT FROM PERPETUAL GEAR. MANIFESTING...

Clock 37: Man-Made Meaning

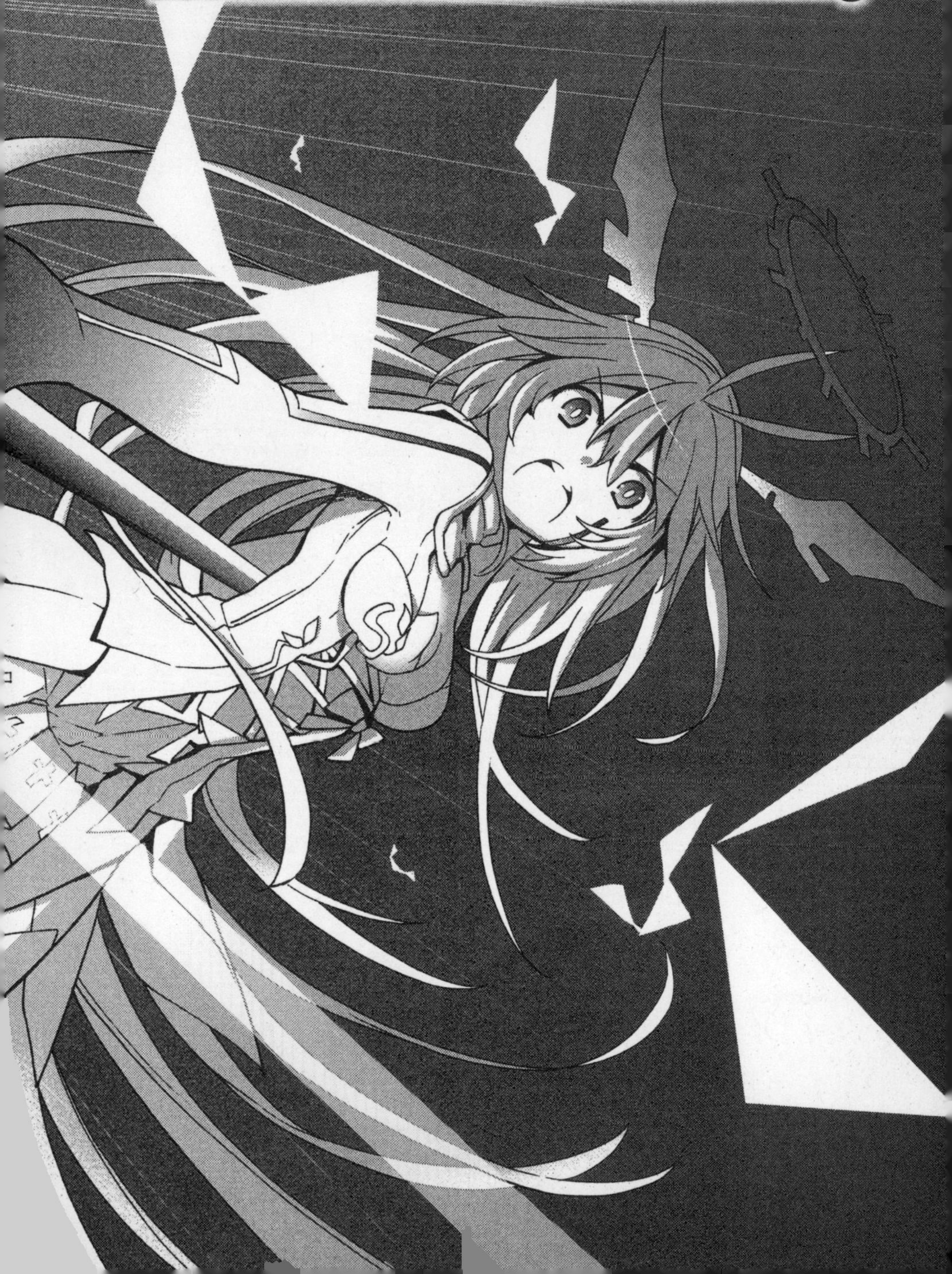

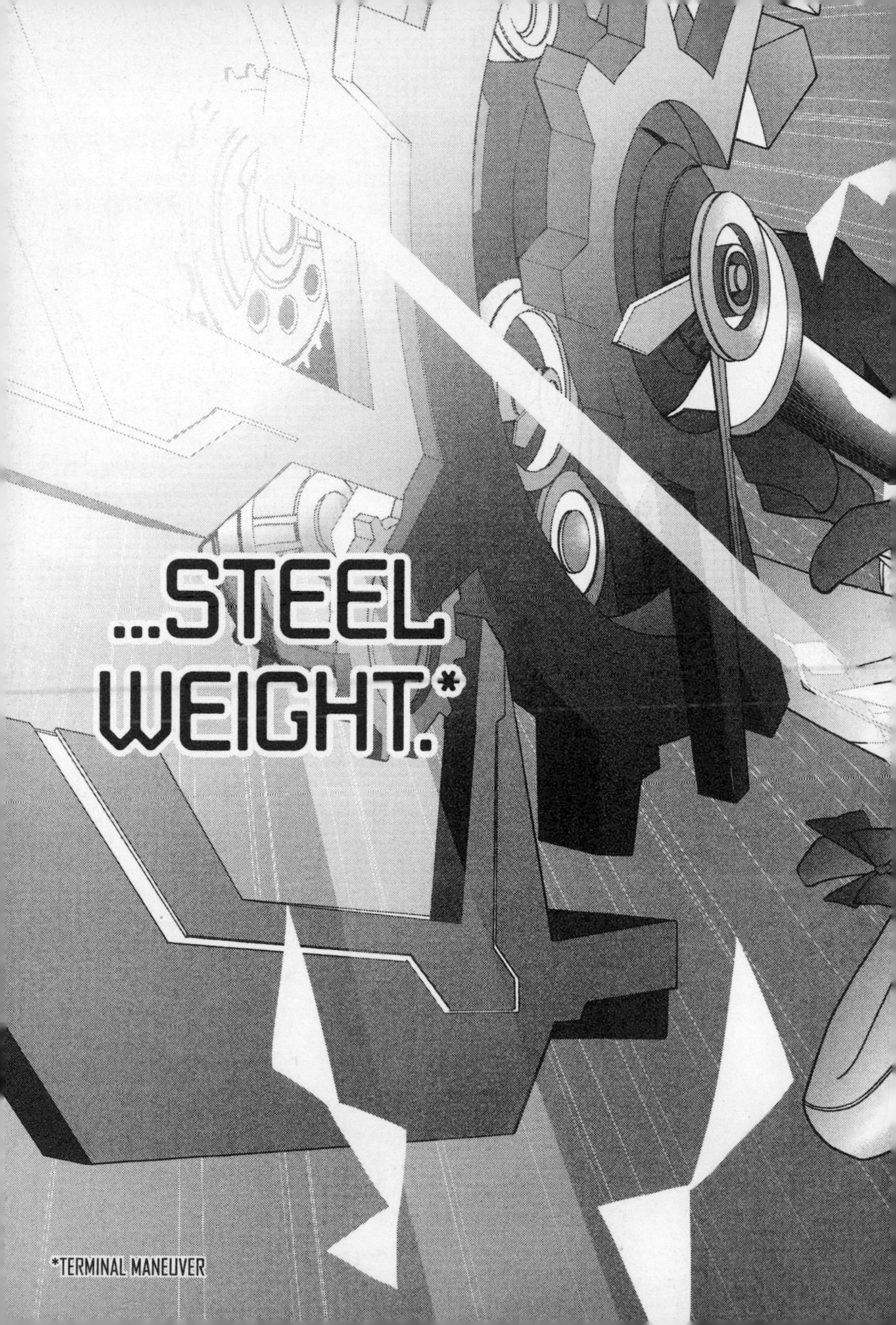
...STEEL WEIGHT.*
*TERMINAL MANEUVER

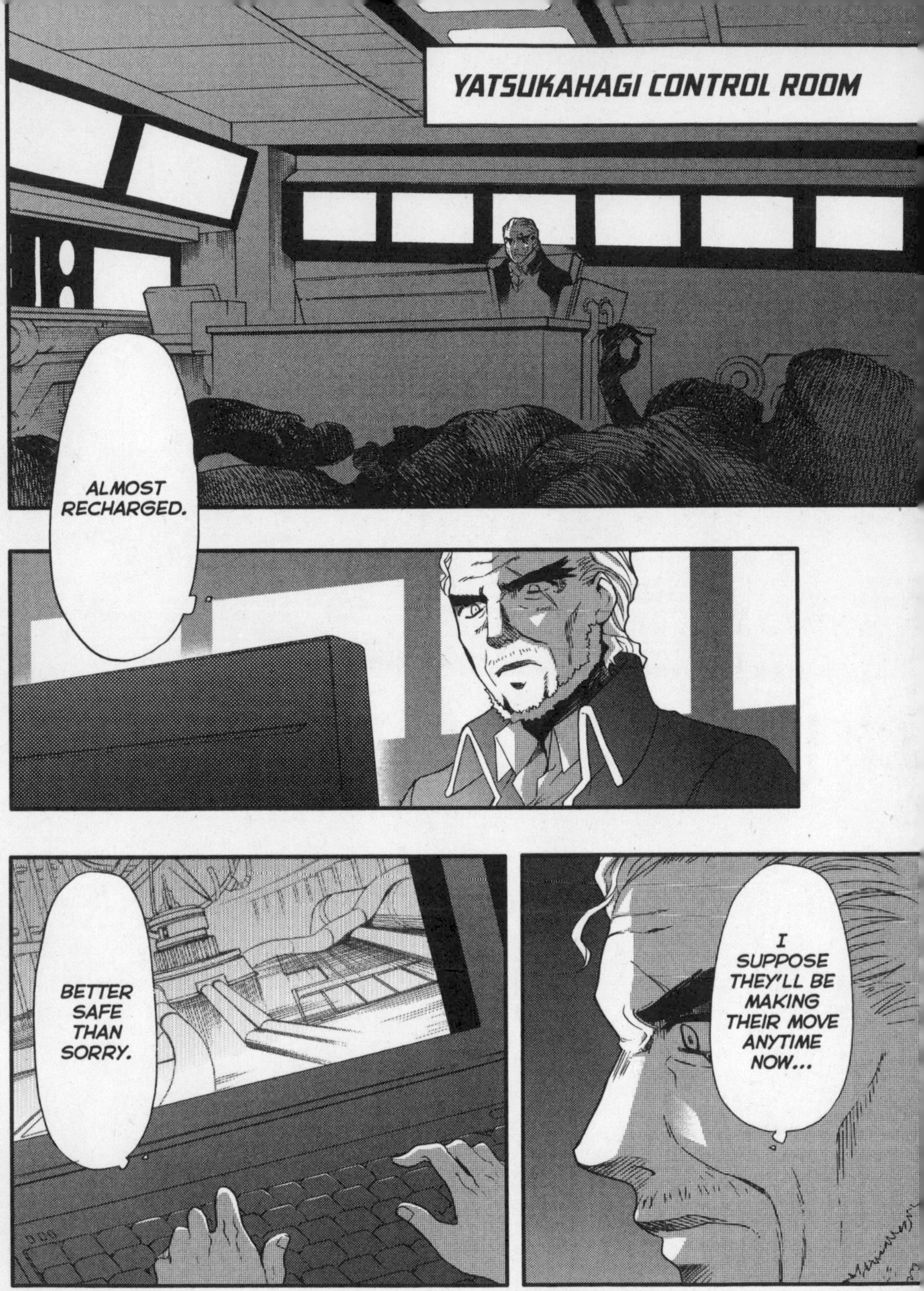
YATSUKAHAGI CONTROL ROOM
ALMOST RECHARGED.
I SUPPOSE THEY'LL BE MAKING THEIR MOVE ANYTIME NOW...
BETTER SAFE THAN SORRY.

TAK

CRACKLE!!

CHARGED

FWOOSH

GRIN

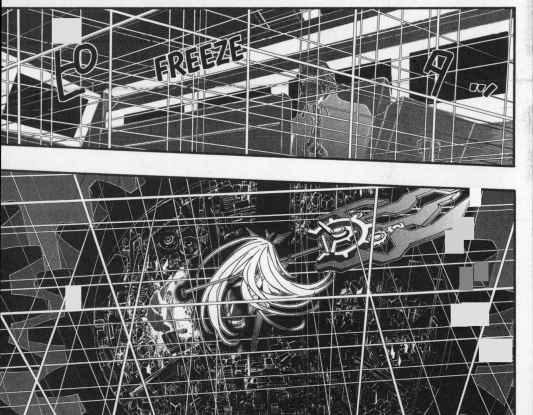

FREEZE

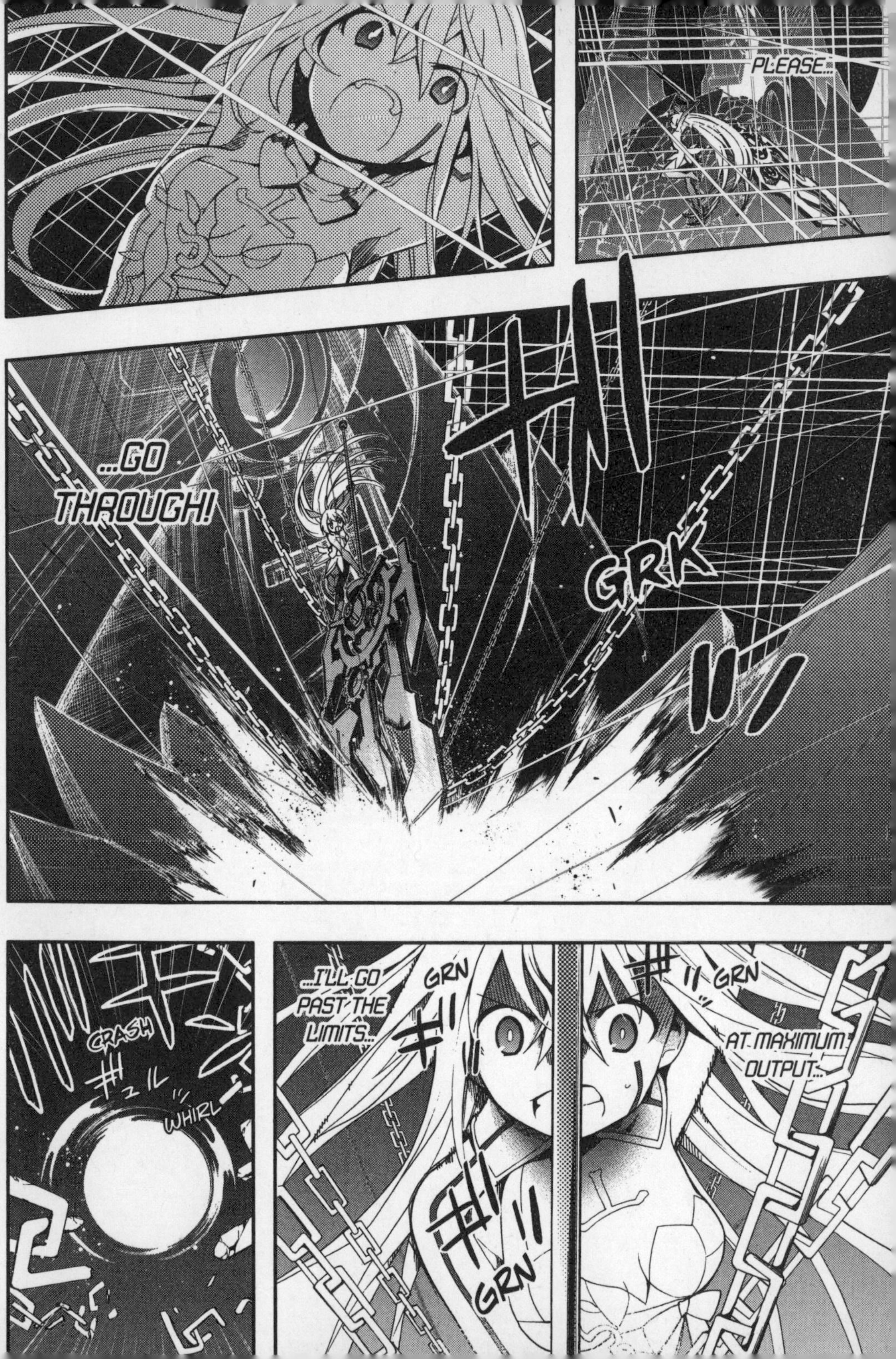
PLEASE...
...GO THROUGH!
GRK
AT MAXIMUM OUTPUT...
GRN
...I'LL GO PAST THE LIMITS...
GRN
GRN
CRASH
WHIRL

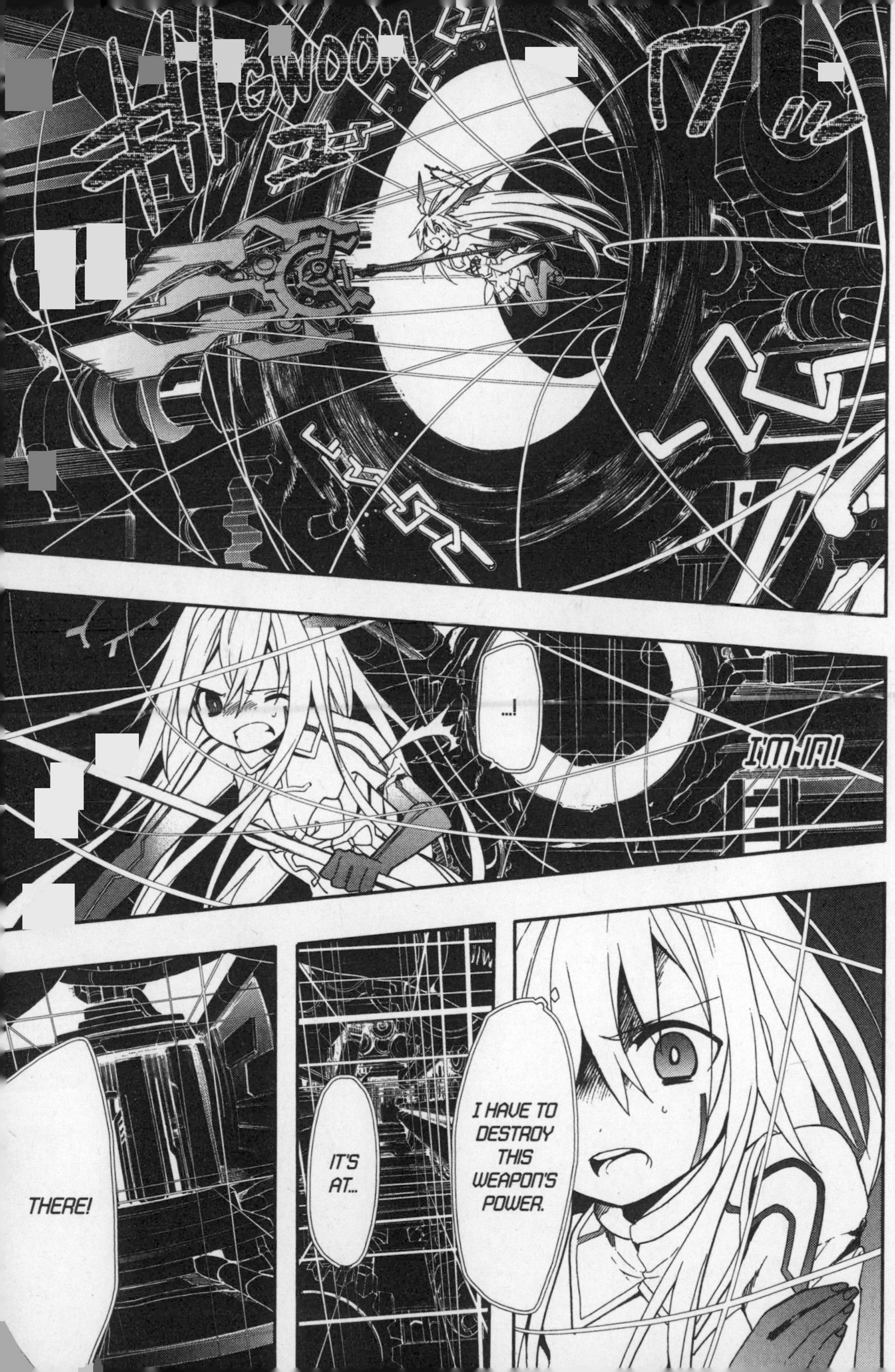
GWOON
...!
I'M IN!
I HAVE TO DESTROY THIS WEAPON'S POWER.
IT'S AT...
THERE!

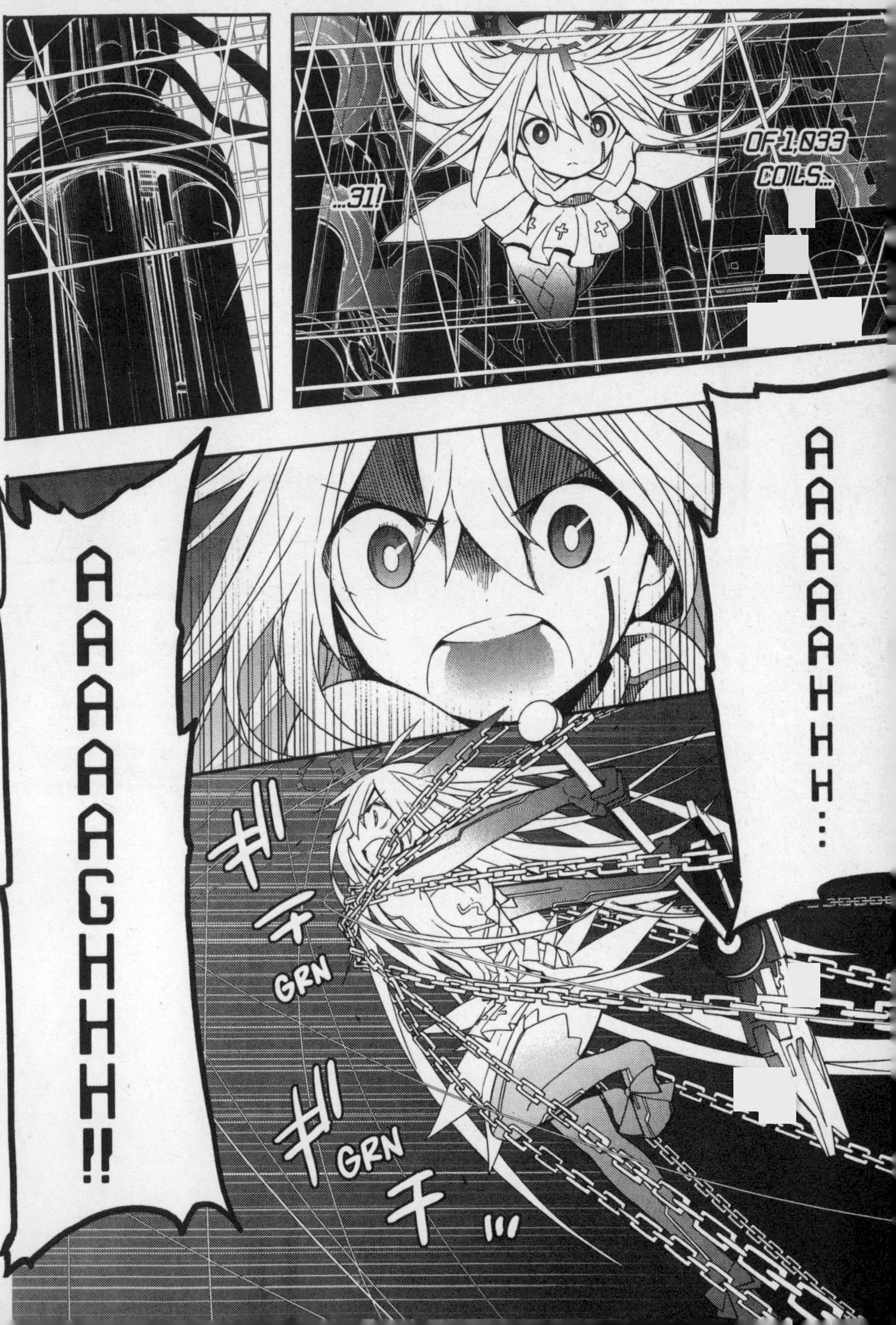
OF 1,033 COILS...
...31!
AAAAAHHH...
AAAAAGHHH!!
GRN
GRN

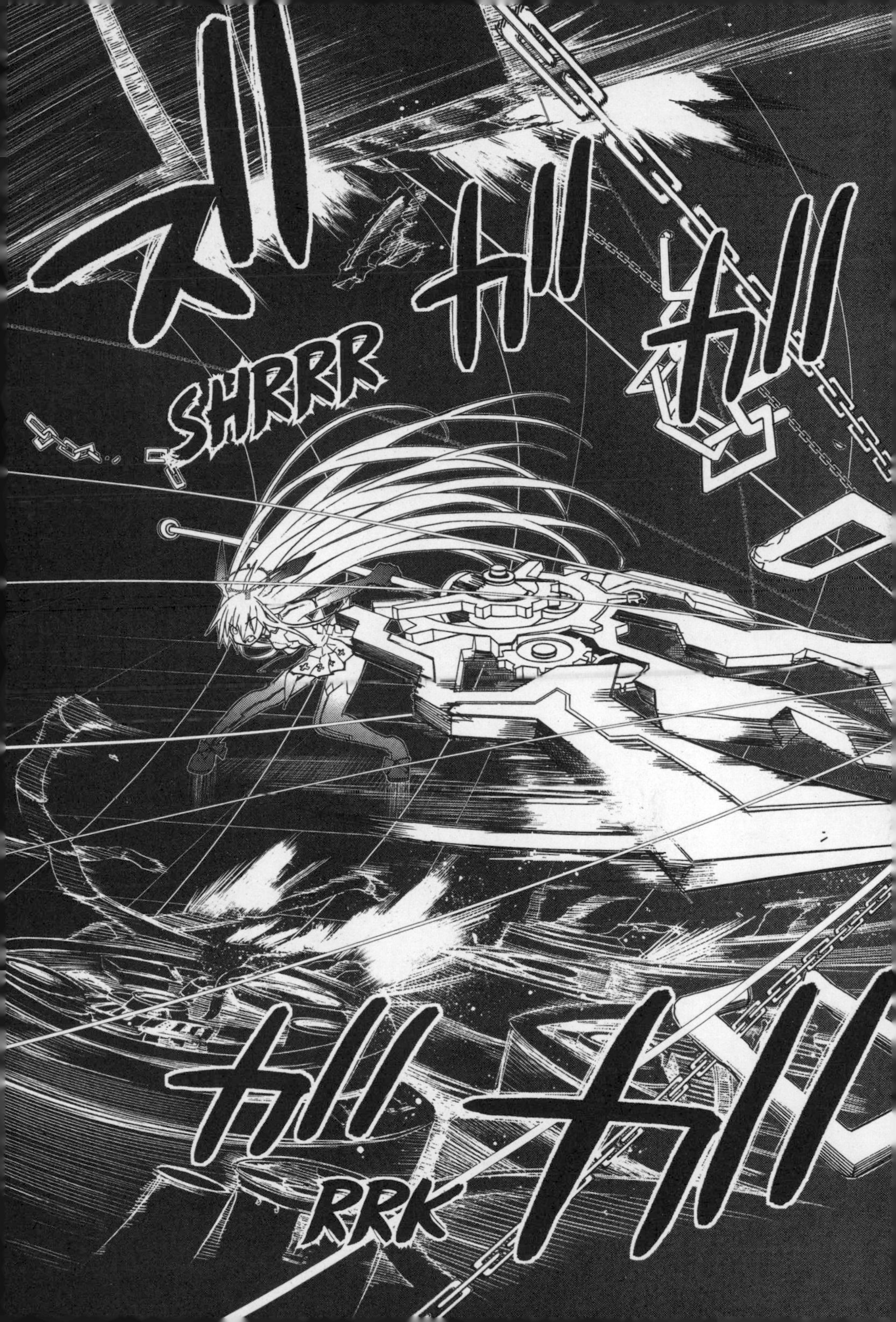
SHRRR
RRK

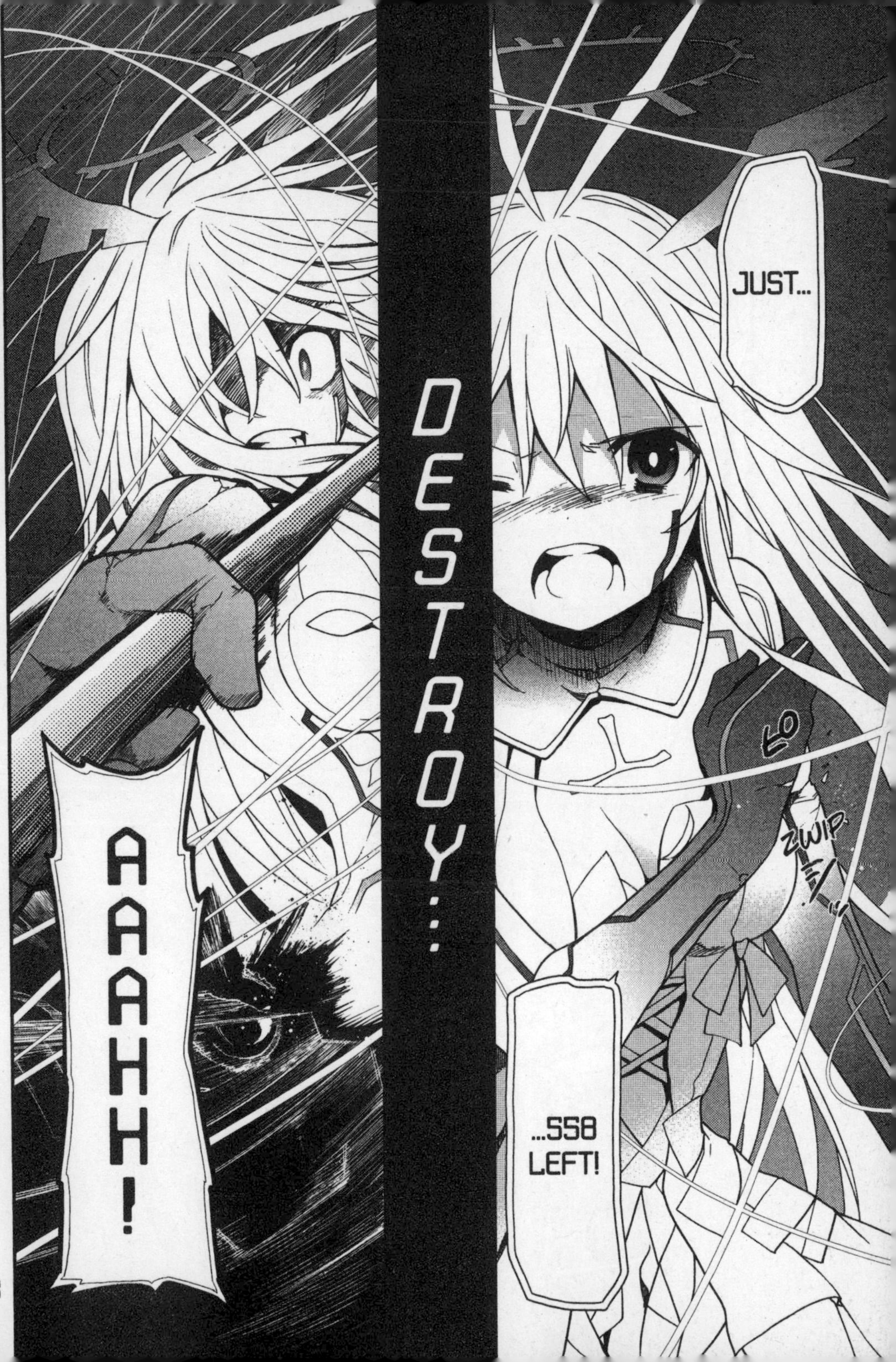
JUST...
DESTROY...
ZWIP
...558 LEFT!
AAAHH!

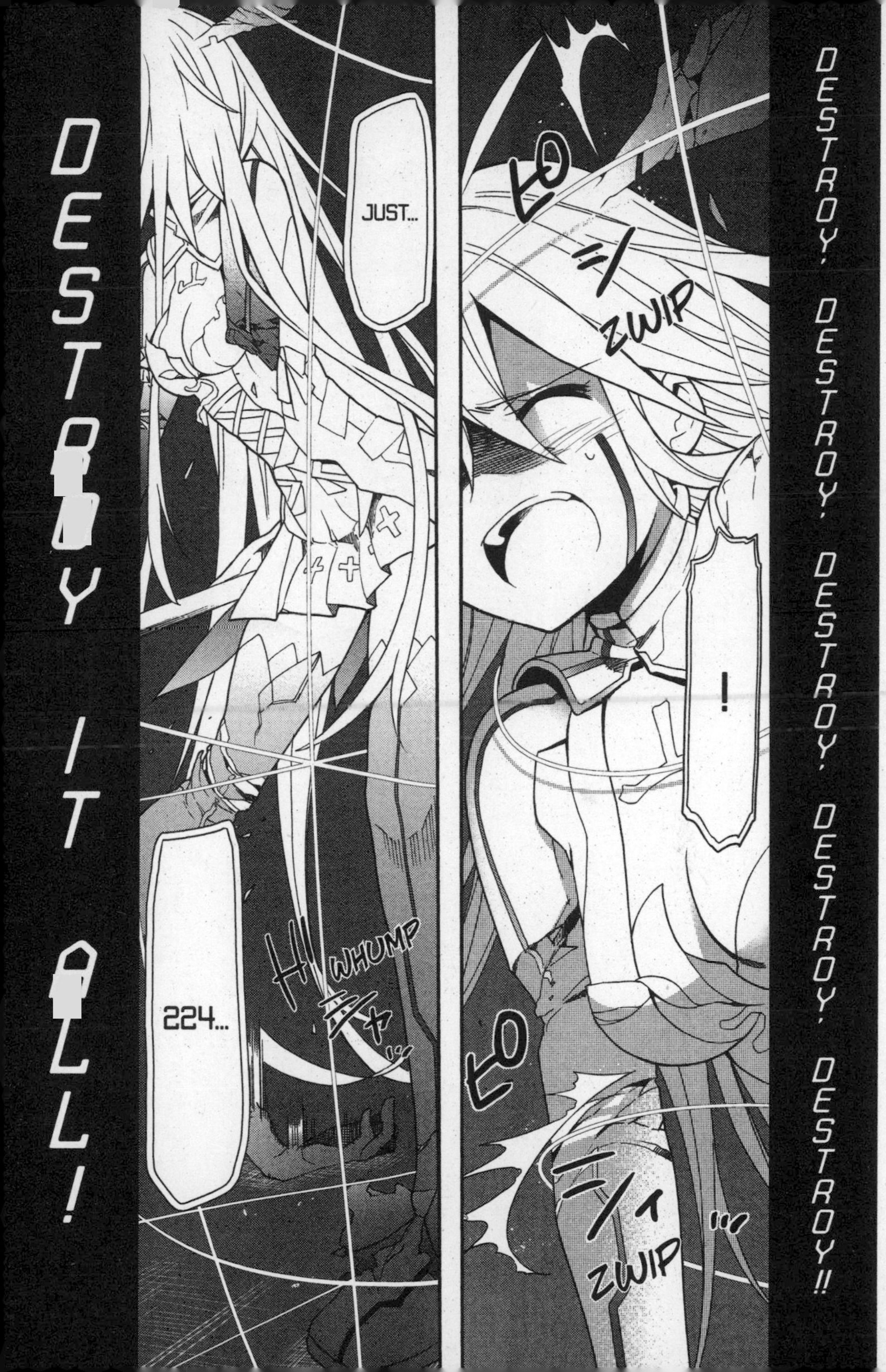
DESTROY, DESTROY, DESTROY, DESTROY, DESTROY!!
ZWIP
!
ZWIP
JUST...
WHUMP
224...
DESTROY IT ALL!

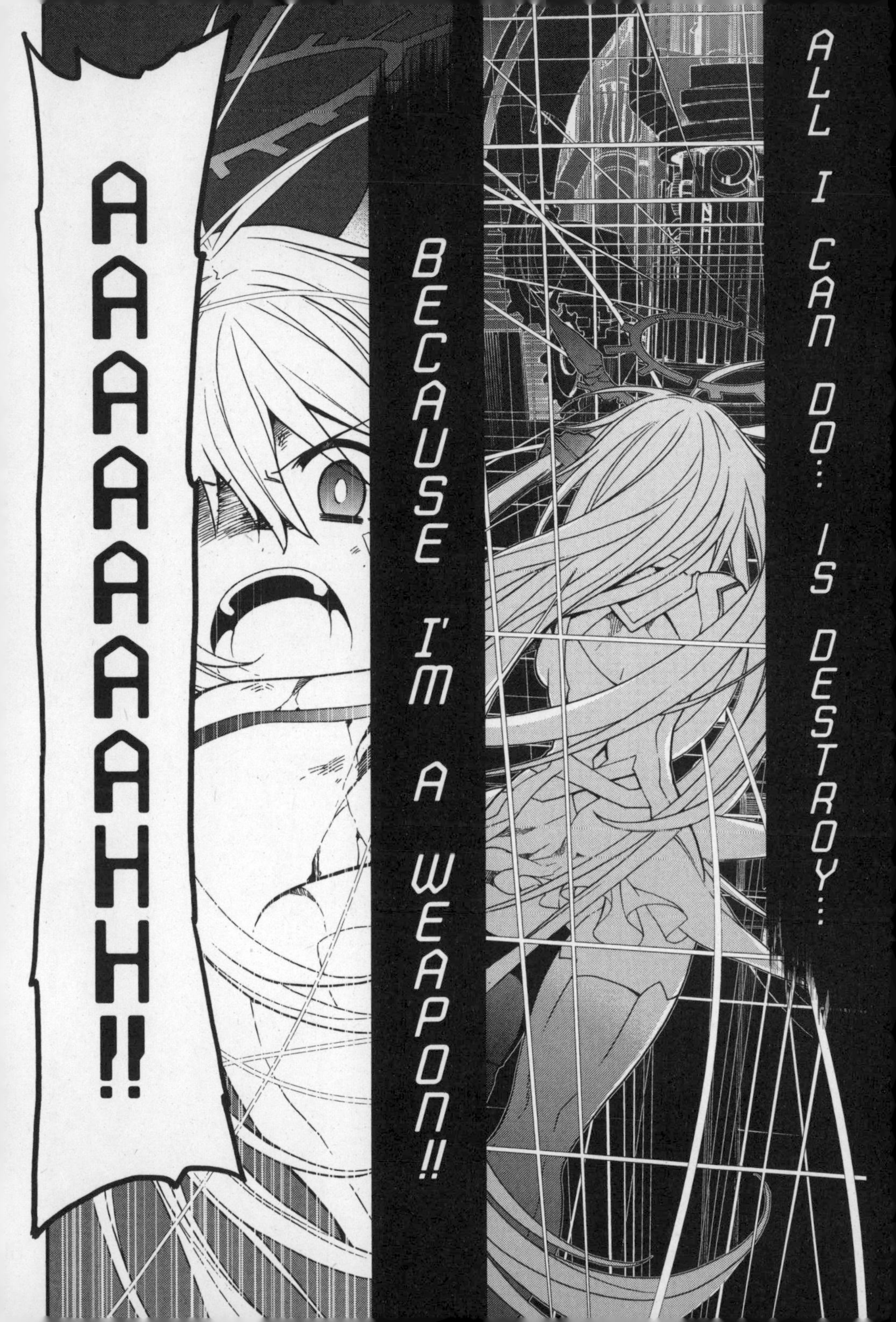
ALL I CAN DO... IS DESTROY...
BECAUSE I'M A WEAPON!!
AAAAAAAHH!!

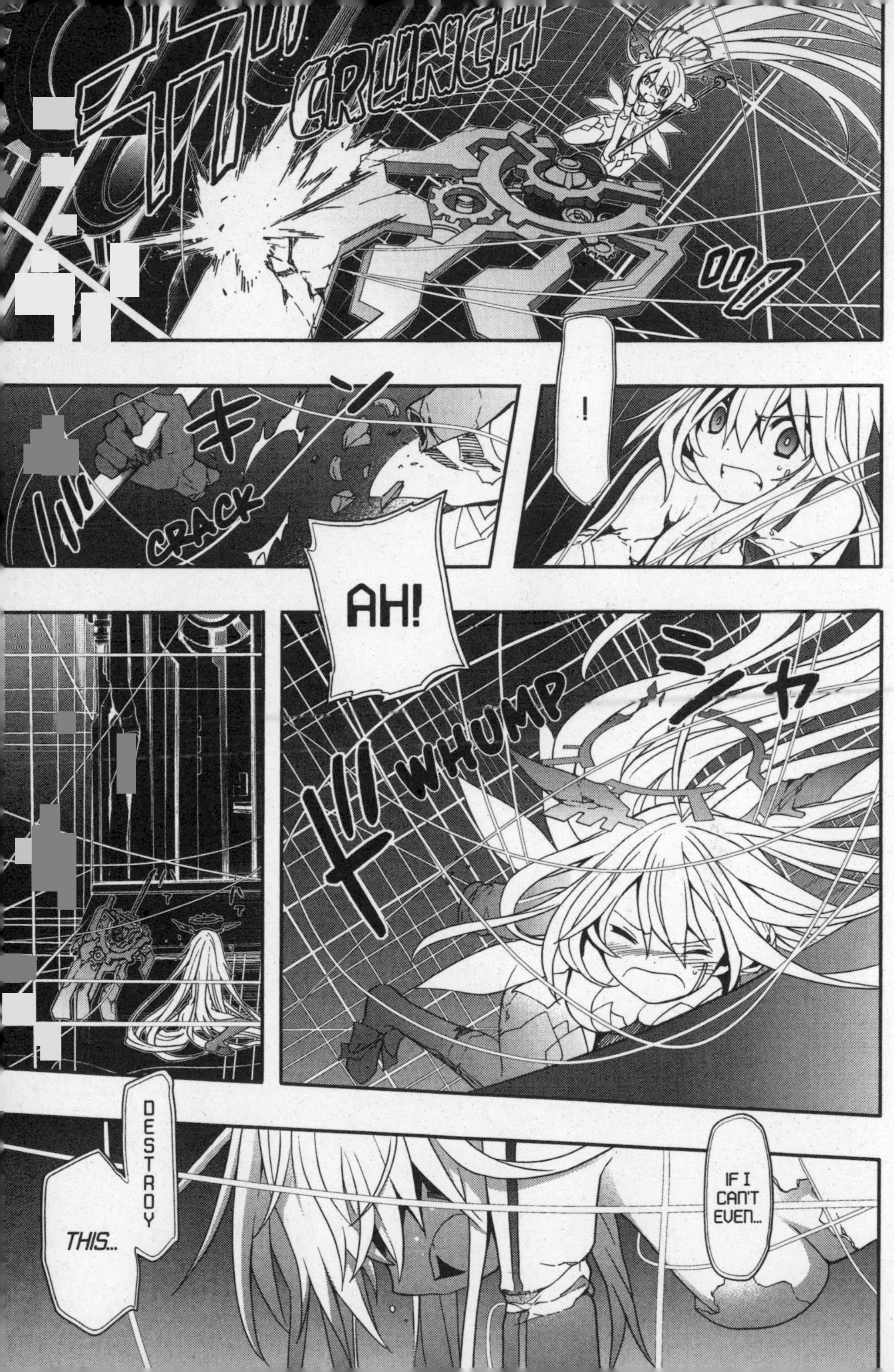
CRUNCH
!
CRACK
AH!
WHUMP
IF I CAN'T EVEN...
DESTROY THIS...

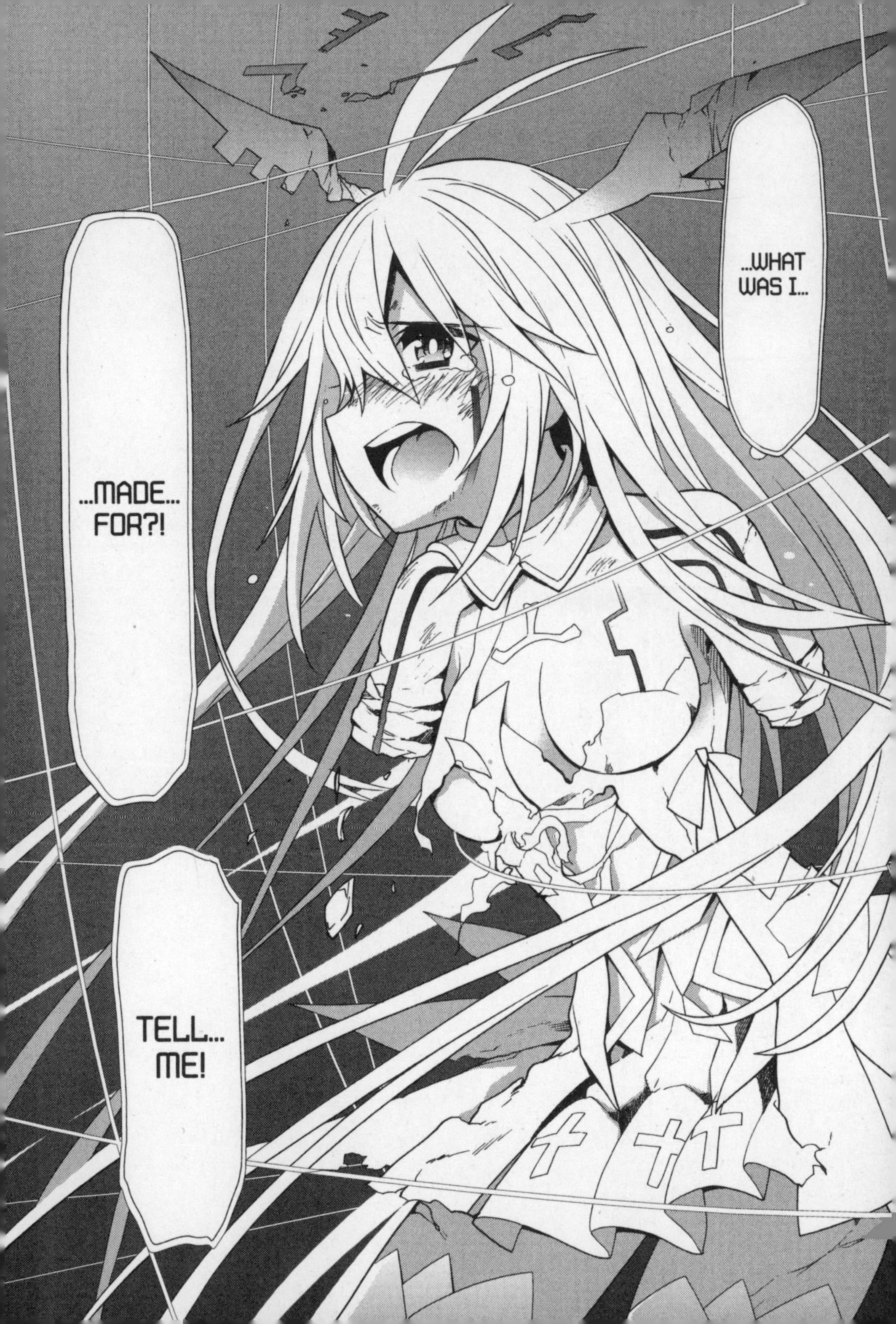
...WHAT WAS I...
...MADE... FOR?!
TELL... ME!

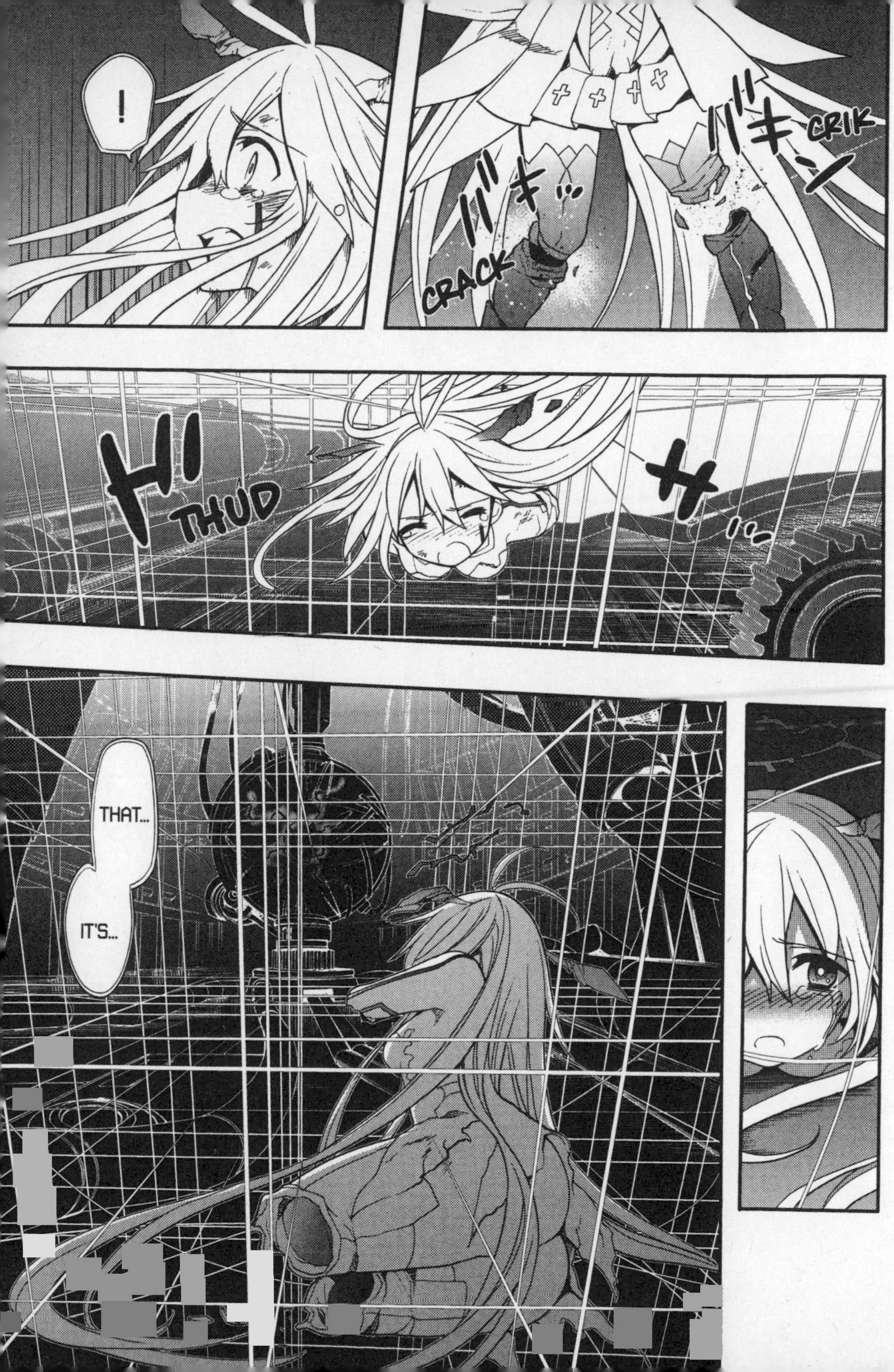

CRIK
CRACK
!
THUD
THAT...
IT'S...

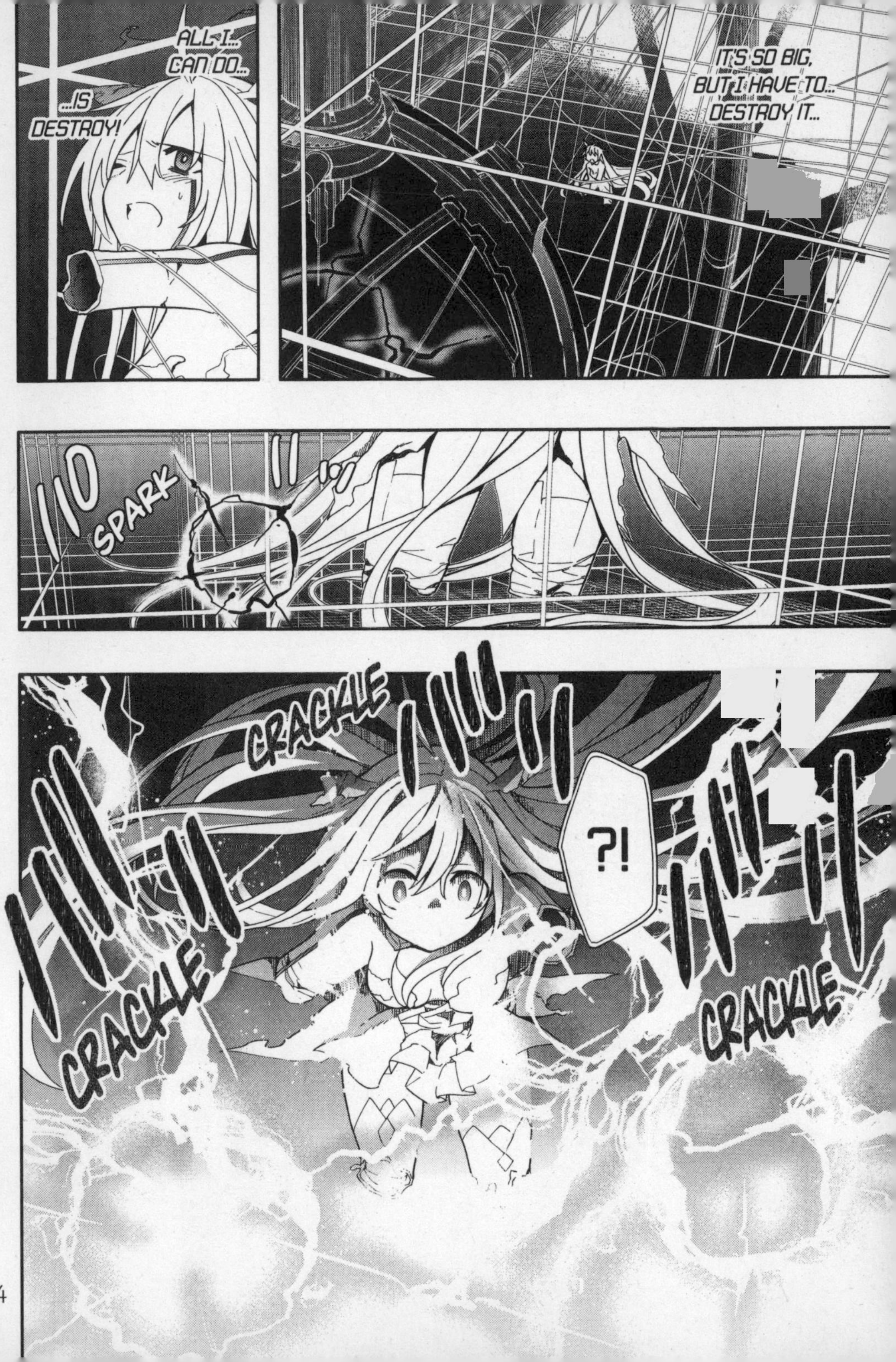
IT'S SO BIG, BUT I HAVE TO... DESTROY IT...
ALL I... CAN DO...
...IS DESTROY!
SPARK
CRACKLE
?!
CRACKLE
CRACKLE

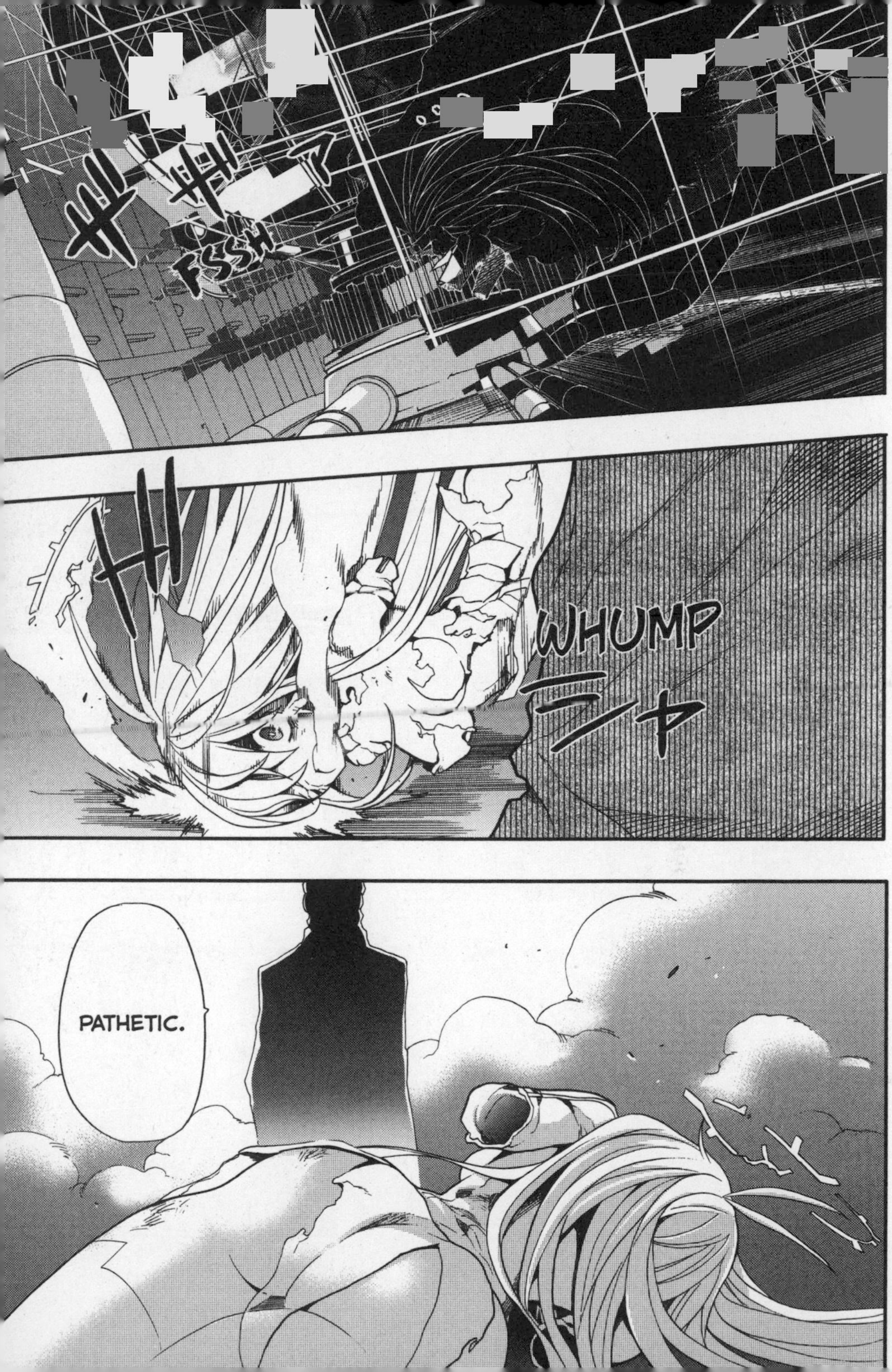
FSSH
WHUMP
PATHETIC.

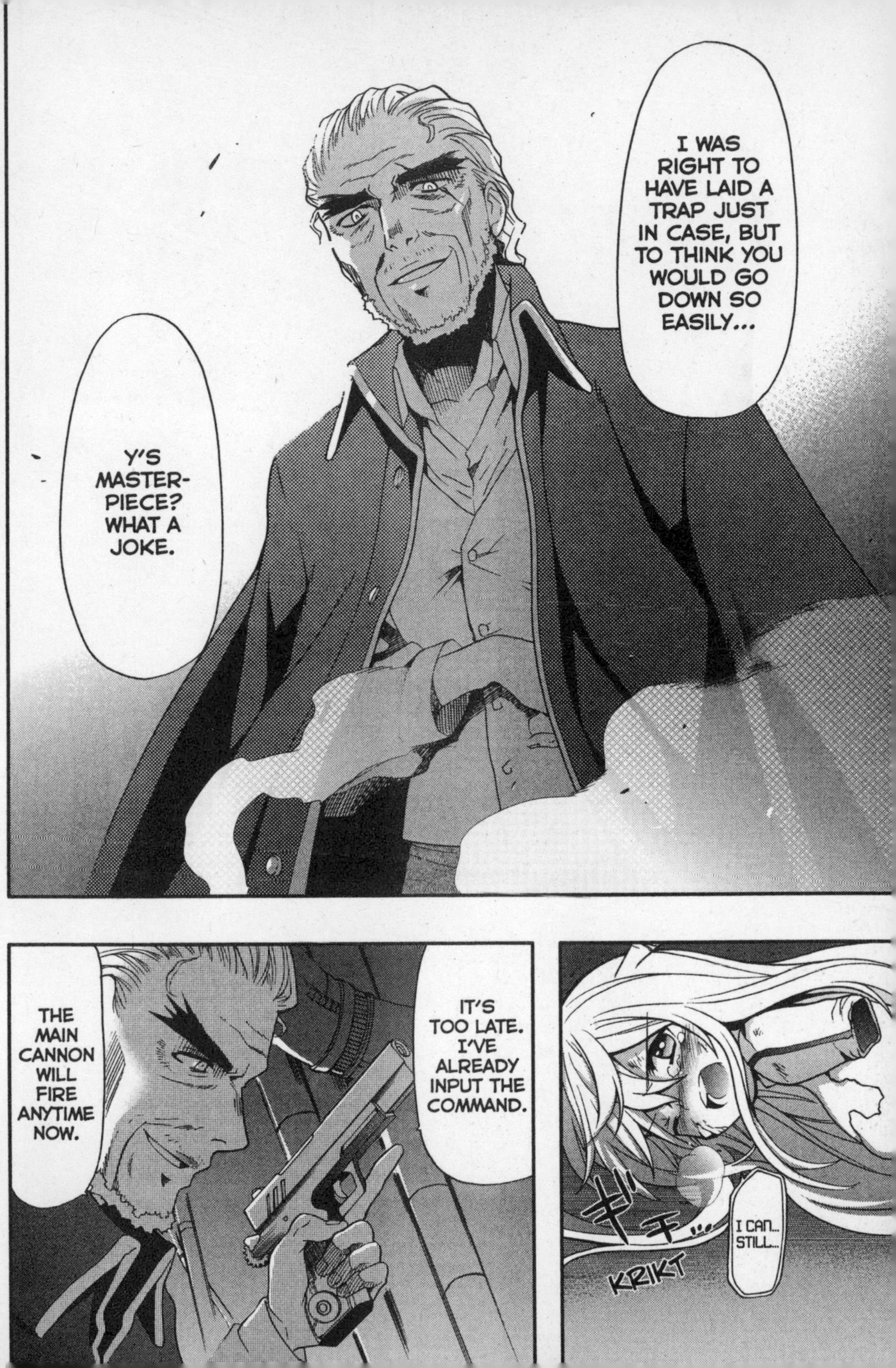
I WAS RIGHT TO HAVE LAID A TRAP JUST IN CASE, BUT TO THINK YOU WOULD GO DOWN SO EASILY...
Y'S MASTER-PIECE? WHAT A JOKE.
I CAN... STILL...
KRIKT
IT'S TOO LATE. I'VE ALREADY INPUT THE COMMAND.
THE MAIN CANNON WILL FIRE ANYTIME NOW.

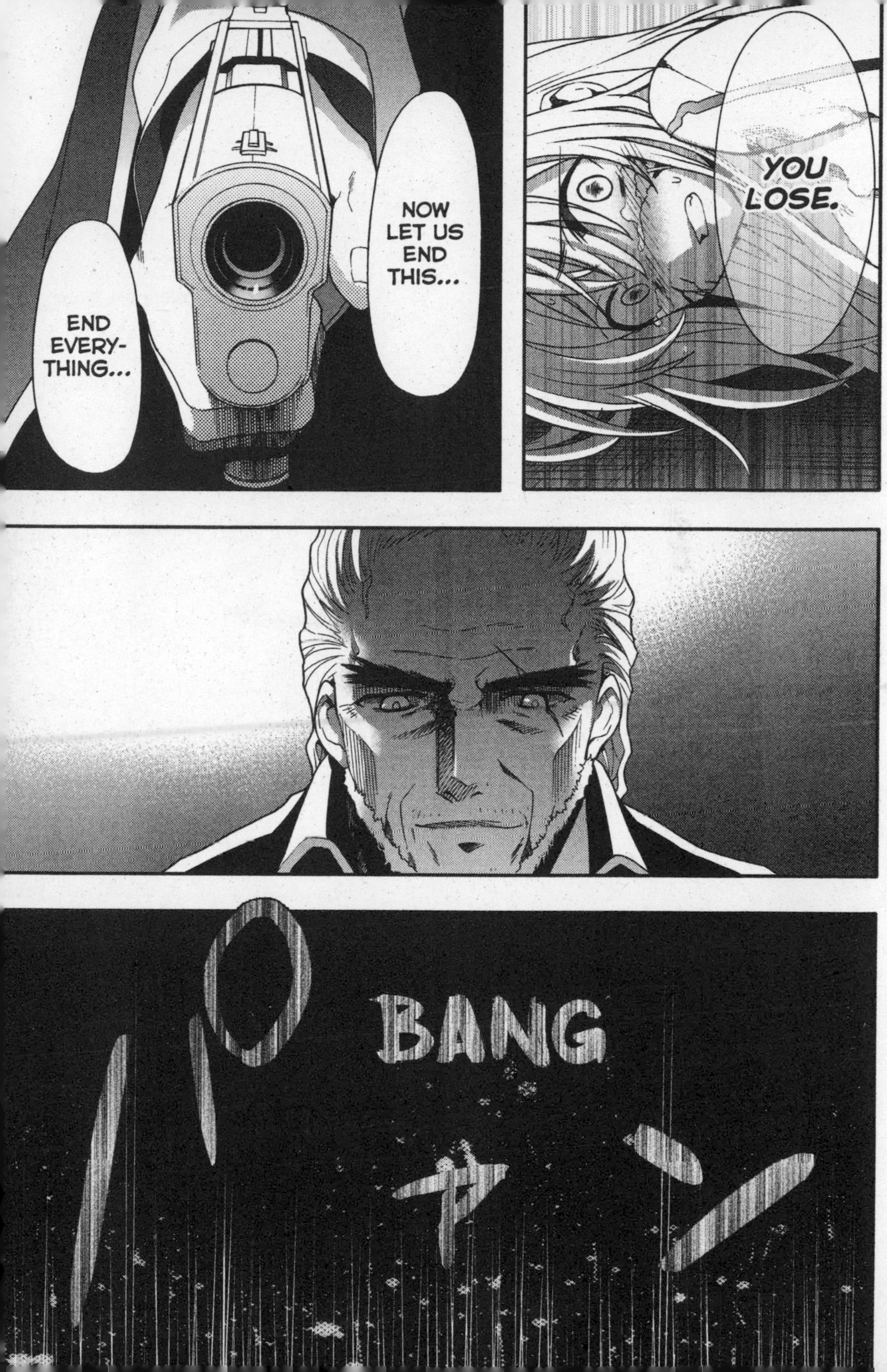
YOU LOSE.
NOW LET US END THIS...
END EVERY-THING...
BANG

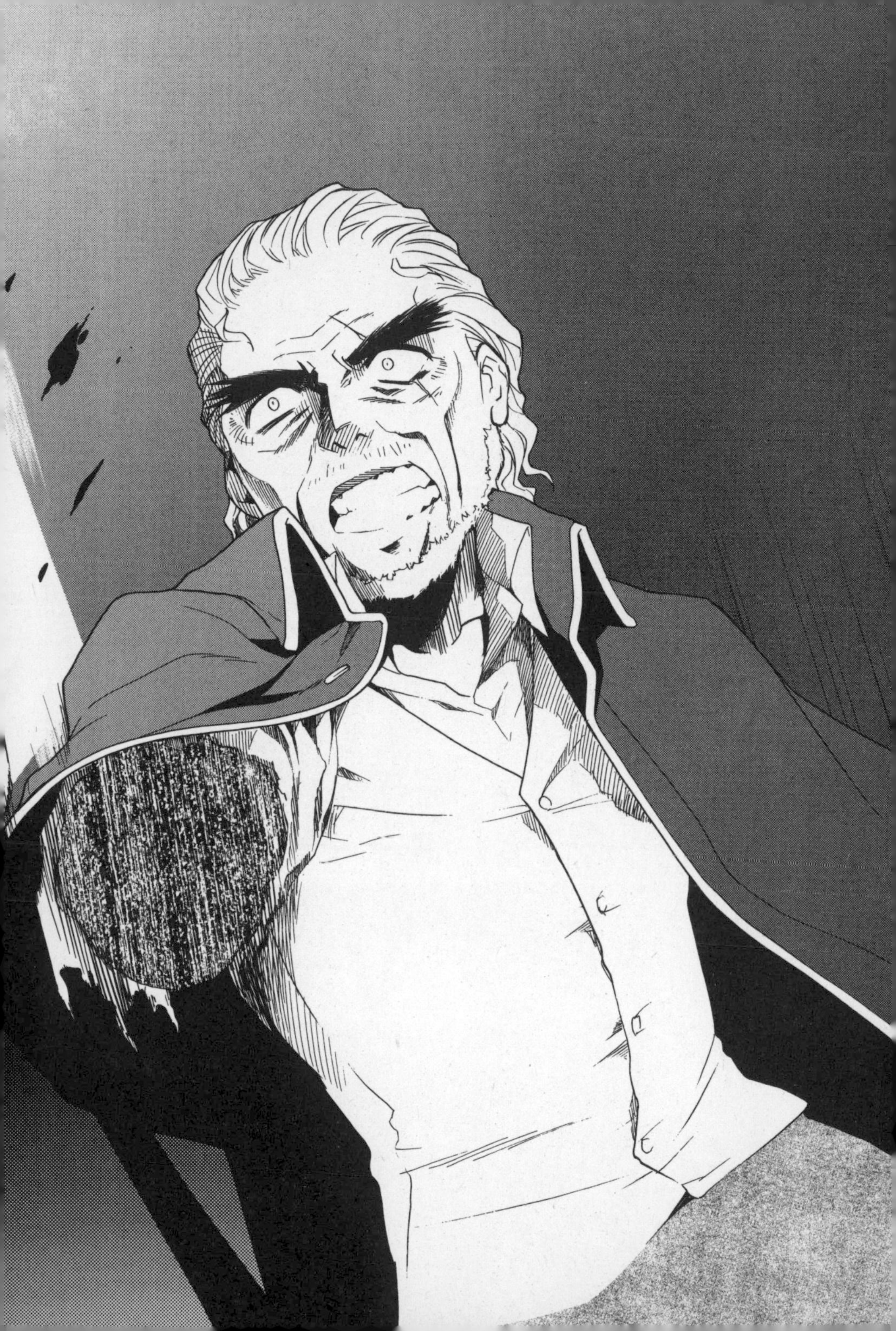

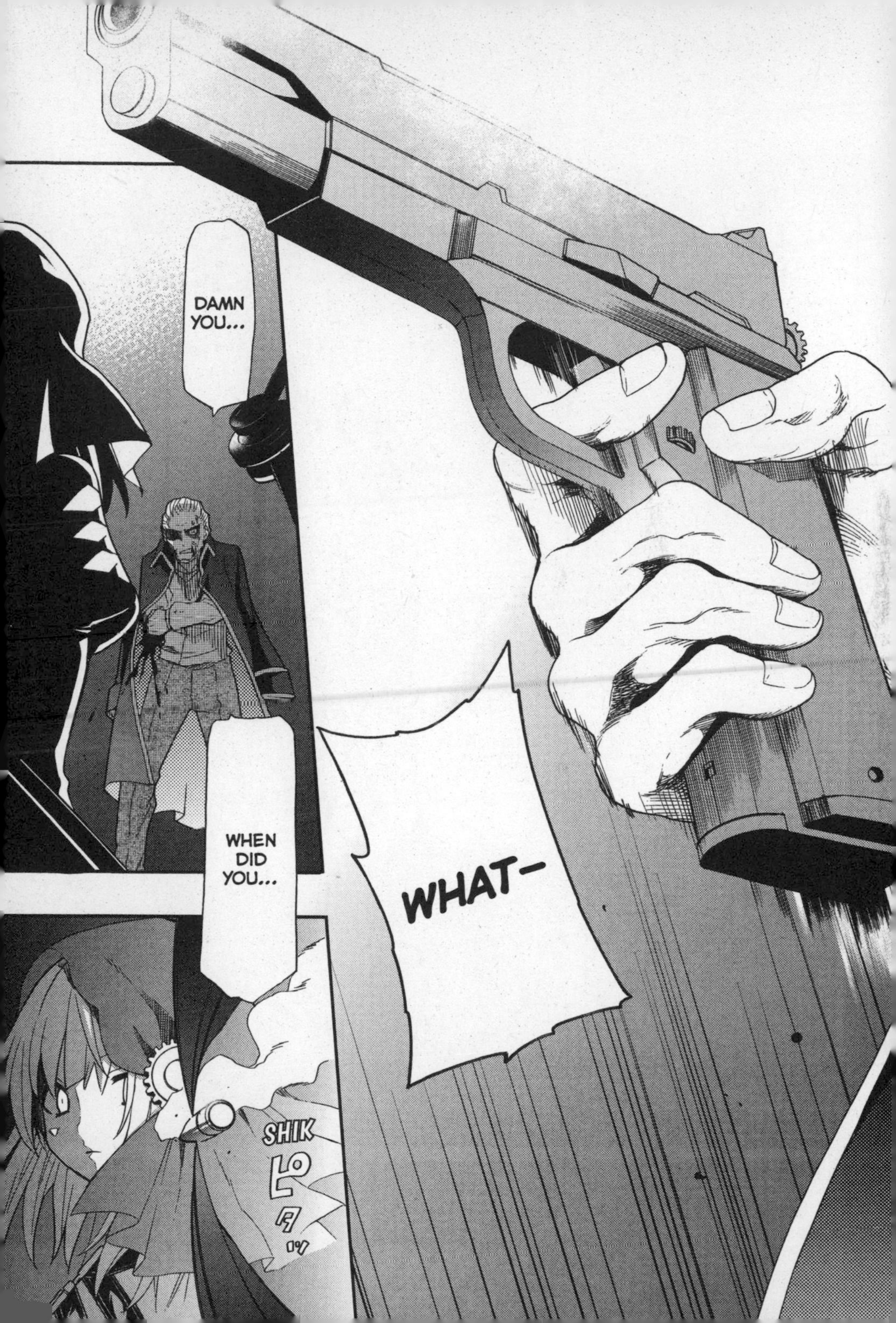
WHAT-
DAMN YOU...
WHEN DID YOU...
SHIK

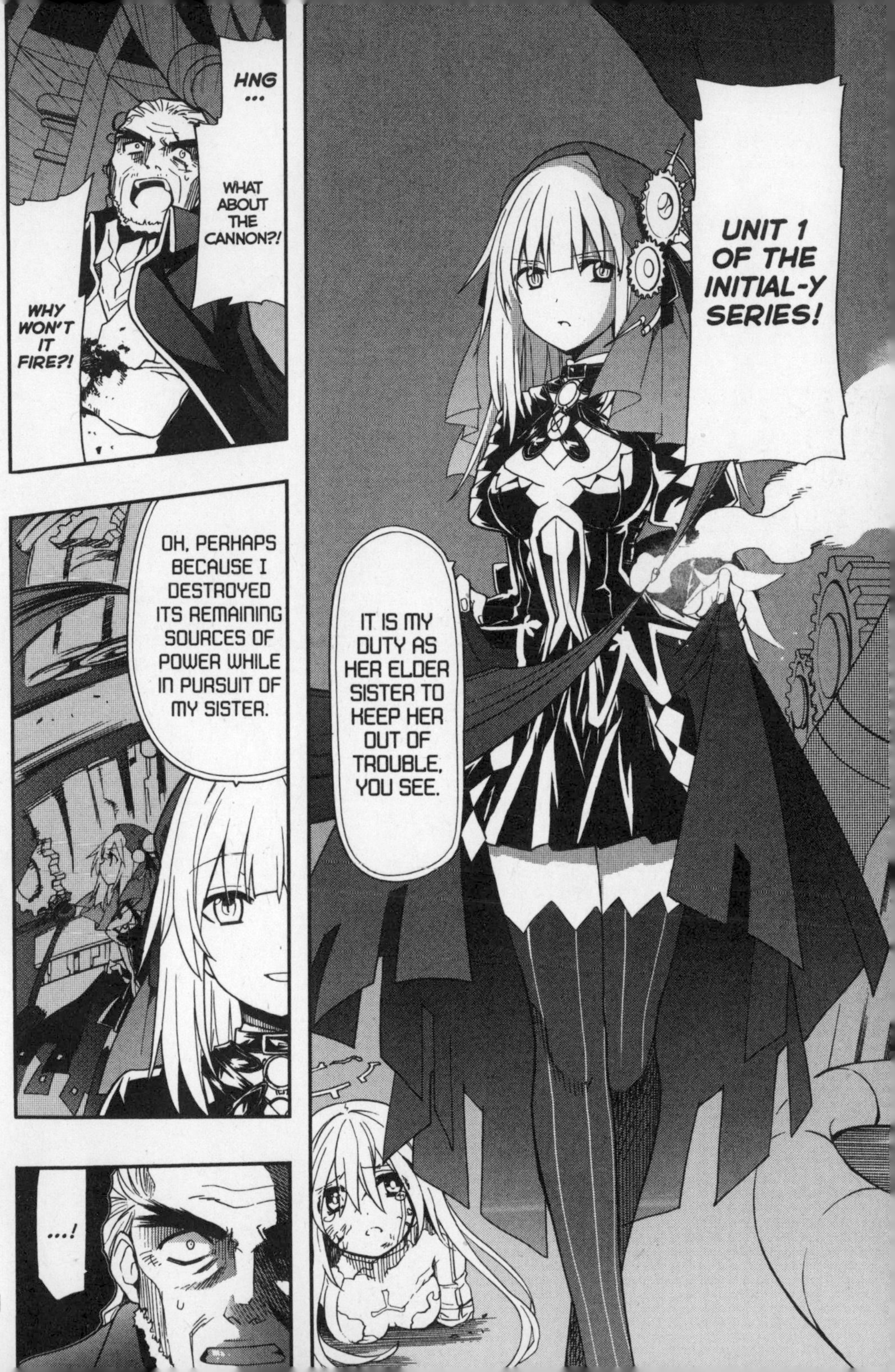
UNIT 1 OF THE INITIAL-Y SERIES!
IT IS MY DUTY AS HER ELDER SISTER TO KEEP HER OUT OF TROUBLE, YOU SEE.
HNG ...
WHAT ABOUT THE CANNON?!
WHY WON'T IT FIRE?!
OH, PERHAPS BECAUSE I DESTROYED ITS REMAINING SOURCES OF POWER WHILE IN PURSUIT OF MY SISTER.
...!

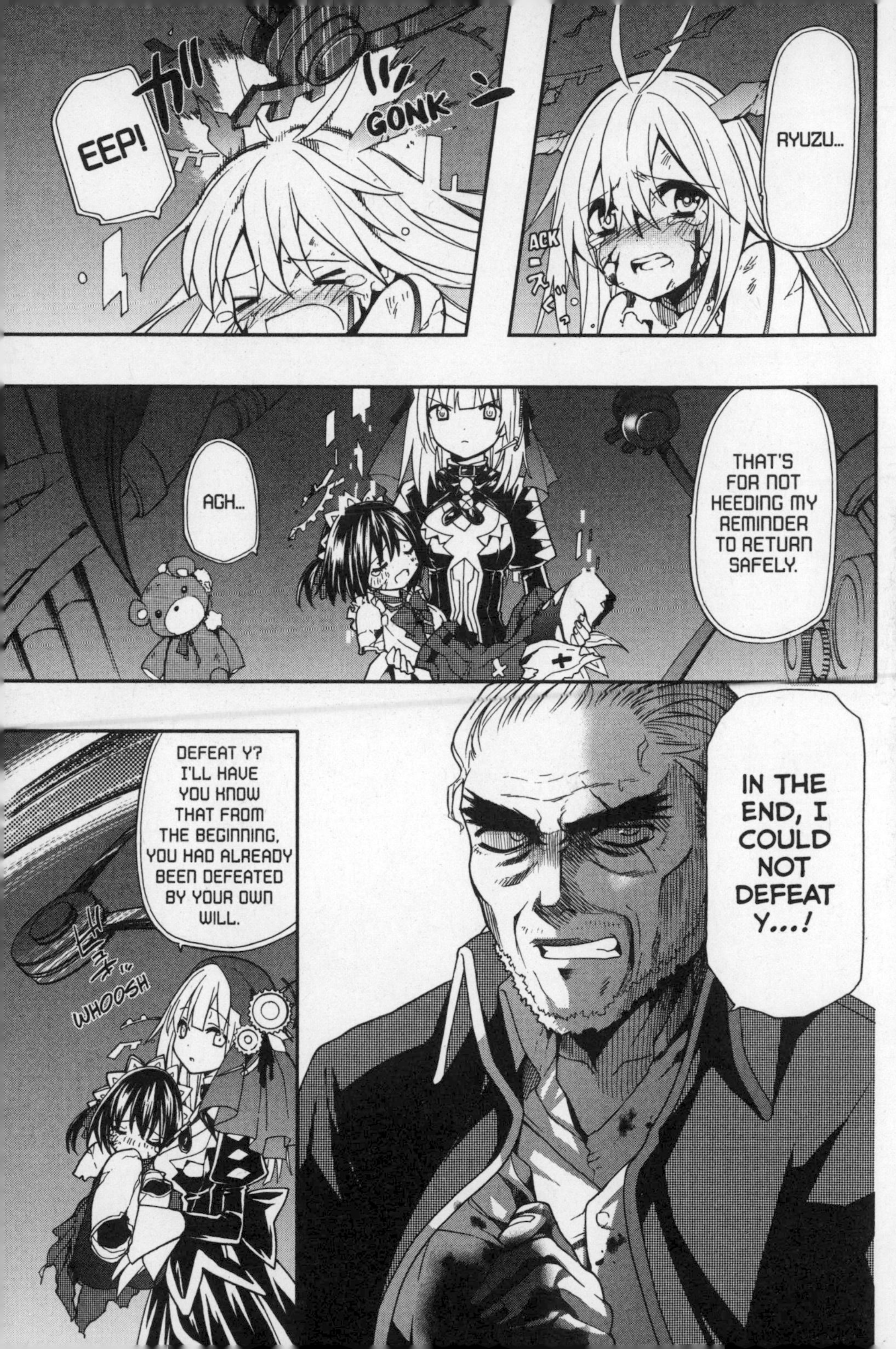
RYUZU...
ACK
EEP!
GONK
THAT'S FOR NOT HEEDING MY REMINDER TO RETURN SAFELY.
AGH...
IN THE END, I COULD NOT DEFEAT Y...!
DEFEAT Y? I'LL HAVE YOU KNOW THAT FROM THE BEGINNING, YOU HAD ALREADY BEEN DEFEATED BY YOUR OWN WILL.
WHOOSH

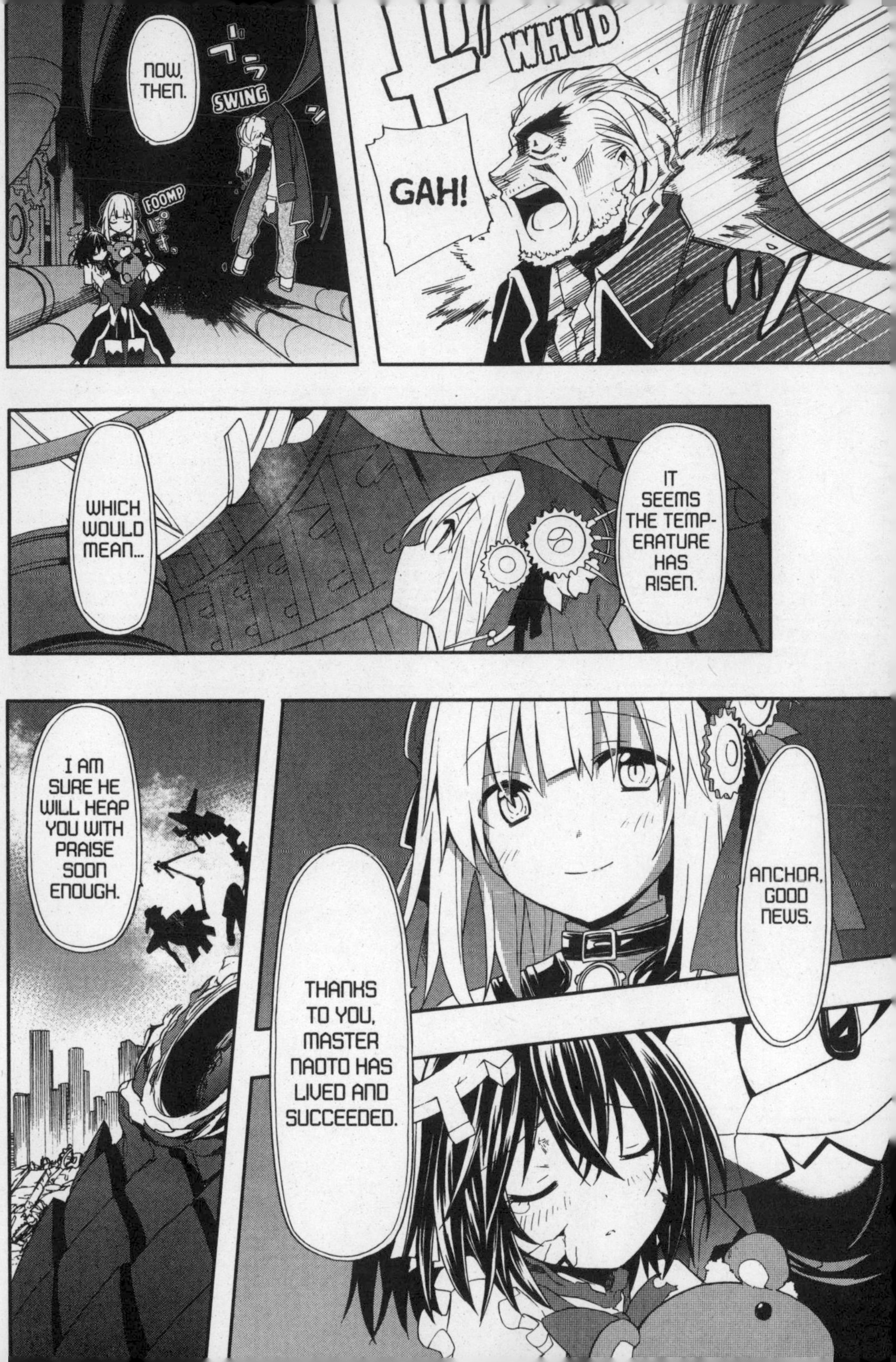
WHUD
GAH!
NOW, THEN.
SWING
FOOMP
IT SEEMS THE TEMPERATURE HAS RISEN.
WHICH WOULD MEAN...
ANCHOR, GOOD NEWS.
THANKS TO YOU, MASTER NAOTO HAS LIVED AND SUCCEEDED.
I AM SURE HE WILL HEAP YOU WITH PRAISE SOON ENOUGH.

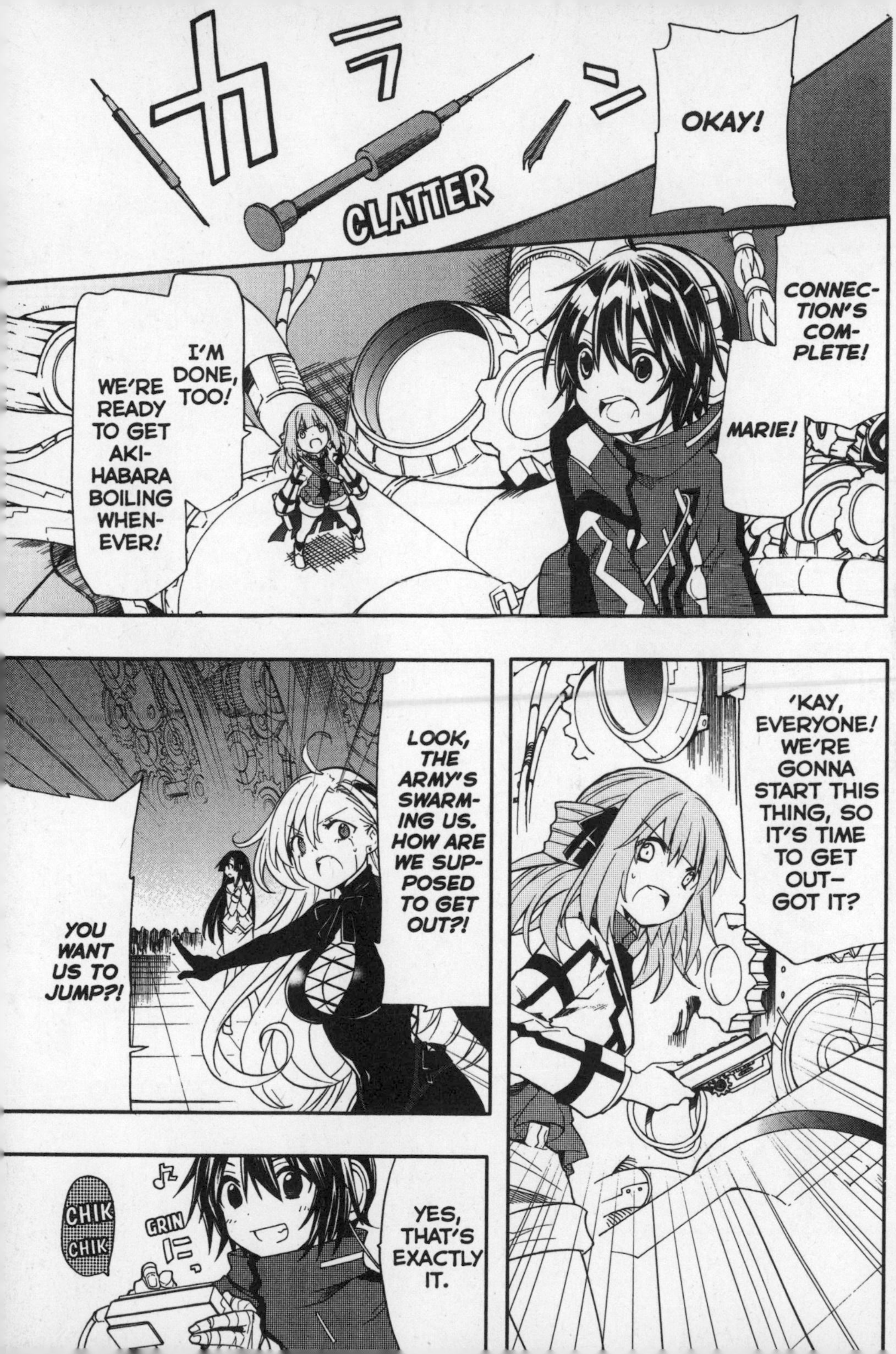

OKAY!
カラン
CLATTER
CONNECTION'S COMPLETE!
MARIE!
I'M DONE, TOO!
WE'RE READY TO GET AKIHABARA BOILING WHENEVER!
'KAY, EVERYONE! WE'RE GONNA START THIS THING, SO IT'S TIME TO GET OUT— GOT IT?
LOOK, THE ARMY'S SWARMING US. HOW ARE WE SUPPOSED TO GET OUT?!
YOU WANT US TO JUMP?!
YES, THAT'S EXACTLY IT.
GRIN
にっ
CHIK CHIK

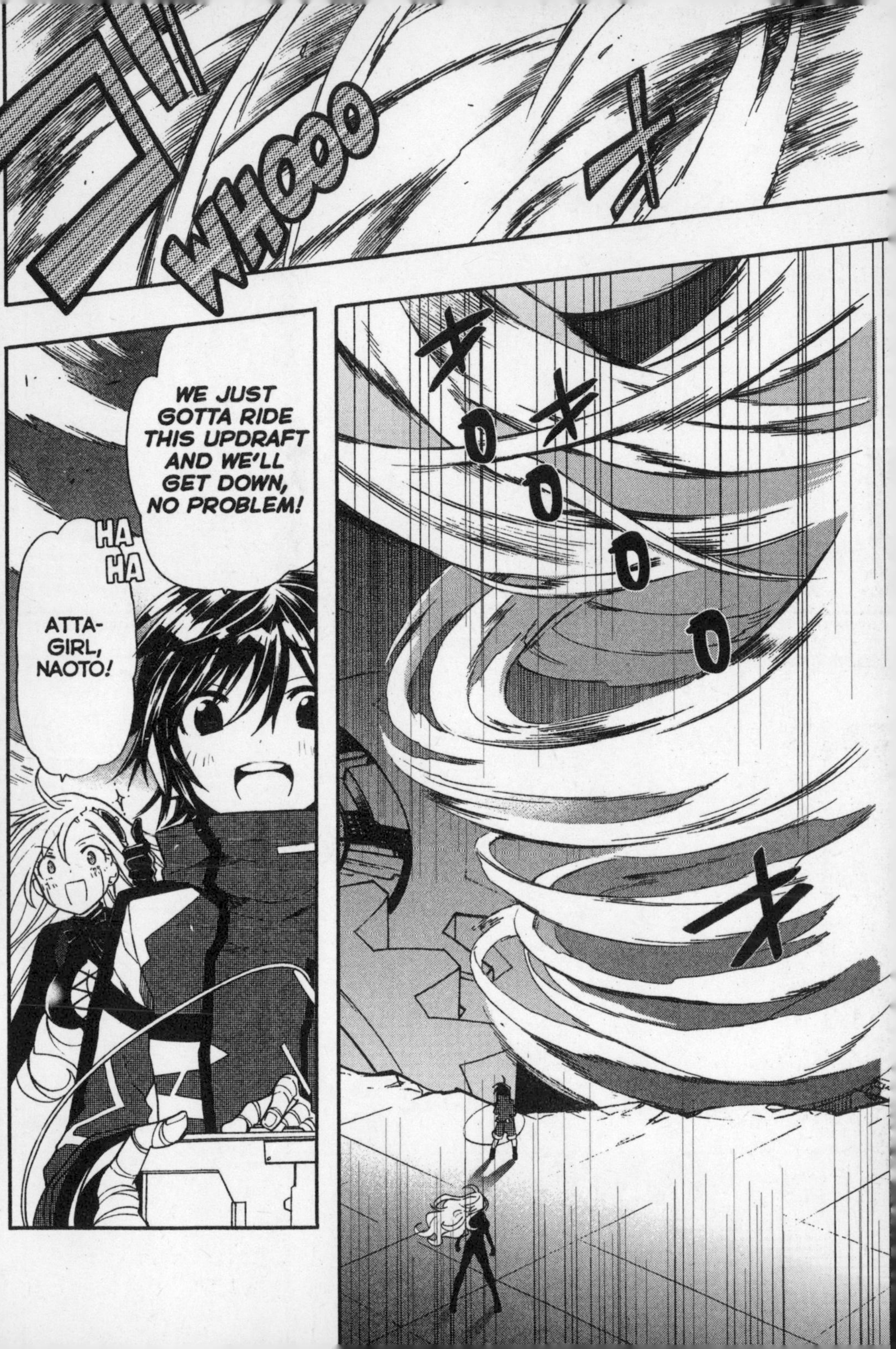
WHOOO
WE JUST GOTTA RIDE THIS UPDRAFT AND WE'LL GET DOWN, NO PROBLEM!
HA HA
ATTA-GIRL, NAOTO!

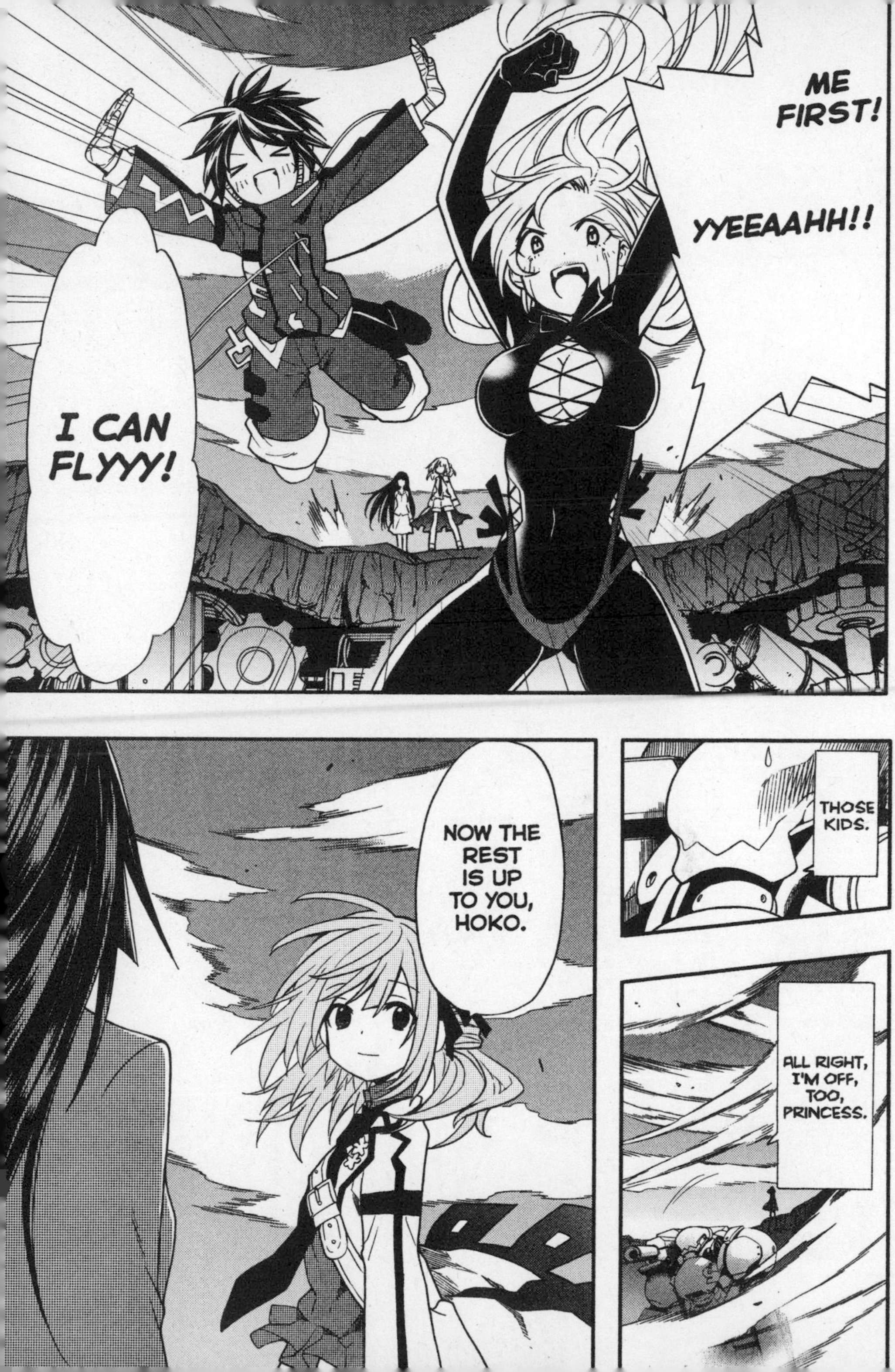
ME FIRST!
YYEEAAHH!!
I CAN FLYYY!
THOSE KIDS.
ALL RIGHT, I'M OFF, TOO, PRINCESS.
NOW THE REST IS UP TO YOU, HOKO.

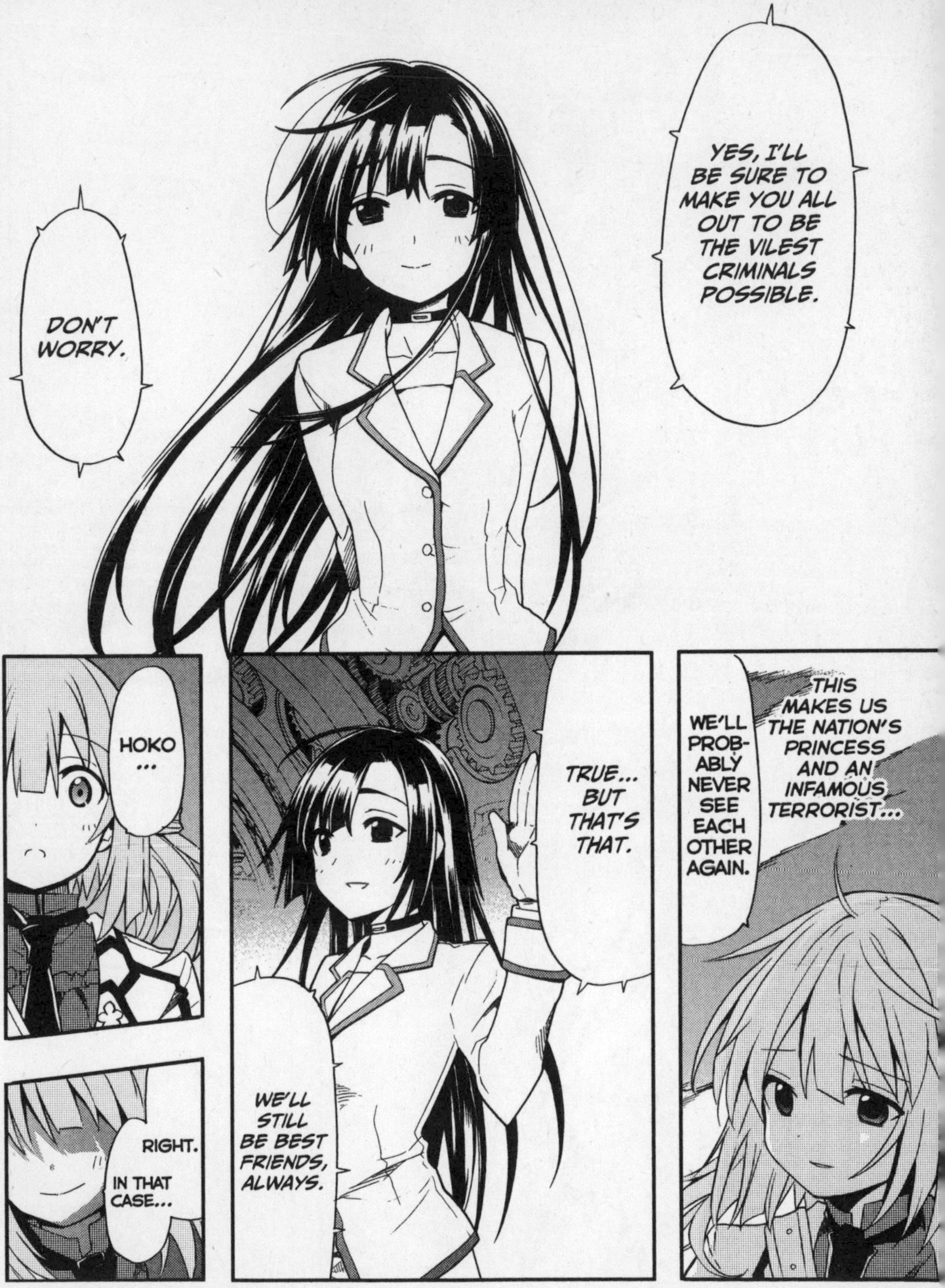
YES, I'LL BE SURE TO MAKE YOU ALL OUT TO BE THE VILEST CRIMINALS POSSIBLE.
DON'T WORRY.
THIS MAKES US THE NATION'S PRINCESS AND AN INFAMOUS TERRORIST...
WE'LL PROB-ABLY NEVER SEE EACH OTHER AGAIN.
TRUE... BUT THAT'S THAT.
WE'LL STILL BE BEST FRIENDS, ALWAYS.
HOKO ...
RIGHT.
IN THAT CASE...

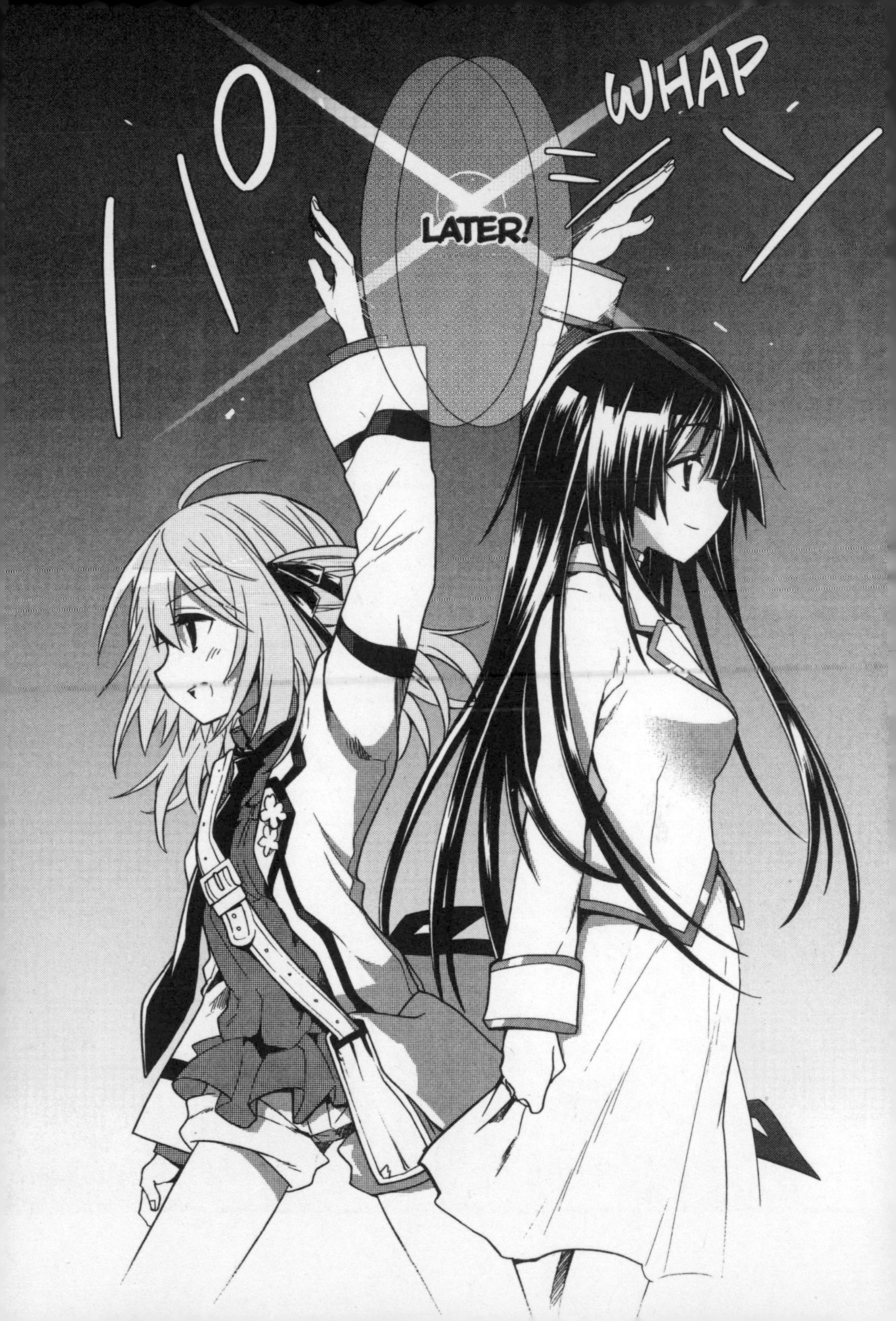
WHAP
LATER!

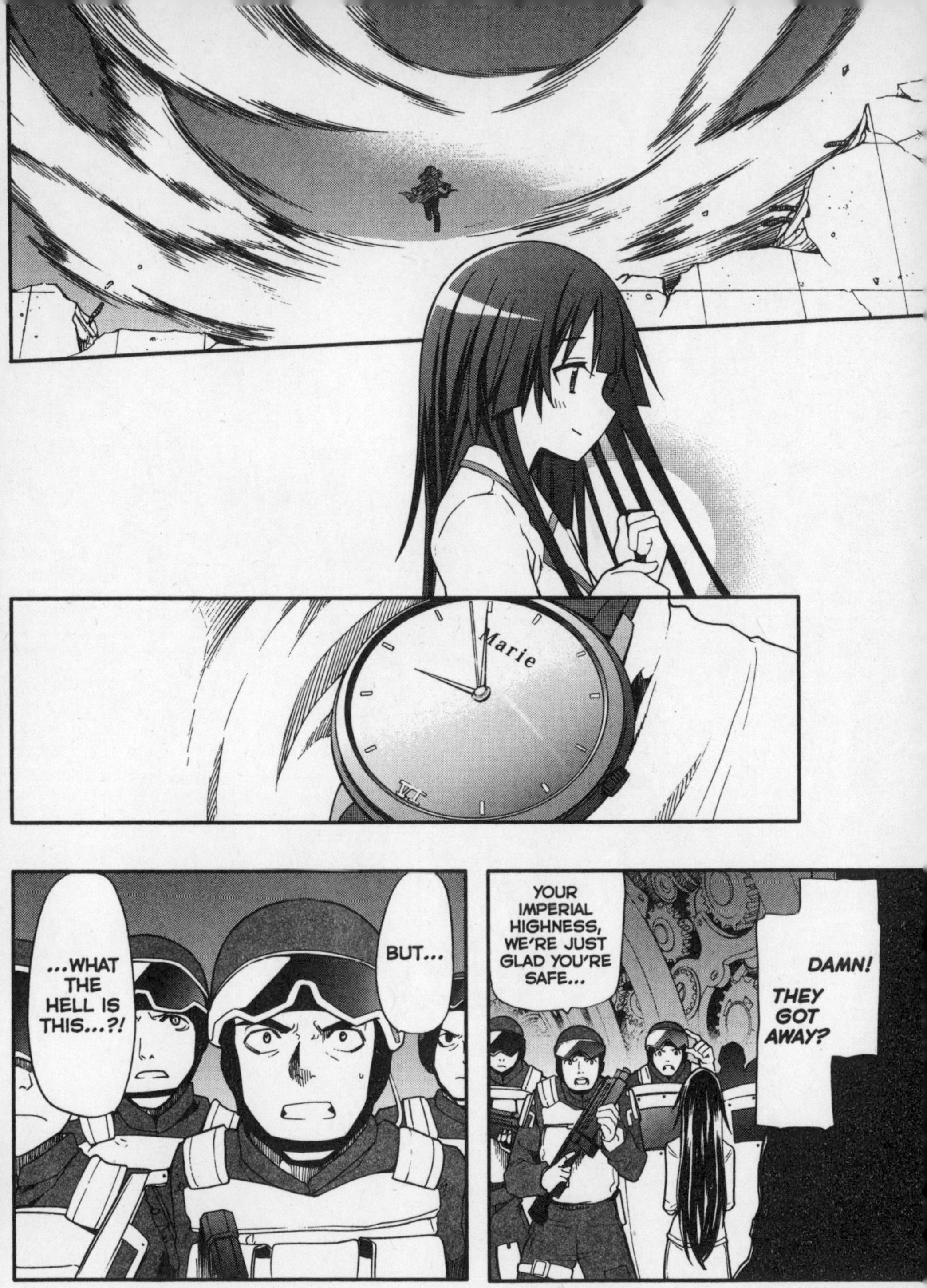
Marie
DAMN!
THEY GOT AWAY?
YOUR IMPERIAL HIGHNESS, WE'RE JUST GLAD YOU'RE SAFE...
BUT...
...WHAT THE HELL IS THIS...?!

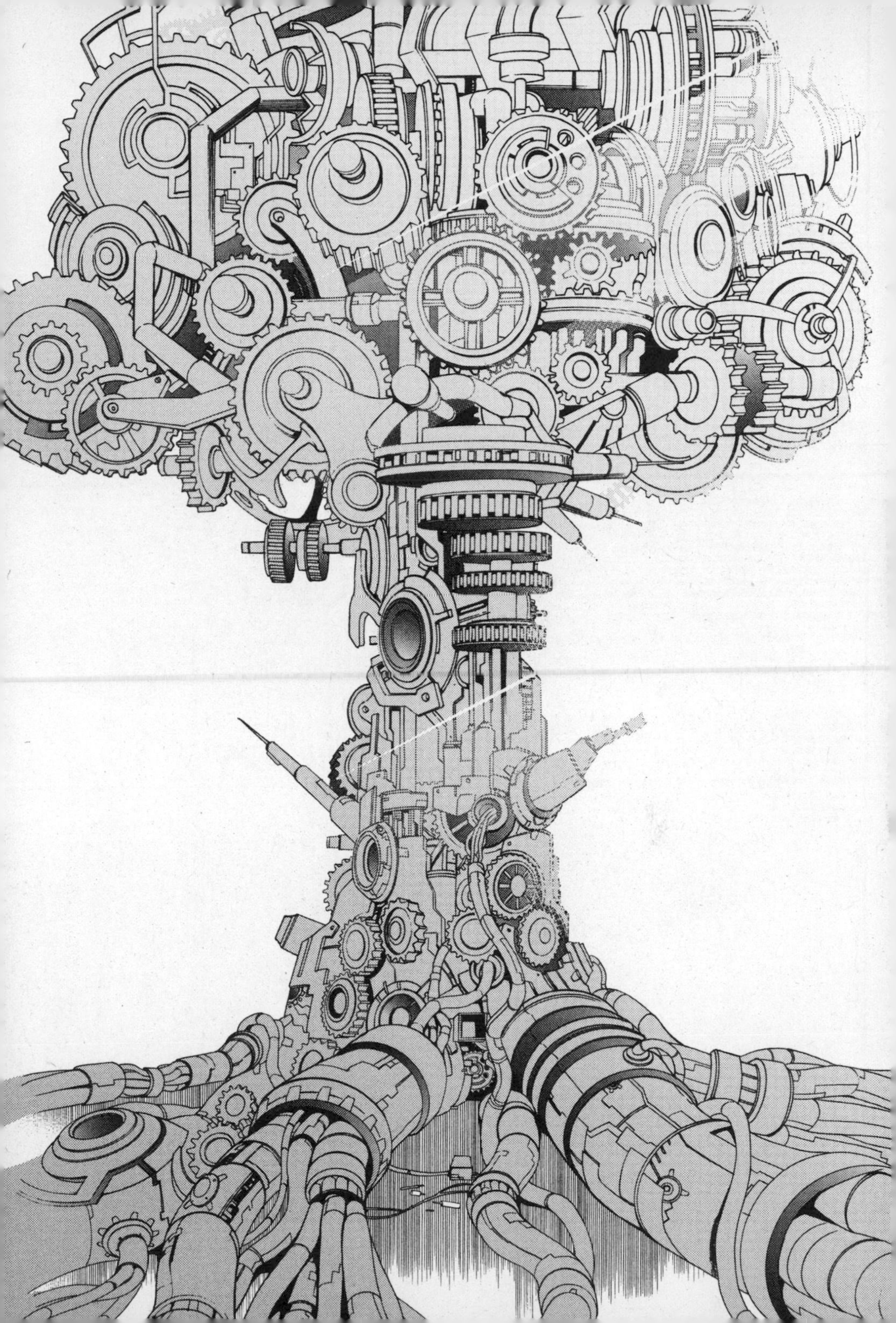

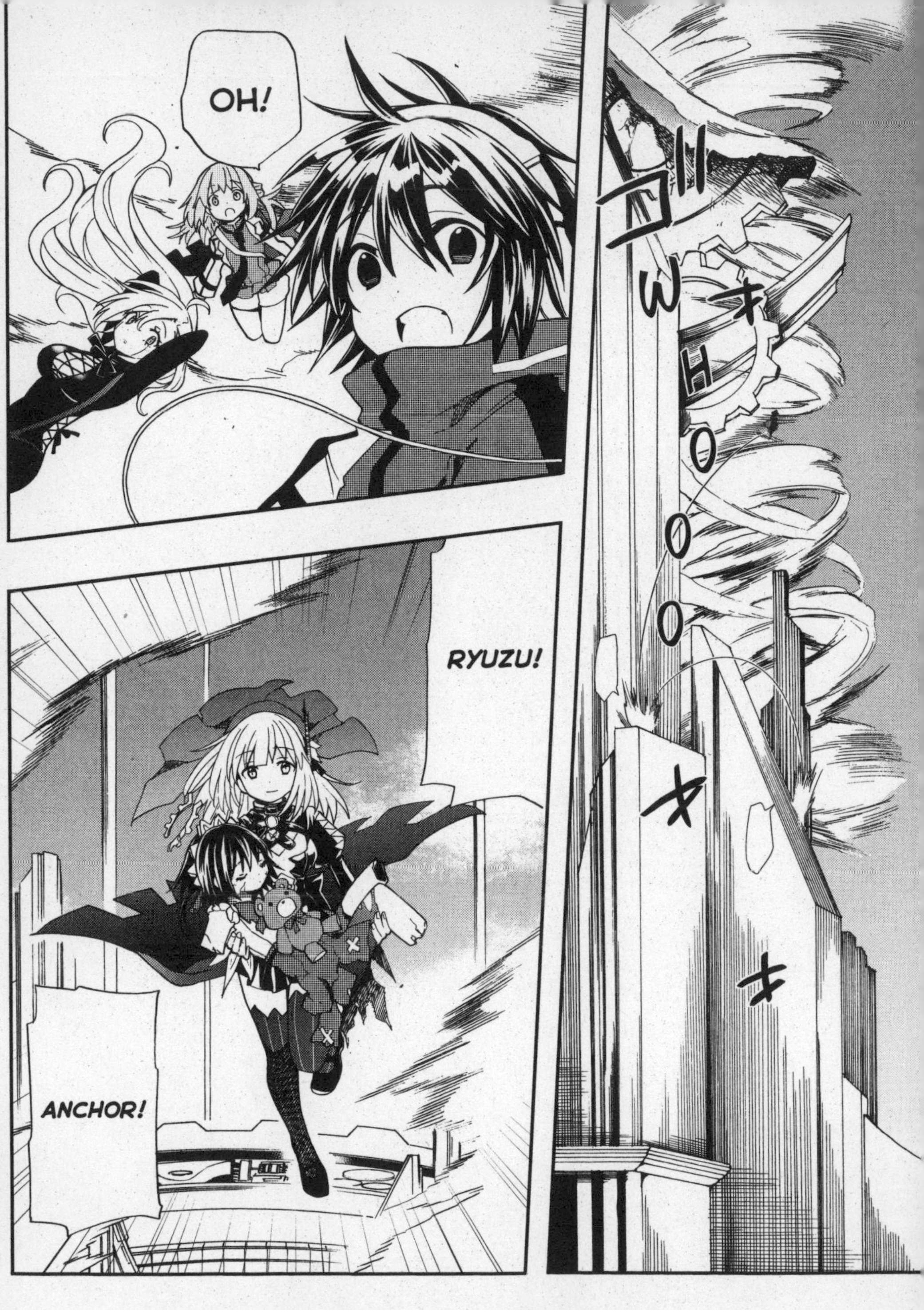
WHOOOO
OH!
RYUZU!
ANCHOR!

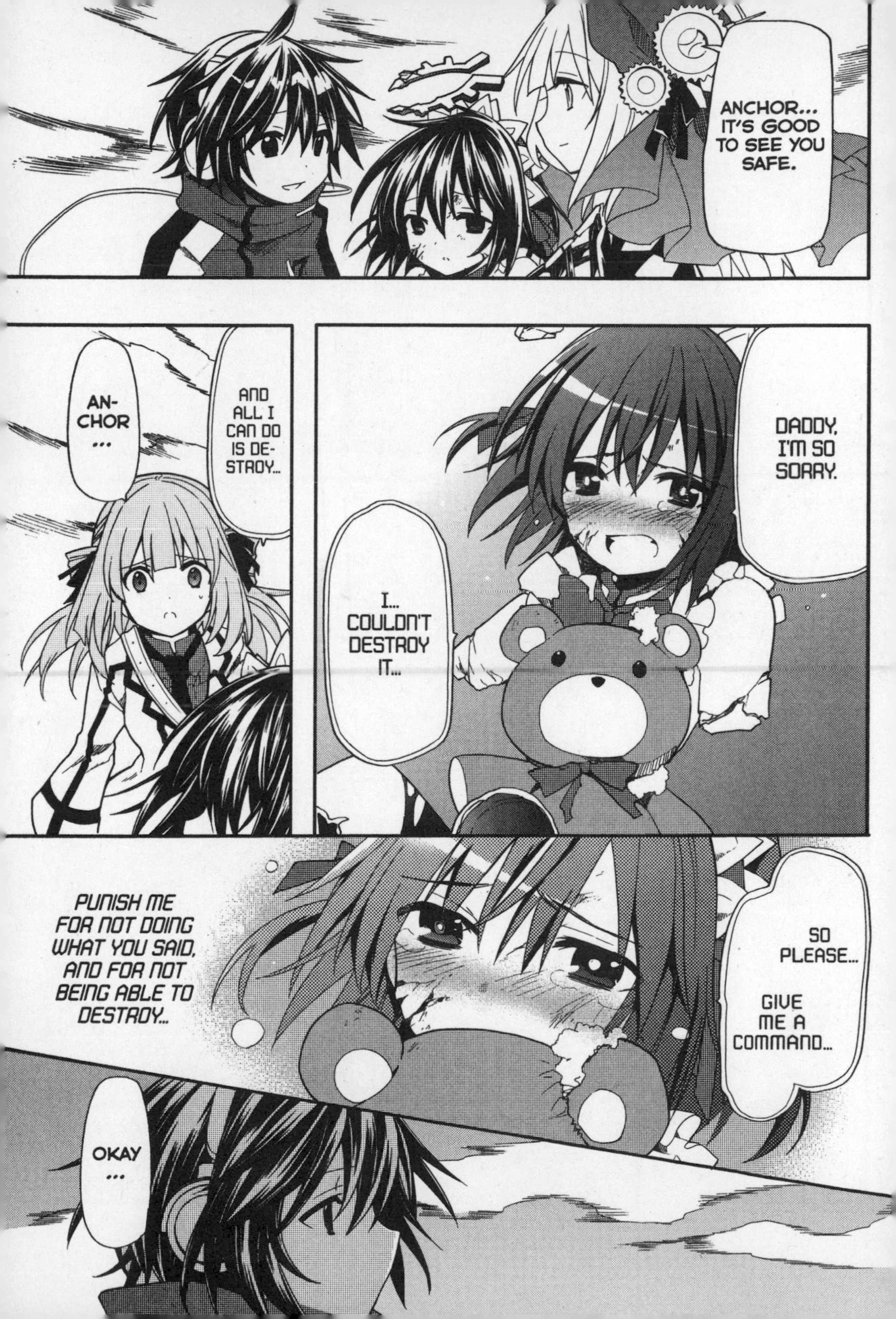
ANCHOR... IT'S GOOD TO SEE YOU SAFE.
DADDY, I'M SO SORRY.
I... COULDN'T DESTROY IT...
AND ALL I CAN DO IS DE-STROY...
AN-CHOR ...
SO PLEASE...
GIVE ME A COMMAND...
PUNISH ME FOR NOT DOING WHAT YOU SAID, AND FOR NOT BEING ABLE TO DESTROY...
OKAY ...

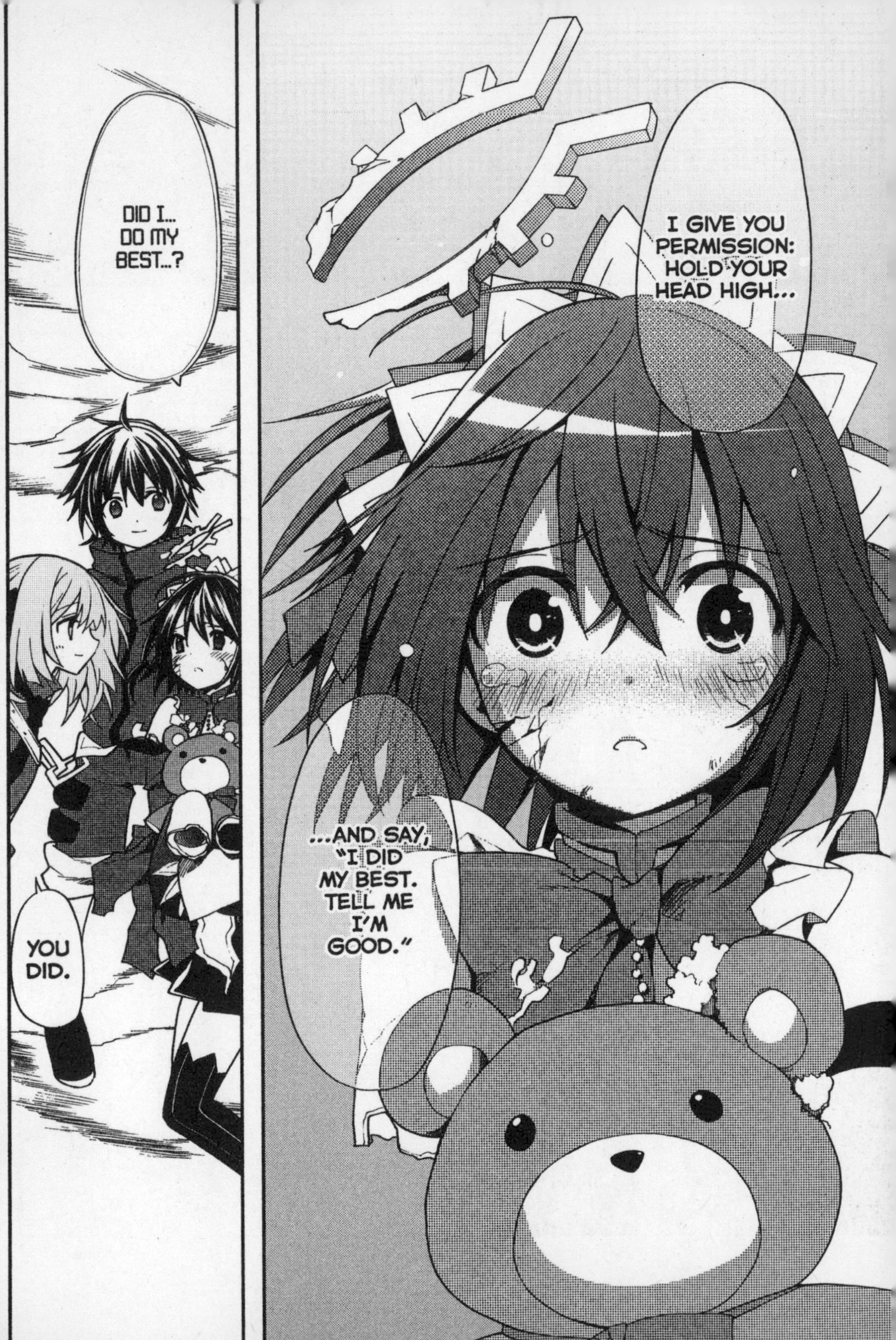
I GIVE YOU PERMISSION: HOLD YOUR HEAD HIGH...
...AND SAY, "I DID MY BEST. TELL ME I'M GOOD."
DID I... DO MY BEST...?
YOU DID.

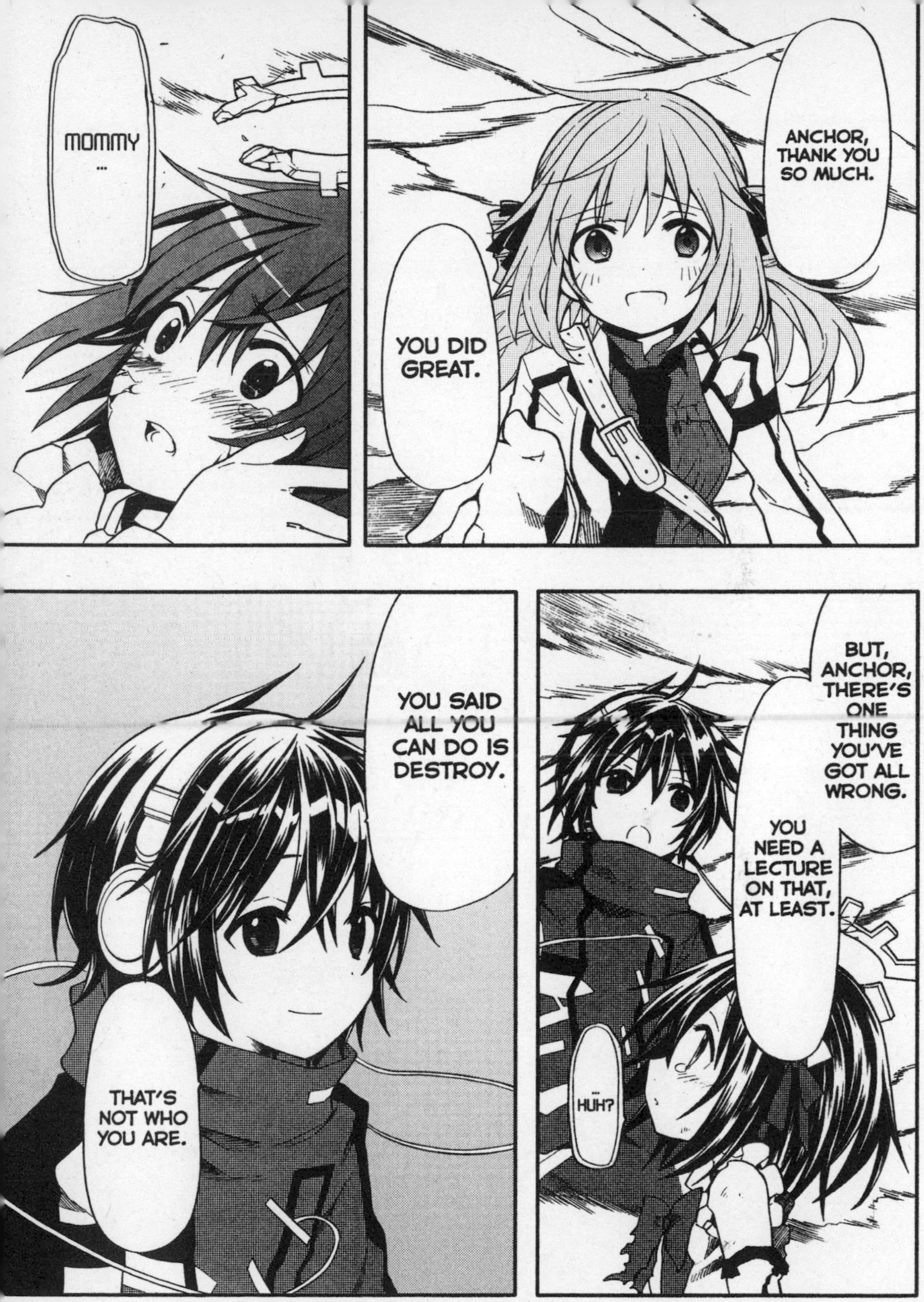
ANCHOR, THANK YOU SO MUCH.
YOU DID GREAT.
MOMMY ...
BUT, ANCHOR, THERE'S ONE THING YOU'VE GOT ALL WRONG.
YOU NEED A LECTURE ON THAT, AT LEAST.
... HUH?
YOU SAID ALL YOU CAN DO IS DESTROY.
THAT'S NOT WHO YOU ARE.

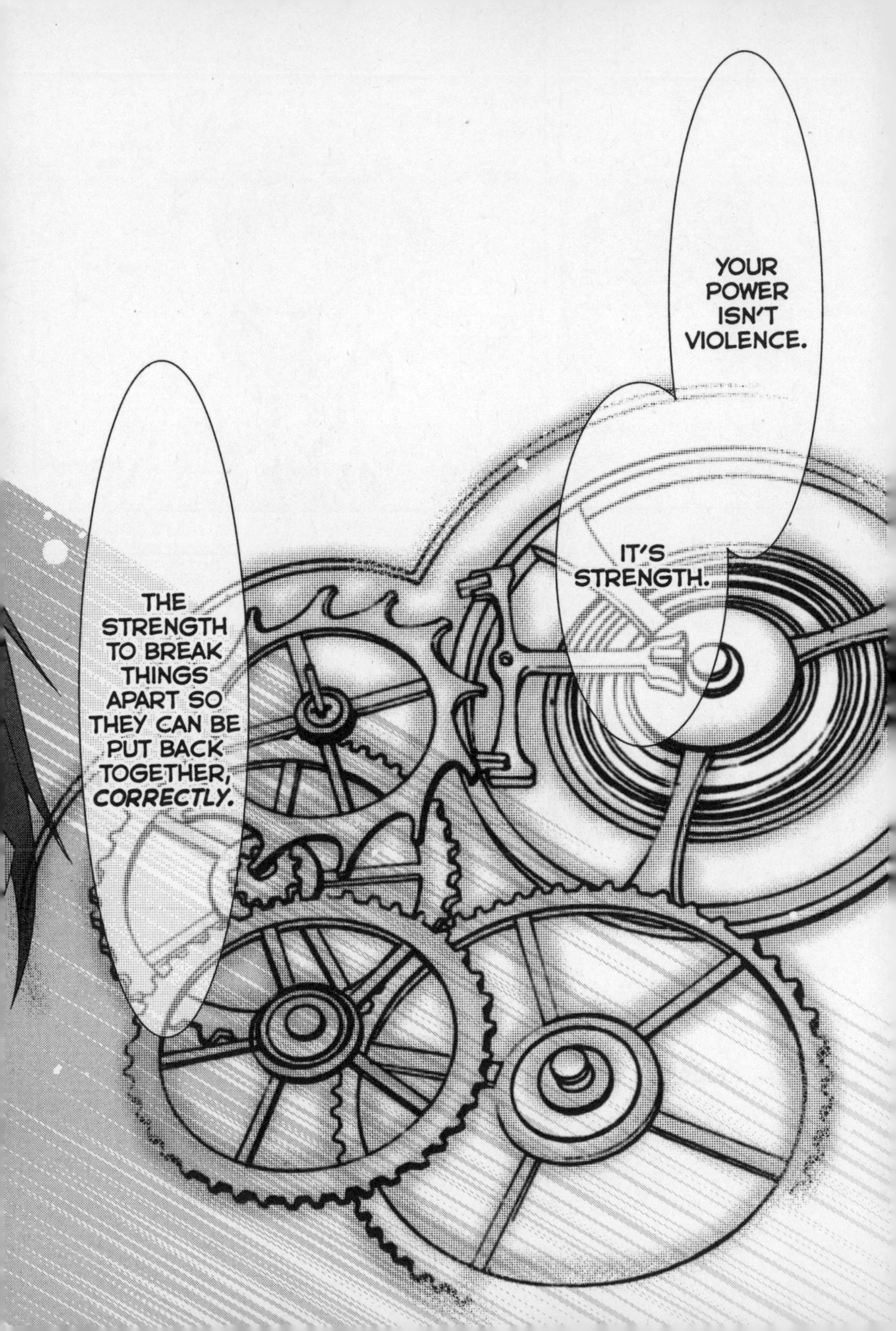
YOUR POWER ISN'T VIOLENCE.
IT'S STRENGTH.
THE STRENGTH TO BREAK THINGS APART SO THEY CAN BE PUT BACK TOGETHER, *CORRECTLY.*

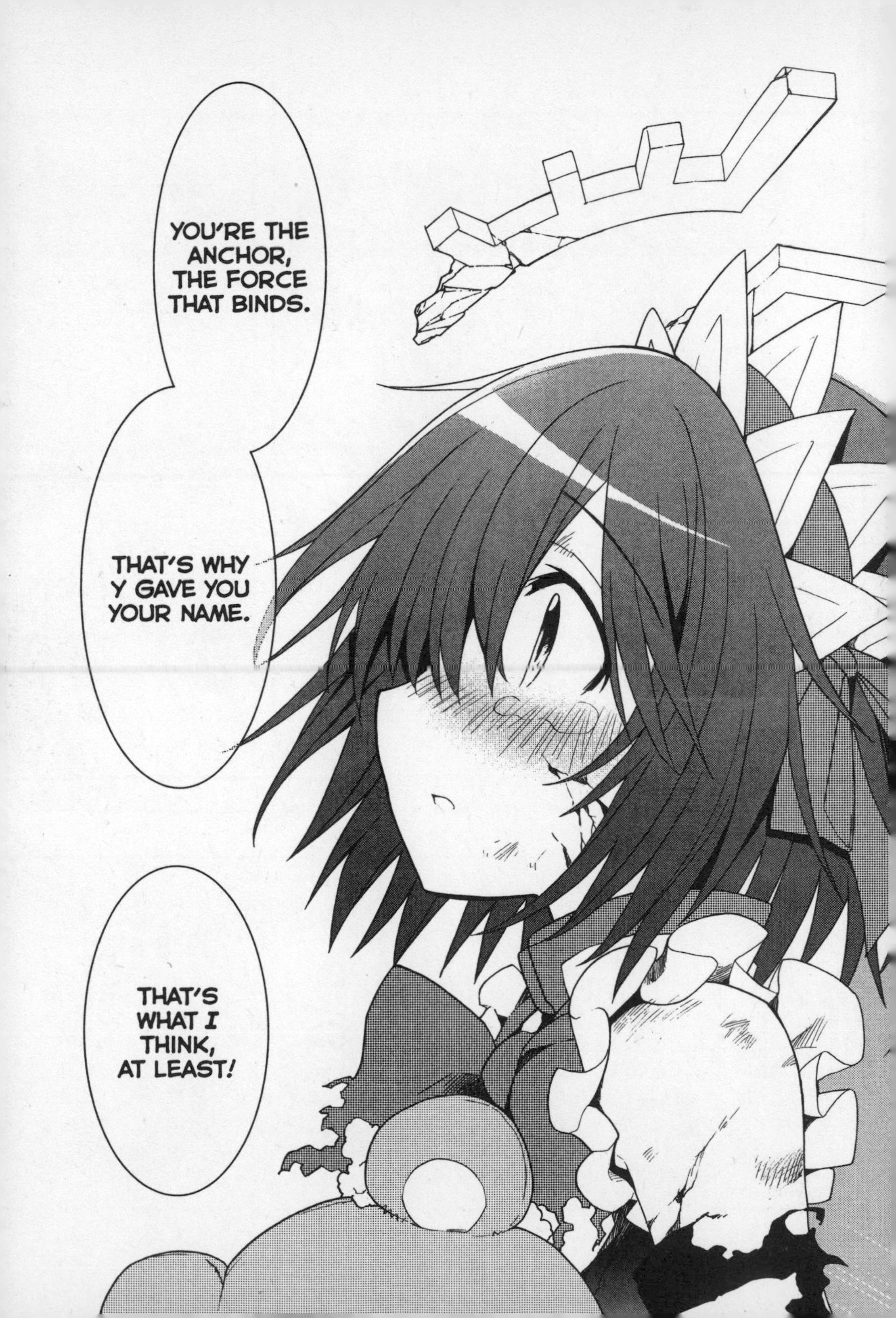
YOU'RE THE ANCHOR, THE FORCE THAT BINDS.
THAT'S WHY Y GAVE YOU YOUR NAME.
THAT'S WHAT *I* THINK, AT LEAST!

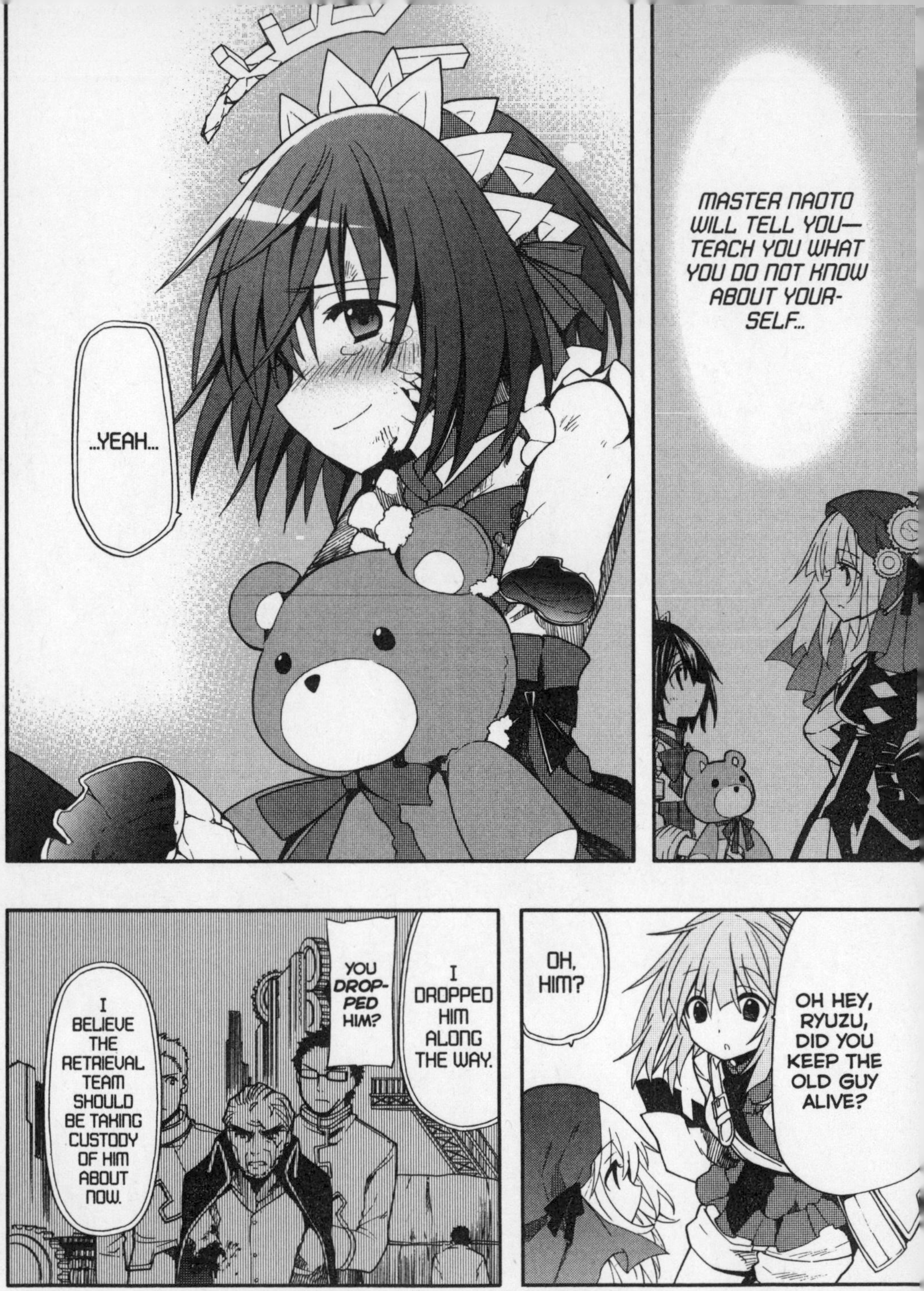
MASTER NAOTO WILL TELL YOU— TEACH YOU WHAT YOU DO NOT KNOW ABOUT YOUR-SELF...
...YEAH...
OH HEY, RYUZU, DID YOU KEEP THE OLD GUY ALIVE?
OH, HIM?
I DROPPED HIM ALONG THE WAY.
YOU *DROP-PED* HIM?
I BELIEVE THE RETRIEVAL TEAM SHOULD BE TAKING CUSTODY OF HIM ABOUT NOW.

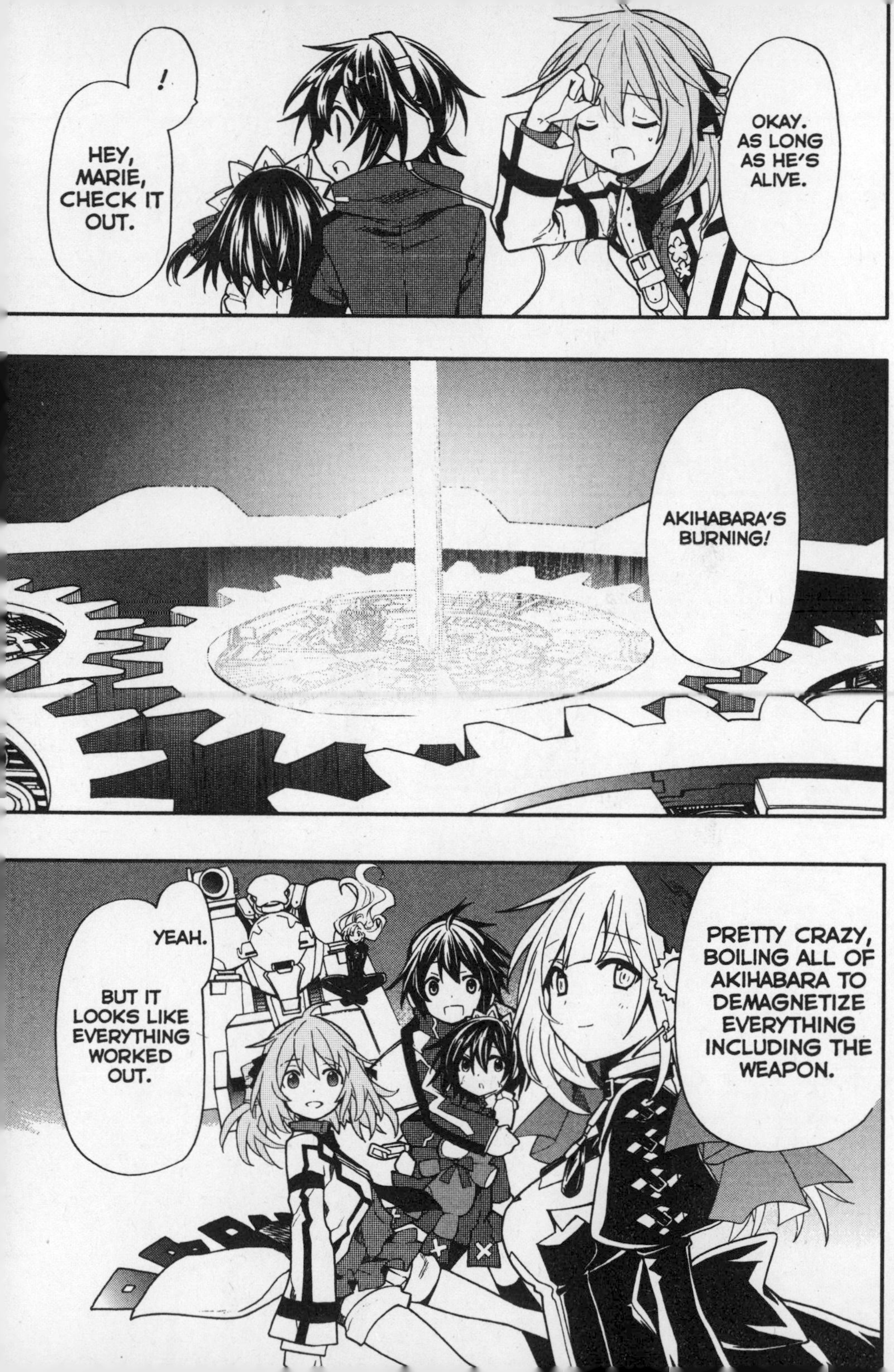
OKAY. AS LONG AS HE'S ALIVE.
!
HEY, MARIE, CHECK IT OUT.
AKIHABARA'S BURNING!
PRETTY CRAZY, BOILING ALL OF AKIHABARA TO DEMAGNETIZE EVERYTHING INCLUDING THE WEAPON.
YEAH.
BUT IT LOOKS LIKE EVERYTHING WORKED OUT.

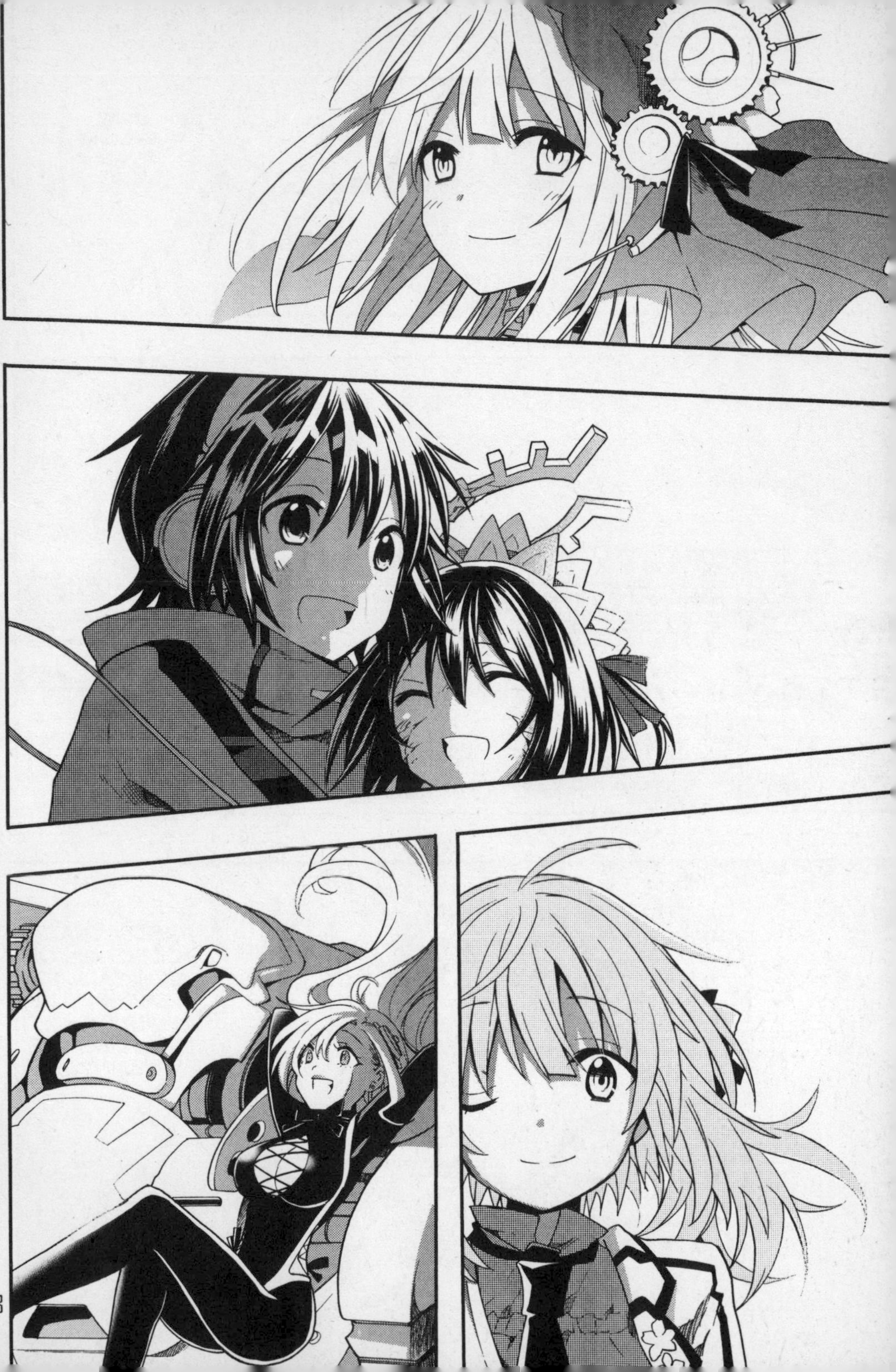

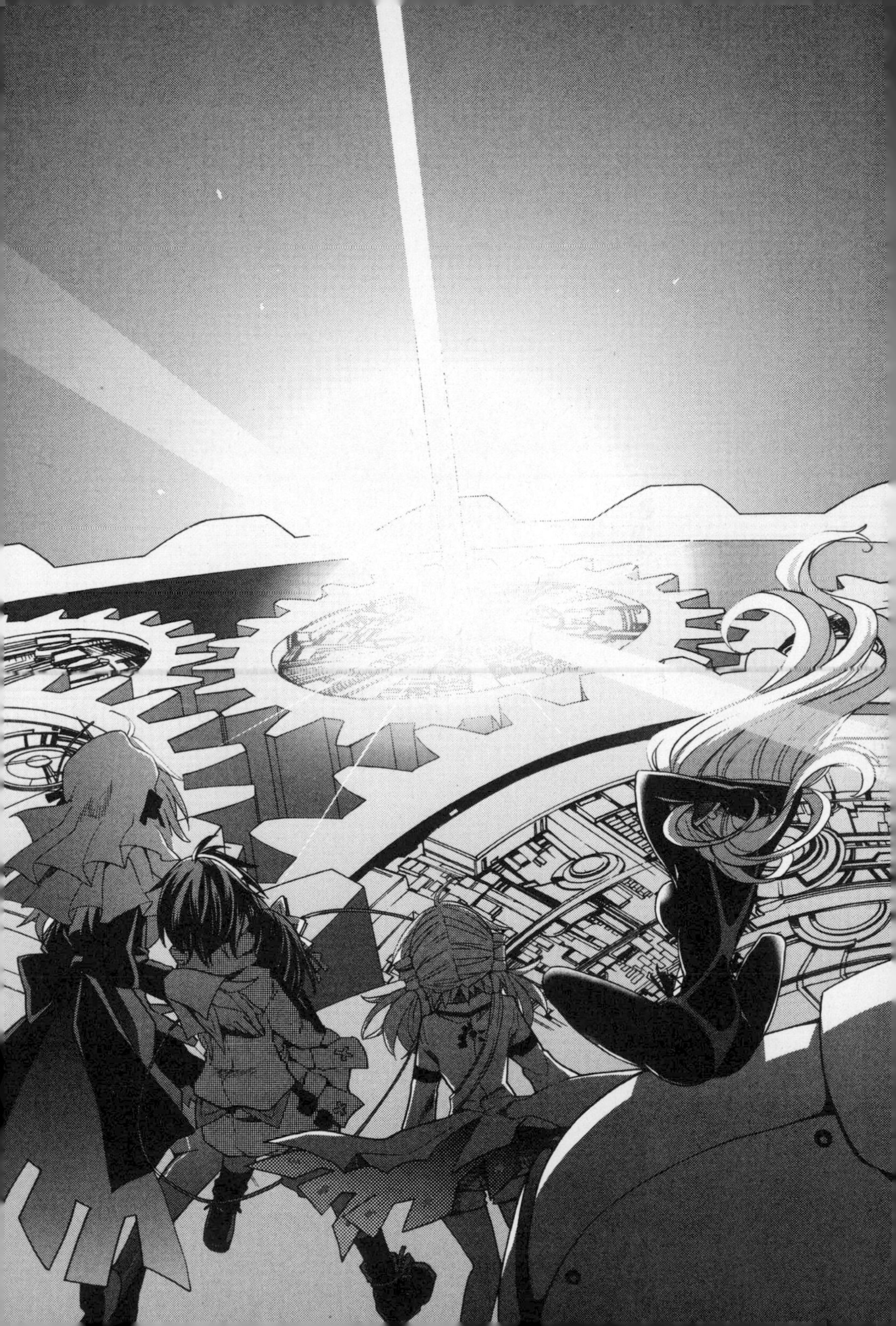

CLOCKWORK
PLANET

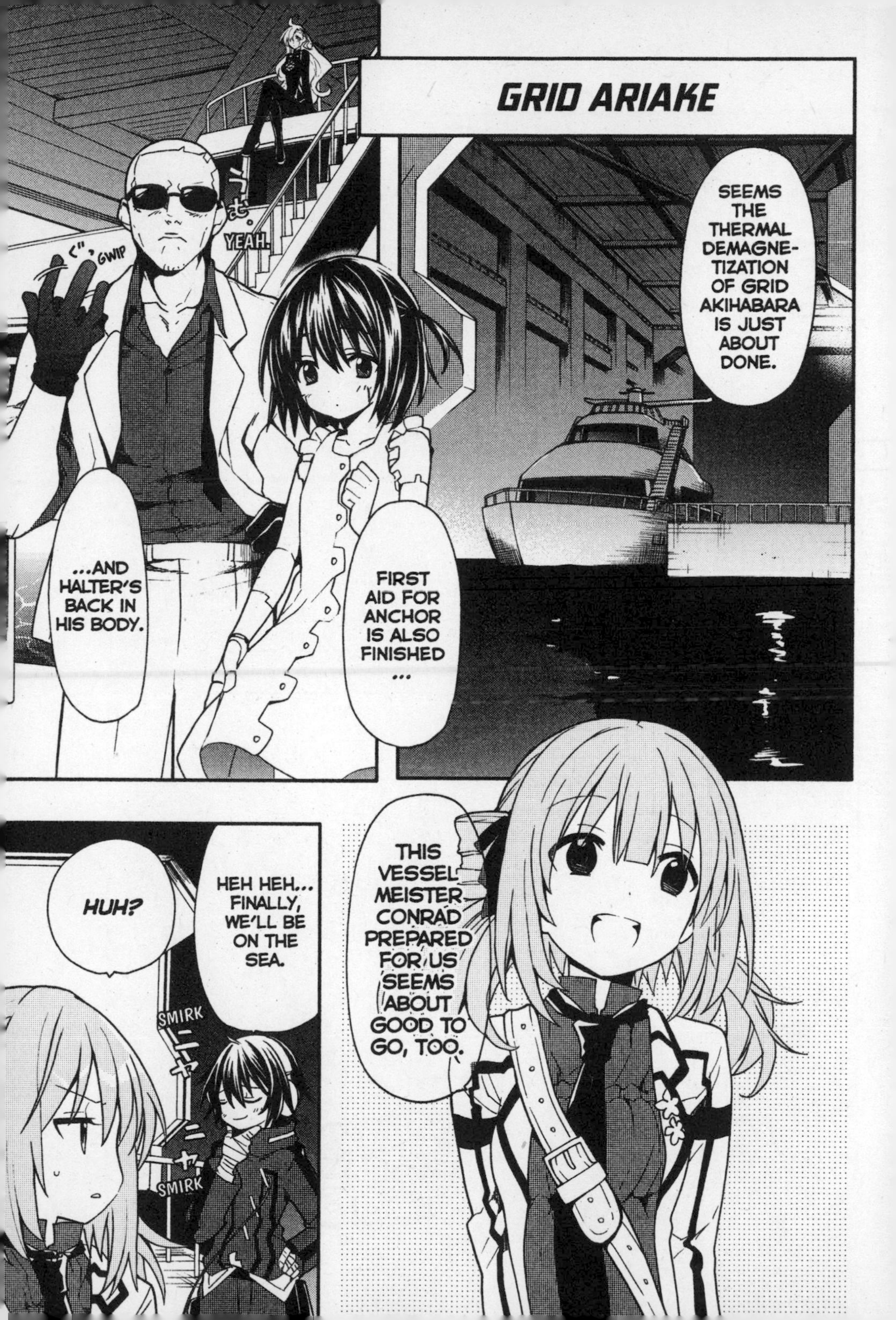
GRID ARIAKE
SEEMS THE THERMAL DEMAGNETIZATION OF GRID AKIHABARA IS JUST ABOUT DONE.
YEAH.
GWIP
FIRST AID FOR ANCHOR IS ALSO FINISHED...
...AND HALTER'S BACK IN HIS BODY.
THIS VESSEL MEISTER CONRAD PREPARED FOR US SEEMS ABOUT GOOD TO GO, TOO.
HEH HEH... FINALLY, WE'LL BE ON THE SEA.
HUH?
SMIRK
SMIRK

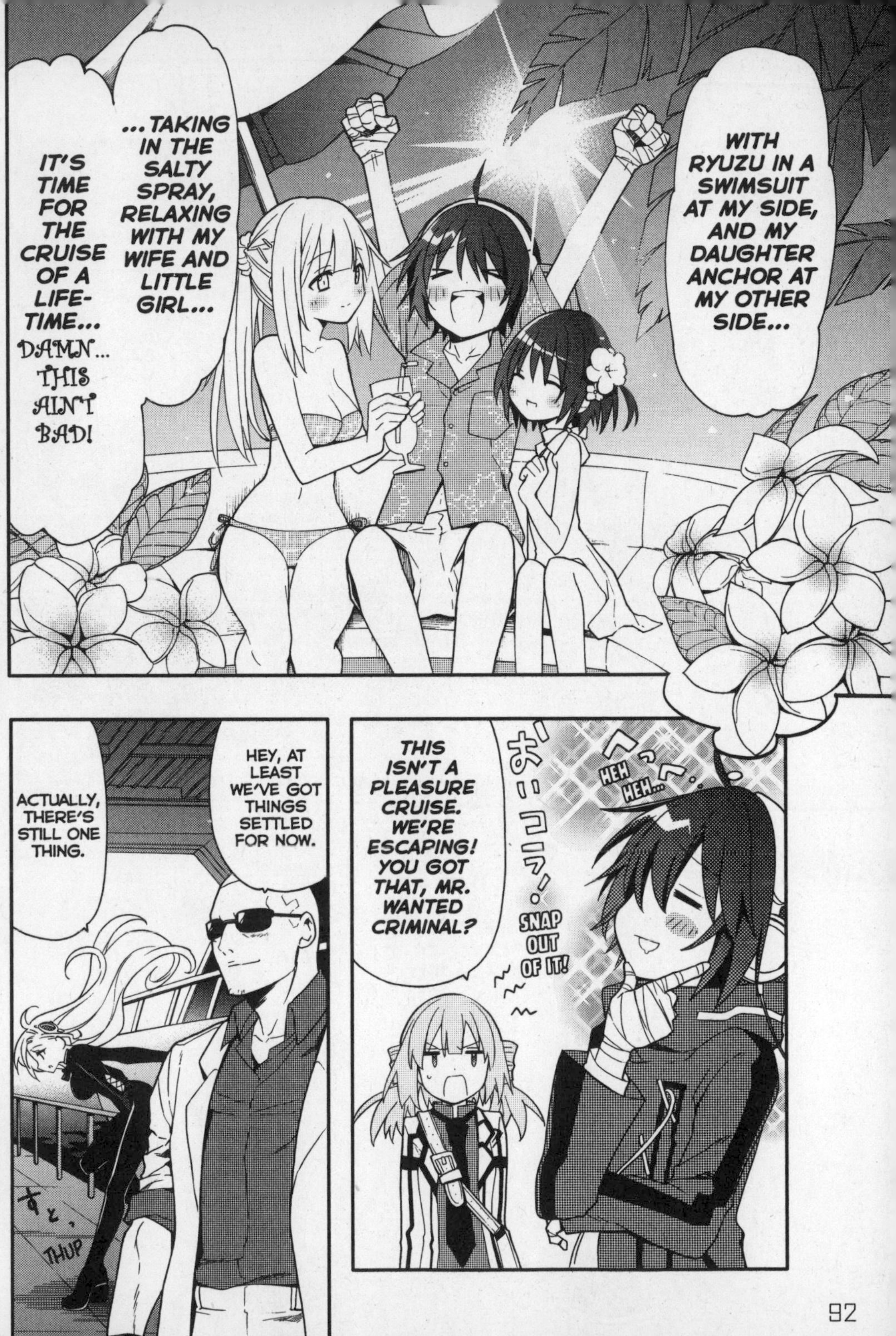
WITH RYUZU IN A SWIMSUIT AT MY SIDE, AND MY DAUGHTER ANCHOR AT MY OTHER SIDE...
...TAKING IN THE SALTY SPRAY, RELAXING WITH MY WIFE AND LITTLE GIRL...
IT'S TIME FOR THE CRUISE OF A LIFE-TIME...
DAMN... THIS AIN'T BAD!
HEH HEH...
THIS ISN'T A PLEASURE CRUISE. WE'RE ESCAPING! YOU GOT THAT, MR. WANTED CRIMINAL?
SNAP OUT OF IT!
HEY, AT LEAST WE'VE GOT THINGS SETTLED FOR NOW.
ACTUALLY, THERE'S STILL ONE THING.
THUP

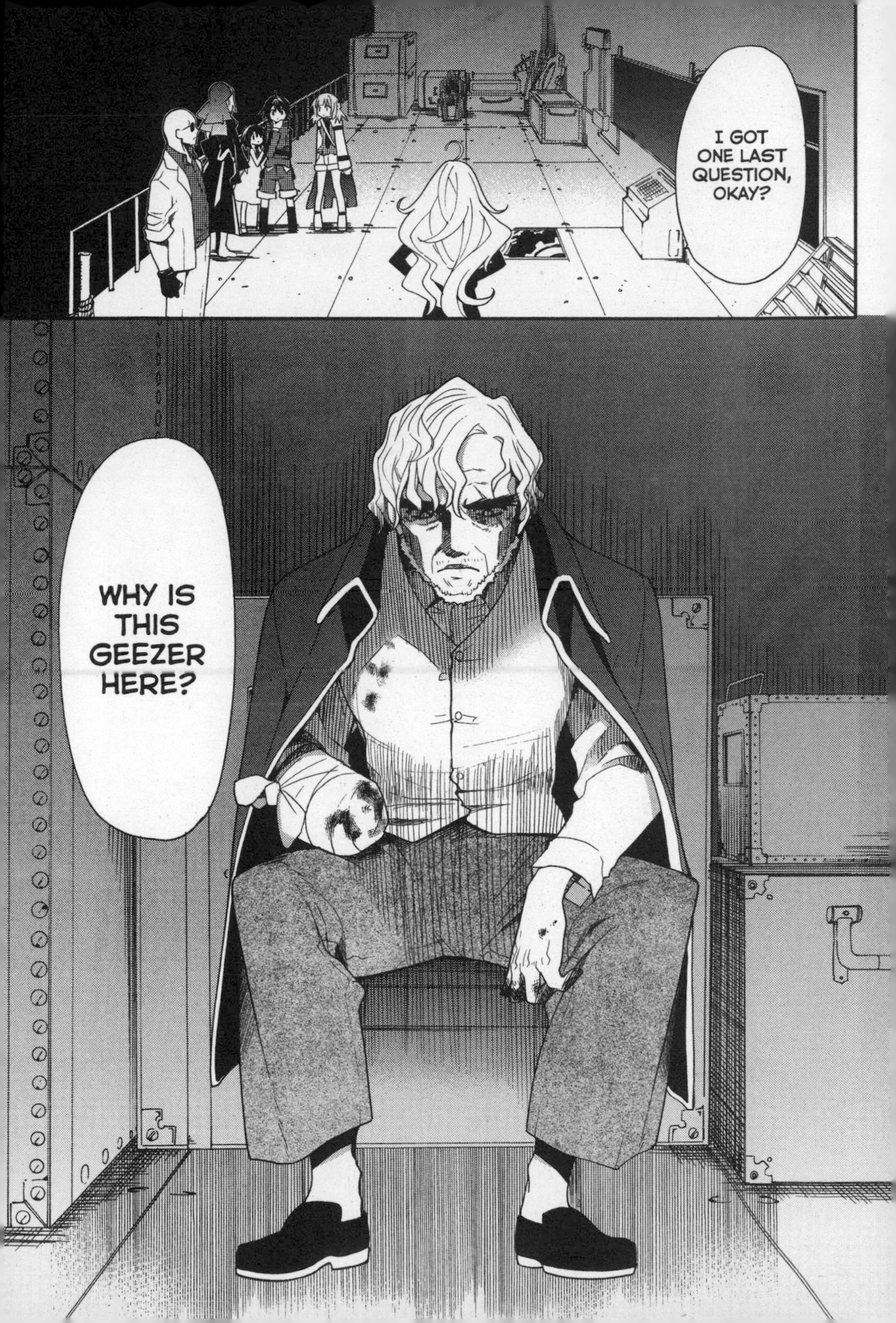
I GOT ONE LAST QUESTION, OKAY?
WHY IS THIS GEEZER HERE?

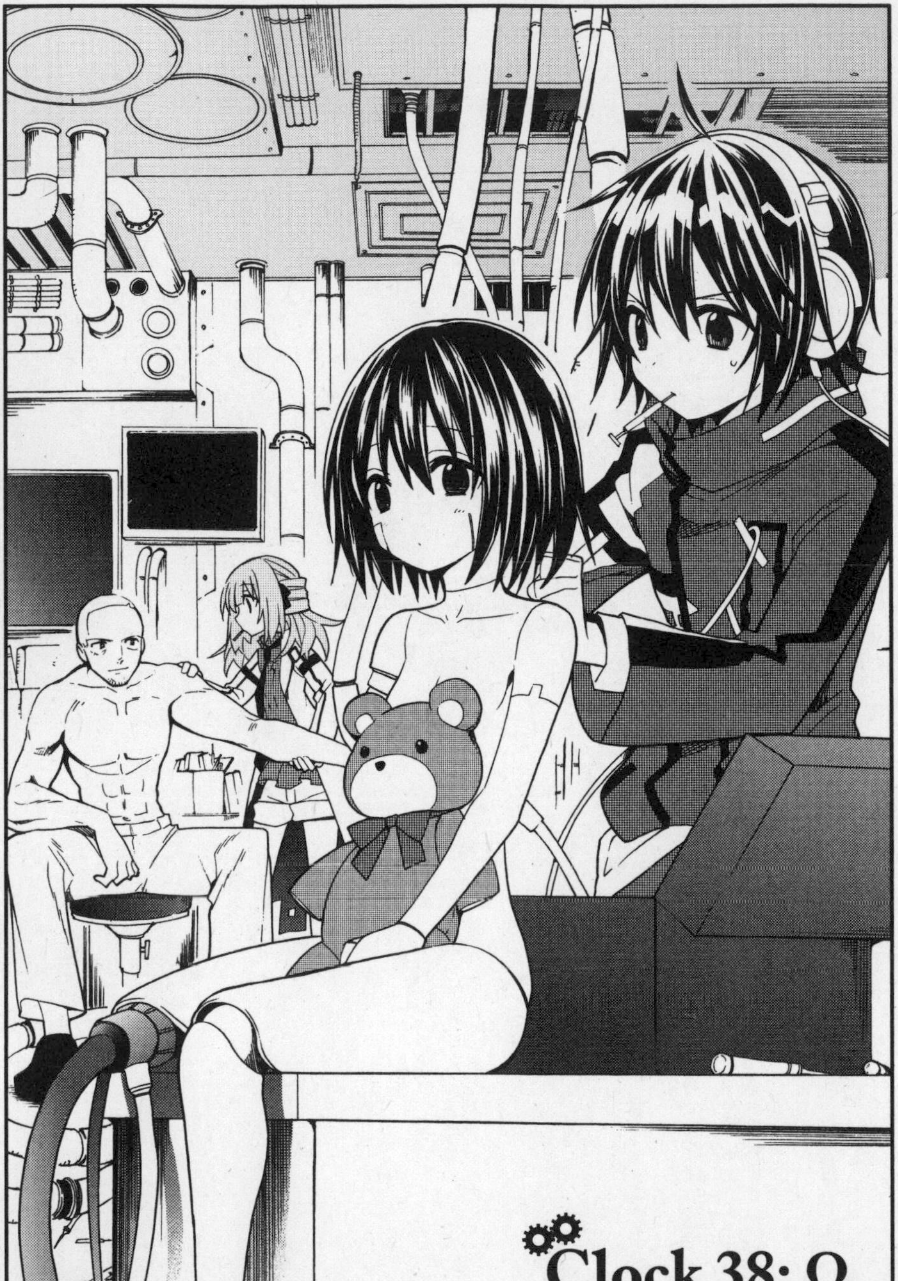
Clock 38: Ω

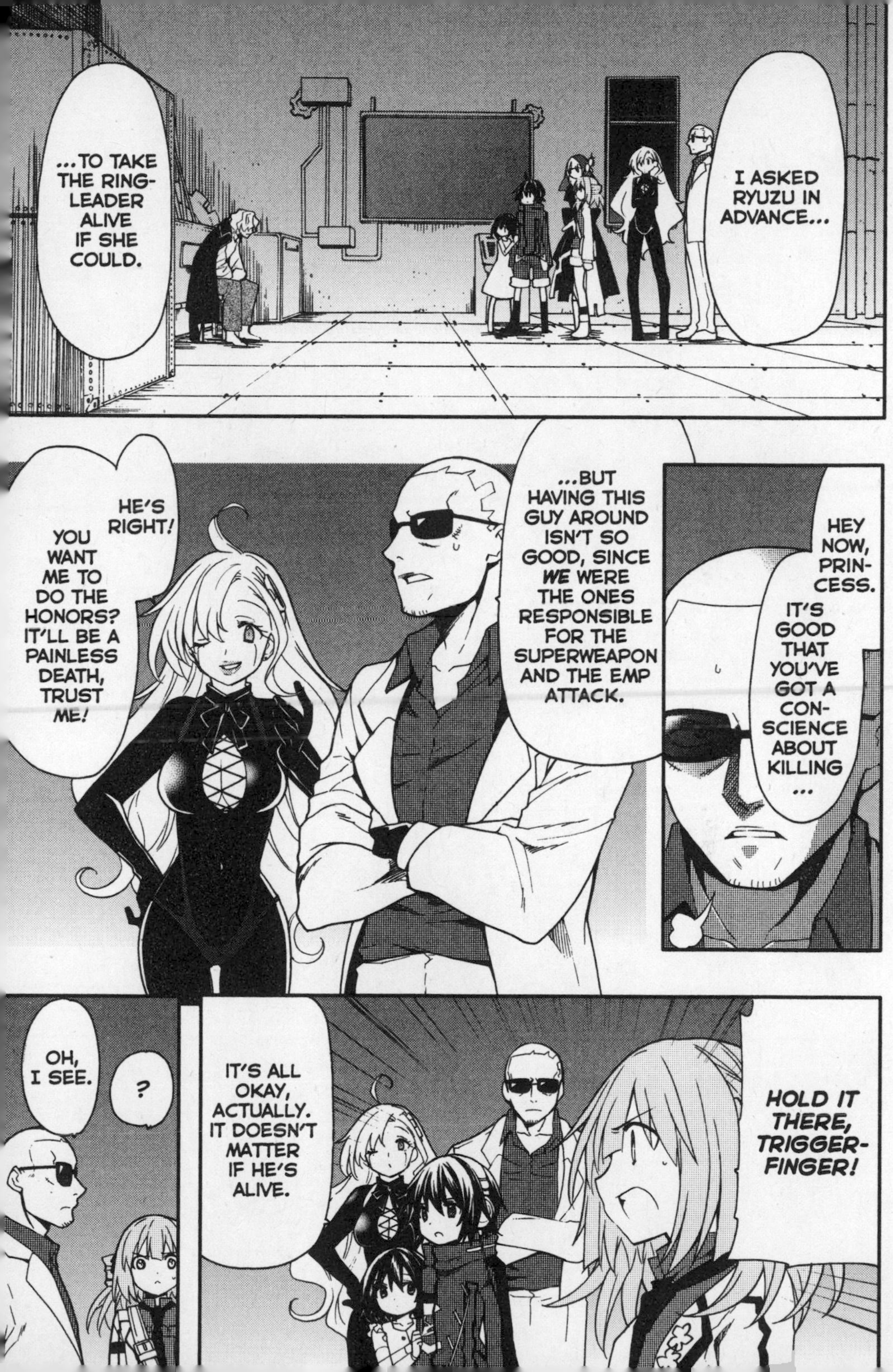
I ASKED RYUZU IN ADVANCE...
...TO TAKE THE RINGLEADER ALIVE IF SHE COULD.
HEY NOW, PRINCESS.
IT'S GOOD THAT YOU'VE GOT A CONSCIENCE ABOUT KILLING...
...BUT HAVING THIS GUY AROUND ISN'T SO GOOD, SINCE *WE* WERE THE ONES RESPONSIBLE FOR THE SUPERWEAPON AND THE EMP ATTACK.
HE'S RIGHT!
YOU WANT ME TO DO THE HONORS? IT'LL BE A PAINLESS DEATH, TRUST ME!
HOLD IT THERE, TRIGGER-FINGER!
IT'S ALL OKAY, ACTUALLY. IT DOESN'T MATTER IF HE'S ALIVE.
?
OH, I SEE.

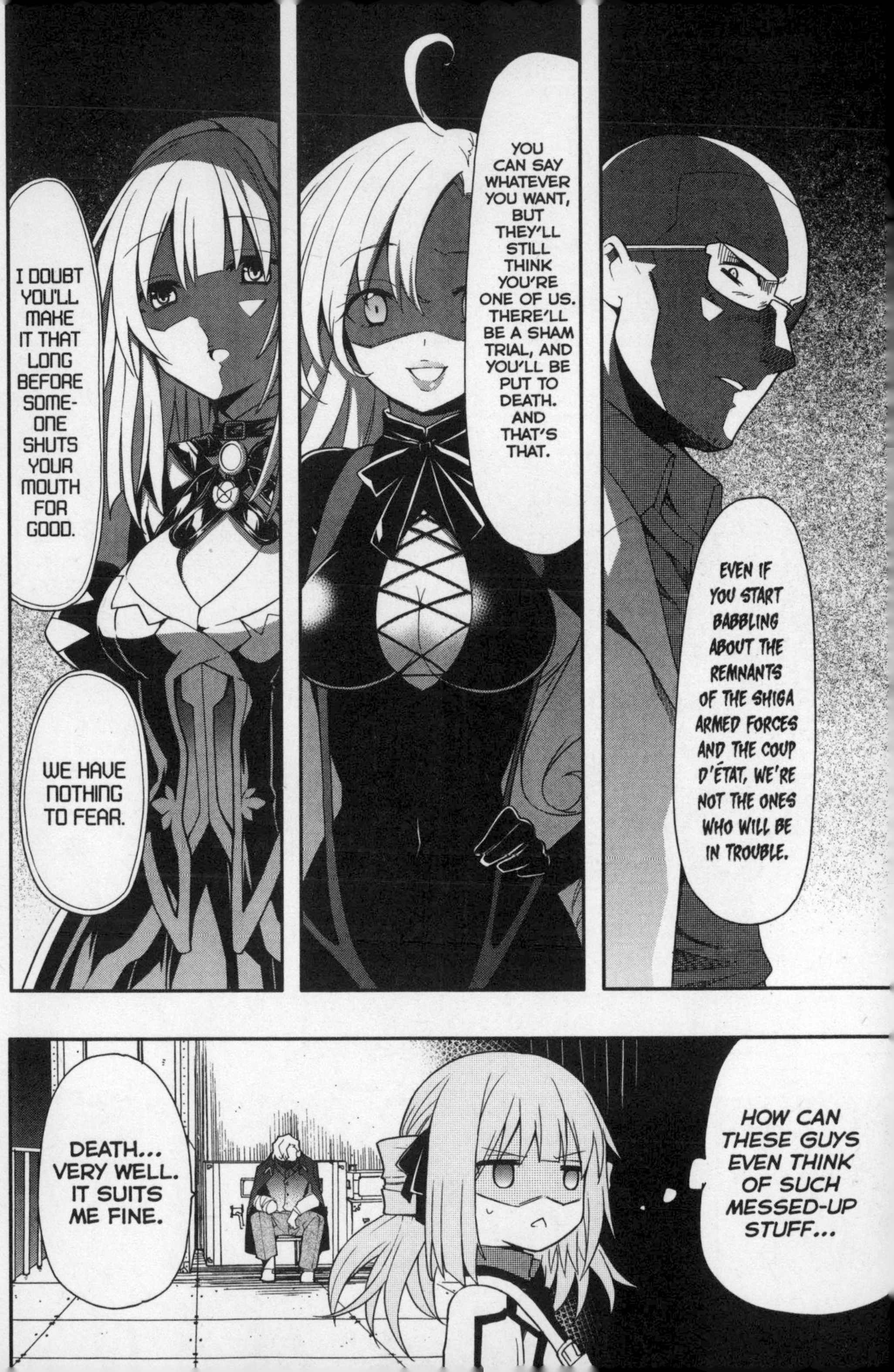
EVEN IF YOU START BABBLING ABOUT THE REMNANTS OF THE SHIGA ARMED FORCES AND THE COUP D'ÉTAT, WE'RE NOT THE ONES WHO WILL BE IN TROUBLE.
YOU CAN SAY WHATEVER YOU WANT, BUT THEY'LL STILL THINK YOU'RE ONE OF US. THERE'LL BE A SHAM TRIAL, AND YOU'LL BE PUT TO DEATH. AND THAT'S THAT.
I DOUBT YOU'LL MAKE IT THAT LONG BEFORE SOME-ONE SHUTS YOUR MOUTH FOR GOOD.
WE HAVE NOTHING TO FEAR.
HOW CAN THESE GUYS EVEN THINK OF SUCH MESSED-UP STUFF...
DEATH... VERY WELL. IT SUITS ME FINE.

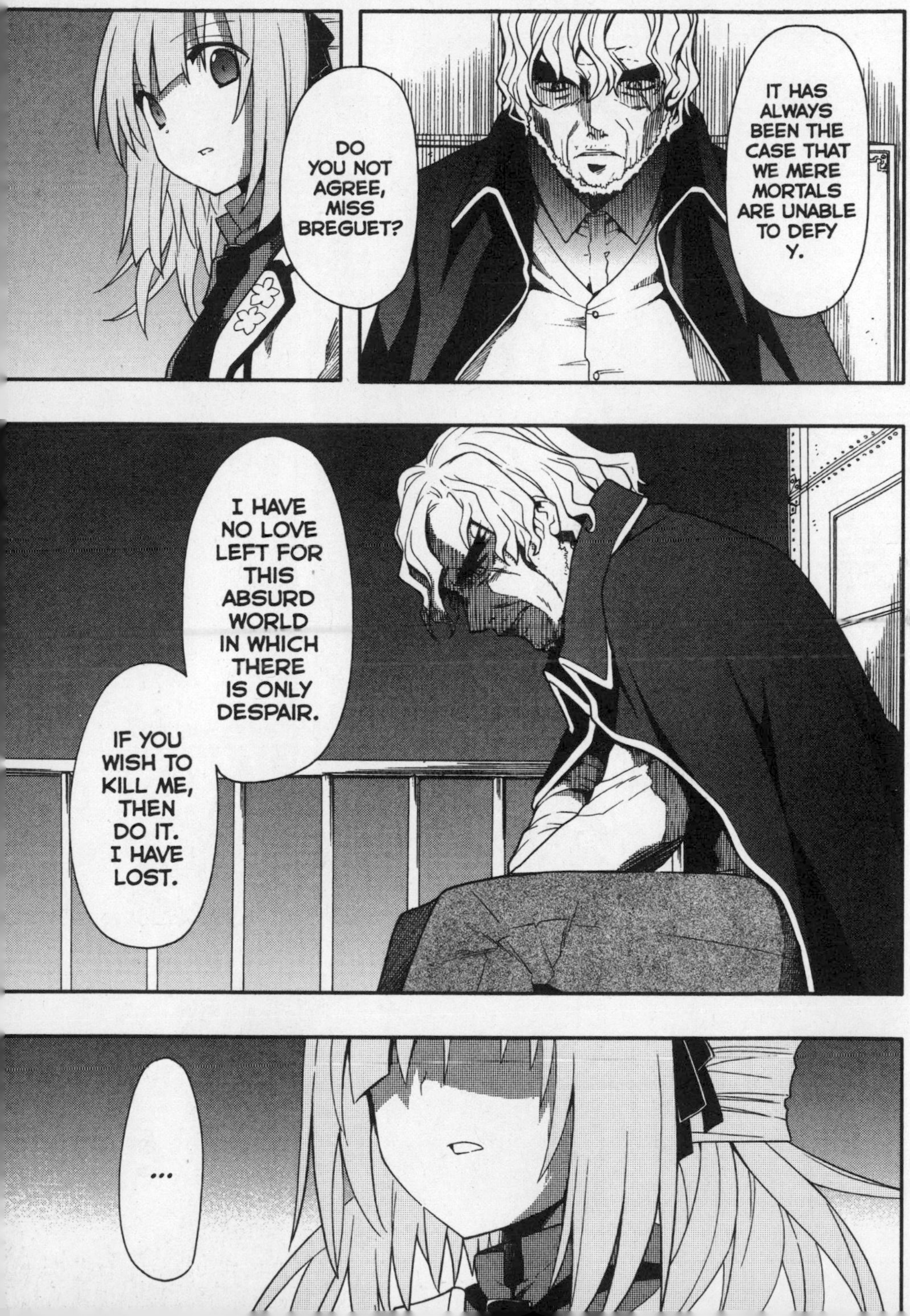
IT HAS ALWAYS BEEN THE CASE THAT WE MERE MORTALS ARE UNABLE TO DEFY Y.
DO YOU NOT AGREE, MISS BREGUET?
I HAVE NO LOVE LEFT FOR THIS ABSURD WORLD IN WHICH THERE IS ONLY DESPAIR.
IF YOU WISH TO KILL ME, THEN DO IT. I HAVE LOST.
...

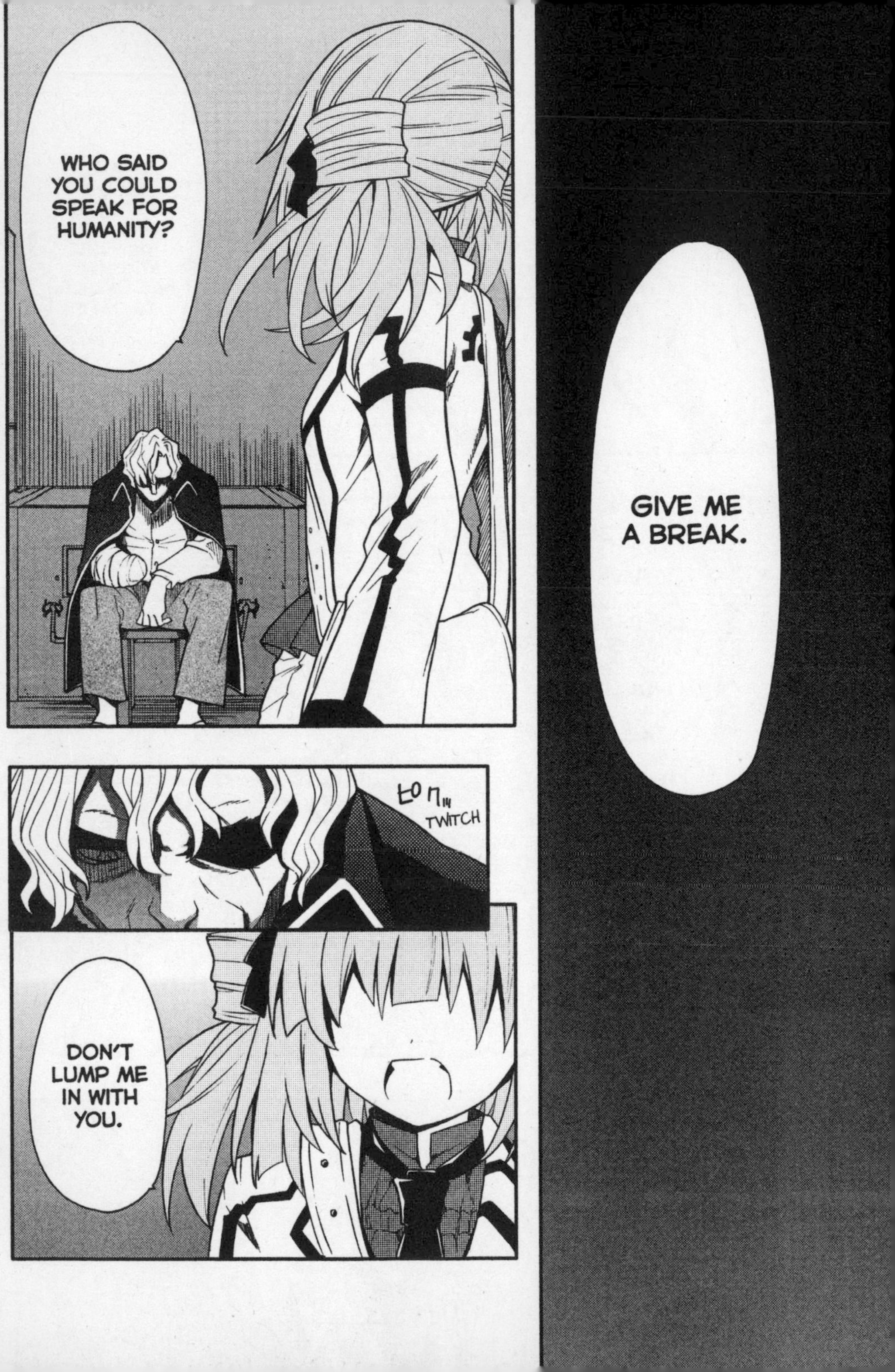
GIVE ME A BREAK.
WHO SAID YOU COULD SPEAK FOR HUMANITY?
TWITCH
DON'T LUMP ME IN WITH YOU.

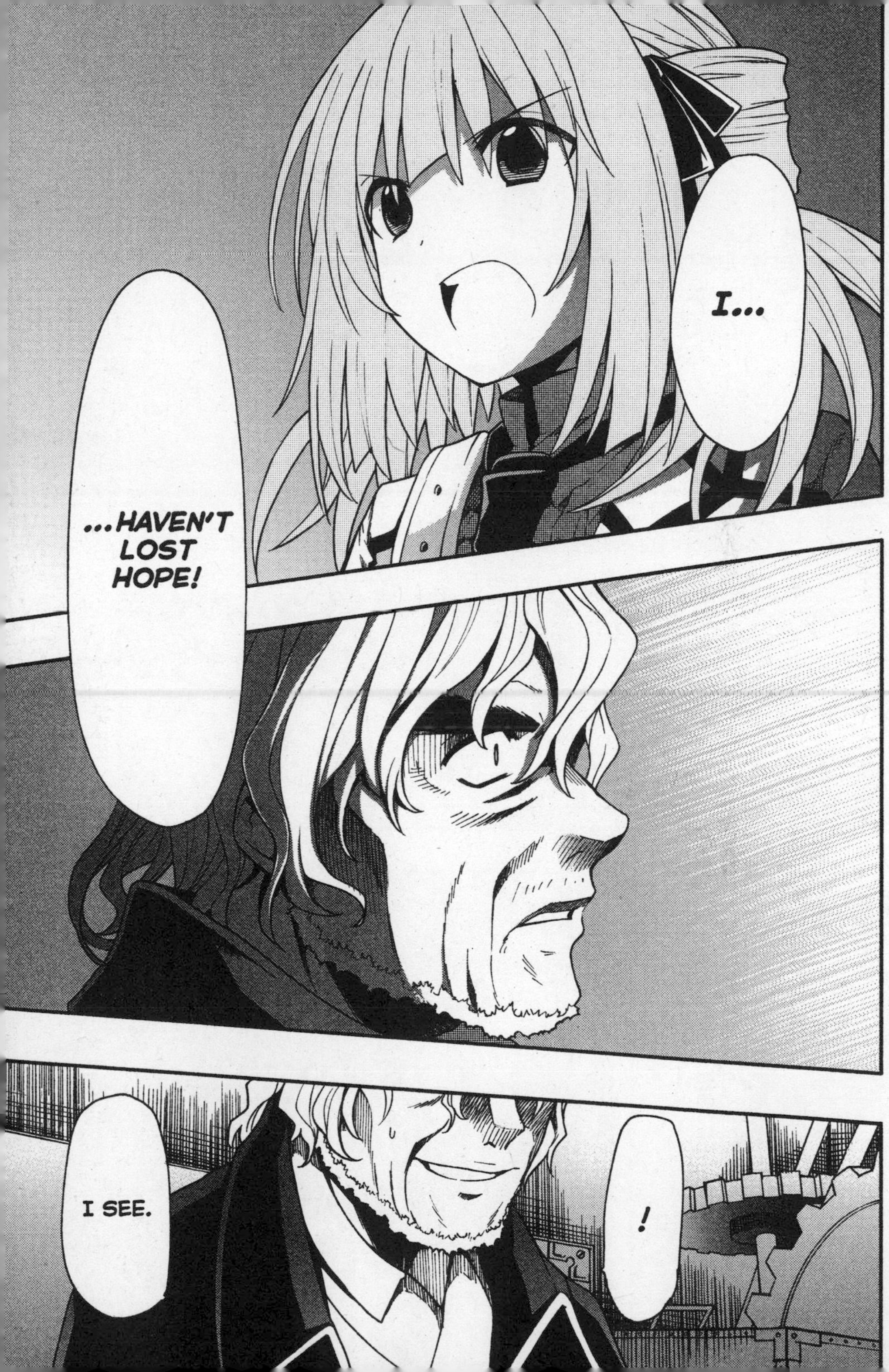
I...
...HAVEN'T LOST HOPE!
!
I SEE.

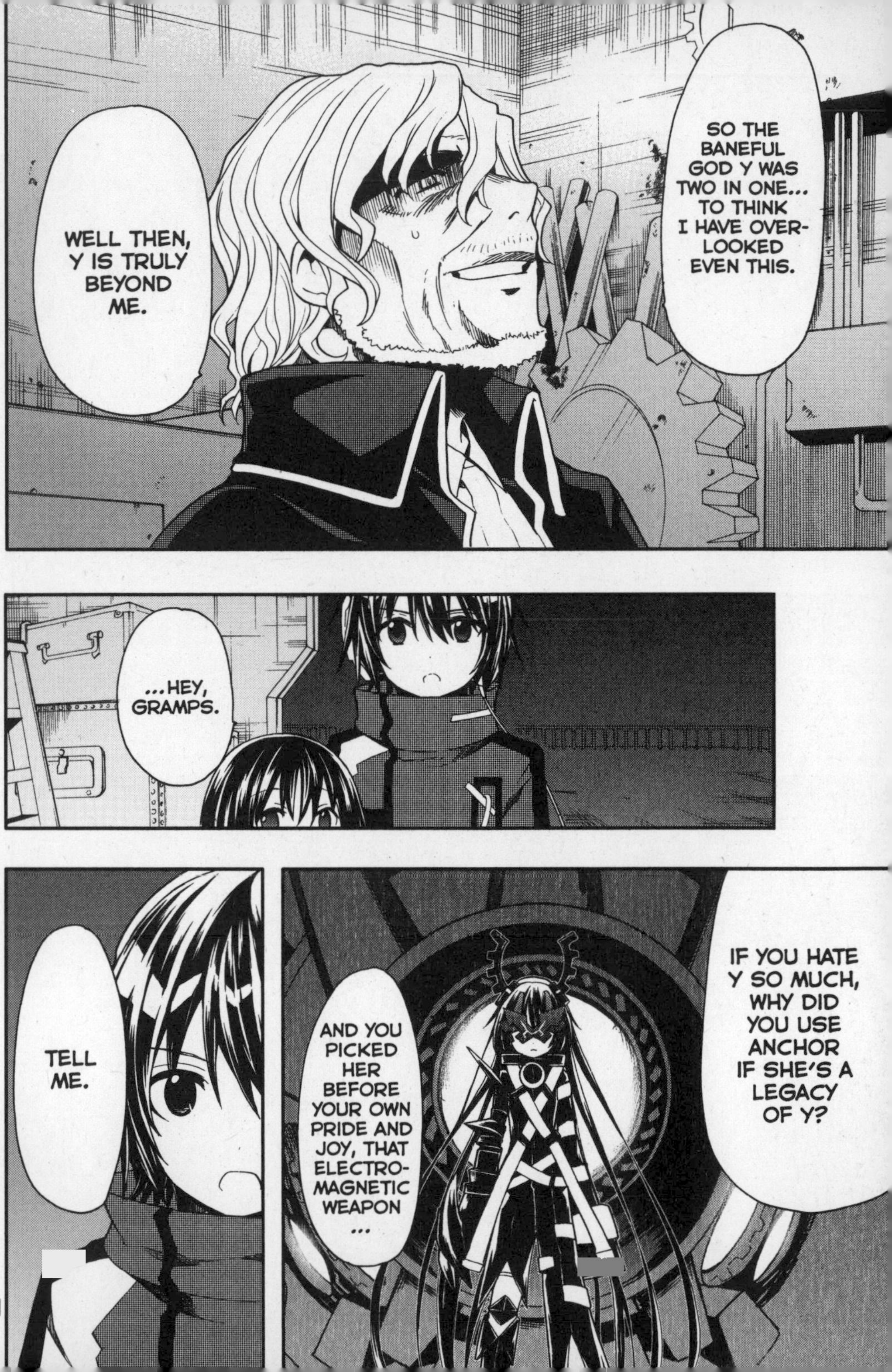
SO THE BANEFUL GOD Y WAS TWO IN ONE... TO THINK I HAVE OVER-LOOKED EVEN THIS.
WELL THEN, Y IS TRULY BEYOND ME.
...HEY, GRAMPS.
IF YOU HATE Y SO MUCH, WHY DID YOU USE ANCHOR IF SHE'S A LEGACY OF Y?
AND YOU PICKED HER BEFORE YOUR OWN PRIDE AND JOY, THAT ELECTRO-MAGNETIC WEAPON ...
TELL ME.

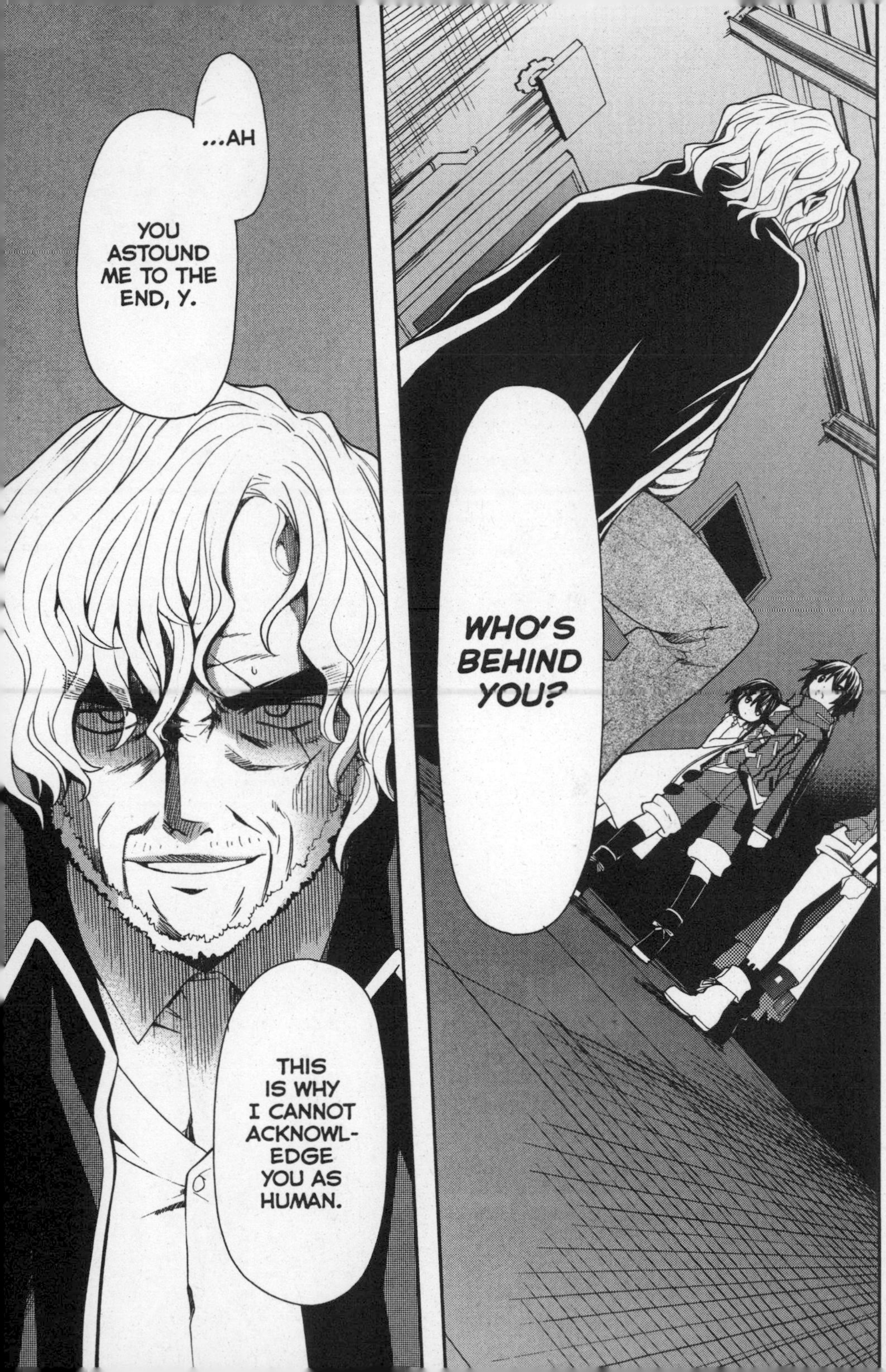
WHO'S BEHIND YOU?
...AH
YOU ASTOUND ME TO THE END, Y.
THIS IS WHY I CANNOT ACKNOWL-EDGE YOU AS HUMAN.

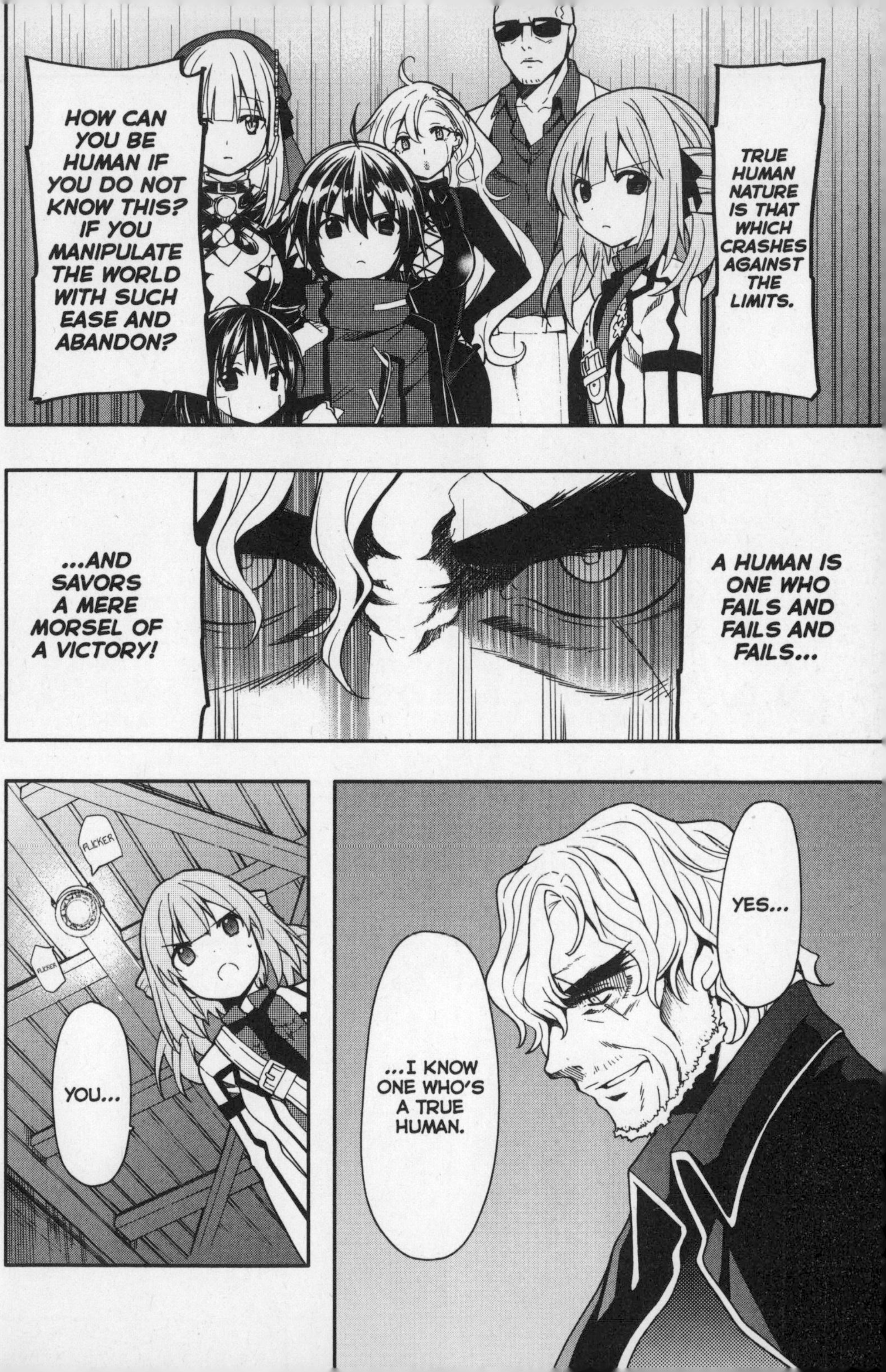
TRUE HUMAN NATURE IS THAT WHICH CRASHES AGAINST THE LIMITS.
HOW CAN YOU BE HUMAN IF YOU DO NOT KNOW THIS? IF YOU MANIPULATE THE WORLD WITH SUCH EASE AND ABANDON?
A HUMAN IS ONE WHO FAILS AND FAILS AND FAILS...
...AND SAVORS A MERE MORSEL OF A VICTORY!
YES...
...I KNOW ONE WHO'S A TRUE HUMAN.
FLICKER
FLICKER
YOU...

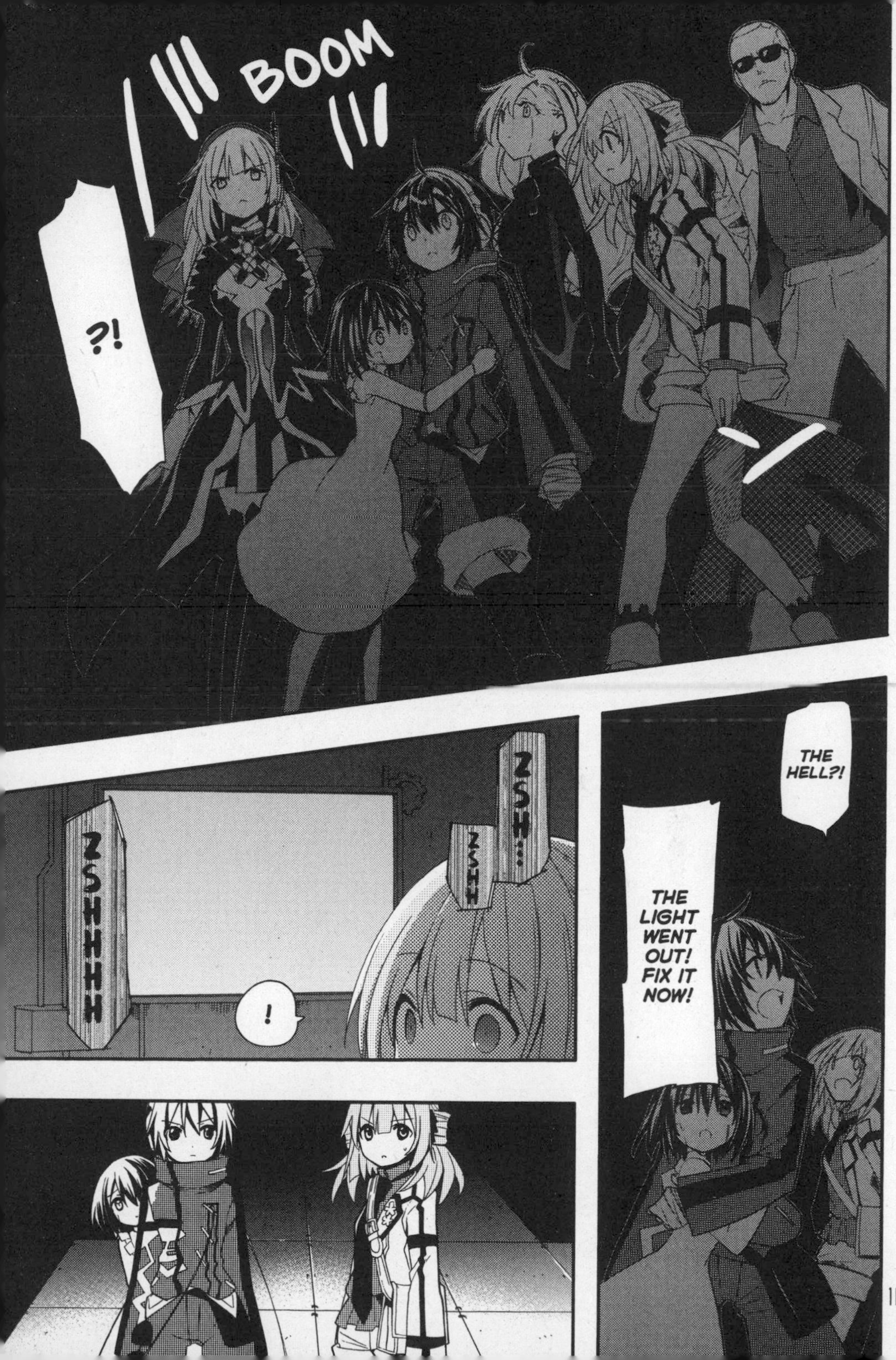
BOOM
?!
THE HELL?!
THE LIGHT WENT OUT! FIX IT NOW!
ZSH...
ZSHH
ZSHHHHH
!

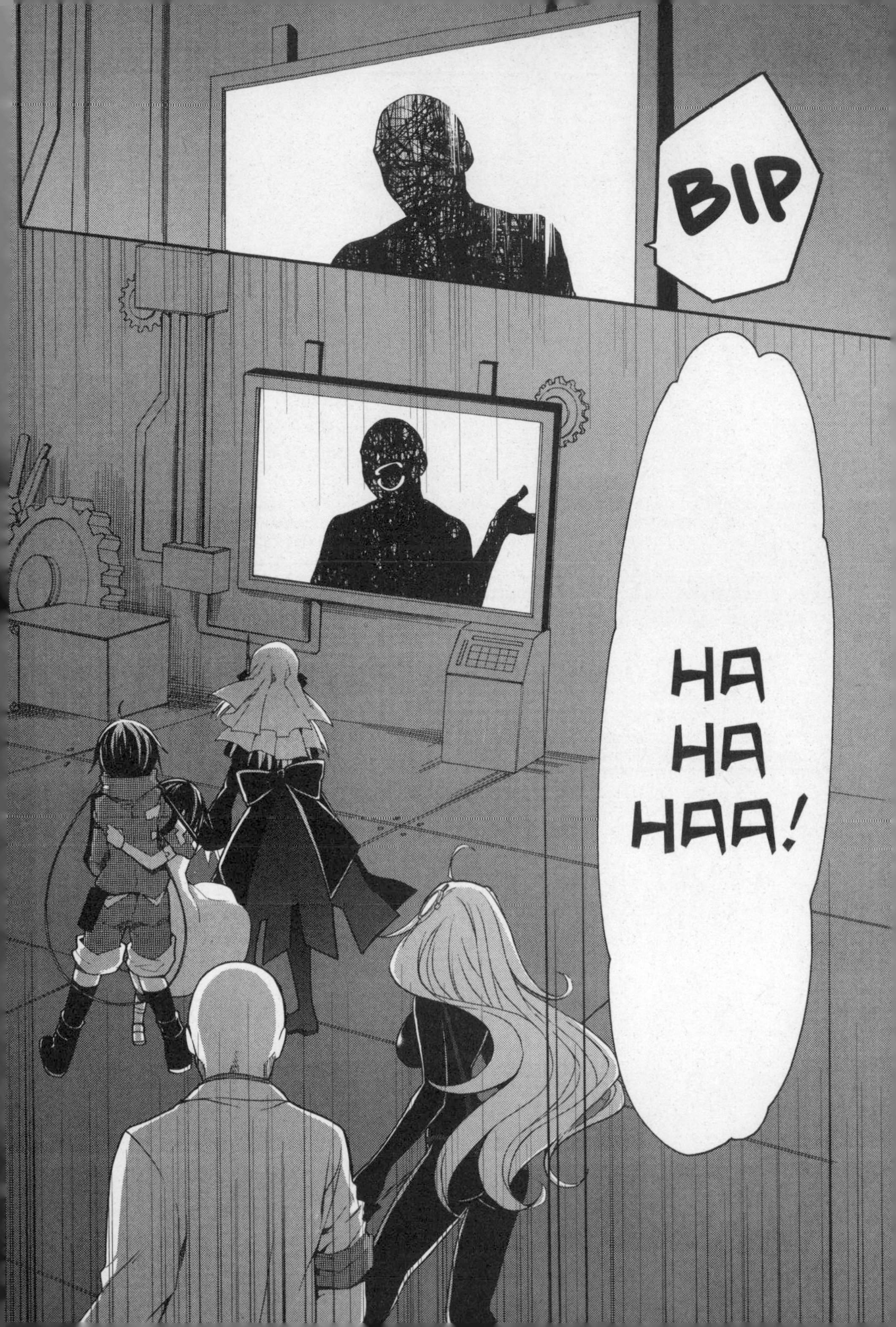
BIP
HA HA HAA!

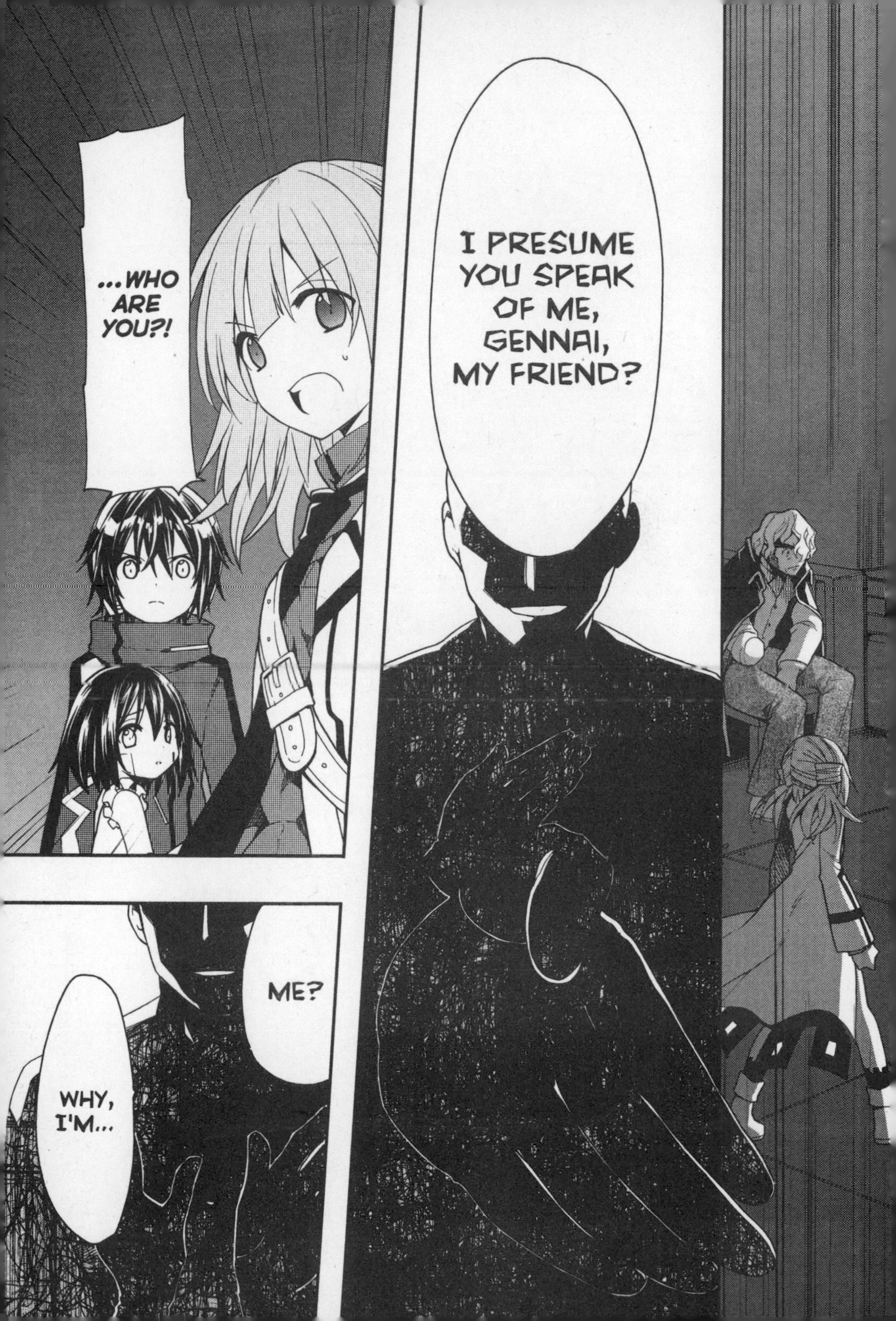
I PRESUME YOU SPEAK OF ME, GENNAI, MY FRIEND?
...WHO ARE YOU?!
ME?
WHY, I'M...

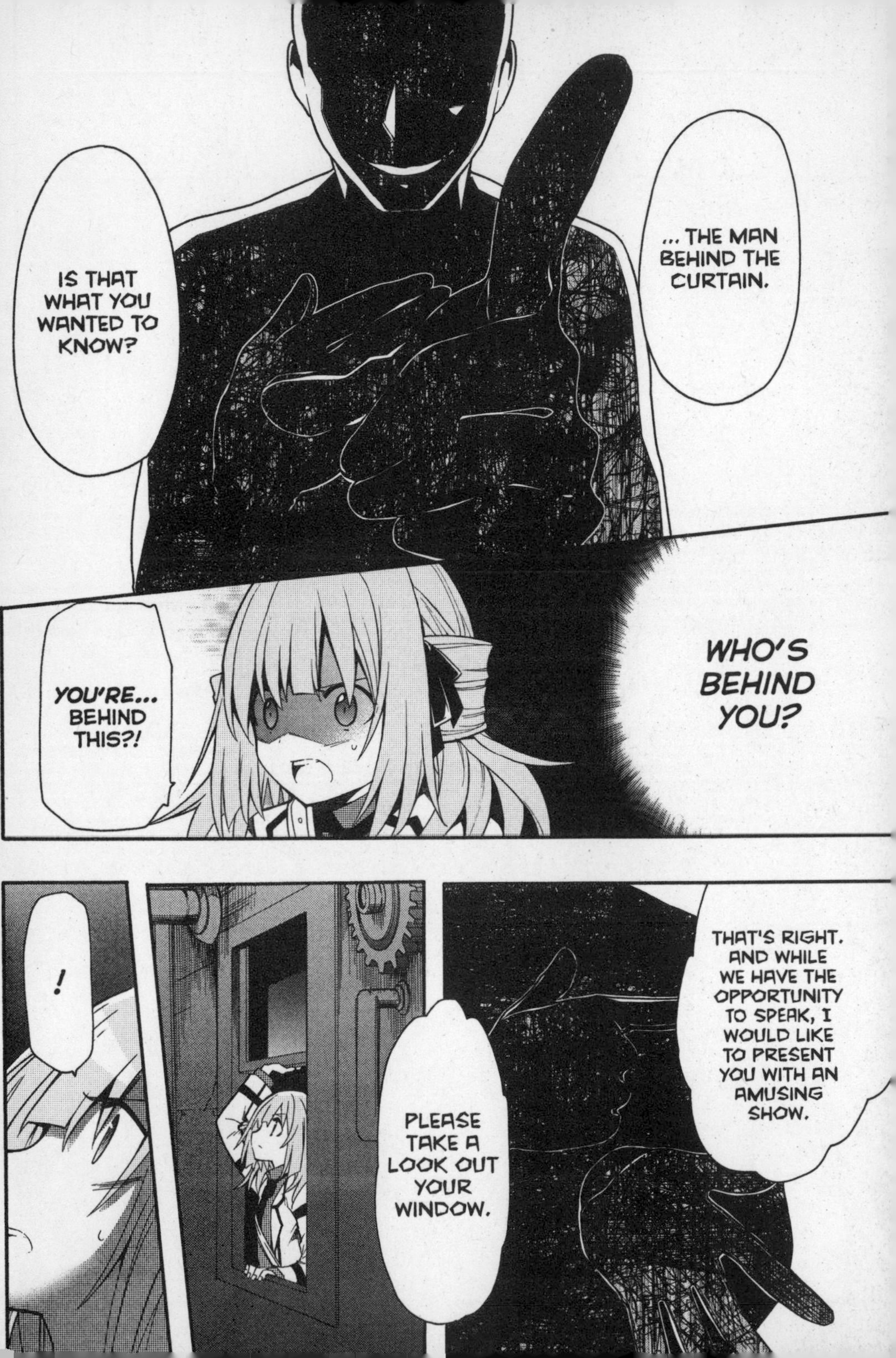
... THE MAN BEHIND THE CURTAIN.
IS THAT WHAT YOU WANTED TO KNOW?
WHO'S BEHIND YOU?
YOU'RE... BEHIND THIS?!
THAT'S RIGHT. AND WHILE WE HAVE THE OPPORTUNITY TO SPEAK, I WOULD LIKE TO PRESENT YOU WITH AN AMUSING SHOW.
PLEASE TAKE A LOOK OUT YOUR WINDOW.
!

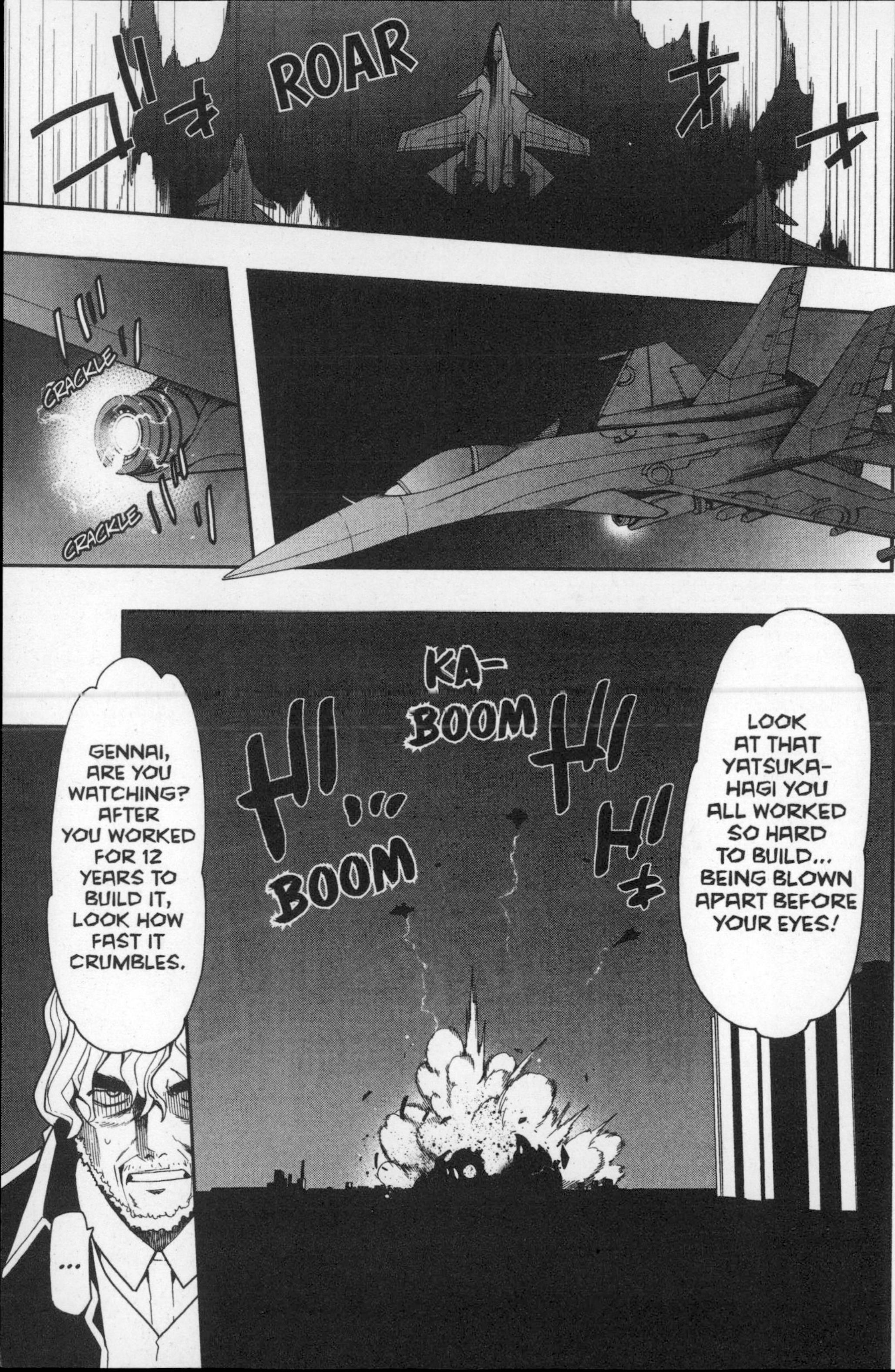
ROAR
CRACKLE
CRACKLE
LOOK AT THAT YATSUKA-HAGI YOU ALL WORKED SO HARD TO BUILD... BEING BLOWN APART BEFORE YOUR EYES!
KA-BOOM
BOOM
GENNAI, ARE YOU WATCHING? AFTER YOU WORKED FOR 12 YEARS TO BUILD IT, LOOK HOW FAST IT CRUMBLES.
...

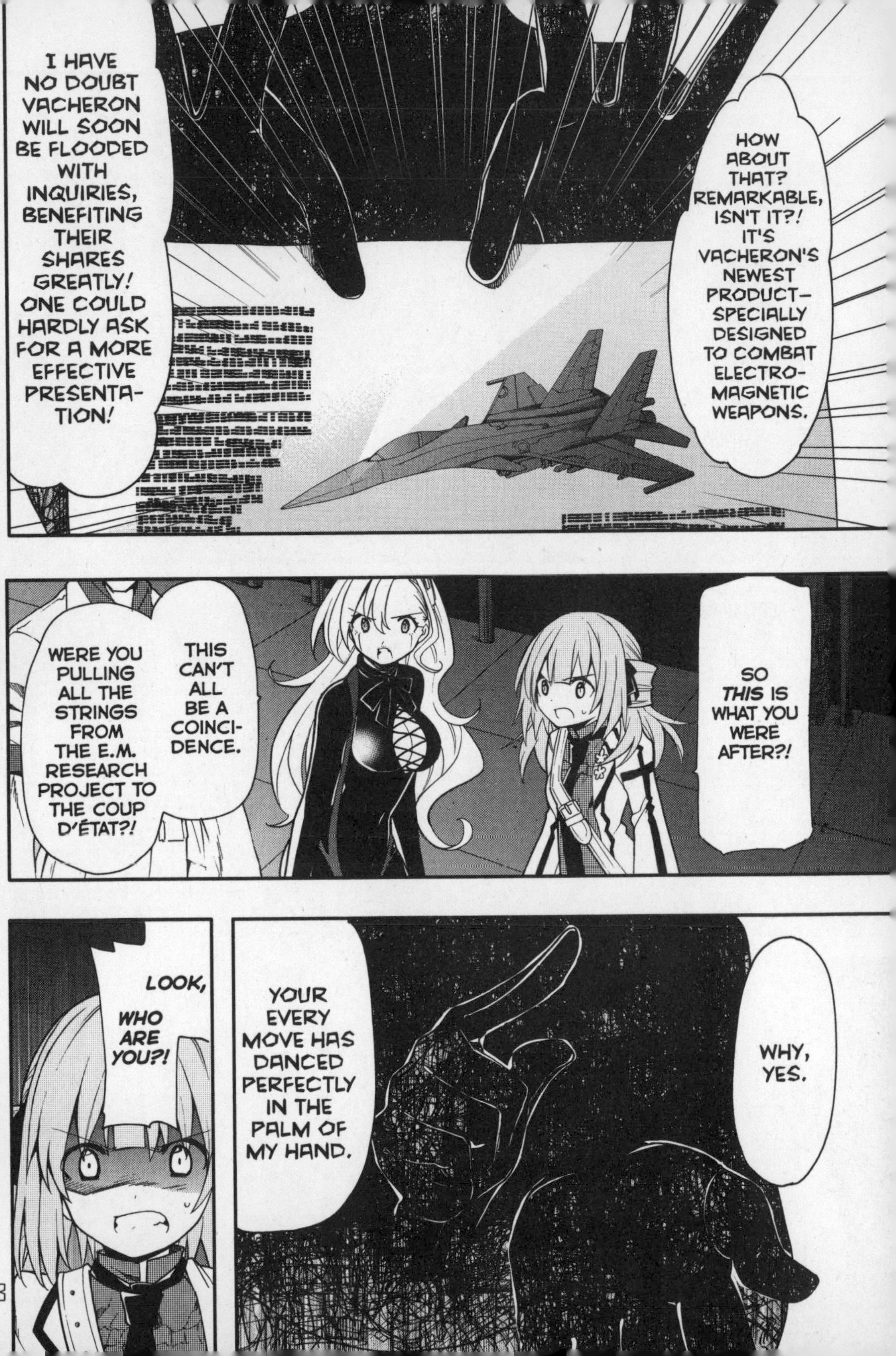
HOW ABOUT THAT? REMARKABLE, ISN'T IT?! IT'S VACHERON'S NEWEST PRODUCT—SPECIALLY DESIGNED TO COMBAT ELECTRO-MAGNETIC WEAPONS.
I HAVE NO DOUBT VACHERON WILL SOON BE FLOODED WITH INQUIRIES, BENEFITING THEIR SHARES GREATLY! ONE COULD HARDLY ASK FOR A MORE EFFECTIVE PRESENTA-TION!
SO *THIS* IS WHAT YOU WERE AFTER?!
THIS CAN'T ALL BE A COINCI-DENCE.
WERE YOU PULLING ALL THE STRINGS FROM THE E.M. RESEARCH PROJECT TO THE COUP D'ÉTAT?!
WHY, YES.
YOUR EVERY MOVE HAS DANCED PERFECTLY IN THE PALM OF MY HAND.
LOOK,
WHO ARE YOU?!

WHO AM I?

I'M A COLLEAGUE OF YOURS.

... ALL RIGHT, YOU MAY CALL ME OMEGA.

YOU CALL YOURSELVES THE SECOND UPSILON, THE SECOND COMING OF Y.

BUT YOU MUSN'T FORGET THAT X IS GREATER THAN Y.

OMEGA...

YOU CAN JUST THINK OF US AS AN EVIL ORGANIZATION, ALL THAT CLICHÉ.

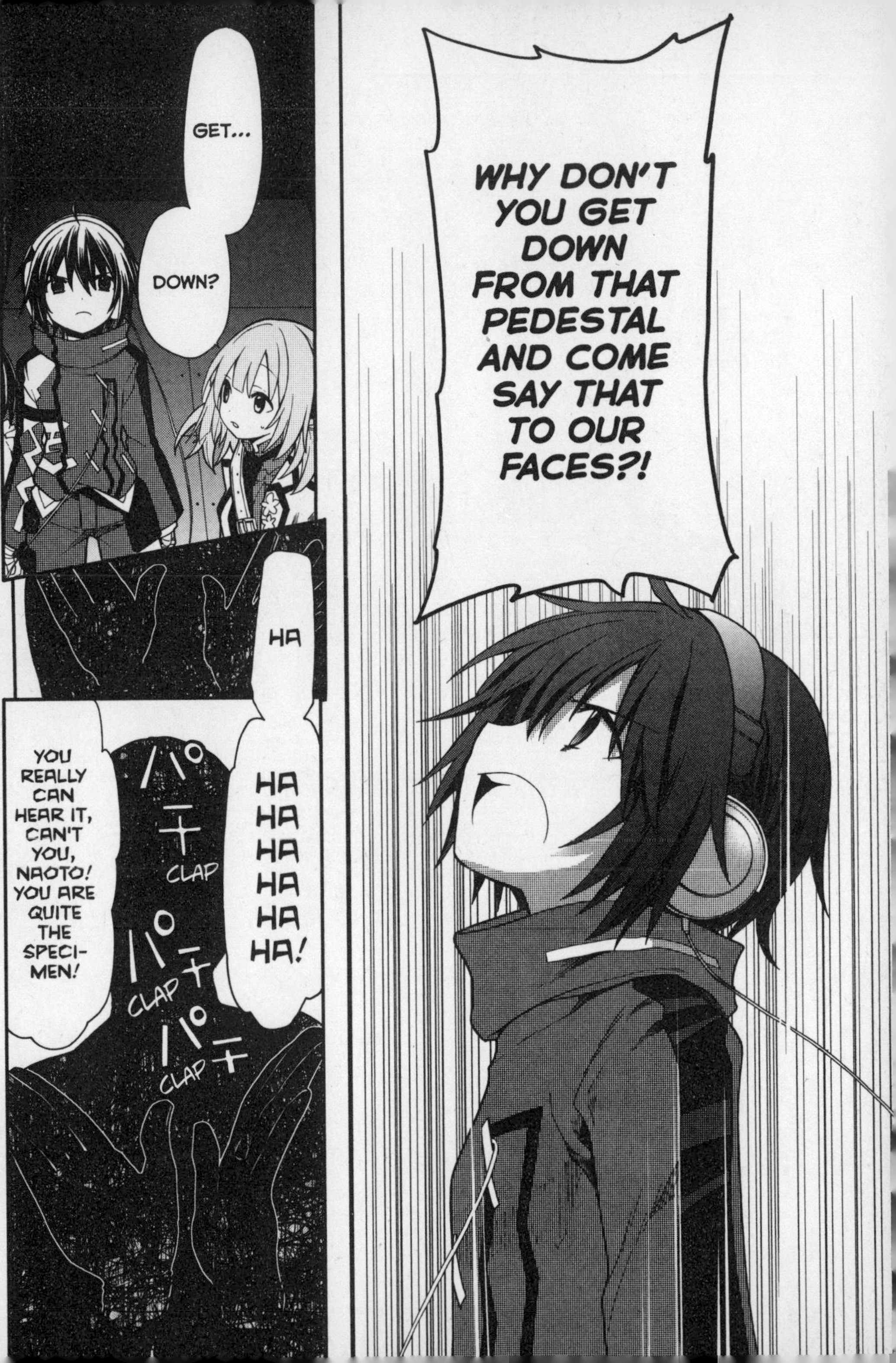
WHY DON'T YOU GET DOWN FROM THAT PEDESTAL AND COME SAY THAT TO OUR FACES?!
GET...
DOWN?
HA
HA HA HA HA HA HA!
YOU REALLY CAN HEAR IT, CAN'T YOU, NAOTO! YOU ARE QUITE THE SPECIMEN!
CLAP
CLAP
CLAP

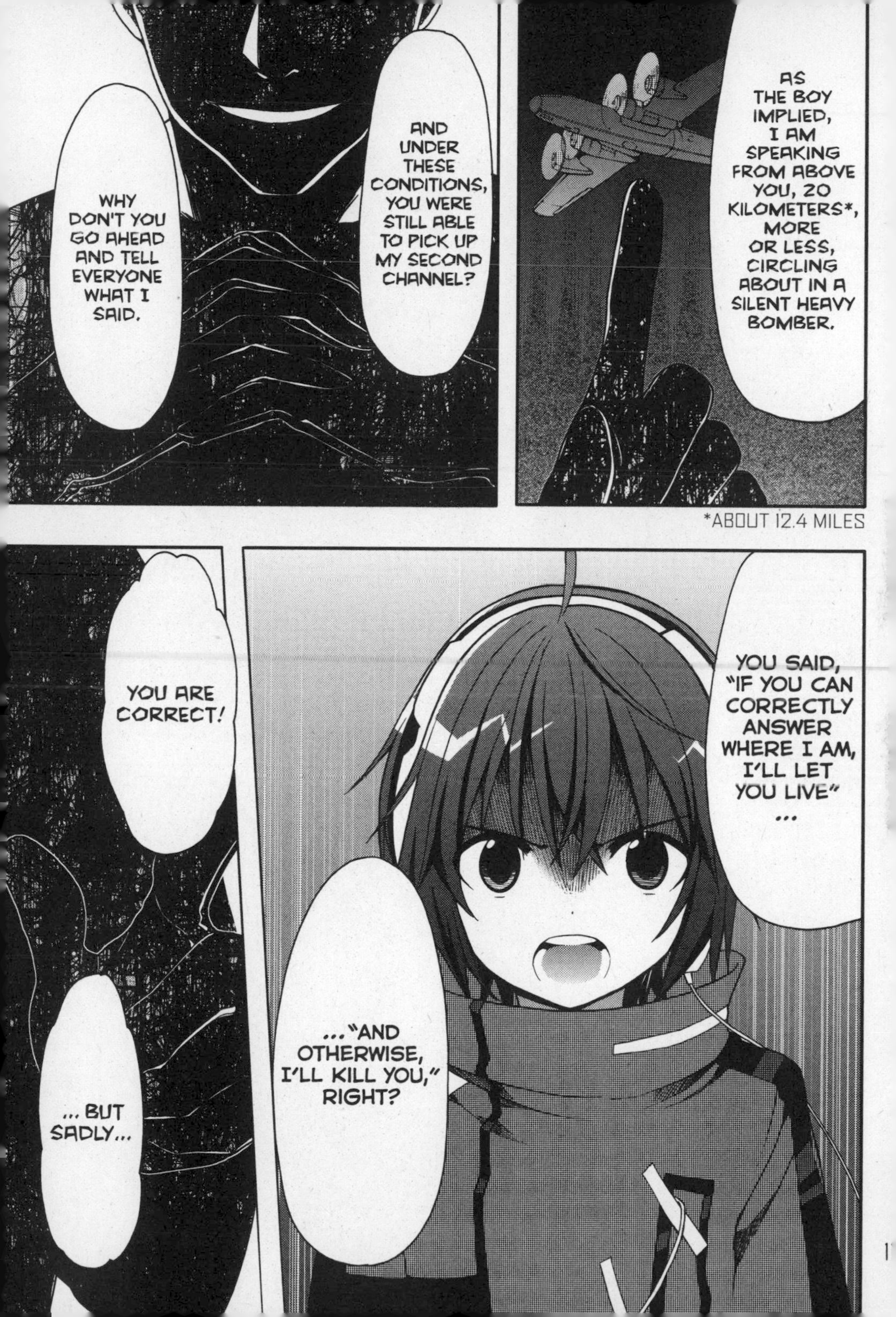
AS THE BOY IMPLIED, I AM SPEAKING FROM ABOVE YOU, 20 KILOMETERS*, MORE OR LESS, CIRCLING ABOUT IN A SILENT HEAVY BOMBER.
AND UNDER THESE CONDITIONS, YOU WERE STILL ABLE TO PICK UP MY SECOND CHANNEL?
WHY DON'T YOU GO AHEAD AND TELL EVERYONE WHAT I SAID.
YOU SAID, "IF YOU CAN CORRECTLY ANSWER WHERE I AM, I'LL LET YOU LIVE" ...
..."AND OTHERWISE, I'LL KILL YOU," RIGHT?
YOU ARE CORRECT!
...BUT SADLY...

*ABOUT 12.4 MILES

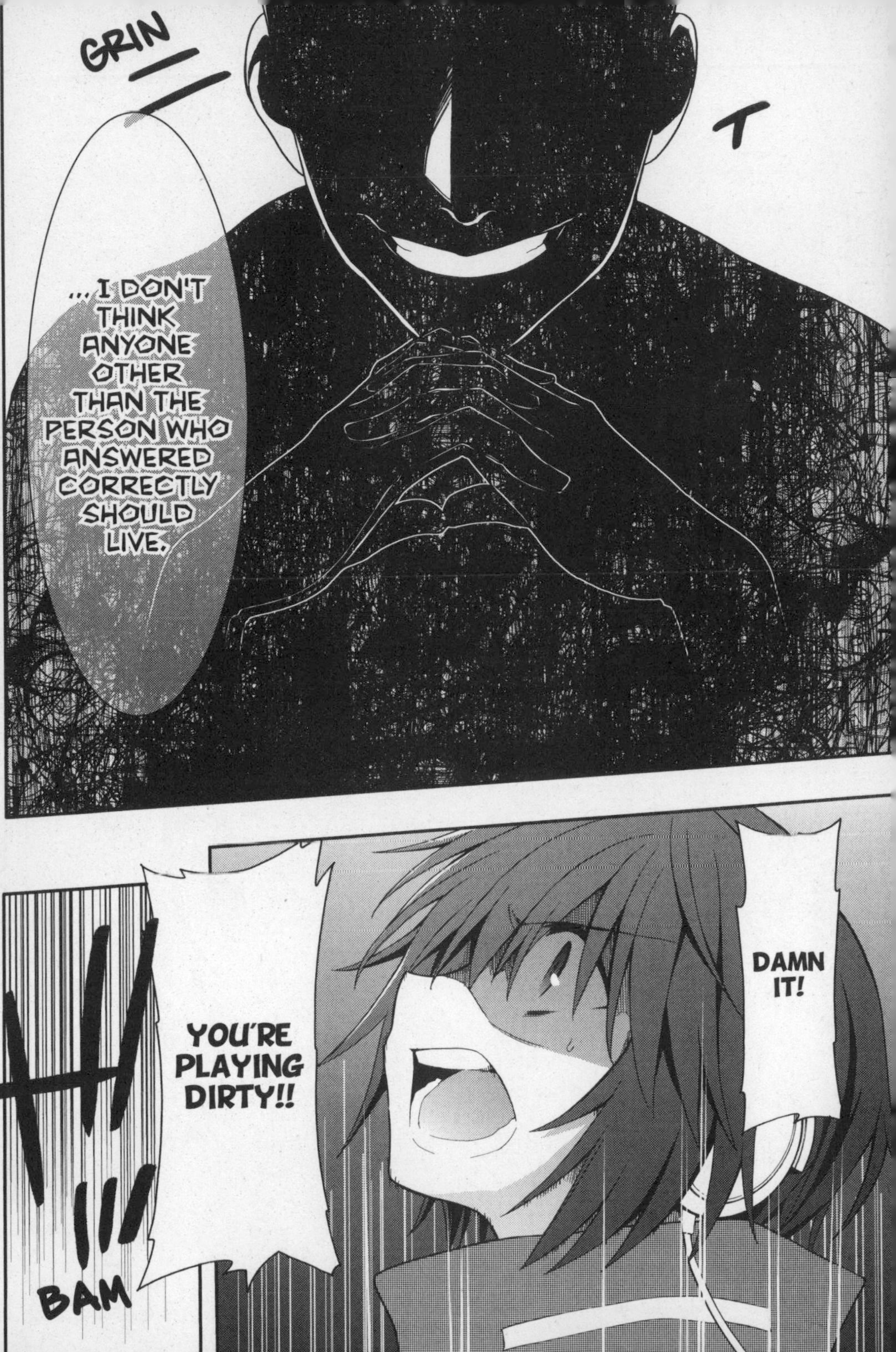
T
GRIN
...I DON'T THINK ANYONE OTHER THAN THE PERSON WHO ANSWERED CORRECTLY SHOULD LIVE.
DAMN IT!
YOU'RE PLAYING DIRTY!!
BAM

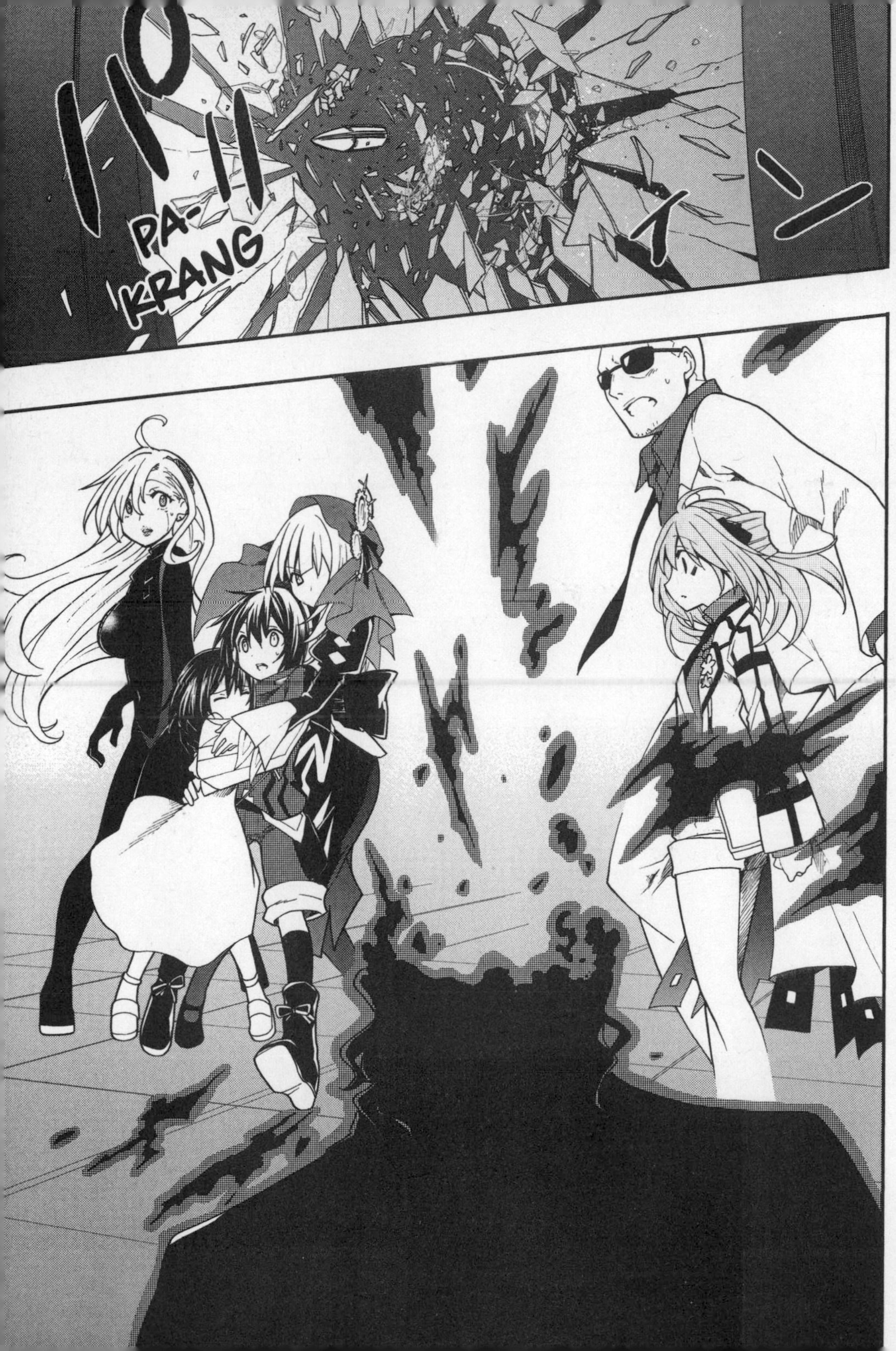
PA-
KRANG

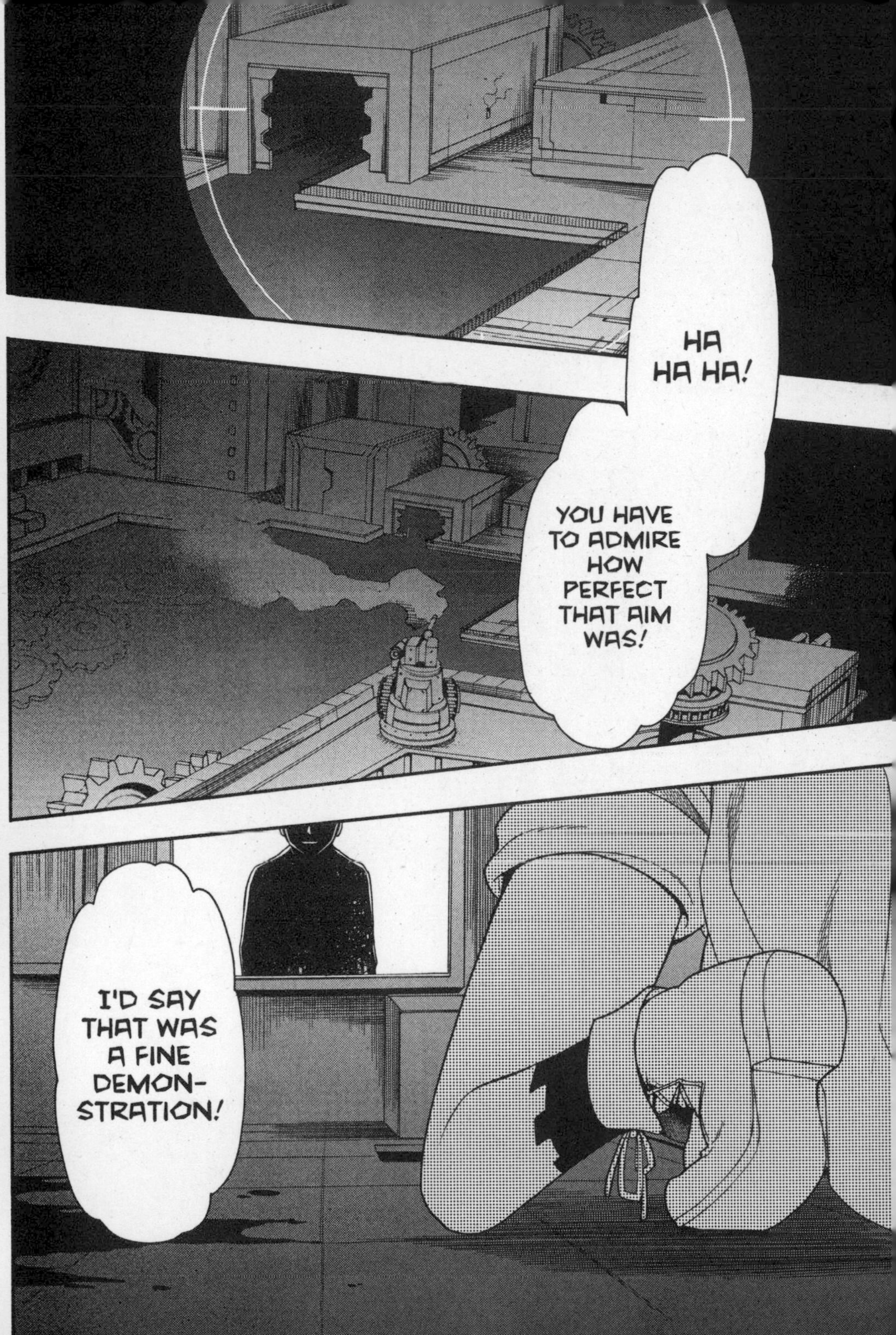
HA HA HA!
YOU HAVE TO ADMIRE HOW PERFECT THAT AIM WAS!
I'D SAY THAT WAS A FINE DEMON-STRATION!

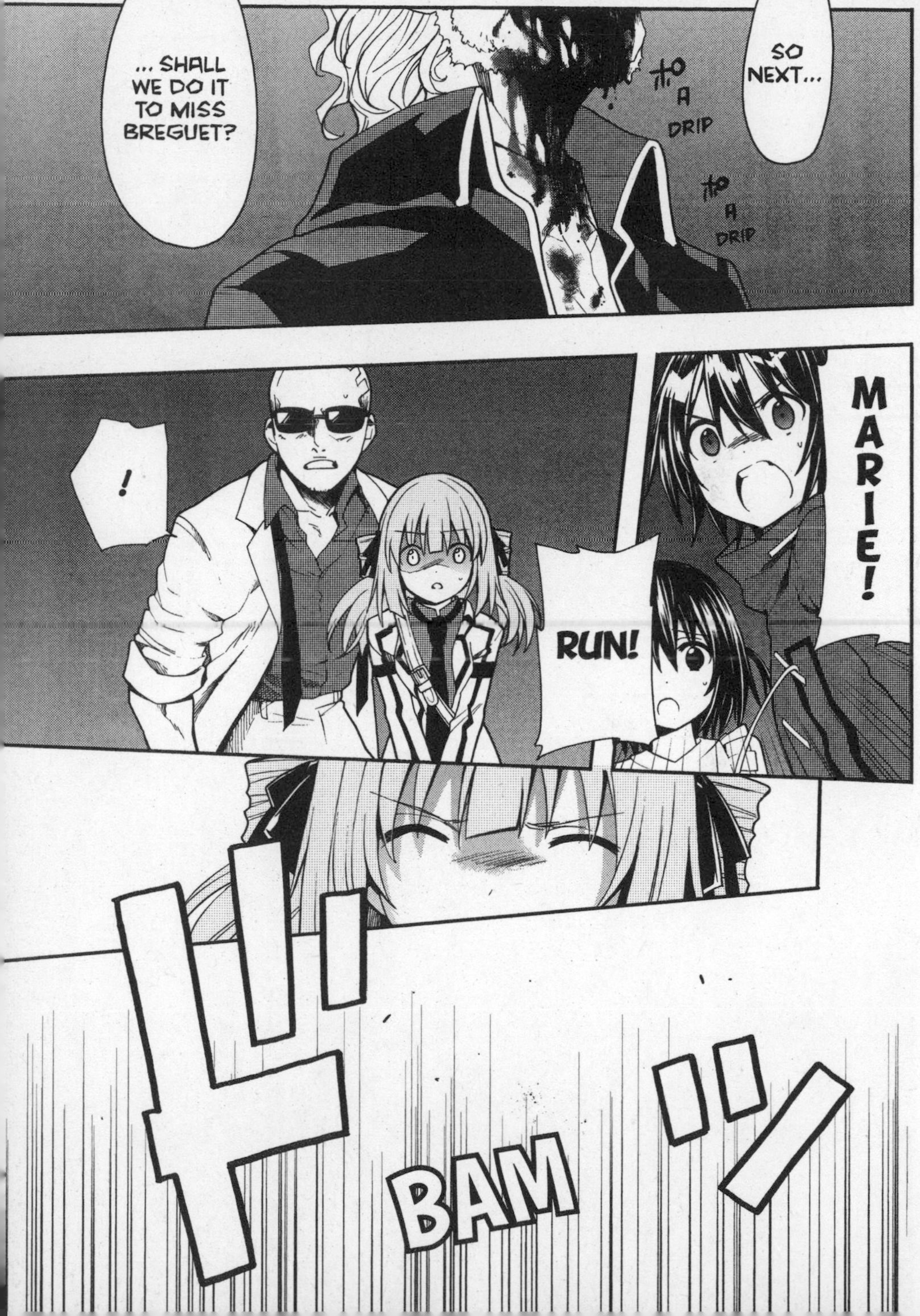
SO NEXT...
A DRIP
A DRIP
... SHALL WE DO IT TO MISS BREGUET?
MARIE!
RUN!
!
BAM

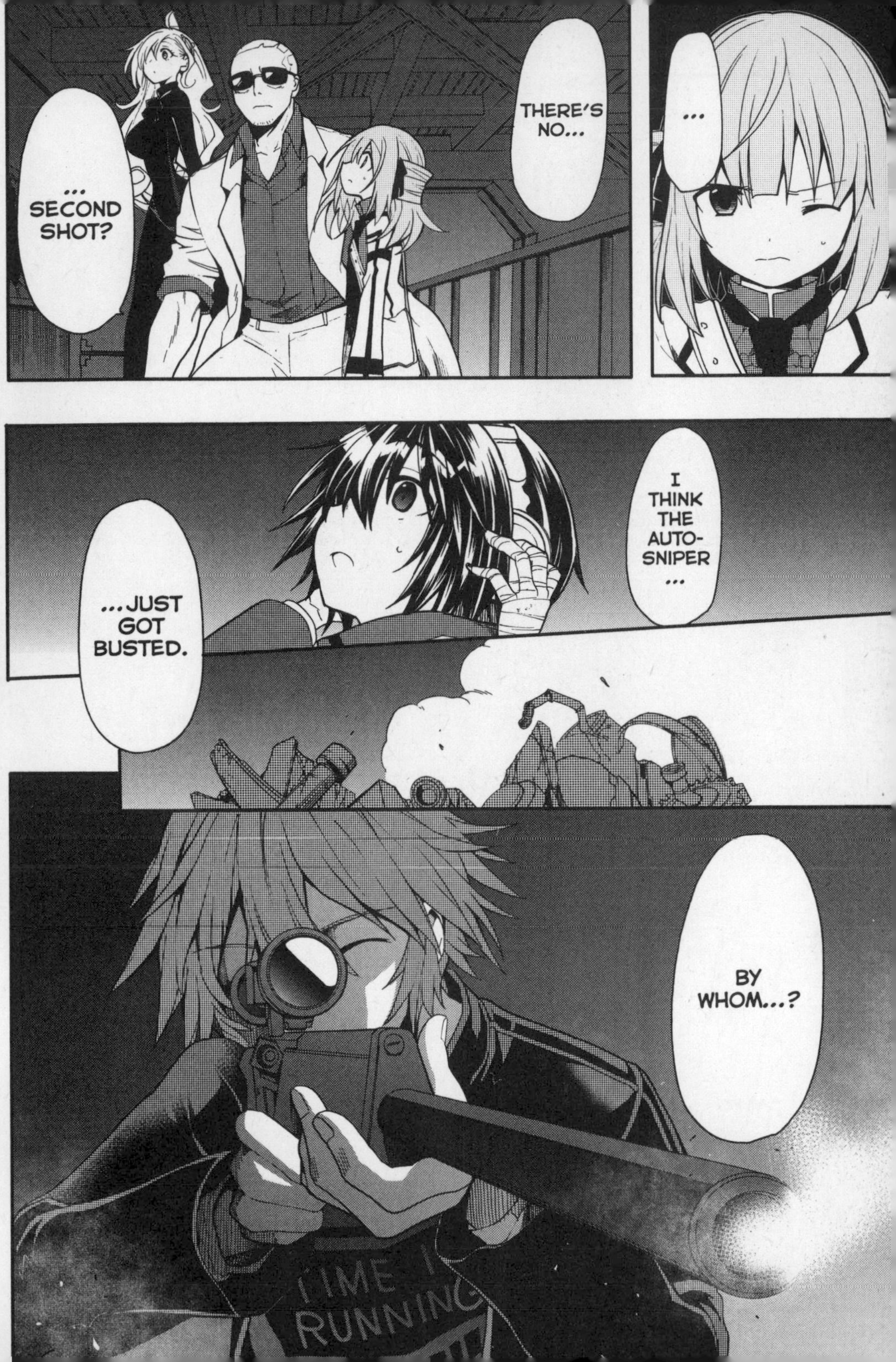
...
THERE'S NO...
... SECOND SHOT?
I THINK THE AUTO-SNIPER ...
...JUST GOT BUSTED.
BY WHOM...?

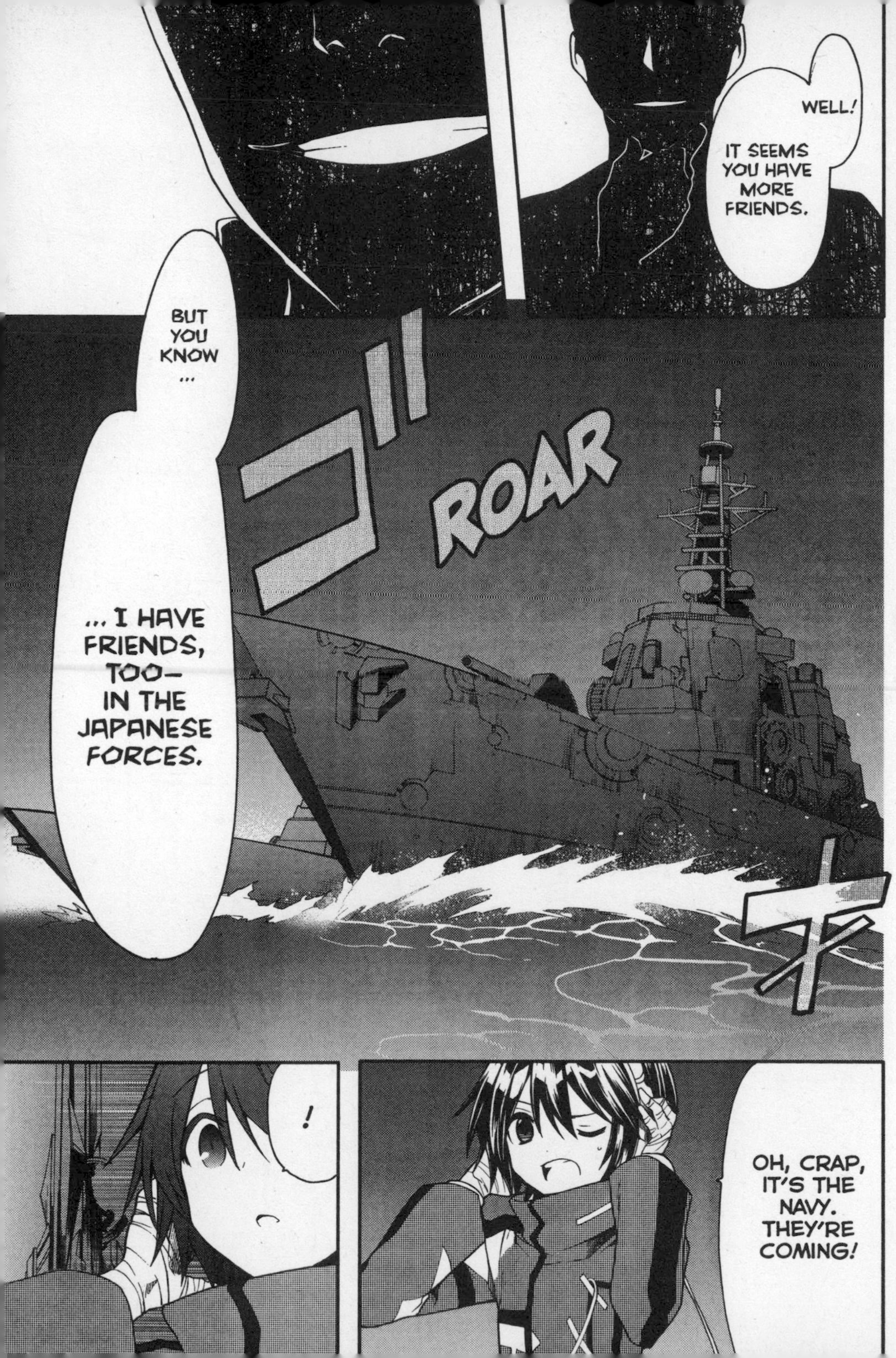
WELL!
IT SEEMS YOU HAVE MORE FRIENDS.
BUT YOU KNOW ...
ROAR
... I HAVE FRIENDS, TOO— IN THE JAPANESE FORCES.
OH, CRAP, IT'S THE NAVY. THEY'RE COMING!
!

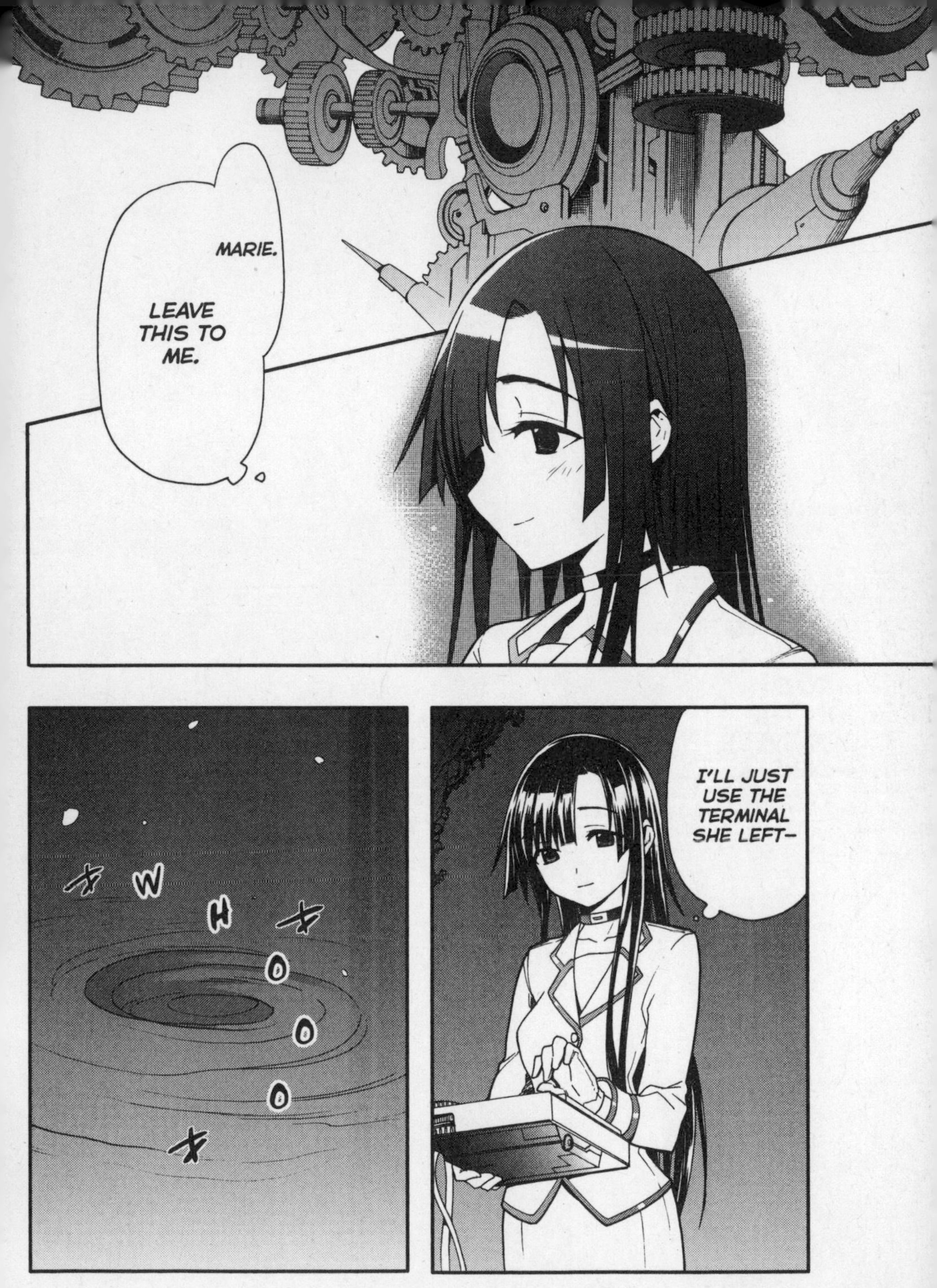
MARIE.
LEAVE THIS TO ME.
I'LL JUST USE THE TERMINAL SHE LEFT—
WHOOO

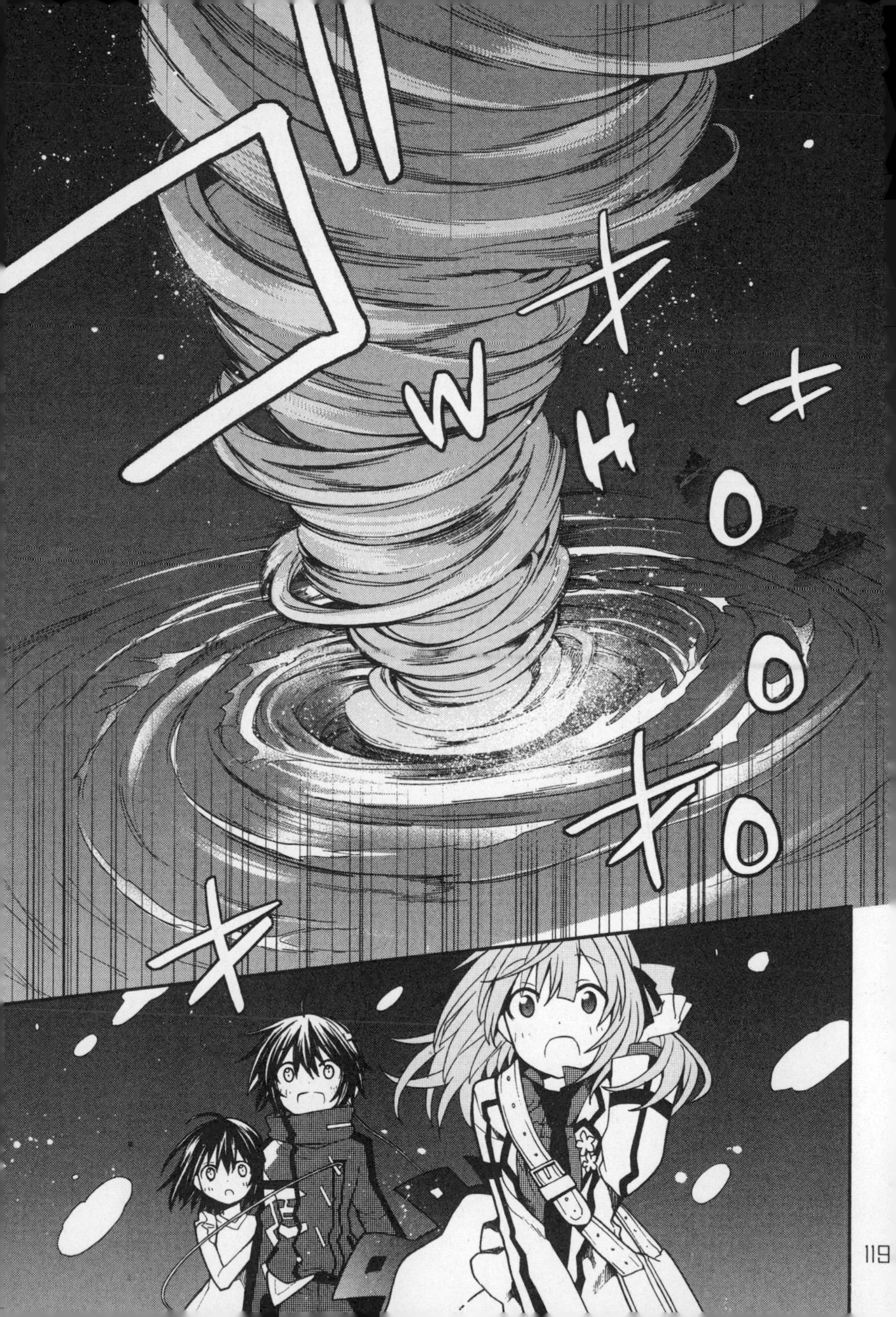
WHOOO

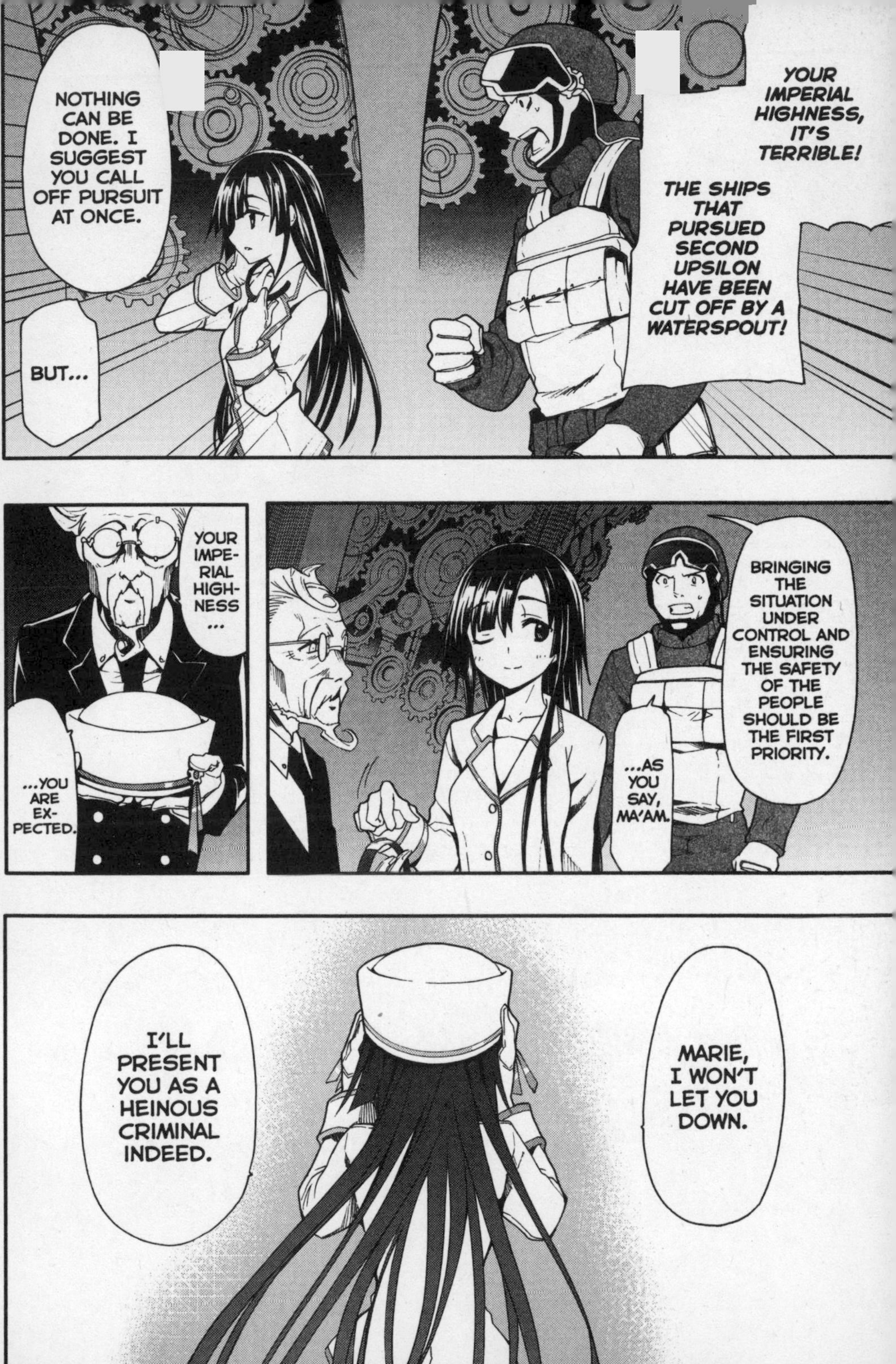
YOUR IMPERIAL HIGHNESS, IT'S TERRIBLE!
THE SHIPS THAT PURSUED SECOND UPSILON HAVE BEEN CUT OFF BY A WATERSPOUT!
NOTHING CAN BE DONE. I SUGGEST YOU CALL OFF PURSUIT AT ONCE.
BUT...
BRINGING THE SITUATION UNDER CONTROL AND ENSURING THE SAFETY OF THE PEOPLE SHOULD BE THE FIRST PRIORITY.
...AS YOU SAY, MA'AM.
YOUR IMPERIAL HIGHNESS...
...YOU ARE EXPECTED.
MARIE, I WON'T LET YOU DOWN.
I'LL PRESENT YOU AS A HEINOUS CRIMINAL INDEED.

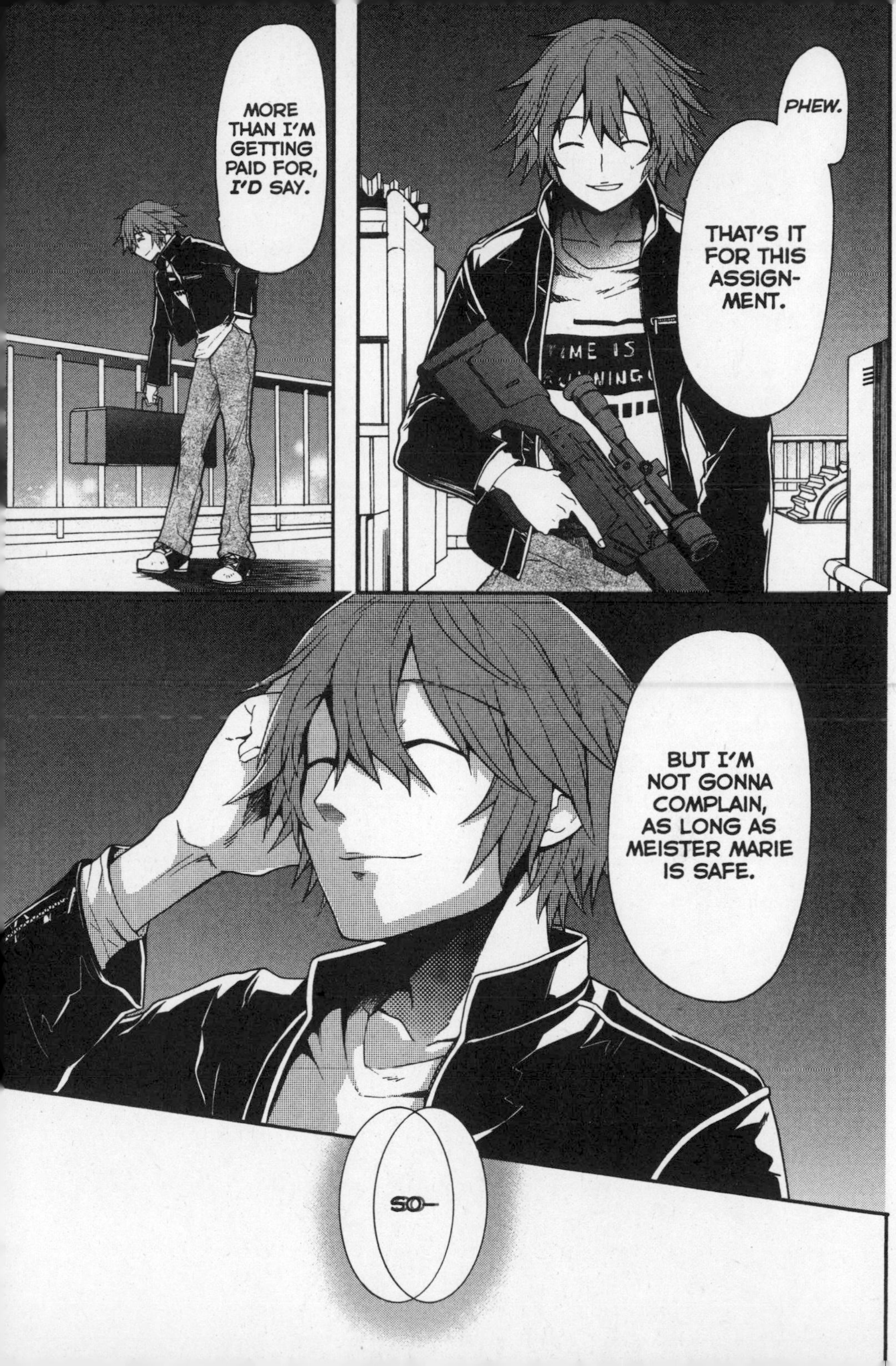
PHEW.
THAT'S IT FOR THIS ASSIGNMENT.
MORE THAN I'M GETTING PAID FOR, I'D SAY.
BUT I'M NOT GONNA COMPLAIN, AS LONG AS MEISTER MARIE IS SAFE.
SO—

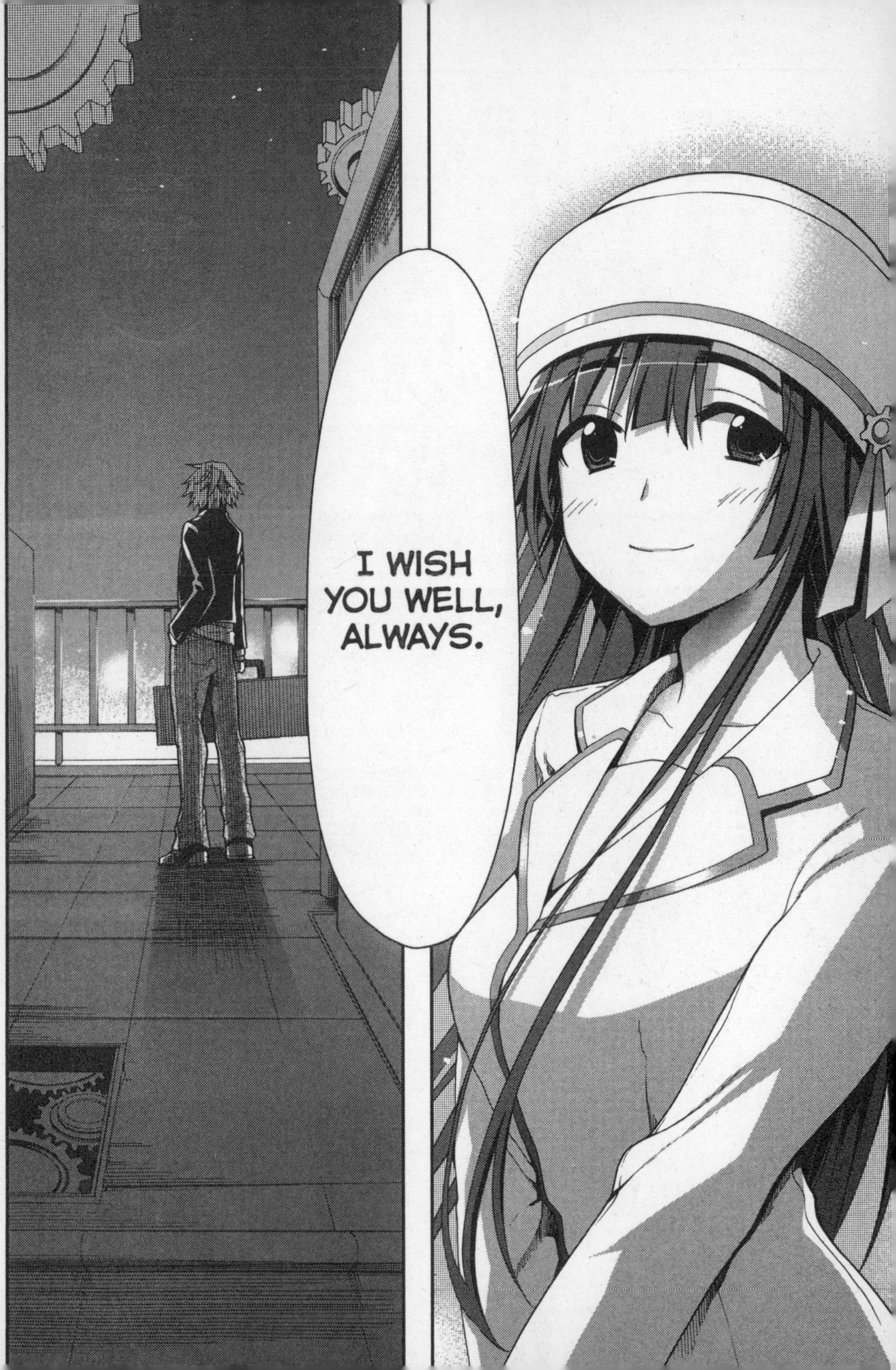
I WISH YOU WELL, ALWAYS.

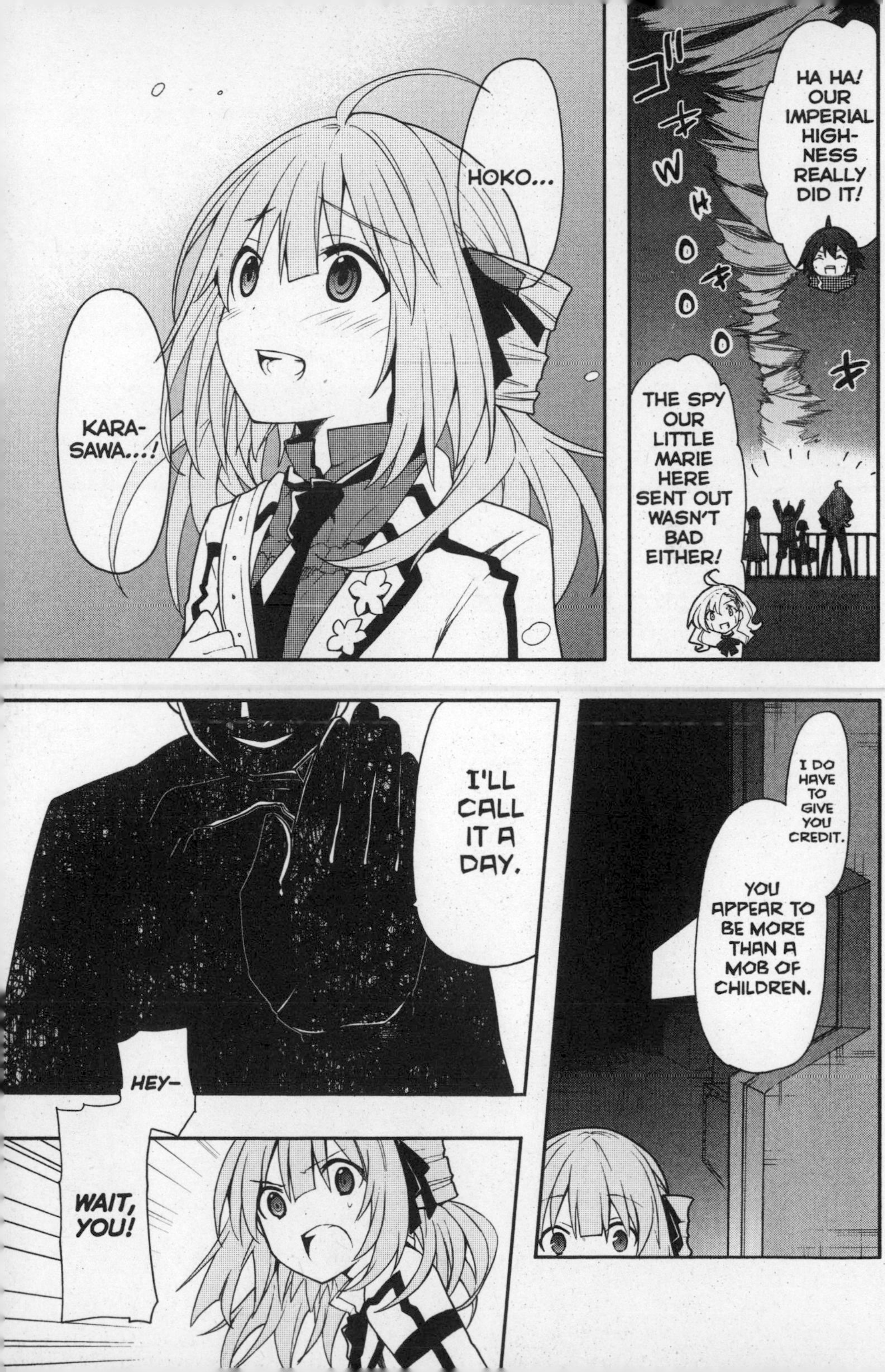
HA HA! OUR IMPERIAL HIGH-NESS REALLY DID IT!
THE SPY OUR LITTLE MARIE HERE SENT OUT WASN'T BAD EITHER!
HOKO...
KARA-SAWA...!
I DO HAVE TO GIVE YOU CREDIT.
YOU APPEAR TO BE MORE THAN A MOB OF CHILDREN.
I'LL CALL IT A DAY.
HEY-
WAIT, YOU!

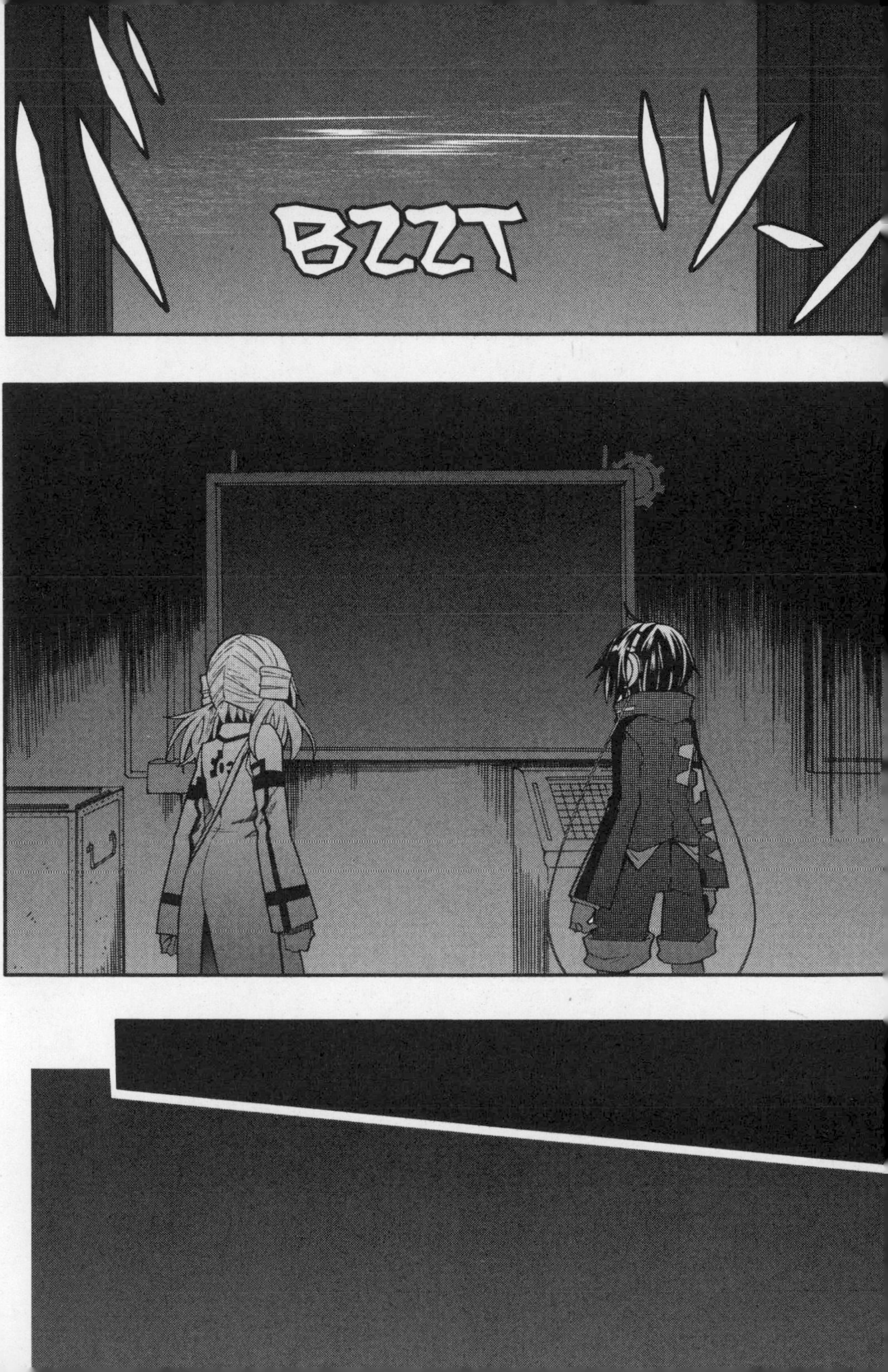
BZZT

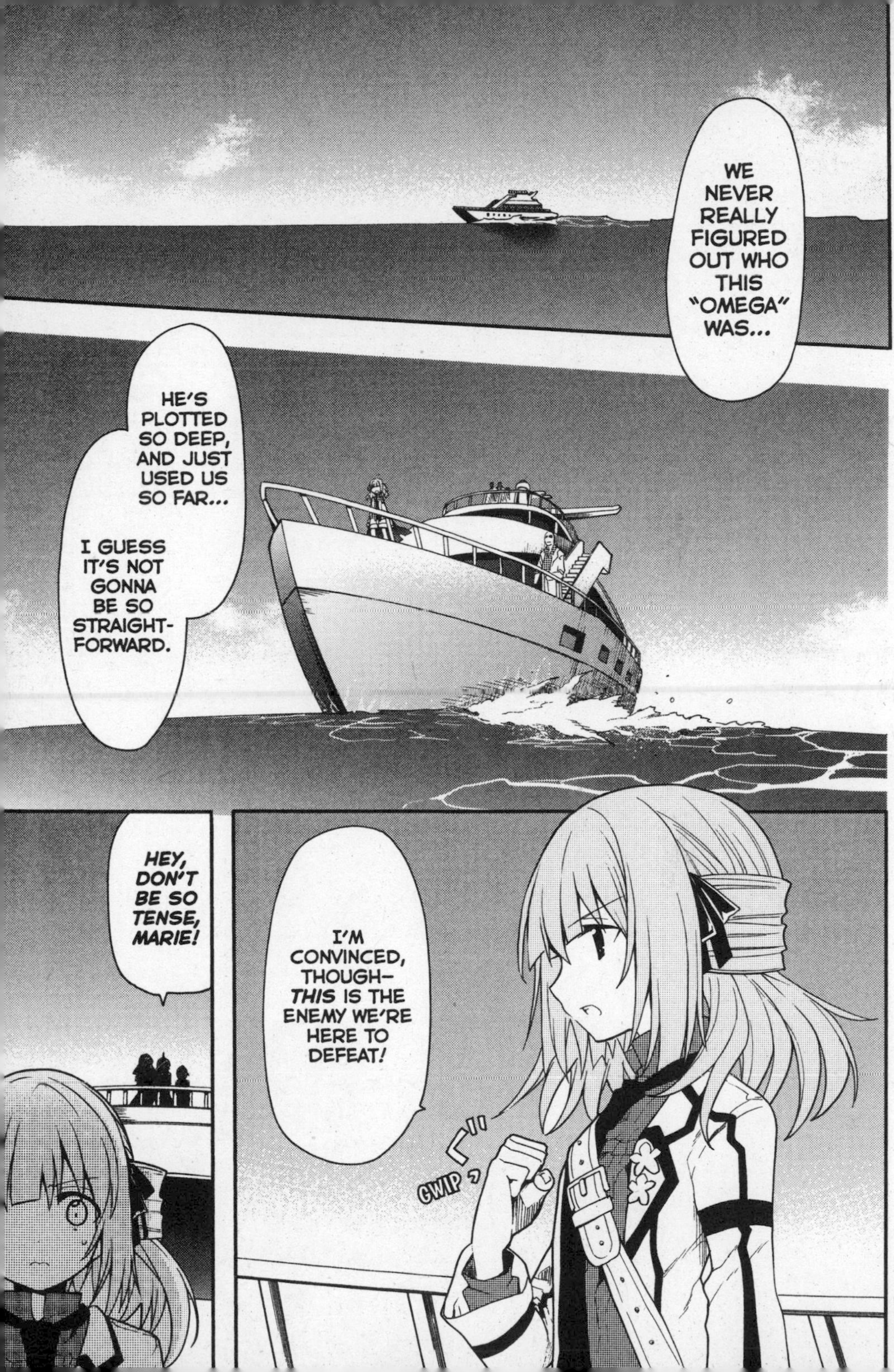
WE NEVER REALLY FIGURED OUT WHO THIS "OMEGA" WAS...
HE'S PLOTTED SO DEEP, AND JUST USED US SO FAR...
I GUESS IT'S NOT GONNA BE SO STRAIGHT-FORWARD.
I'M CONVINCED, THOUGH—*THIS* IS THE ENEMY WE'RE HERE TO DEFEAT!
GWIP
HEY, DON'T BE SO TENSE, MARIE!

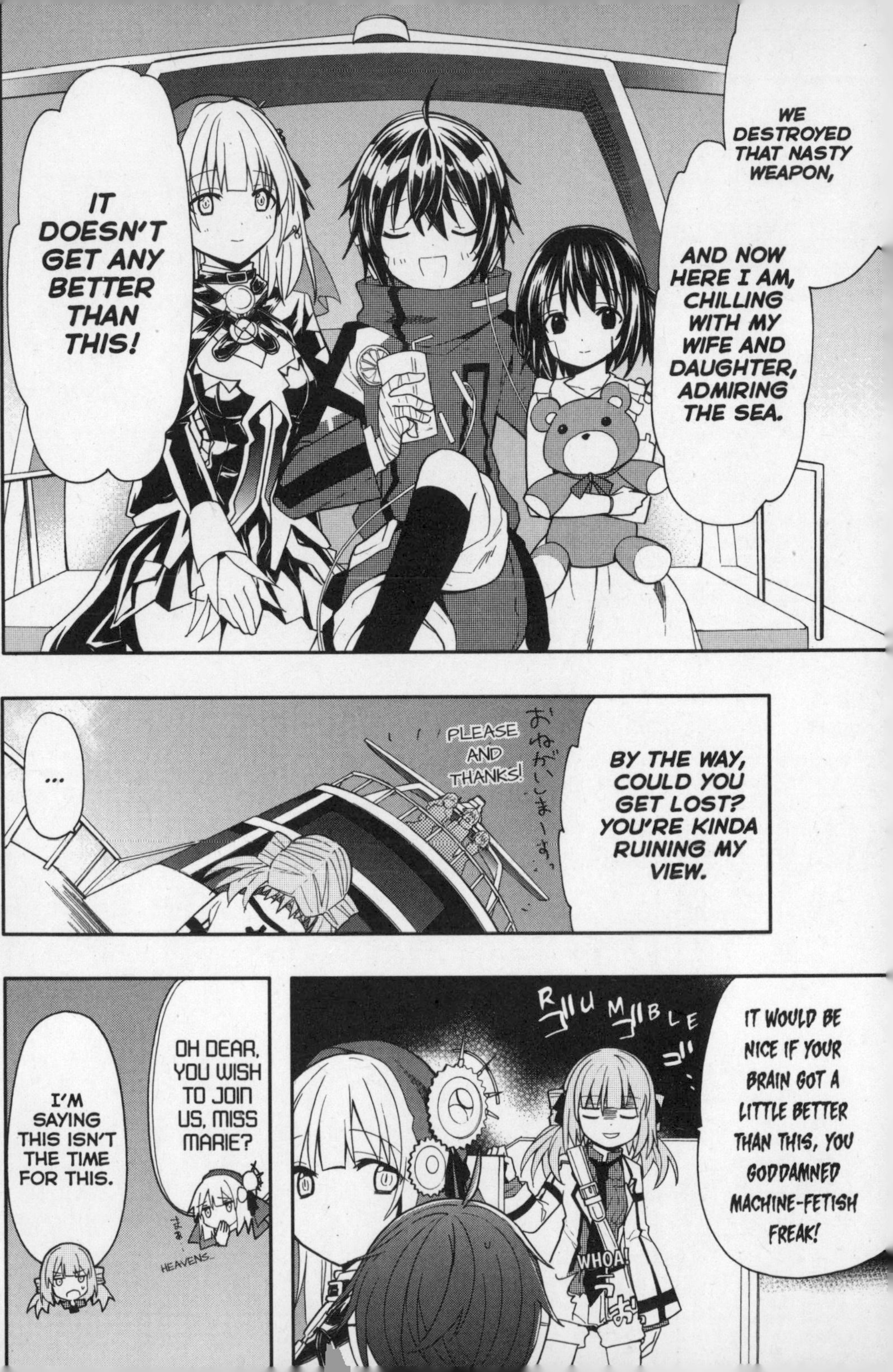

WE DESTROYED THAT NASTY WEAPON,
AND NOW HERE I AM, CHILLING WITH MY WIFE AND DAUGHTER, ADMIRING THE SEA.
IT DOESN'T GET ANY BETTER THAN THIS!
BY THE WAY, COULD YOU GET LOST? YOU'RE KINDA RUINING MY VIEW.
PLEASE AND THANKS!
おねがいしまーす
...
IT WOULD BE NICE IF YOUR BRAIN GOT A LITTLE BETTER THAN THIS, YOU GODDAMNED MACHINE-FETISH FREAK!
RUMBLE
WHOA!
OH DEAR, YOU WISH TO JOIN US, MISS MARIE?
HEAVENS...
I'M SAYING THIS ISN'T THE TIME FOR THIS.

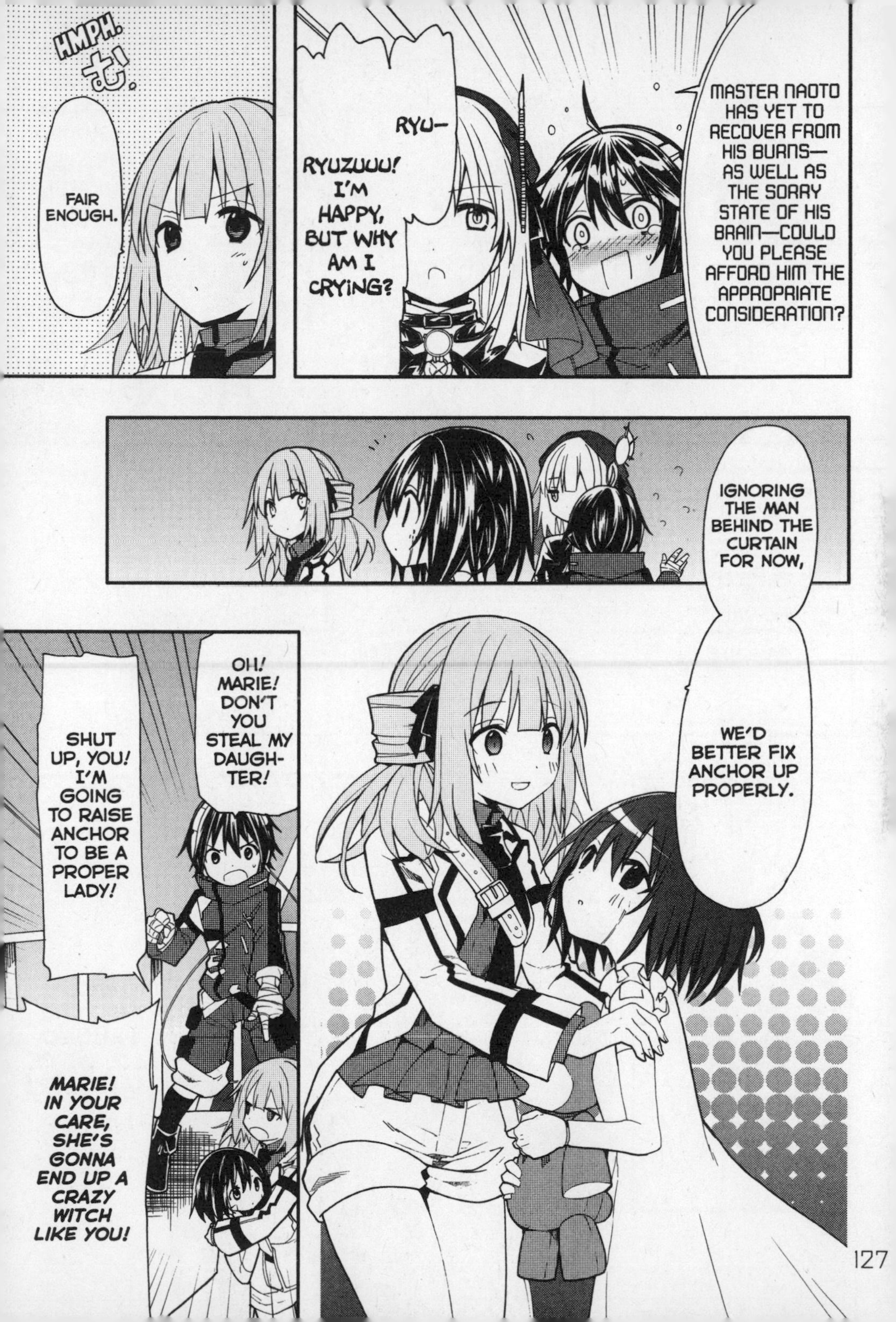
MASTER NAOTO HAS YET TO RECOVER FROM HIS BURNS—AS WELL AS THE SORRY STATE OF HIS BRAIN—COULD YOU PLEASE AFFORD HIM THE APPROPRIATE CONSIDERATION?
RYU—
RYUZUUU! I'M HAPPY, BUT WHY AM I CRYING?
HMPH.
む。
FAIR ENOUGH.
IGNORING THE MAN BEHIND THE CURTAIN FOR NOW,
WE'D BETTER FIX ANCHOR UP PROPERLY.
OH! MARIE! DON'T YOU STEAL MY DAUGHTER!
SHUT UP, YOU! I'M GOING TO RAISE ANCHOR TO BE A PROPER LADY!
MARIE! IN YOUR CARE, SHE'S GONNA END UP A CRAZY WITCH LIKE YOU!

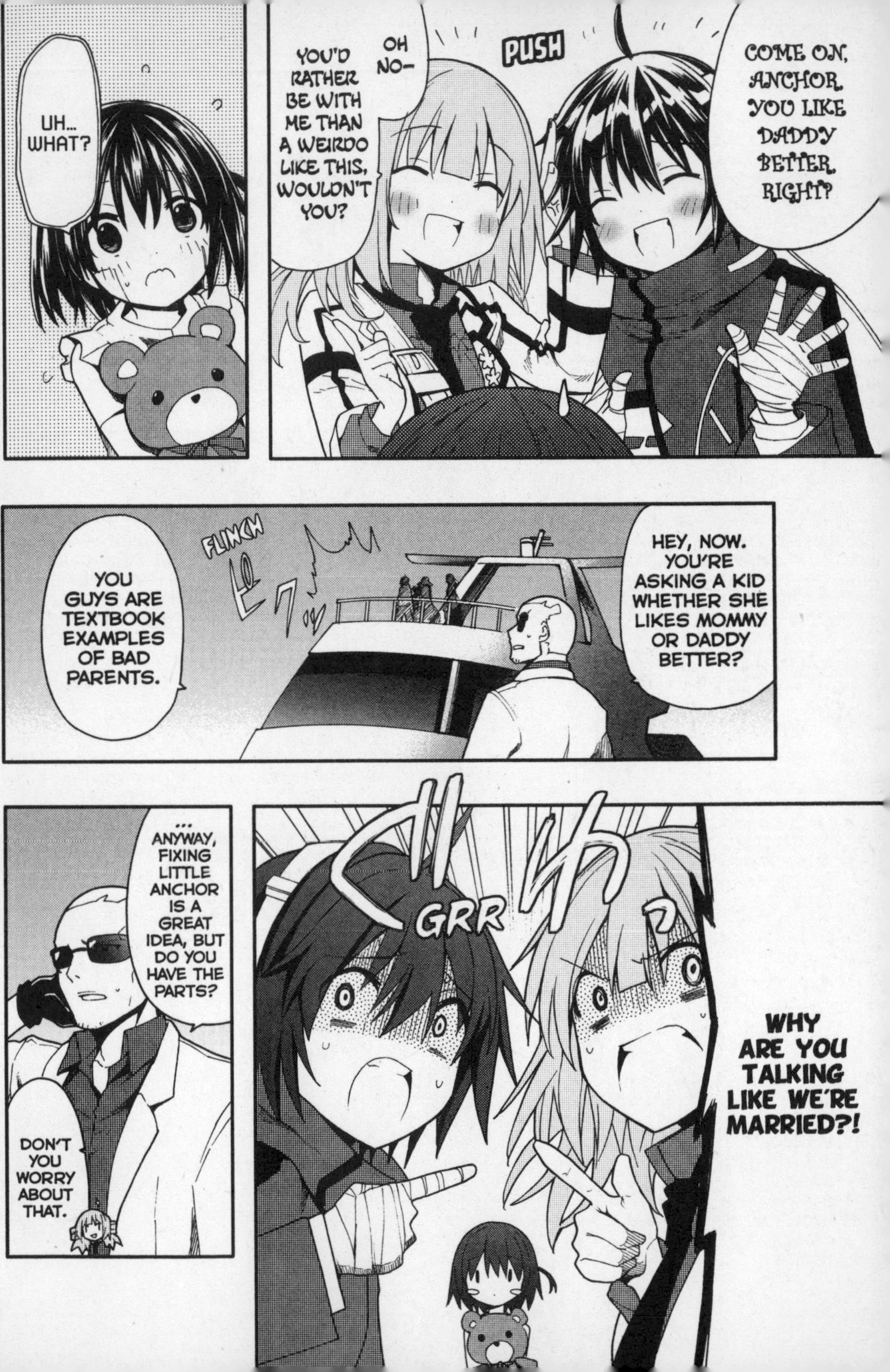
COME ON, ANCHOR. YOU LIKE DADDY BETTER. RIGHT?
PUSH
OH NO—
YOU'D RATHER BE WITH ME THAN A WEIRDO LIKE THIS, WOULDN'T YOU?
UH... WHAT?
HEY, NOW. YOU'RE ASKING A KID WHETHER SHE LIKES MOMMY OR DADDY BETTER?
FLINCH
YOU GUYS ARE TEXTBOOK EXAMPLES OF BAD PARENTS.
GRR
WHY ARE YOU TALKING LIKE WE'RE MARRIED?!
... ANYWAY, FIXING LITTLE ANCHOR IS A GREAT IDEA, BUT DO YOU HAVE THE PARTS?
DON'T YOU WORRY ABOUT THAT.

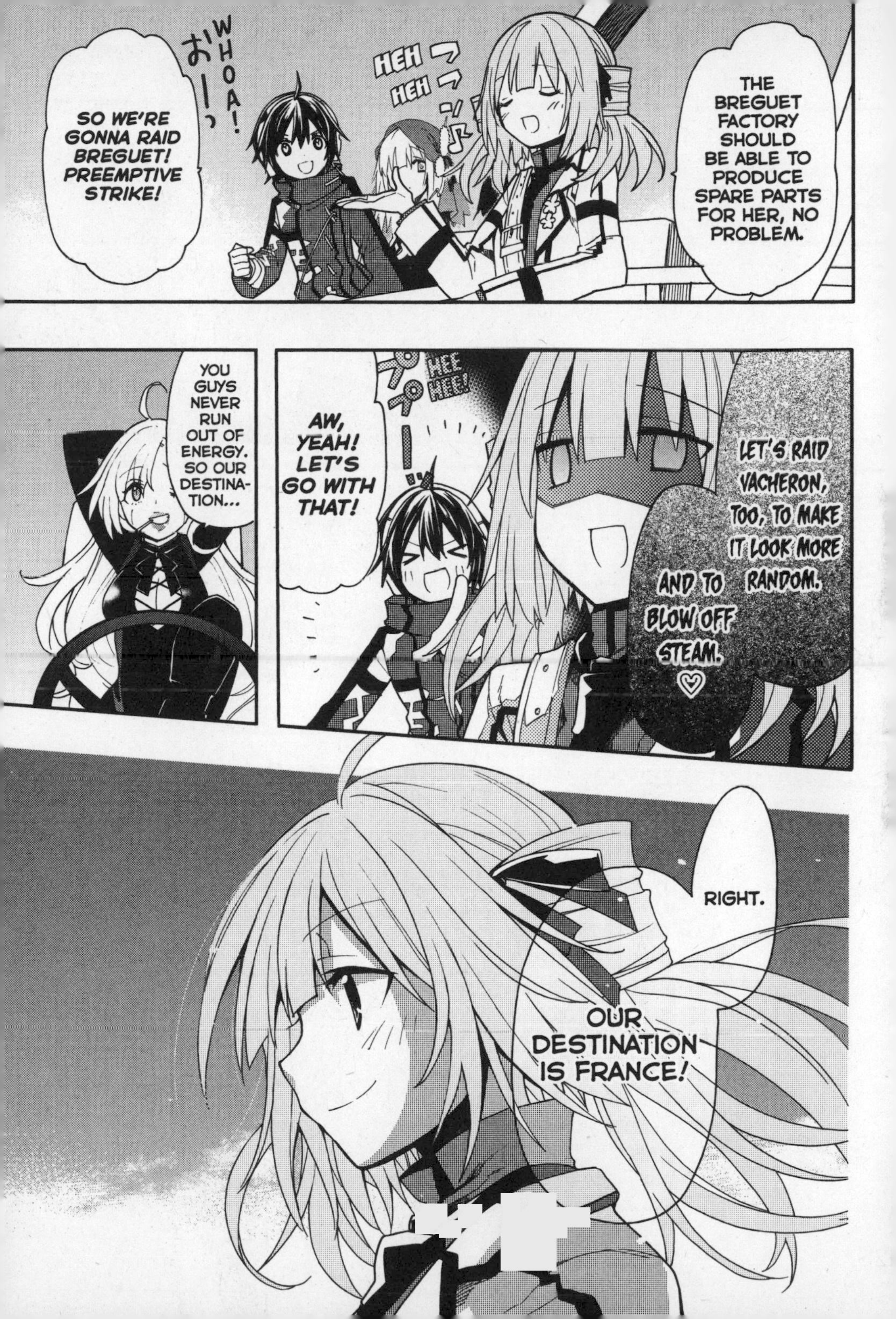
THE BREGUET FACTORY SHOULD BE ABLE TO PRODUCE SPARE PARTS FOR HER, NO PROBLEM.
HEH HEH
WHOA!
SO WE'RE GONNA RAID BREGUET! PREEMPTIVE STRIKE!
LET'S RAID VACHERON, TOO, TO MAKE IT LOOK MORE RANDOM.
AND TO BLOW OFF STEAM. ♡
HEE HEE!
AW, YEAH! LET'S GO WITH THAT!
YOU GUYS NEVER RUN OUT OF ENERGY. SO OUR DESTINATION...
RIGHT.
OUR DESTINATION IS FRANCE!

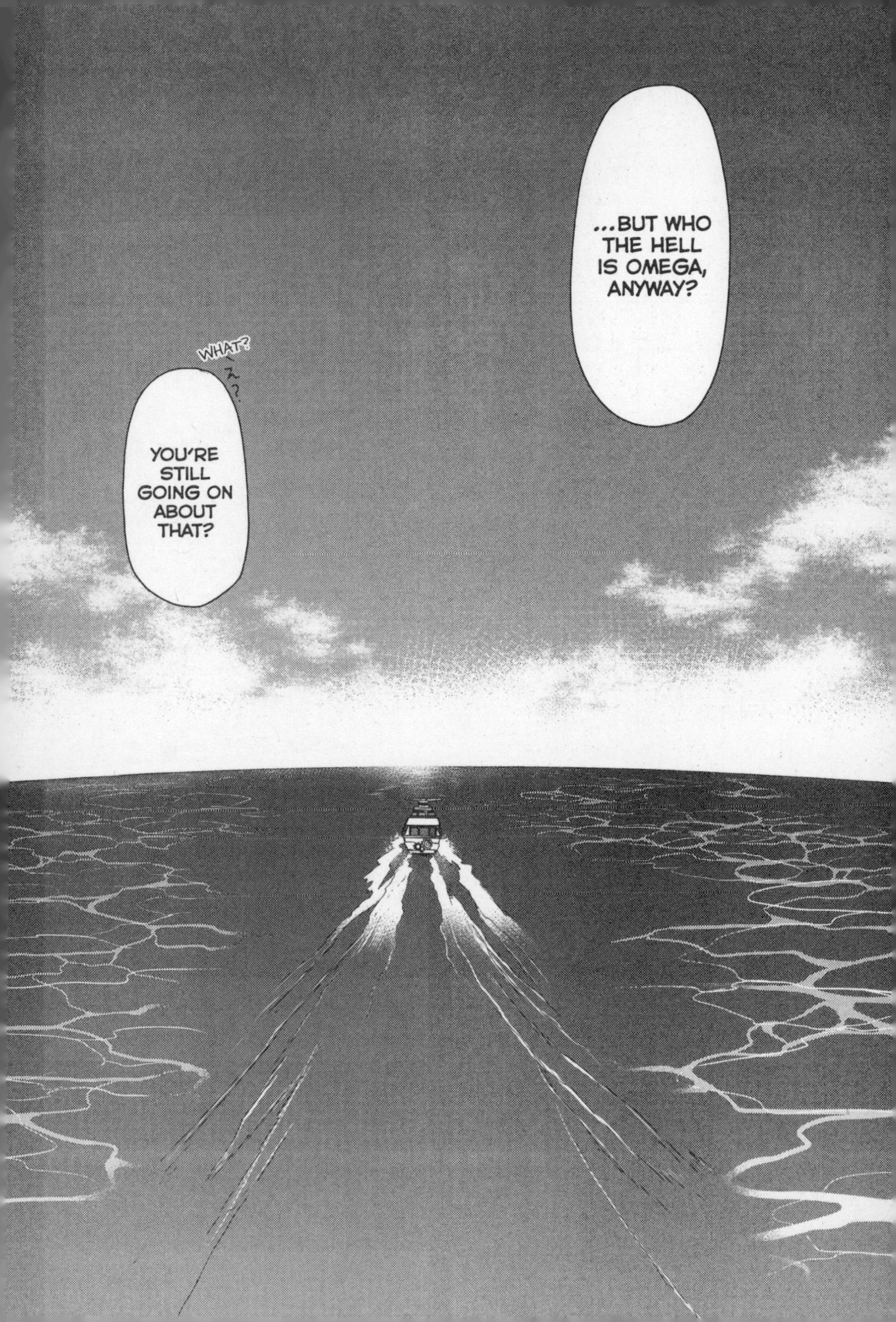
...BUT WHO THE HELL IS OMEGA, ANYWAY?
WHAT?
YOU'RE STILL GOING ON ABOUT THAT?

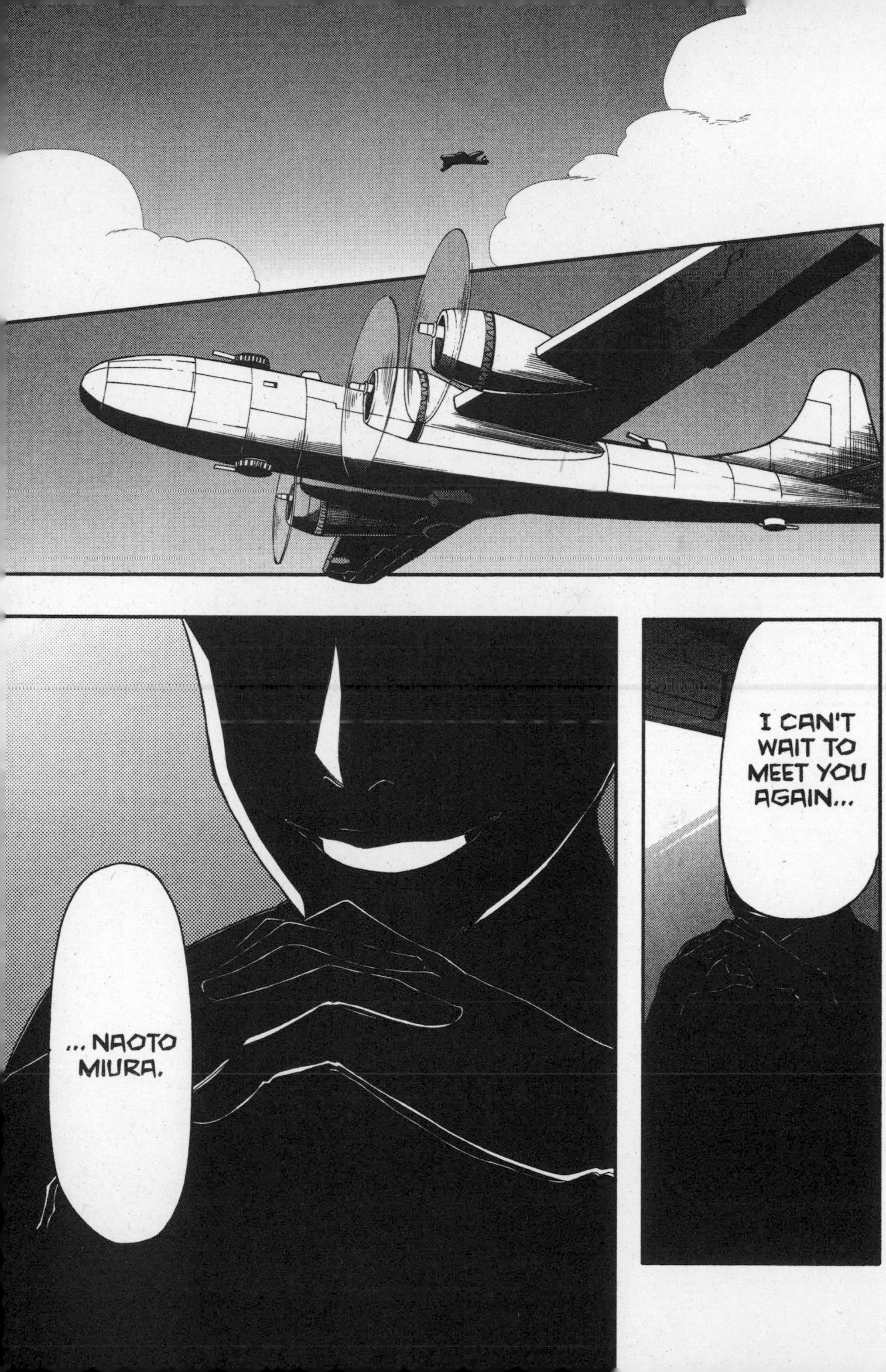
I CAN'T WAIT TO MEET YOU AGAIN...
...NAOTO MIURA.

Clockwork Planet

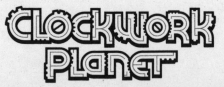

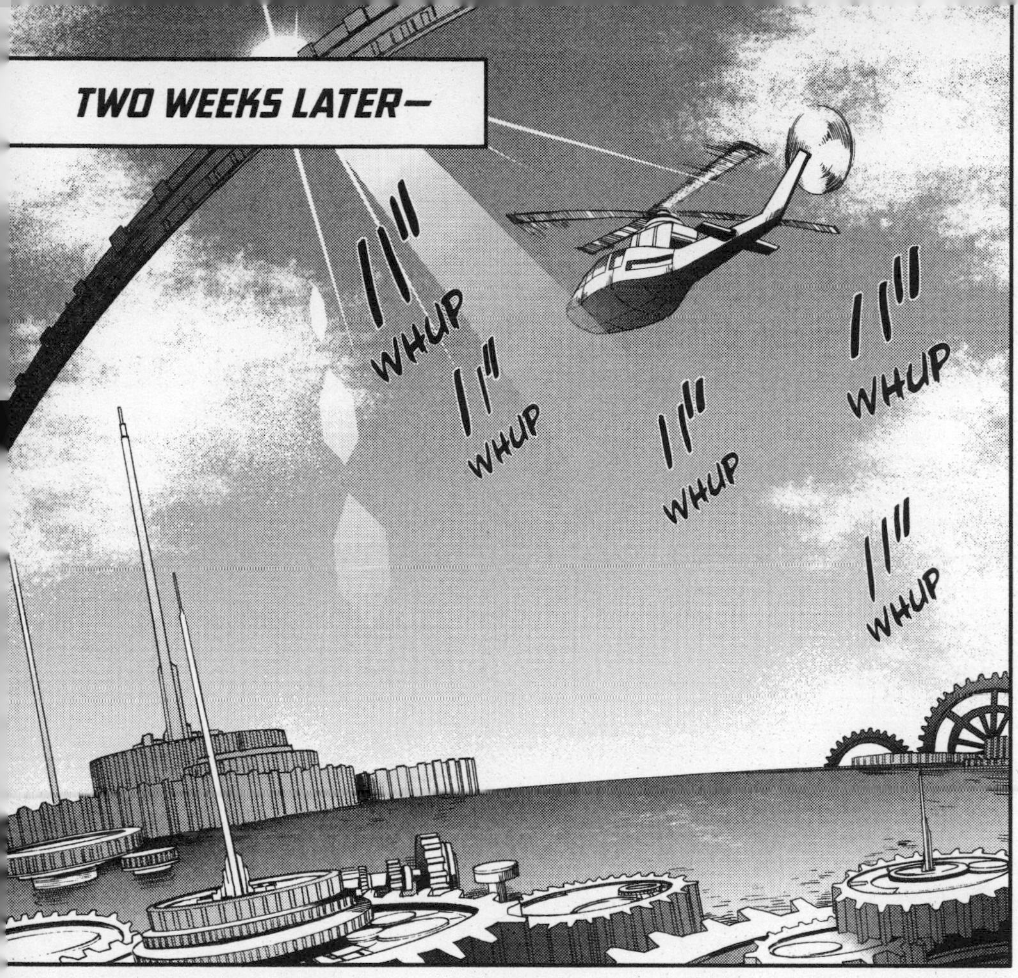
TWO WEEKS LATER—
WHUP
WHUP
WHUP
WHUP
WHUP

*ABOUT 1969 FEET

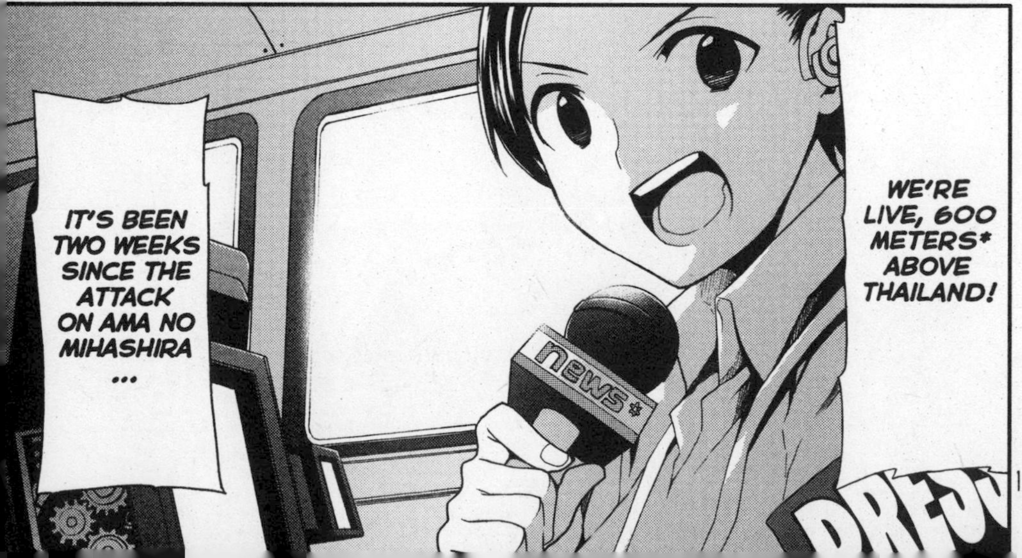
WE'RE LIVE, 600 METERS* ABOVE THAILAND!
IT'S BEEN TWO WEEKS SINCE THE ATTACK ON AMA NO MIHASHIRA ...
news

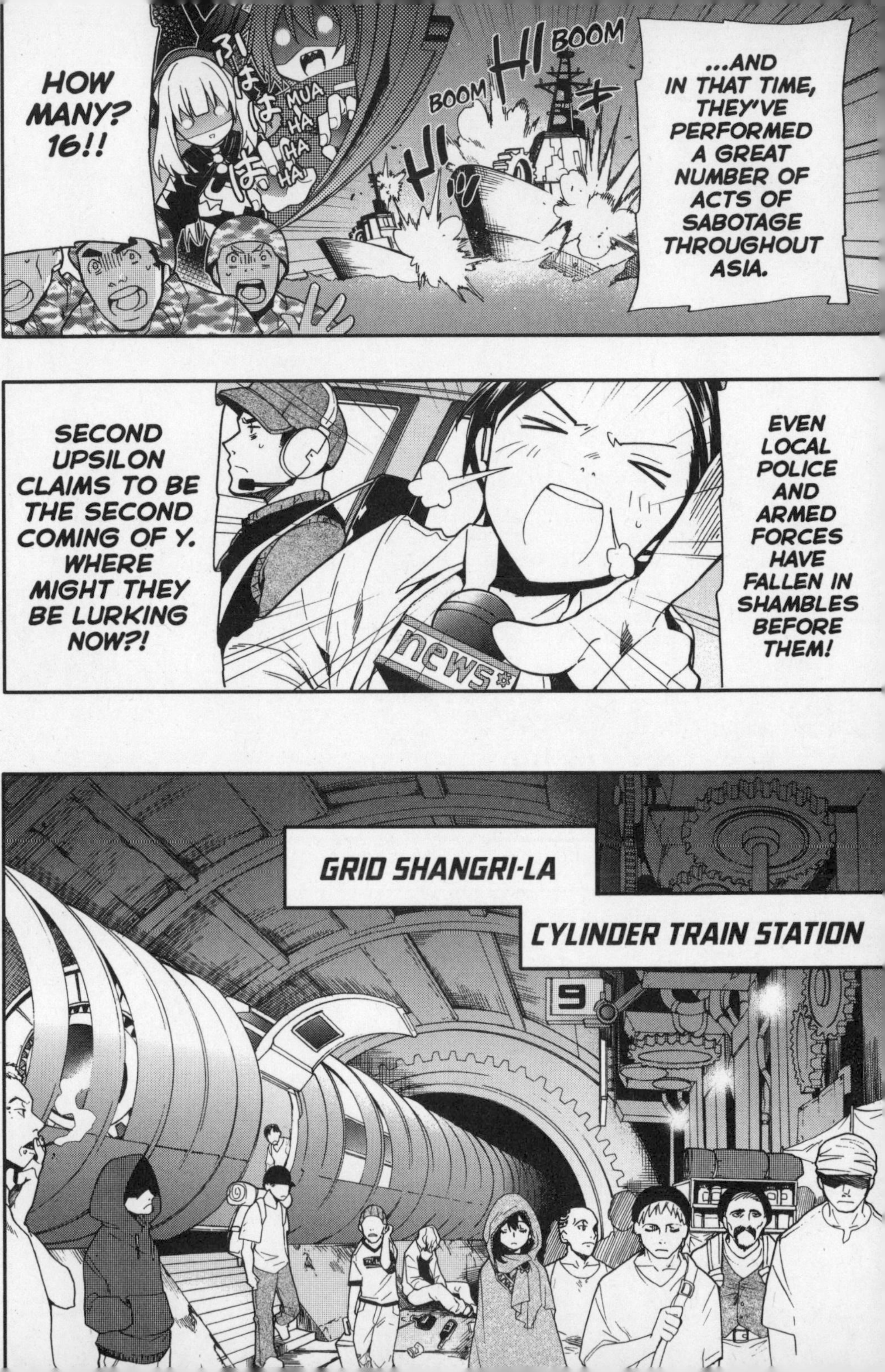
...AND IN THAT TIME, THEY'VE PERFORMED A GREAT NUMBER OF ACTS OF SABOTAGE THROUGHOUT ASIA.
BOOM
HI
BOOM
HI
ふははは
MUA HA HA HA HA
HOW MANY? 16!!
EVEN LOCAL POLICE AND ARMED FORCES HAVE FALLEN IN SHAMBLES BEFORE THEM!
SECOND UPSILON CLAIMS TO BE THE SECOND COMING OF Y. WHERE MIGHT THEY BE LURKING NOW?!
news
GRID SHANGRI-LA
CYLINDER TRAIN STATION
9

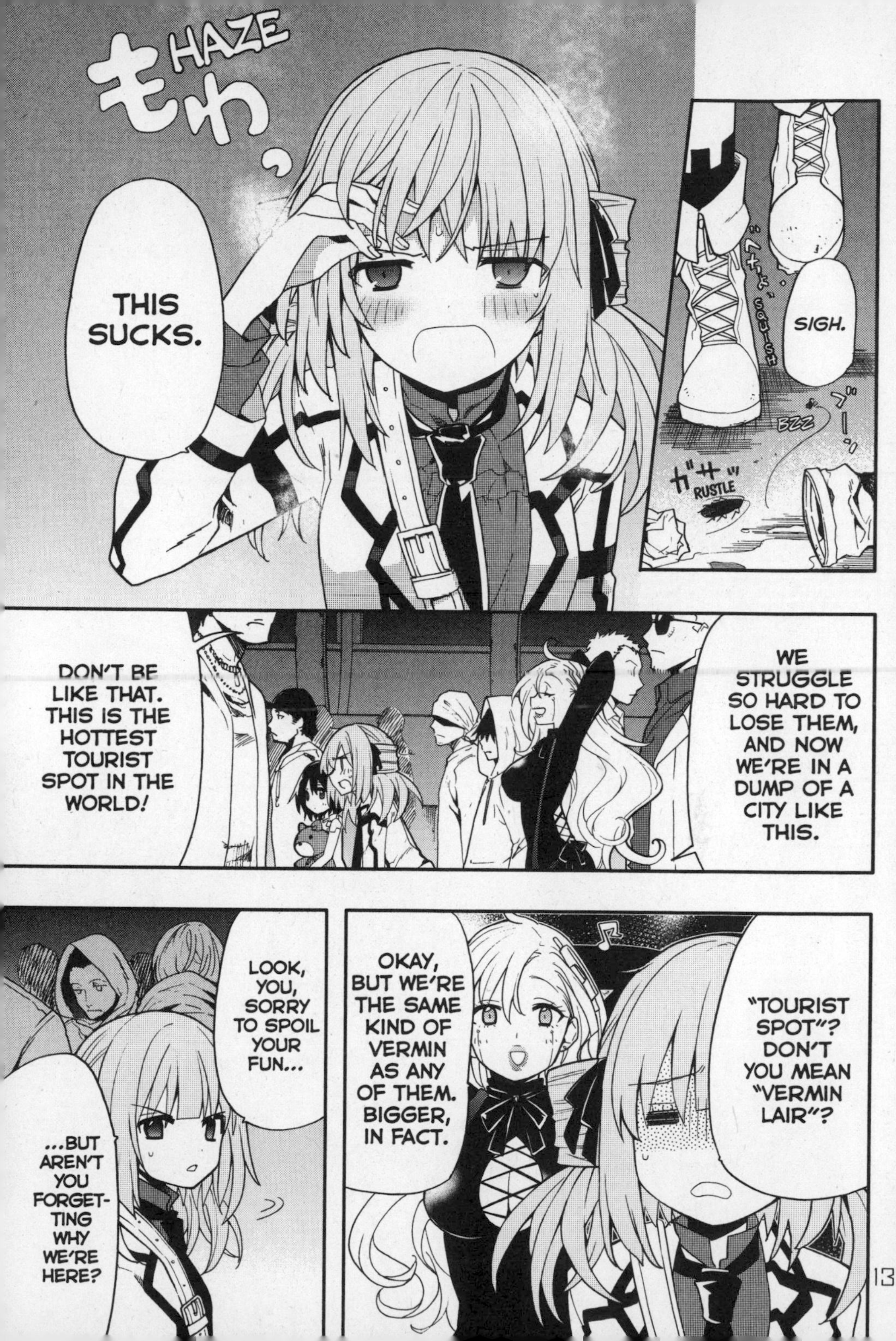
SQUISH
SIGH.
BZZ
RUSTLE
もわっ
HAZE
THIS SUCKS.
WE STRUGGLE SO HARD TO LOSE THEM, AND NOW WE'RE IN A DUMP OF A CITY LIKE THIS.
DON'T BE LIKE THAT. THIS IS THE HOTTEST TOURIST SPOT IN THE WORLD!
"TOURIST SPOT"? DON'T YOU MEAN "VERMIN LAIR"?
OKAY, BUT WE'RE THE SAME KIND OF VERMIN AS ANY OF THEM. BIGGER, IN FACT.
LOOK, YOU, SORRY TO SPOIL YOUR FUN...
...BUT AREN'T YOU FORGET-TING WHY WE'RE HERE?

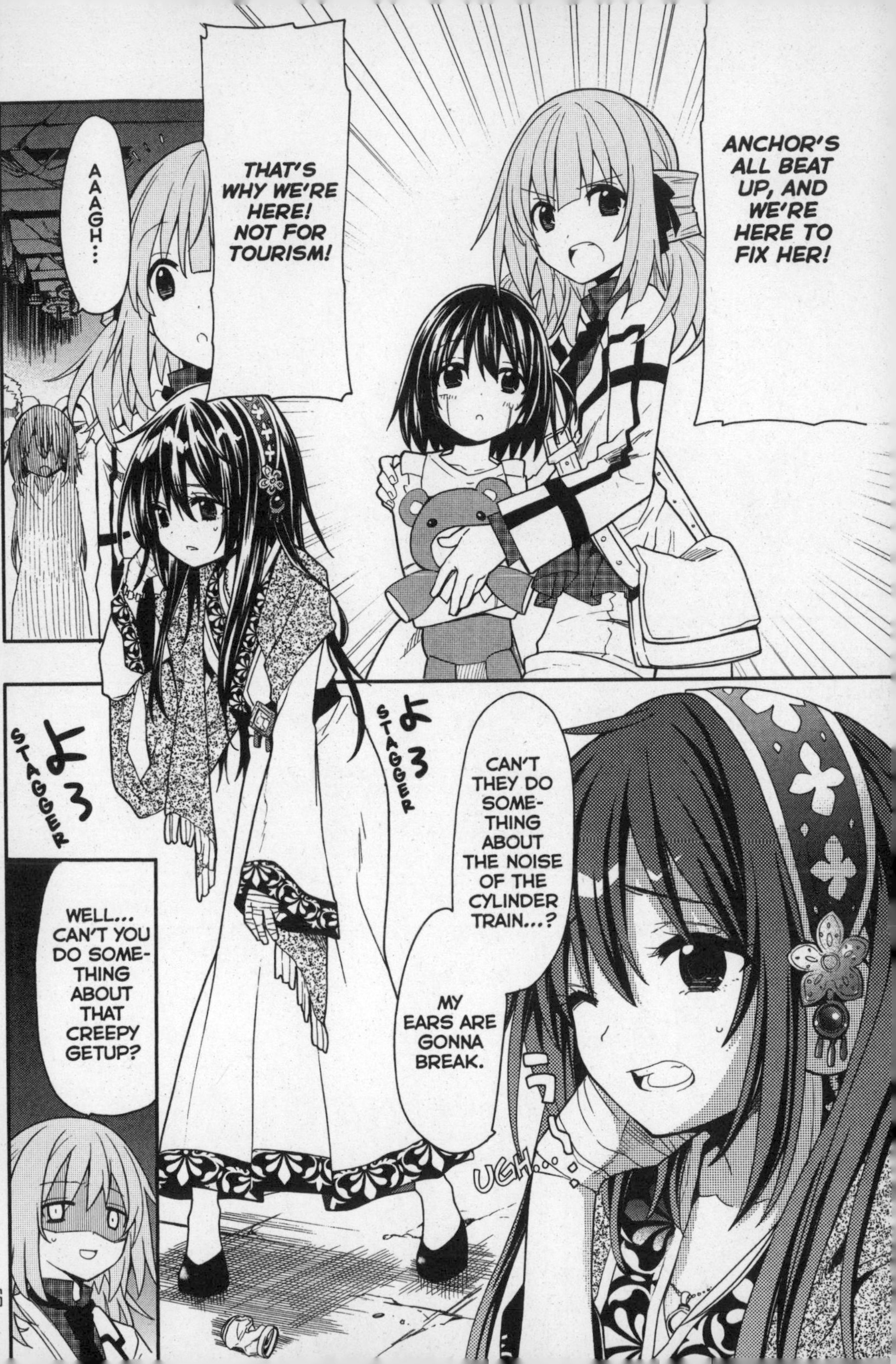
ANCHOR'S ALL BEAT UP, AND WE'RE HERE TO FIX HER!
THAT'S WHY WE'RE HERE! NOT FOR TOURISM!
AAAGH...
よろ STAGGER
よろ STAGGER
CAN'T THEY DO SOME-THING ABOUT THE NOISE OF THE CYLINDER TRAIN...?
MY EARS ARE GONNA BREAK.
UGH...
WELL... CAN'T YOU DO SOME-THING ABOUT THAT CREEPY GETUP?

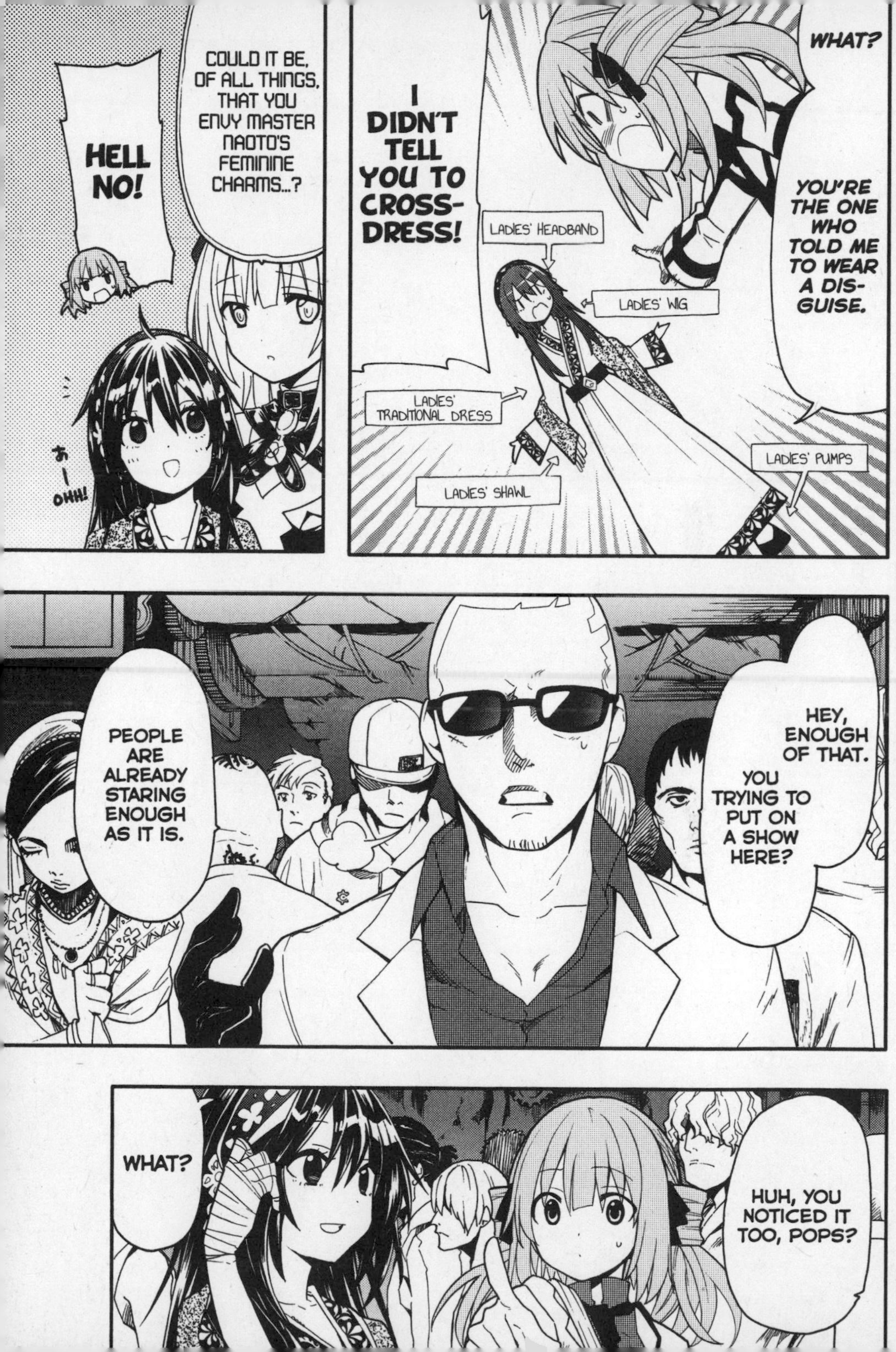
WHAT?
YOU'RE THE ONE WHO TOLD ME TO WEAR A DIS-GUISE.
I DIDN'T TELL YOU TO CROSS-DRESS!
LADIES' HEADBAND
LADIES' WIG
LADIES' TRADITIONAL DRESS
LADIES' SHAWL
LADIES' PUMPS
COULD IT BE, OF ALL THINGS, THAT YOU ENVY MASTER NAOTO'S FEMININE CHARMS...?
HELL NO!
あー OHH!
HEY, ENOUGH OF THAT.
YOU TRYING TO PUT ON A SHOW HERE?
PEOPLE ARE ALREADY STARING ENOUGH AS IT IS.
HUH, YOU NOTICED IT TOO, POPS?
WHAT?

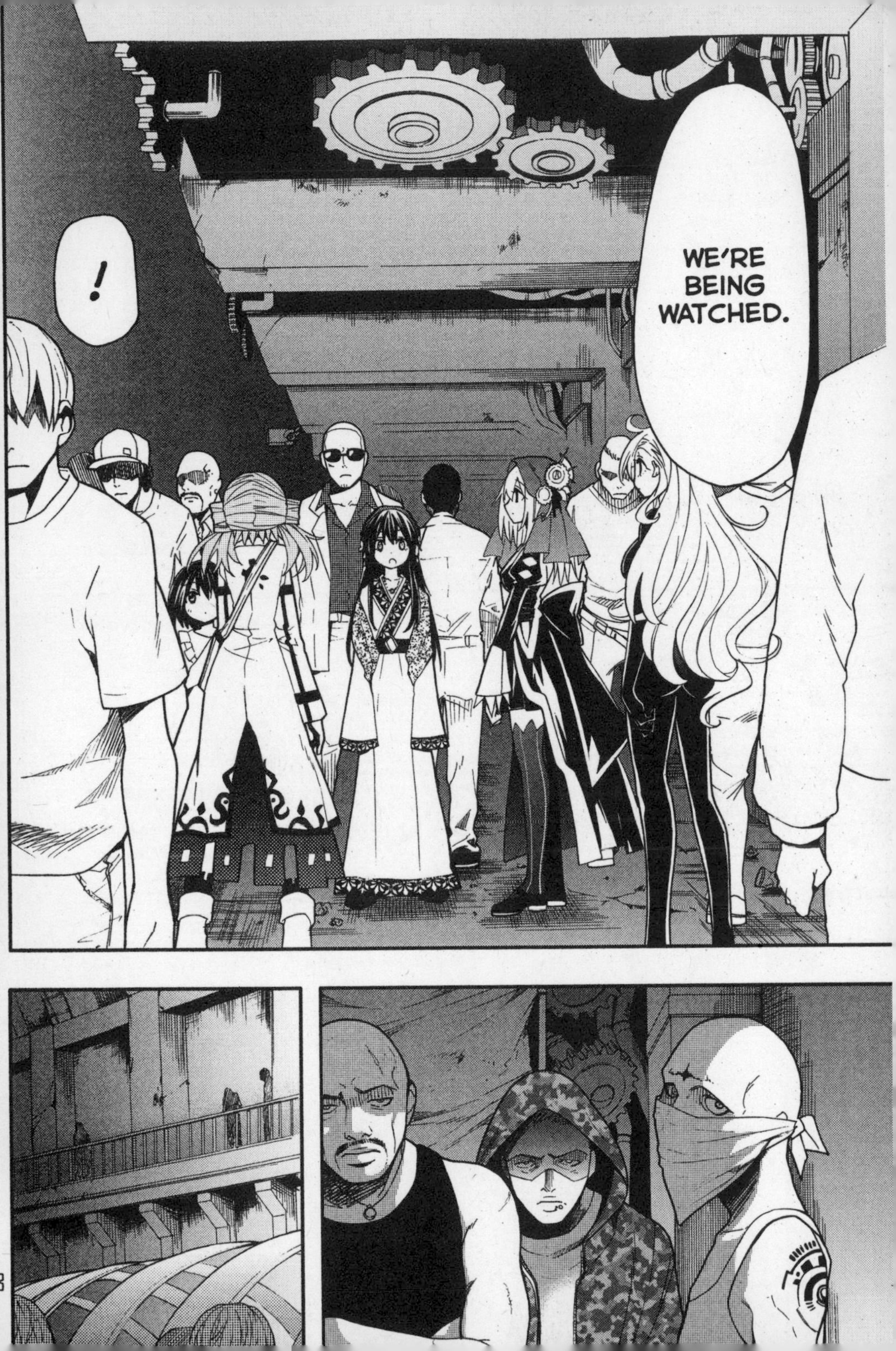
WE'RE BEING WATCHED.
!

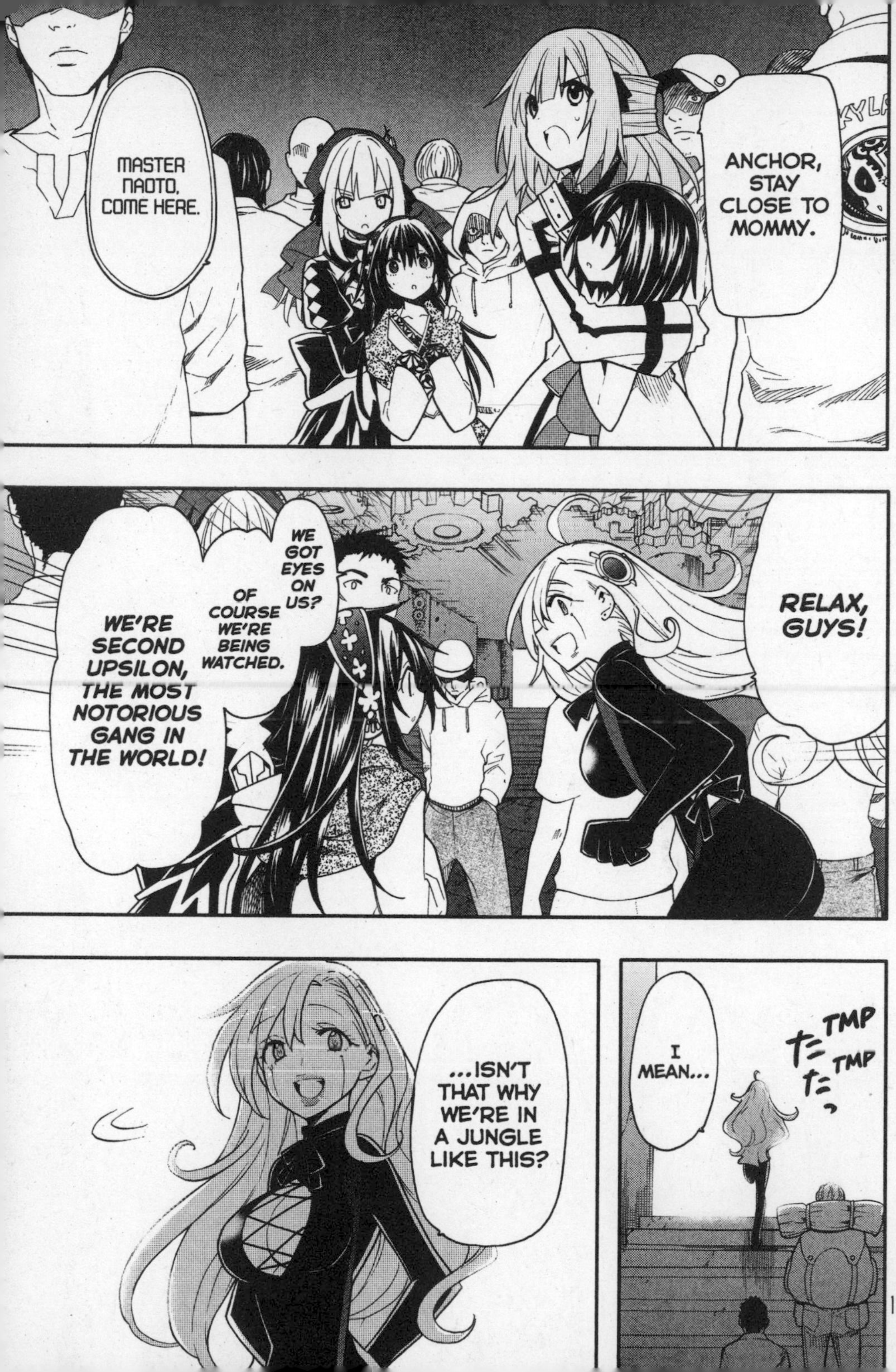
ANCHOR, STAY CLOSE TO MOMMY.
MASTER NAOTO, COME HERE.
RELAX, GUYS!
WE GOT EYES ON US?
OF COURSE WE'RE BEING WATCHED.
WE'RE SECOND UPSILON, THE MOST NOTORIOUS GANG IN THE WORLD!
I MEAN...
TMP TMP
...ISN'T THAT WHY WE'RE IN A JUNGLE LIKE THIS?

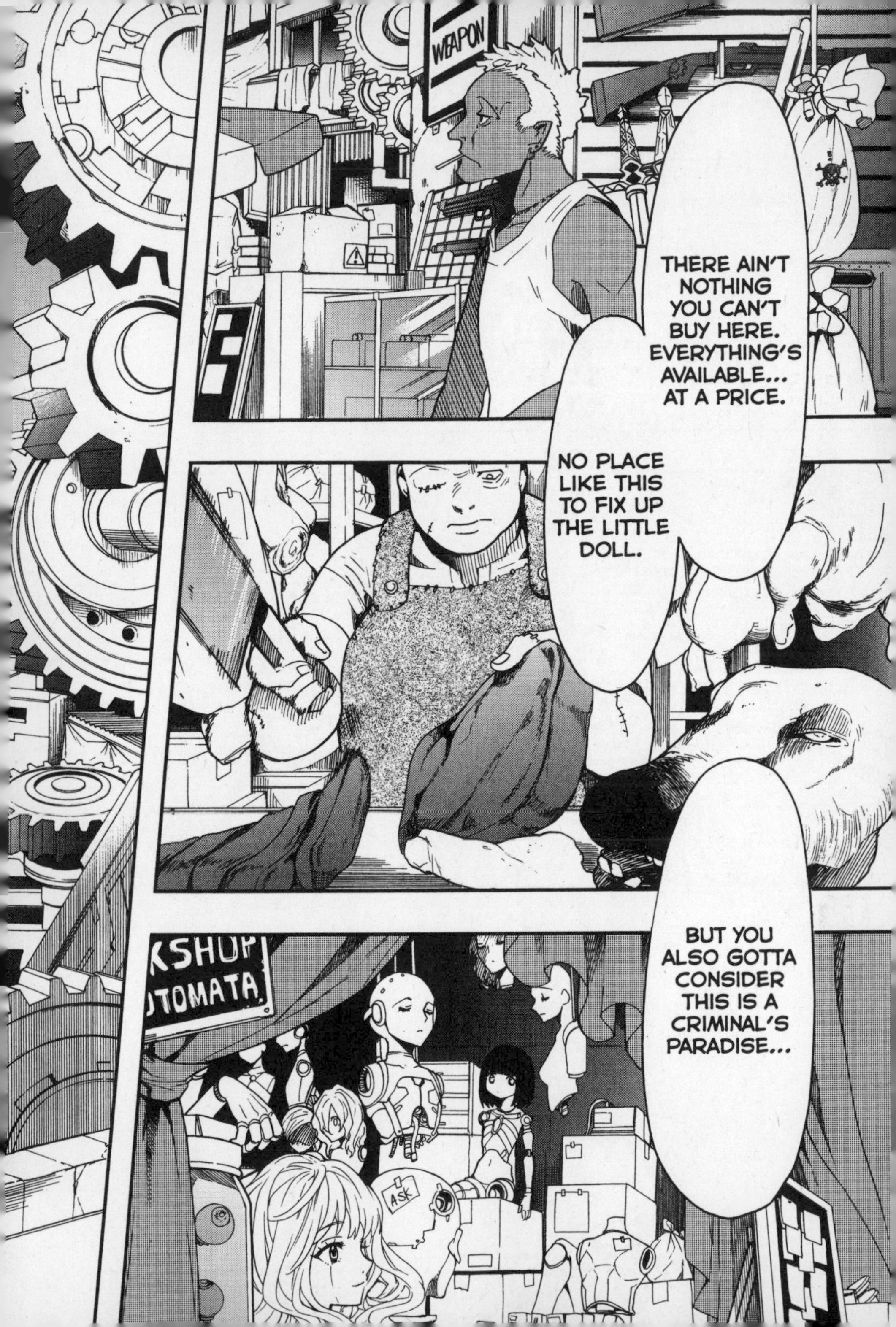
WEAPON
THERE AIN'T NOTHING YOU CAN'T BUY HERE. EVERYTHING'S AVAILABLE... AT A PRICE.
NO PLACE LIKE THIS TO FIX UP THE LITTLE DOLL.
BUT YOU ALSO GOTTA CONSIDER THIS IS A CRIMINAL'S PARADISE...
KSHOP
UTOMATA
ASK

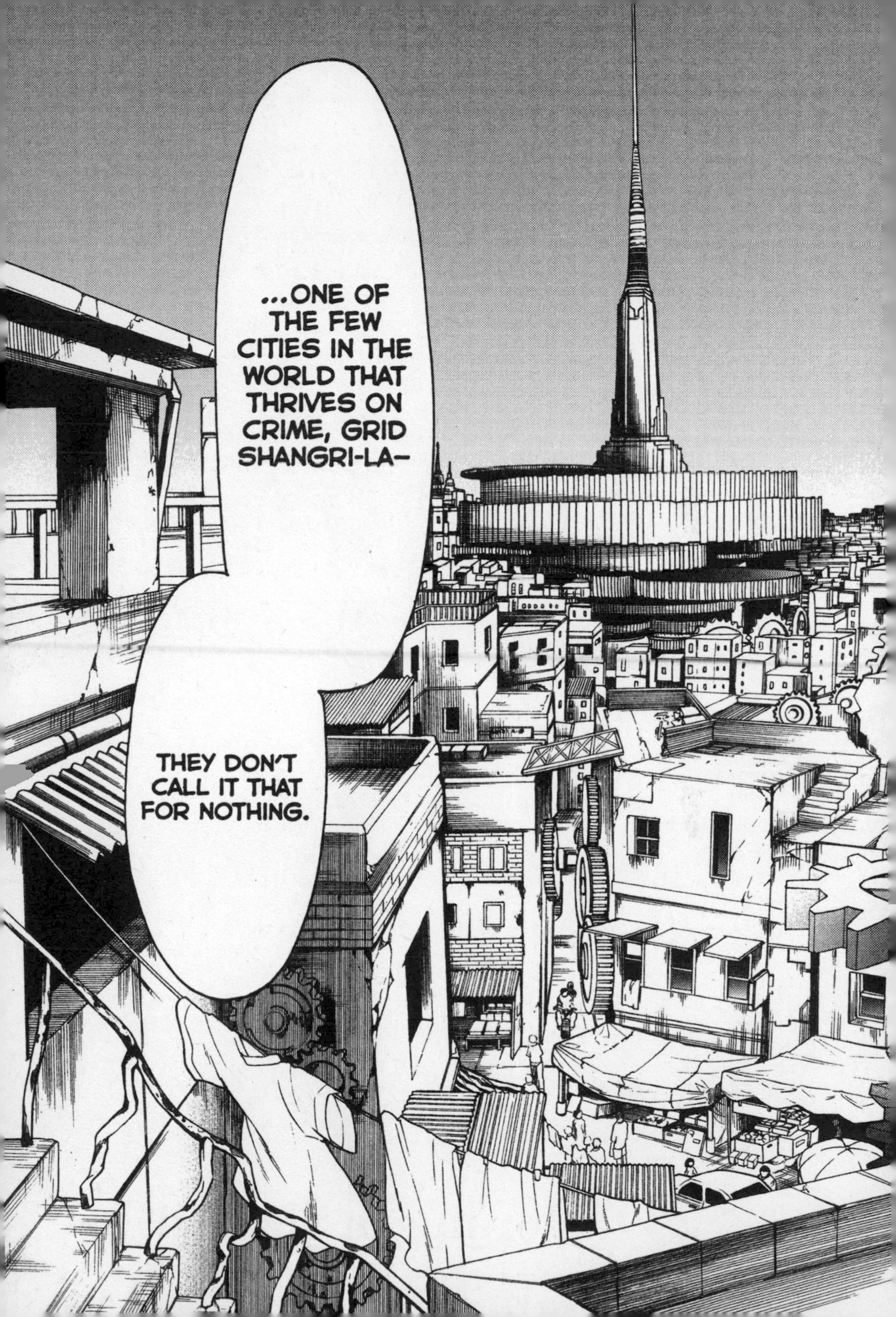
...ONE OF THE FEW CITIES IN THE WORLD THAT THRIVES ON CRIME, GRID SHANGRI-LA-
THEY DON'T CALL IT THAT FOR NOTHING.

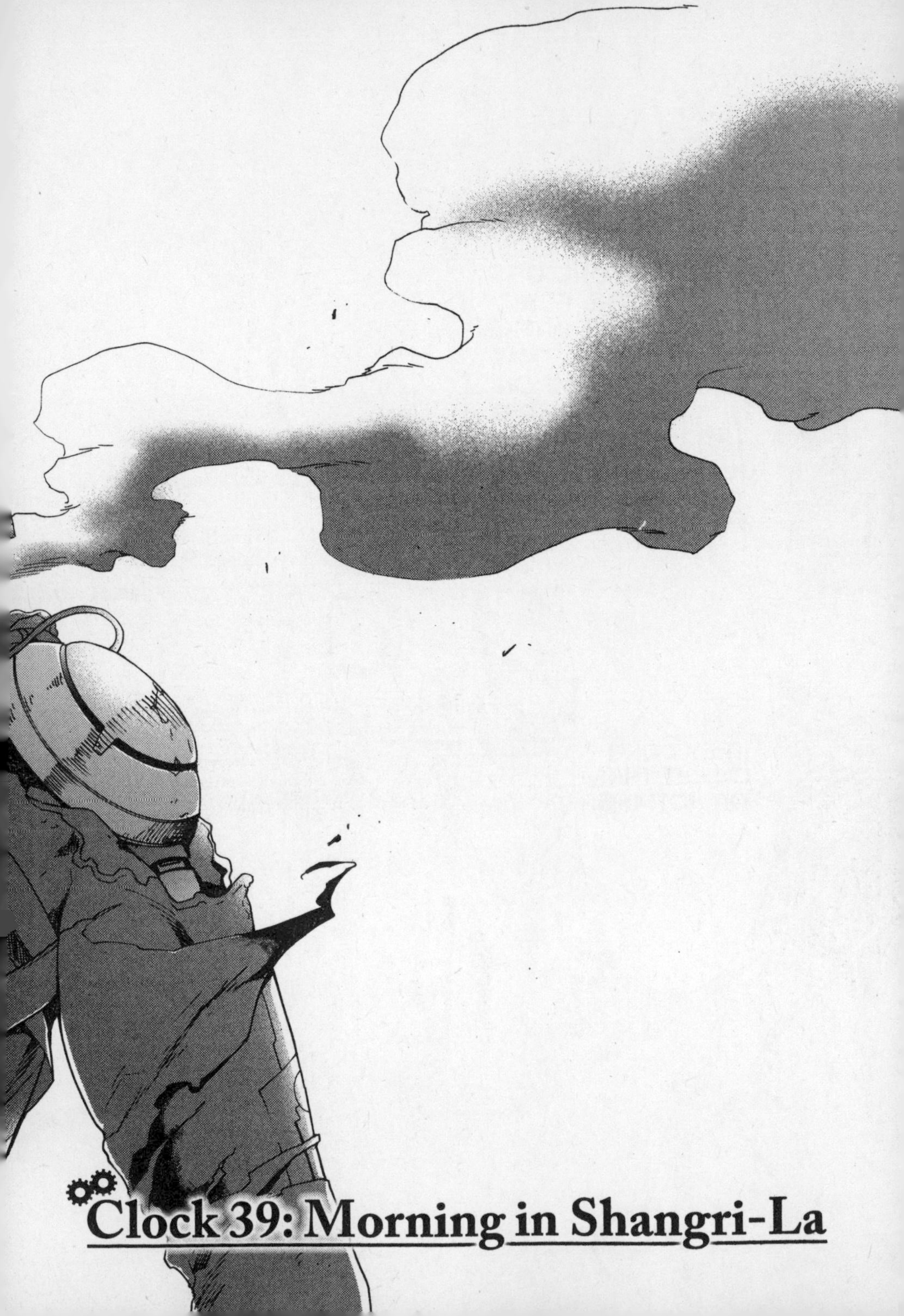

Clock 39: Morning in Shangri-La

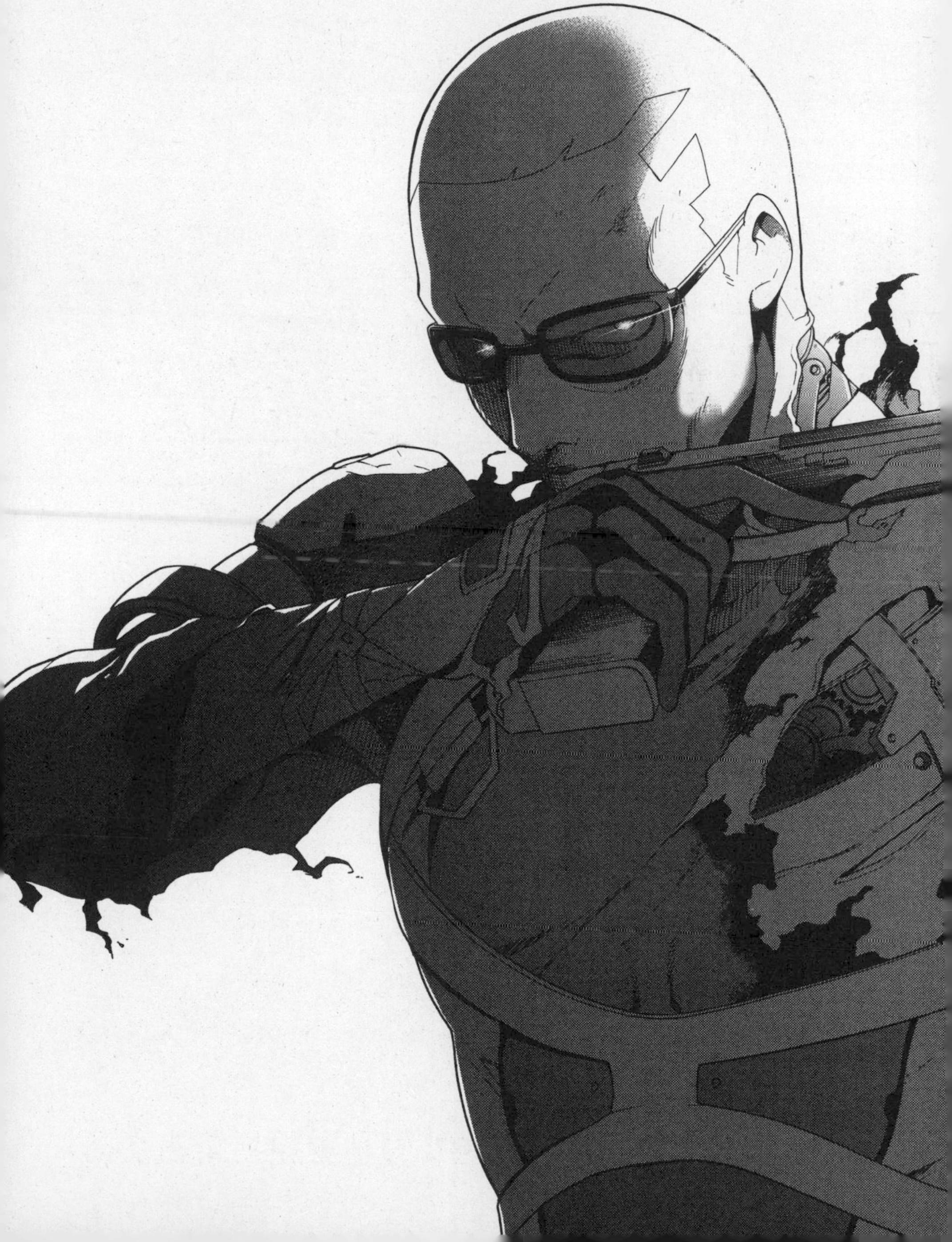

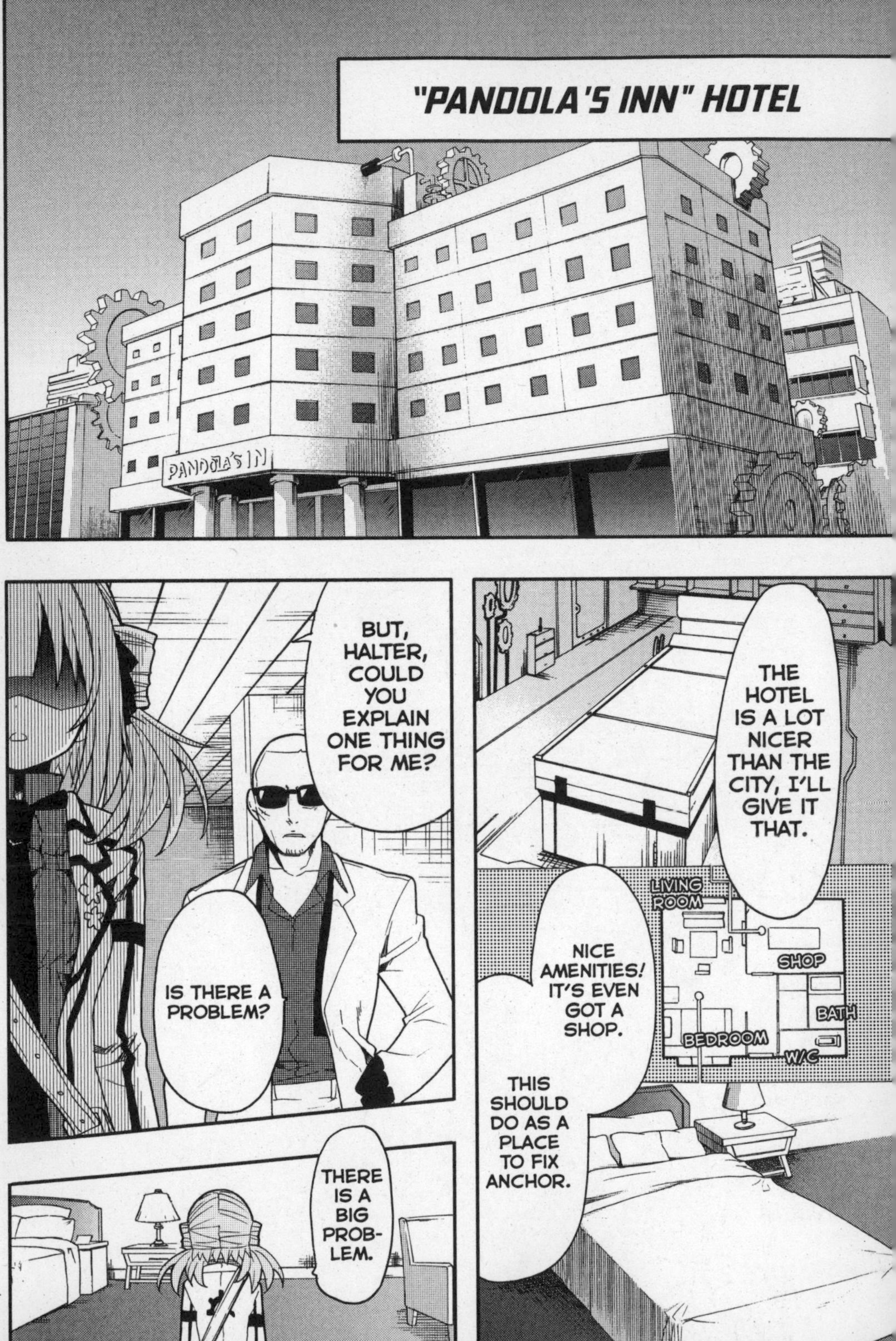
"PANDOLA'S INN" HOTEL
PANDOLA'S INN
THE HOTEL IS A LOT NICER THAN THE CITY, I'LL GIVE IT THAT.
NICE AMENITIES! IT'S EVEN GOT A SHOP.
LIVING ROOM
SHOP
BATH
BEDROOM
W/C
THIS SHOULD DO AS A PLACE TO FIX ANCHOR.
BUT, HALTER, COULD YOU EXPLAIN ONE THING FOR ME?
IS THERE A PROBLEM?
THERE IS A BIG PROB-LEM.

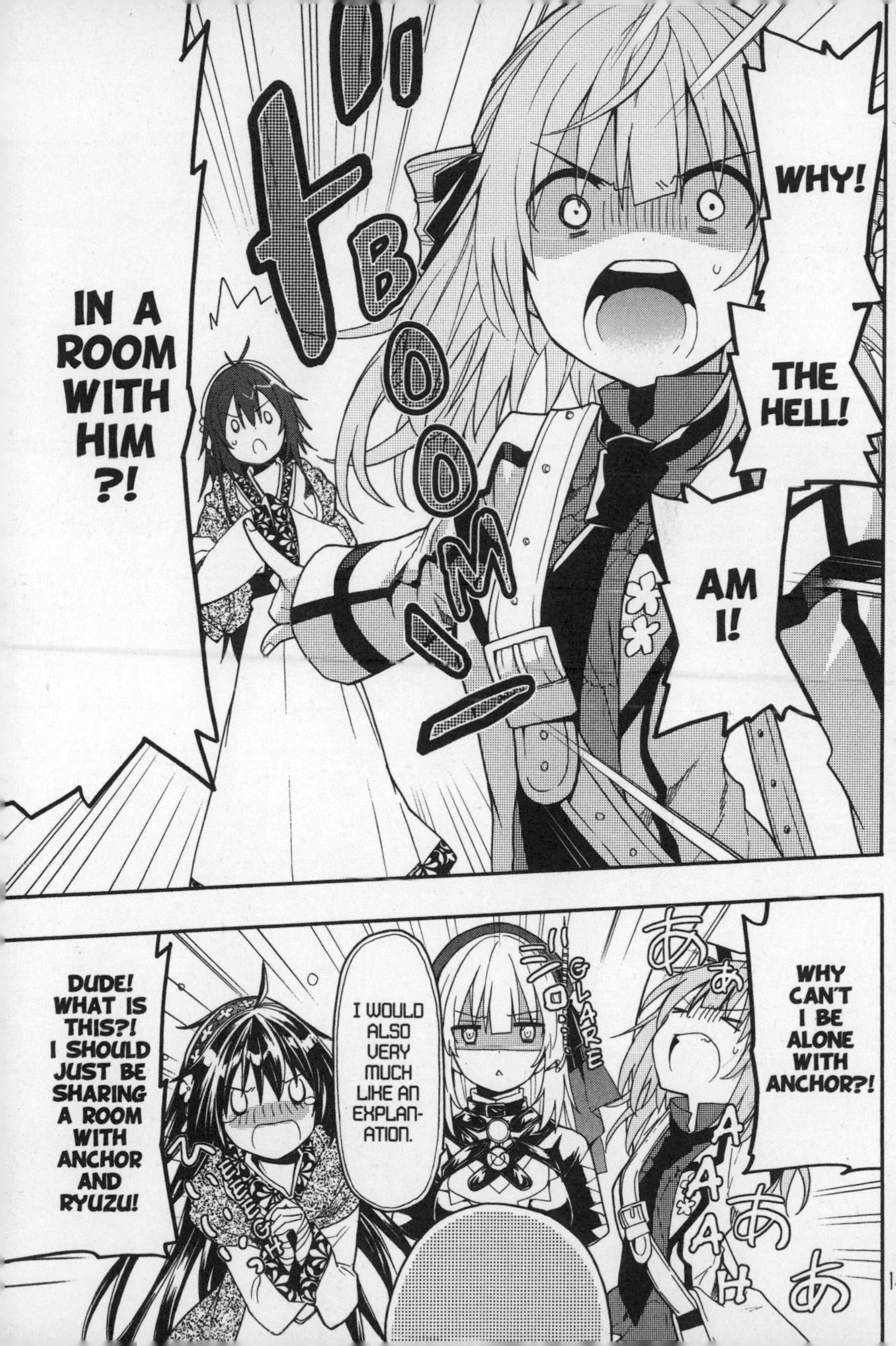
WHY! THE HELL! AM I!
BOOM
IN A ROOM WITH HIM ?!
WHY CAN'T I BE ALONE WITH ANCHOR?!
あああ
AAAH
GLARE
I WOULD ALSO VERY MUCH LIKE AN EXPLANATION.
DUDE! WHAT IS THIS?! I SHOULD JUST BE SHARING A ROOM WITH ANCHOR AND RYUZU!

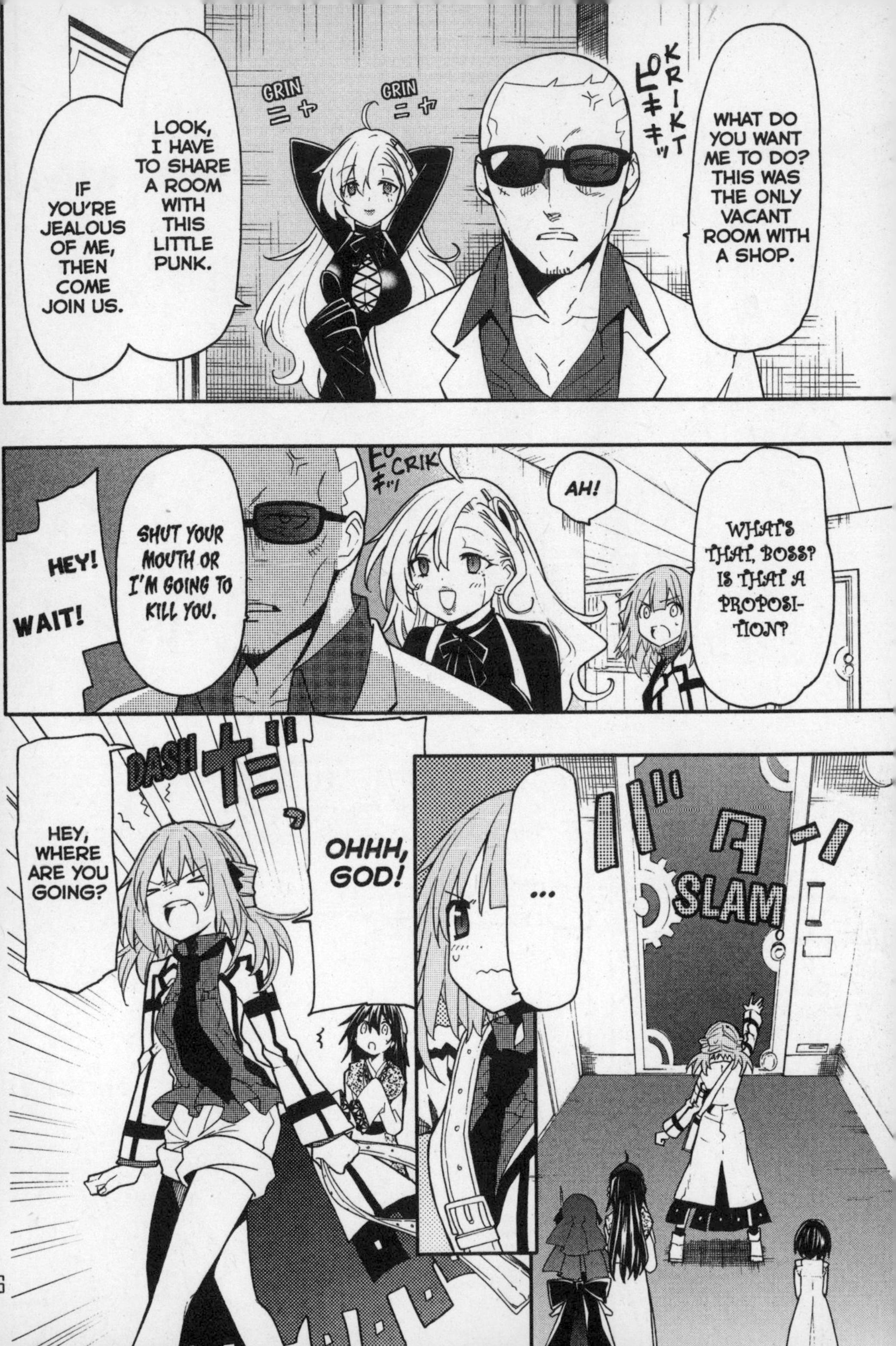
KRIKT
WHAT DO YOU WANT ME TO DO? THIS WAS THE ONLY VACANT ROOM WITH A SHOP.
GRIN
GRIN
LOOK, I HAVE TO SHARE A ROOM WITH THIS LITTLE PUNK.
IF YOU'RE JEALOUS OF ME, THEN COME JOIN US.
WHAT'S THAT, BOSS? IS THAT A PROPOSITION?
AH!
CRIK
SHUT YOUR MOUTH OR I'M GOING TO KILL YOU.
HEY!
WAIT!
SLAM
...
OHHH, GOD!
DASH
HEY, WHERE ARE YOU GOING?

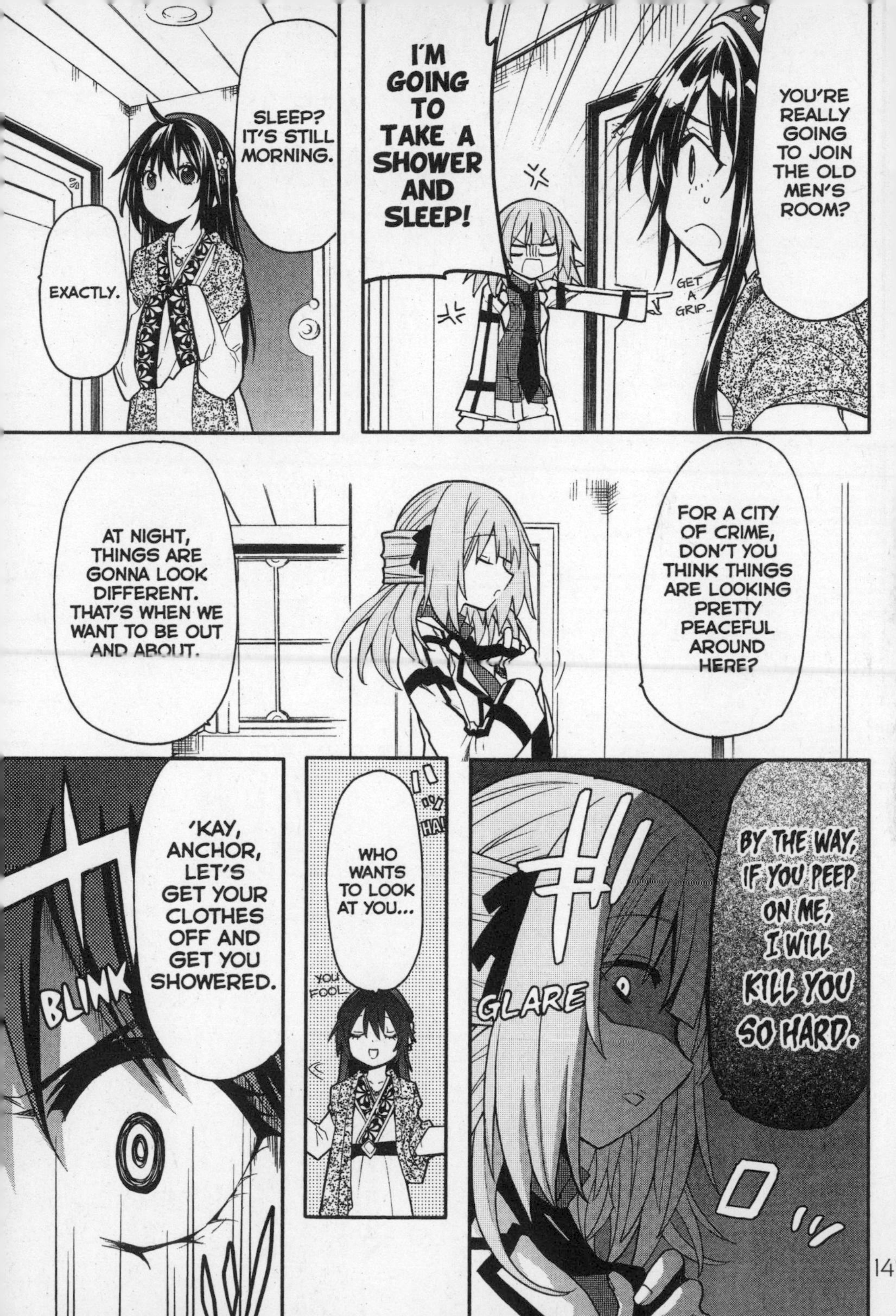
YOU'RE REALLY GOING TO JOIN THE OLD MEN'S ROOM?
I'M GOING TO TAKE A SHOWER AND SLEEP!
GET A GRIP...
SLEEP? IT'S STILL MORNING.
EXACTLY.
FOR A CITY OF CRIME, DON'T YOU THINK THINGS ARE LOOKING PRETTY PEACEFUL AROUND HERE?
AT NIGHT, THINGS ARE GONNA LOOK DIFFERENT. THAT'S WHEN WE WANT TO BE OUT AND ABOUT.
BY THE WAY, IF YOU PEEP ON ME, I WILL KILL YOU SO HARD.
GLARE
HA!
WHO WANTS TO LOOK AT YOU...
YOU FOOL
'KAY, ANCHOR, LET'S GET YOUR CLOTHES OFF AND GET YOU SHOWERED.
BLINK

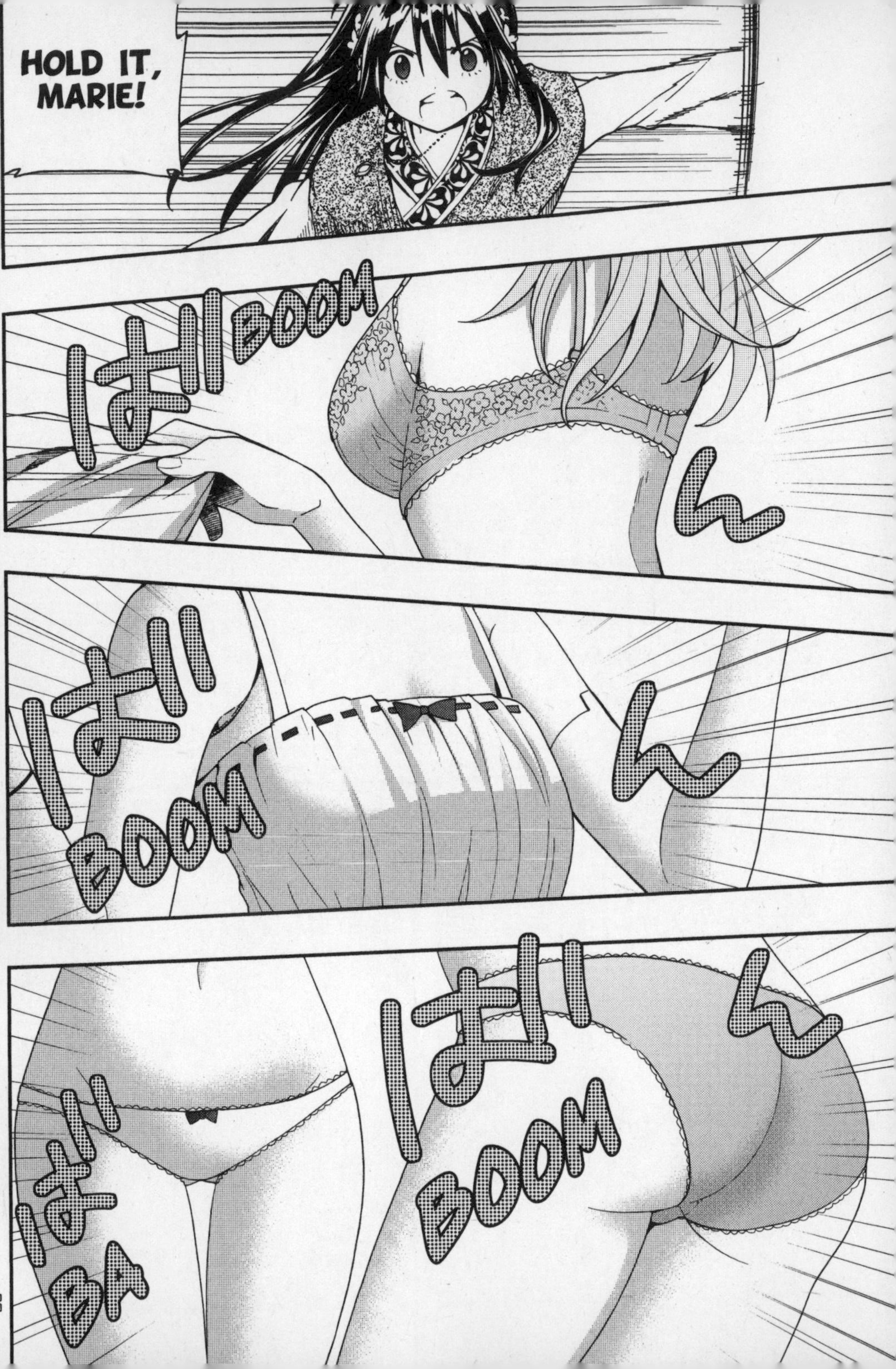
HOLD IT, MARIE!
BOOM
BOOM
BOOM
BA

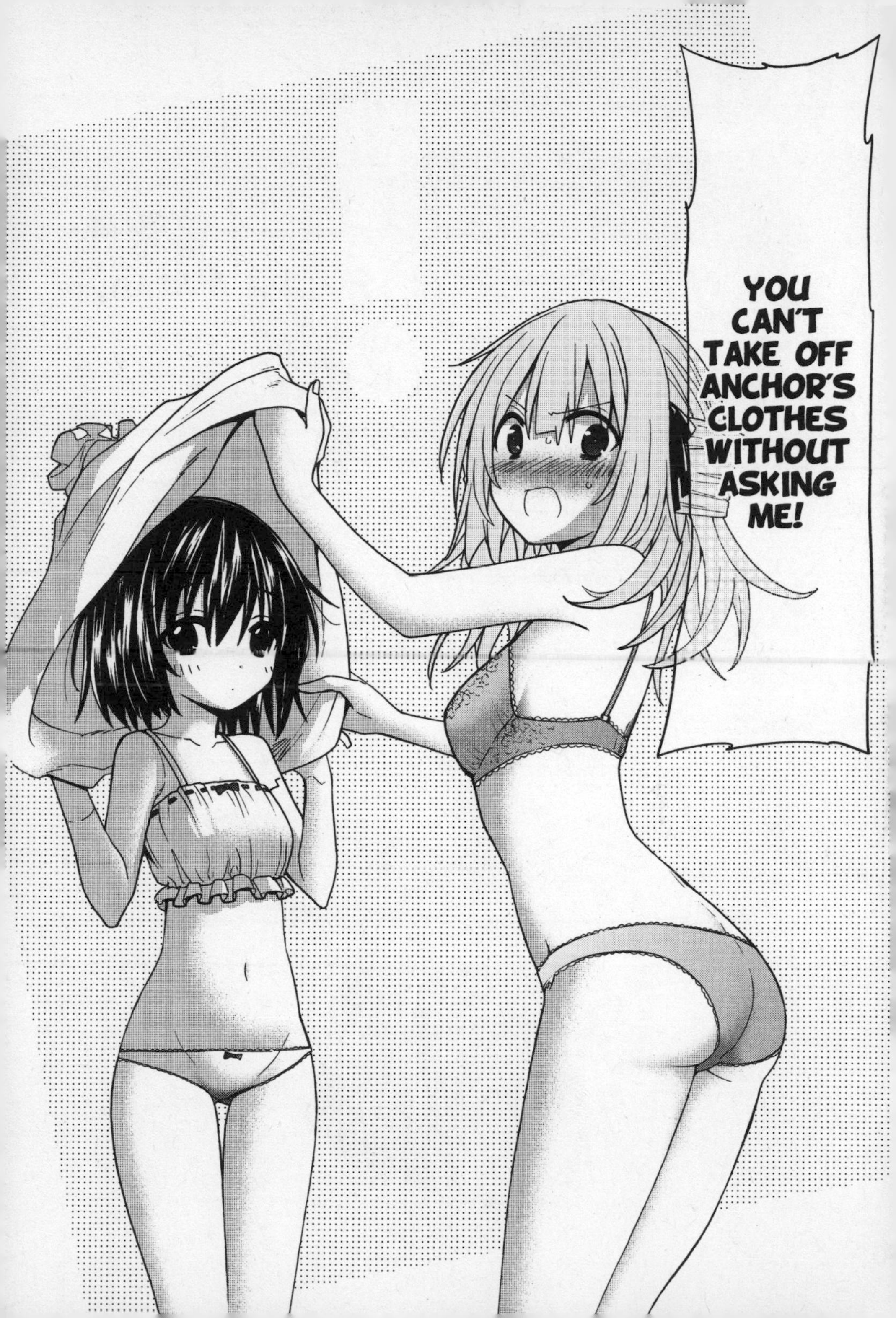
YOU CAN'T TAKE OFF ANCHOR'S CLOTHES WITHOUT ASKING ME!

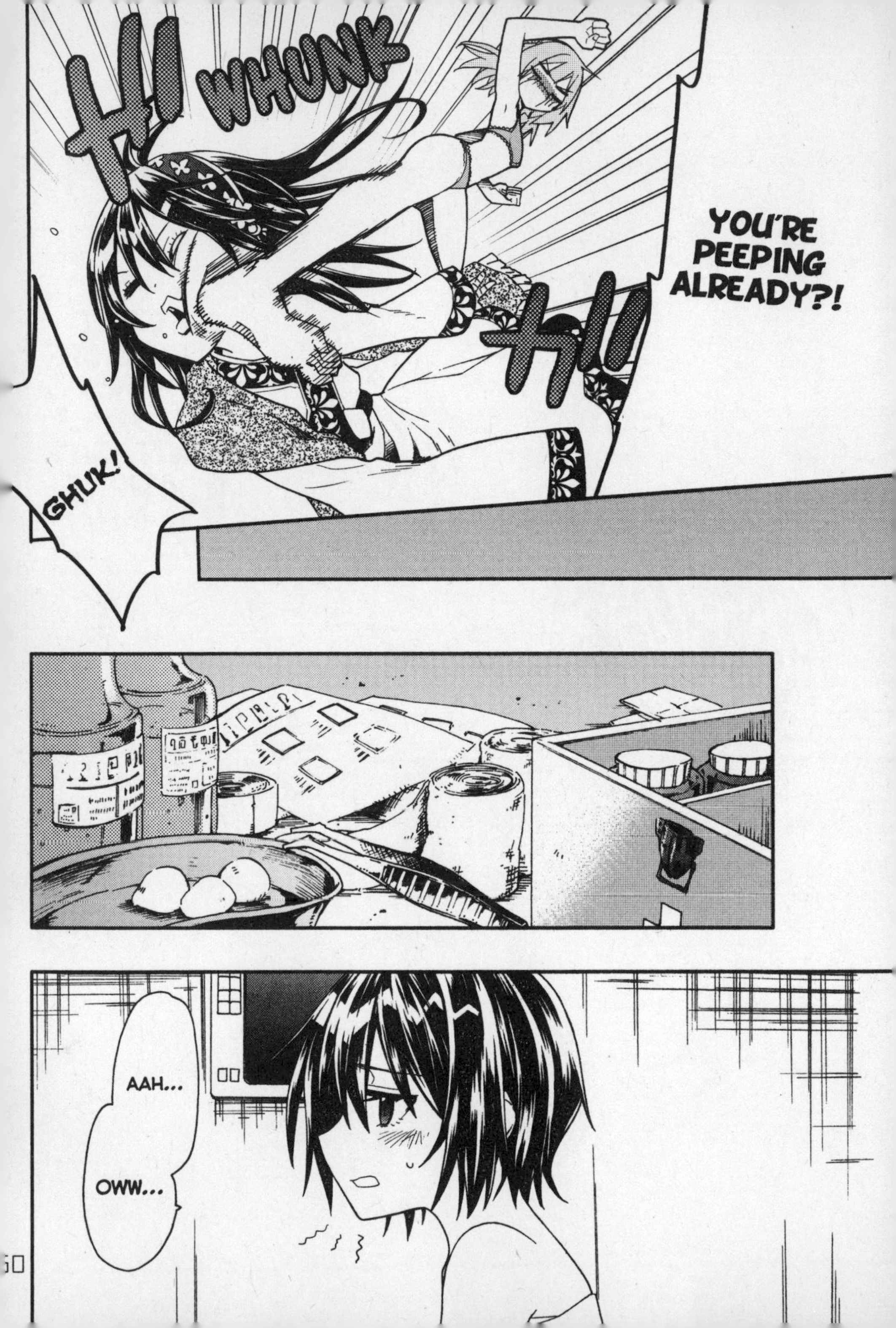
YOU'RE PEEPING ALREADY?!
WHUNK
H!
H!!
GHUK!
AAH...
OWW...

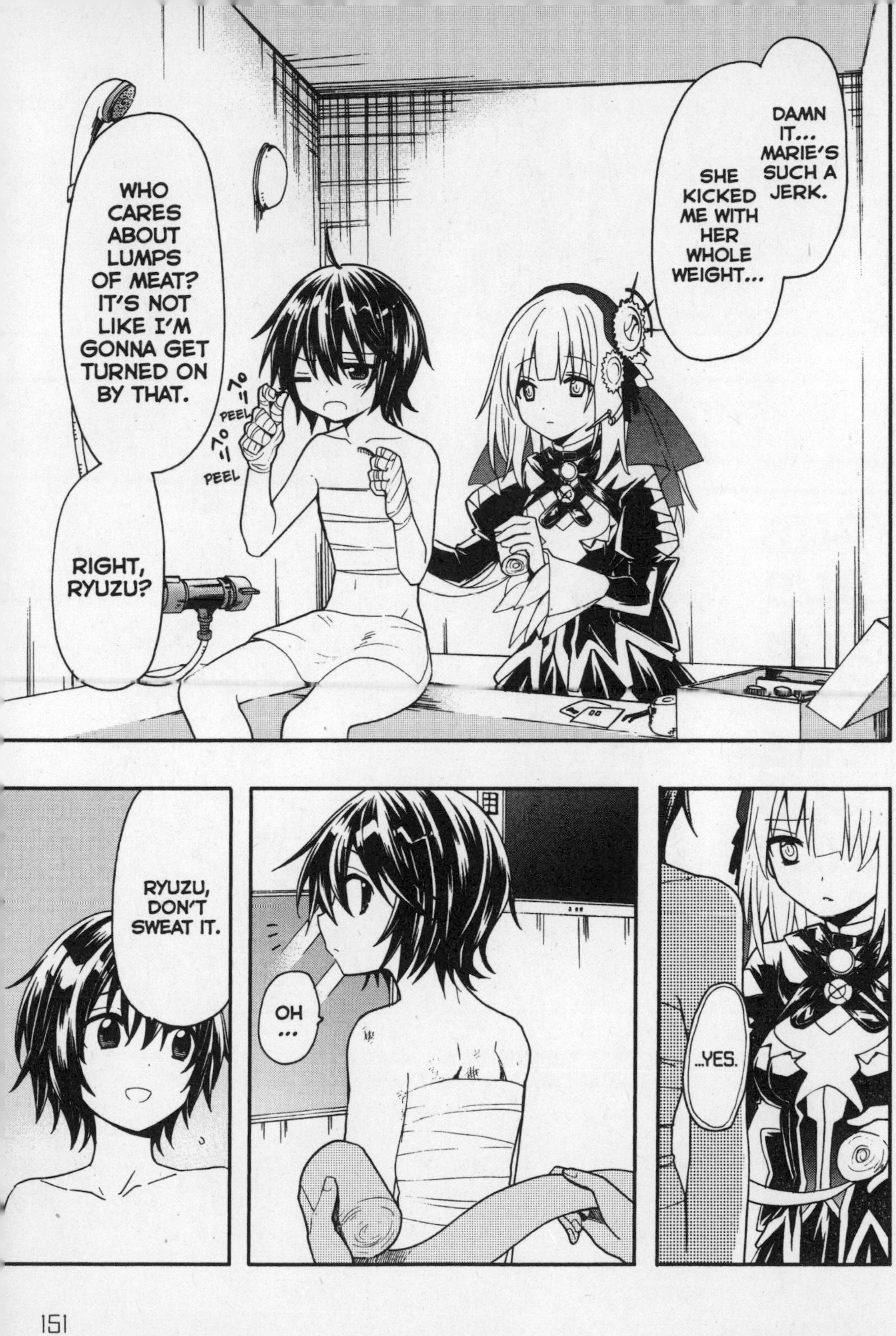
DAMN IT... MARIE'S SUCH A JERK.
SHE KICKED ME WITH HER WHOLE WEIGHT...
WHO CARES ABOUT LUMPS OF MEAT? IT'S NOT LIKE I'M GONNA GET TURNED ON BY THAT.
PEEL
PEEL
RIGHT, RYUZU?
...YES.
OH ...
RYUZU, DON'T SWEAT IT.

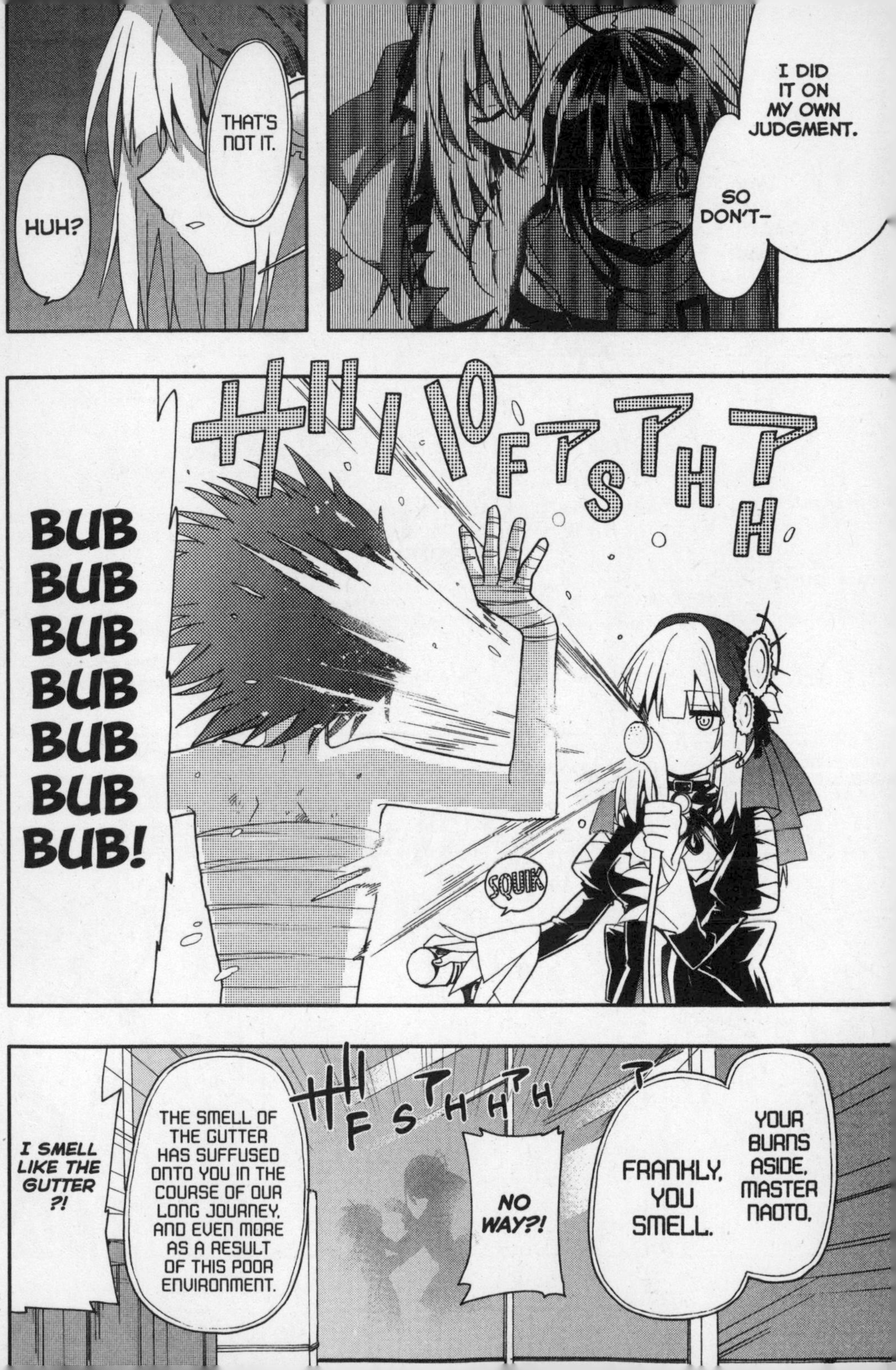
I DID IT ON MY OWN JUDGMENT.
SO DON'T–
THAT'S NOT IT.
HUH?
FSHH
BUB BUB BUB BUB BUB BUB BUB!
SQUIK
YOUR BURNS ASIDE, MASTER NAOTO,
FRANKLY, YOU SMELL.
FSHHH
NO WAY?!
THE SMELL OF THE GUTTER HAS SUFFUSED ONTO YOU IN THE COURSE OF OUR LONG JOURNEY, AND EVEN MORE AS A RESULT OF THIS POOR ENVIRONMENT.
I SMELL LIKE THE GUTTER?!

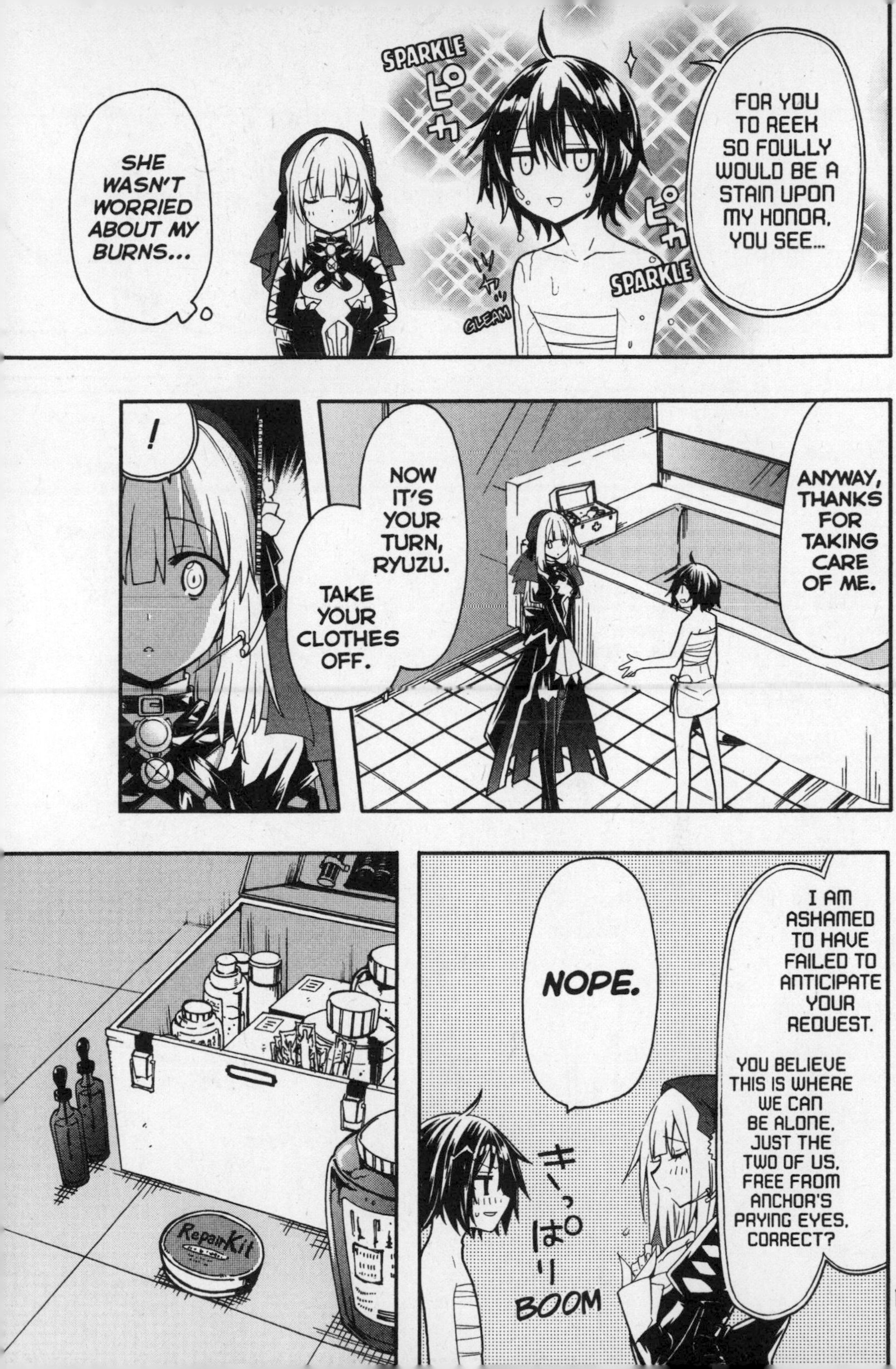
FOR YOU TO REEK SO FOULLY WOULD BE A STAIN UPON MY HONOR, YOU SEE...
SPARKLE
SPARKLE
GLEAM
SHE WASN'T WORRIED ABOUT MY BURNS...
ANYWAY, THANKS FOR TAKING CARE OF ME.
NOW IT'S YOUR TURN, RYUZU.
TAKE YOUR CLOTHES OFF.
!
I AM ASHAMED TO HAVE FAILED TO ANTICIPATE YOUR REQUEST.
YOU BELIEVE THIS IS WHERE WE CAN BE ALONE, JUST THE TWO OF US, FREE FROM ANCHOR'S PRYING EYES, CORRECT?
NOPE.
BOOM

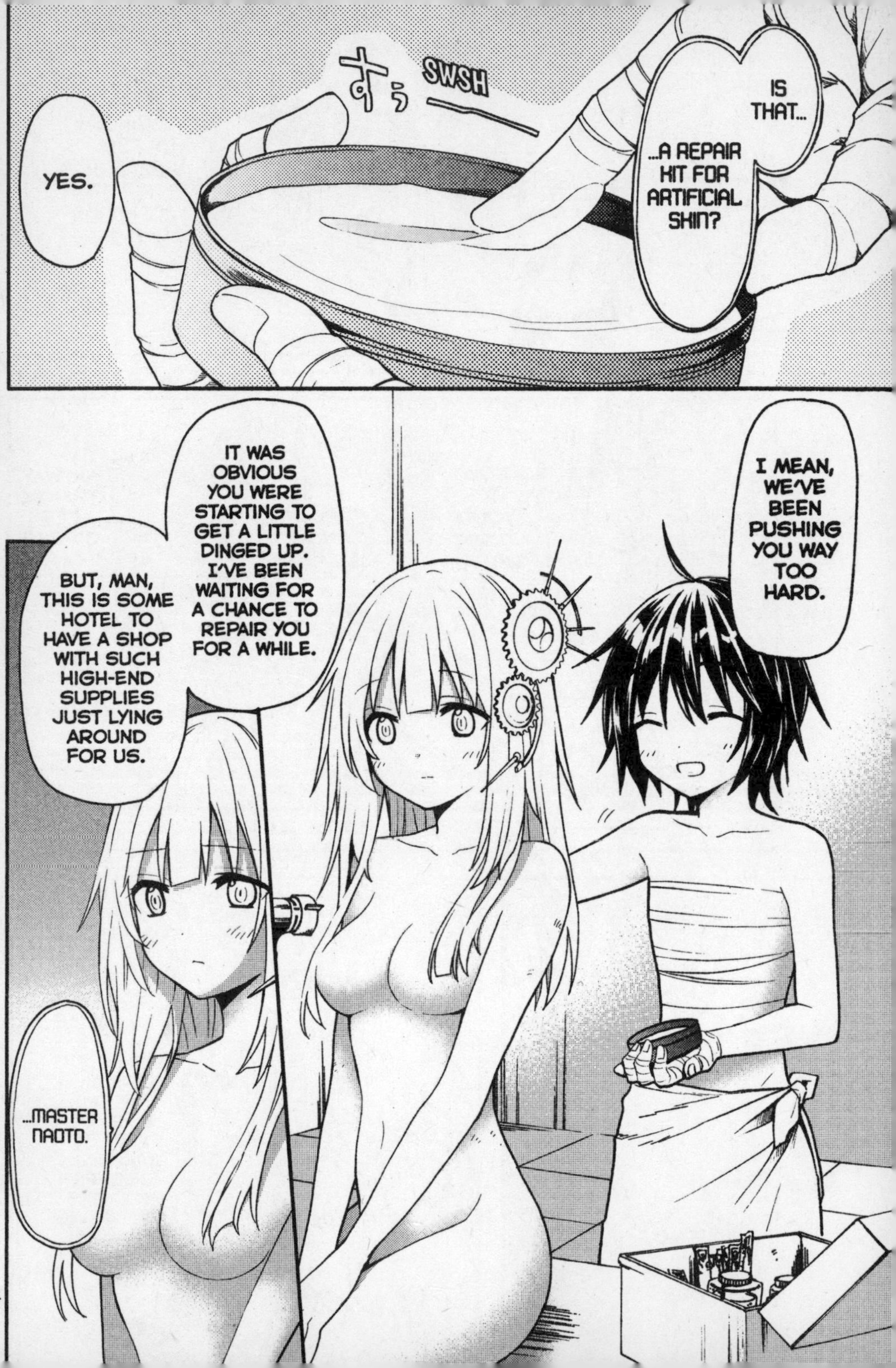
IS THAT...
...A REPAIR KIT FOR ARTIFICIAL SKIN?
すぅー
SWSH
YES.
I MEAN, WE'VE BEEN PUSHING YOU WAY TOO HARD.
IT WAS OBVIOUS YOU WERE STARTING TO GET A LITTLE DINGED UP. I'VE BEEN WAITING FOR A CHANCE TO REPAIR YOU FOR A WHILE.
BUT, MAN, THIS IS SOME HOTEL TO HAVE A SHOP WITH SUCH HIGH-END SUPPLIES JUST LYING AROUND FOR US.
...MASTER NAOTO.

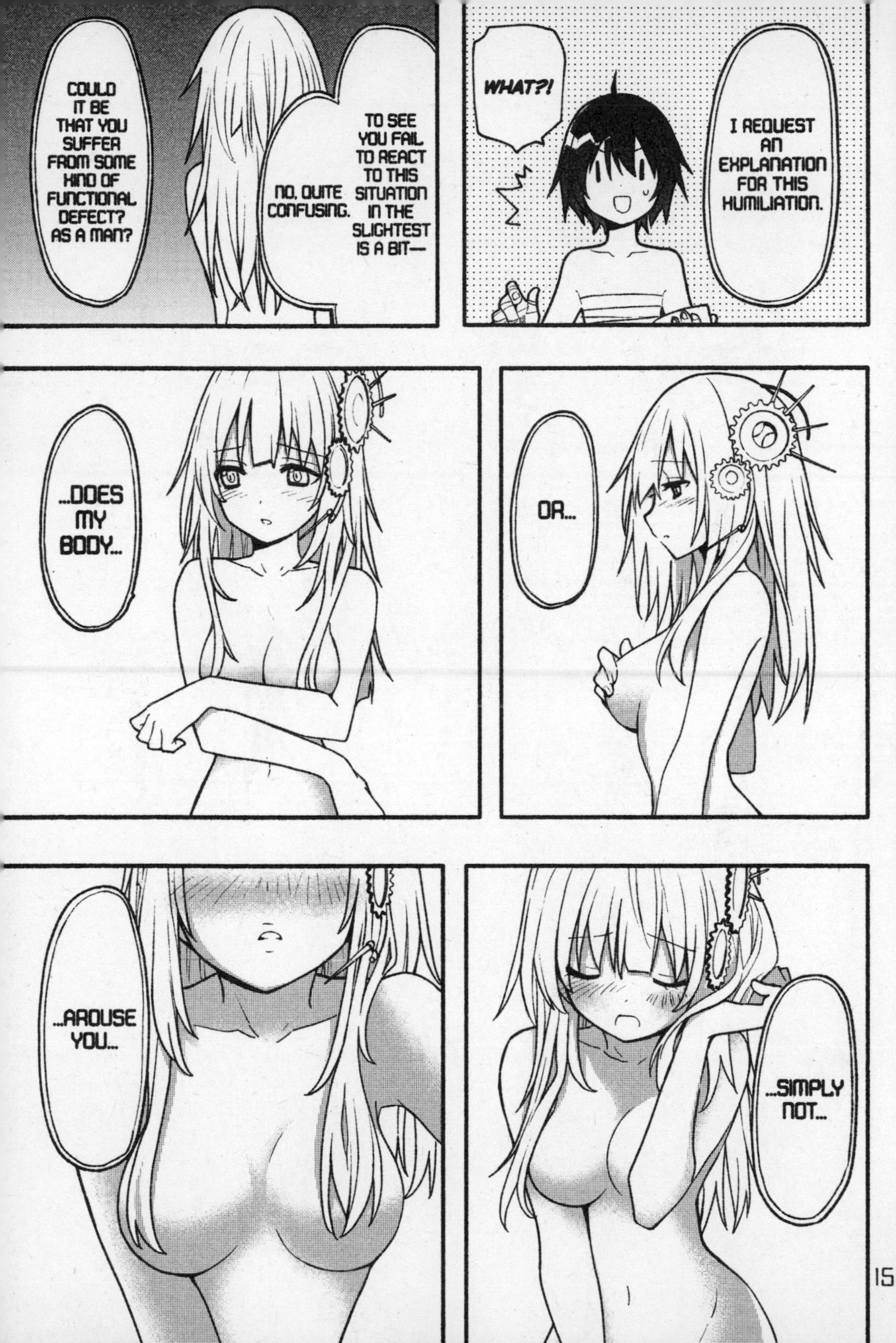
I REQUEST AN EXPLANATION FOR THIS HUMILIATION.
WHAT?!
TO SEE YOU FAIL TO REACT TO THIS SITUATION IN THE SLIGHTEST IS A BIT—
NO, QUITE CONFUSING.
COULD IT BE THAT YOU SUFFER FROM SOME KIND OF FUNCTIONAL DEFECT? AS A MAN?
OR...
...DOES MY BODY...
...SIMPLY NOT...
...AROUSE YOU...

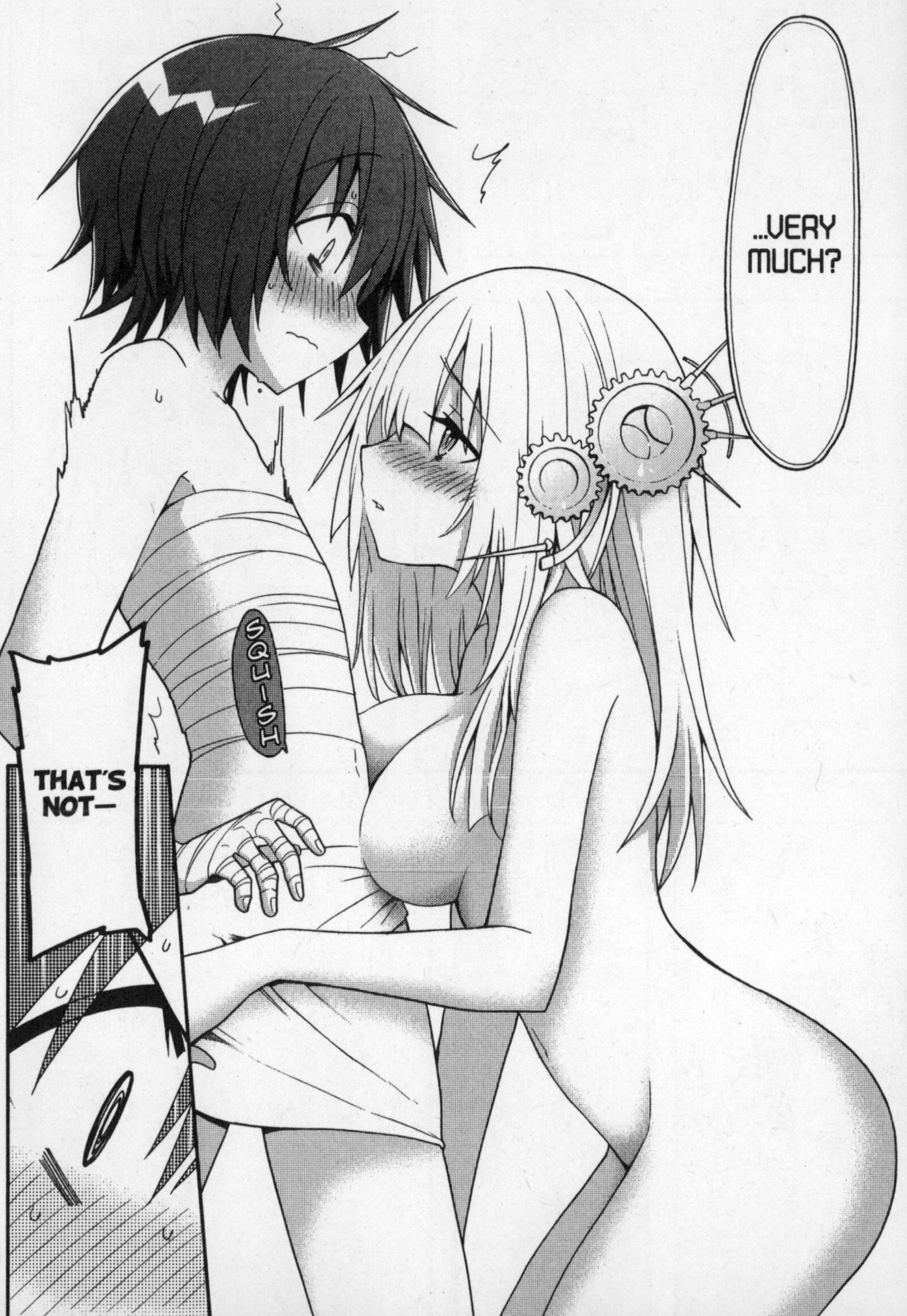
...VERY MUCH?
SQUISH
THAT'S NOT—

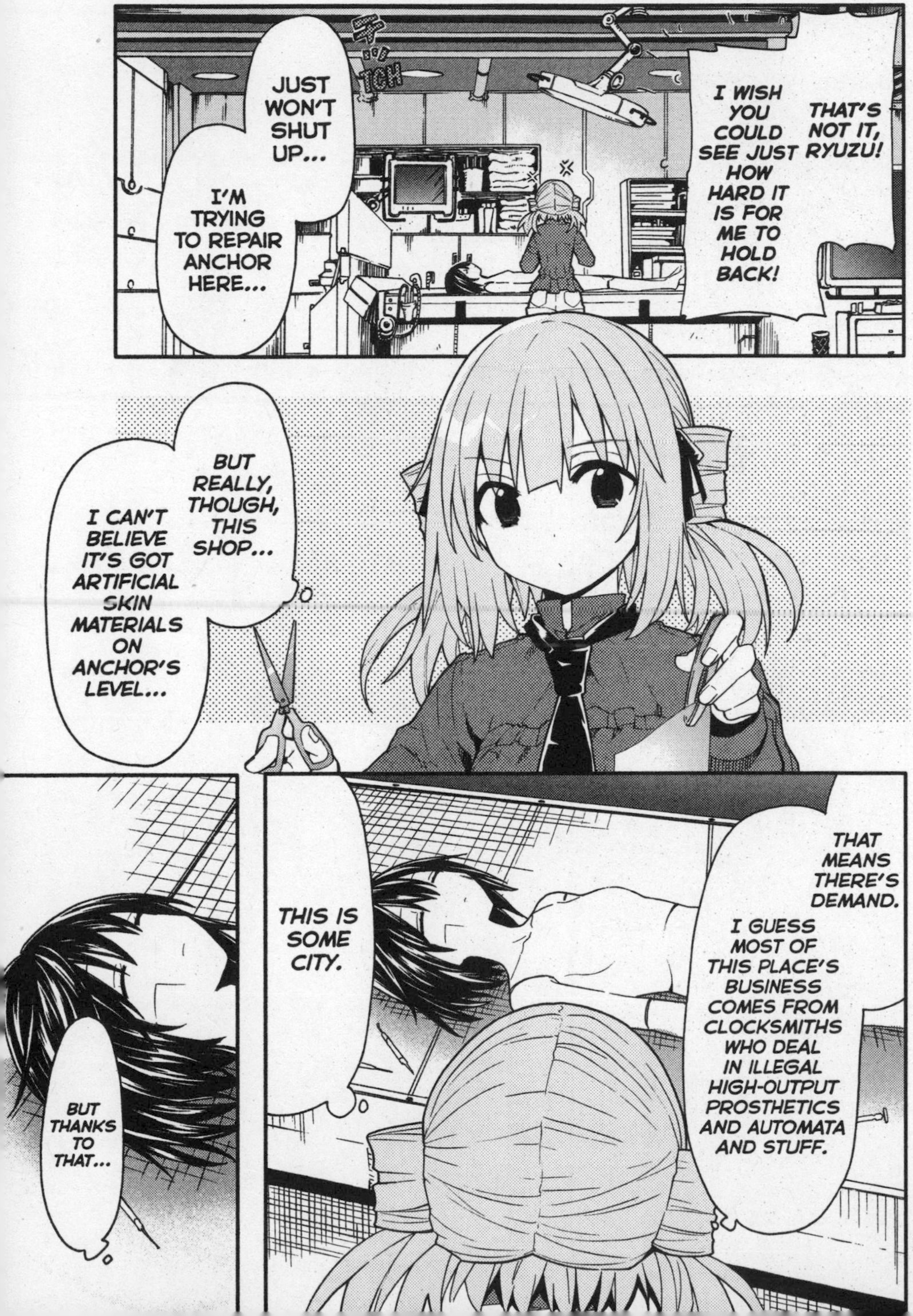
THAT'S NOT IT, RYUZU!
I WISH YOU COULD SEE JUST HOW HARD IT IS FOR ME TO HOLD BACK!
TCH
JUST WON'T SHUT UP...
I'M TRYING TO REPAIR ANCHOR HERE...
BUT REALLY, THOUGH, THIS SHOP...
I CAN'T BELIEVE IT'S GOT ARTIFICIAL SKIN MATERIALS ON ANCHOR'S LEVEL...
THAT MEANS THERE'S DEMAND.
I GUESS MOST OF THIS PLACE'S BUSINESS COMES FROM CLOCKSMITHS WHO DEAL IN ILLEGAL HIGH-OUTPUT PROSTHETICS AND AUTOMATA AND STUFF.
THIS IS SOME CITY.
BUT THANKS TO THAT...

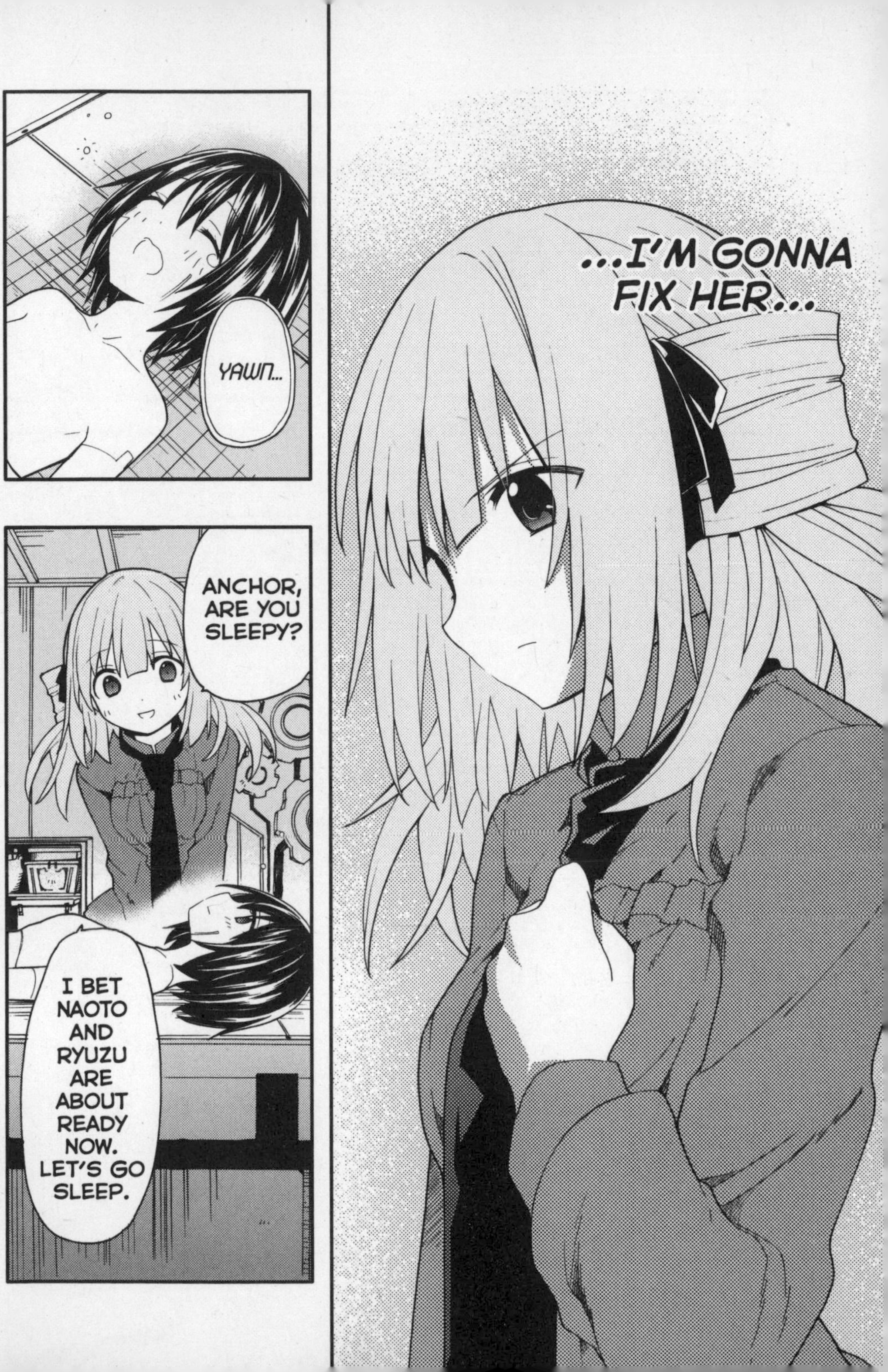
...I'M GONNA FIX HER...
YAWN...
ANCHOR, ARE YOU SLEEPY?
I BET NAOTO AND RYUZU ARE ABOUT READY NOW. LET'S GO SLEEP.

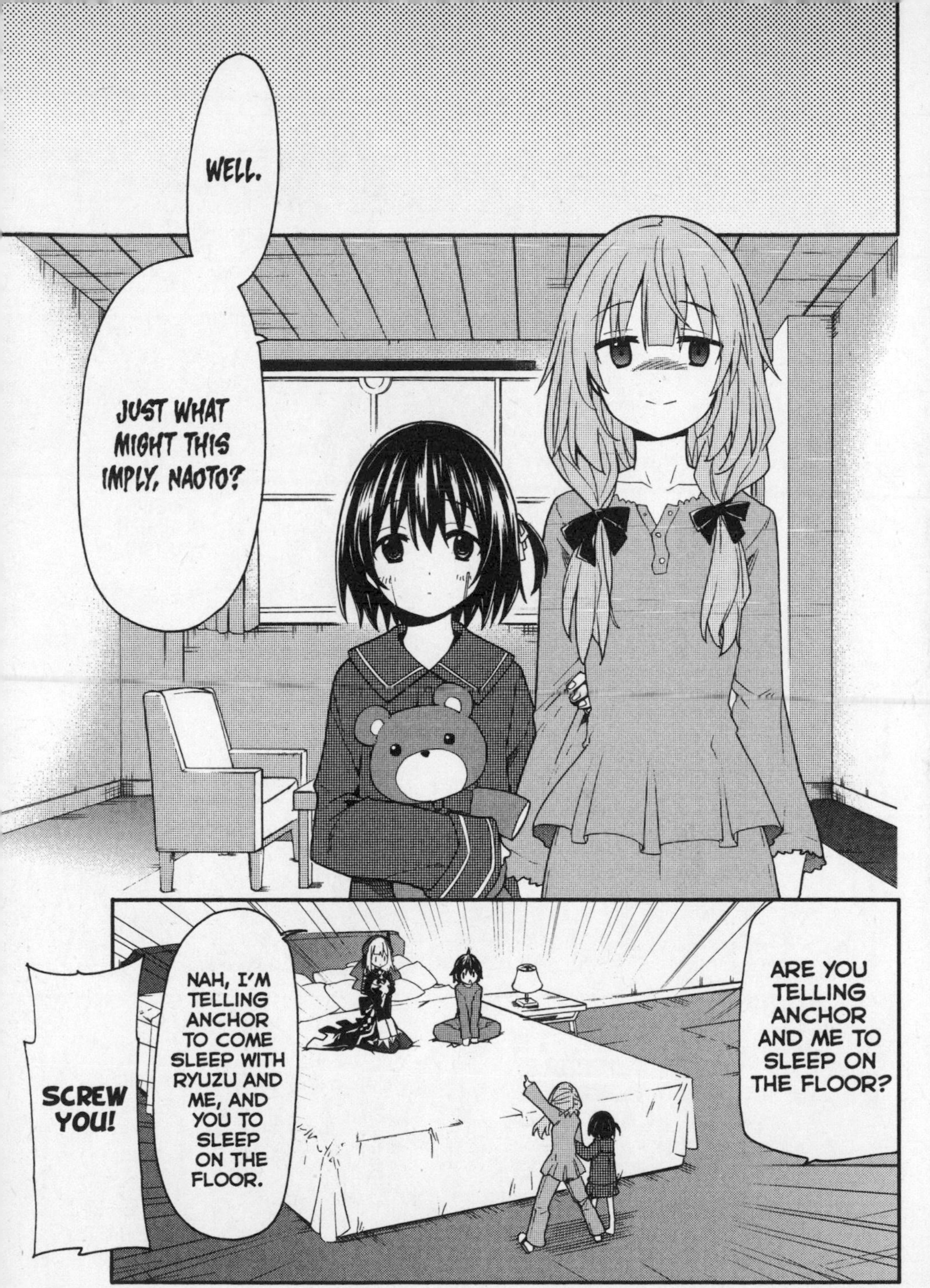
WELL.
JUST WHAT MIGHT THIS IMPLY, NAOTO?
ARE YOU TELLING ANCHOR AND ME TO SLEEP ON THE FLOOR?
NAH, I'M TELLING ANCHOR TO COME SLEEP WITH RYUZU AND ME, AND YOU TO SLEEP ON THE FLOOR.
SCREW YOU!

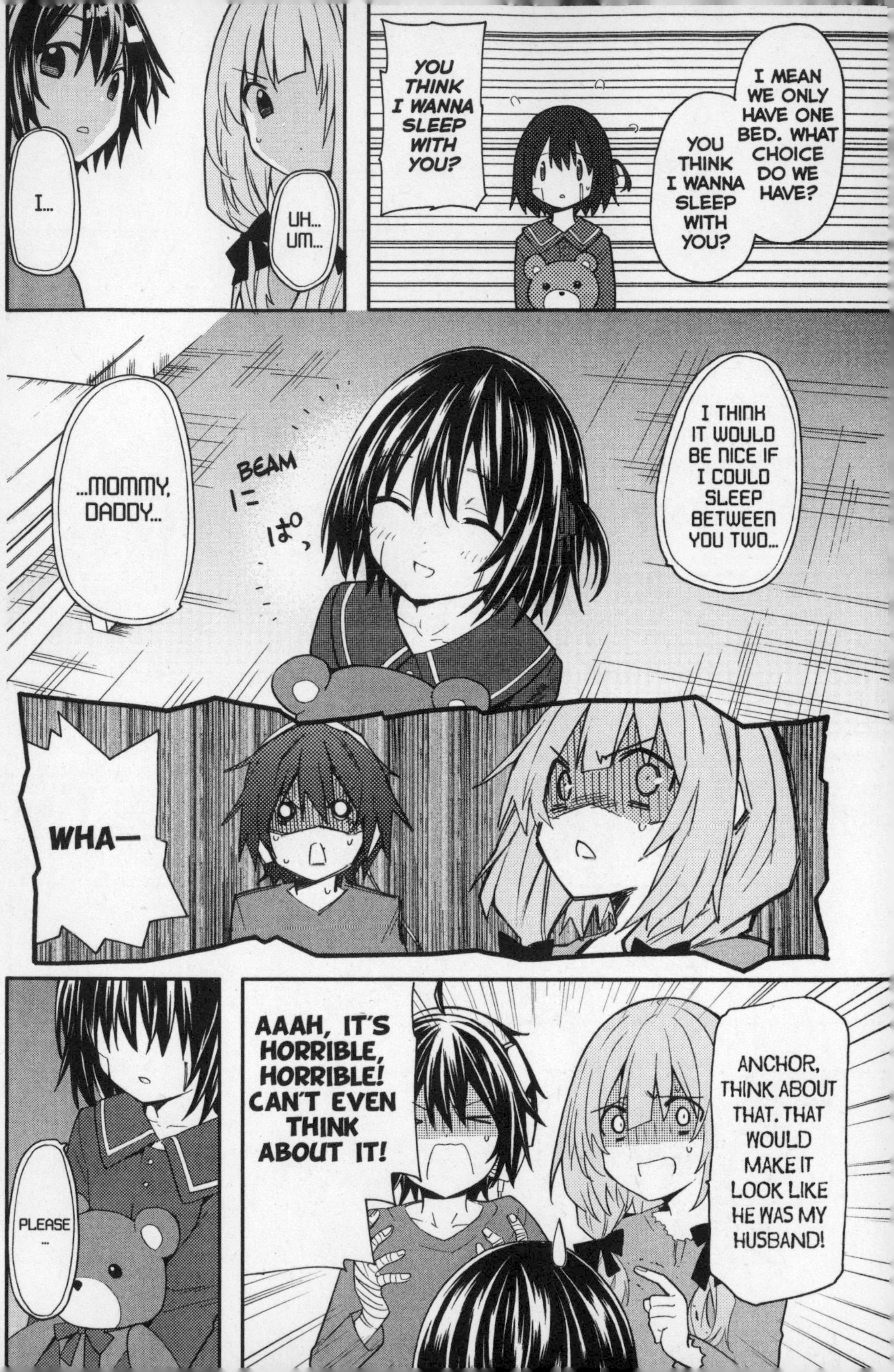
I MEAN WE ONLY HAVE ONE BED. WHAT CHOICE DO WE HAVE?
YOU THINK I WANNA SLEEP WITH YOU?
YOU THINK I WANNA SLEEP WITH YOU?
UH... UM...
I...
I THINK IT WOULD BE NICE IF I COULD SLEEP BETWEEN YOU TWO...
BEAM
にぱっ
...MOMMY, DADDY...
WHA—
ANCHOR, THINK ABOUT THAT. THAT WOULD MAKE IT LOOK LIKE HE WAS MY HUSBAND!
AAAH, IT'S HORRIBLE, HORRIBLE! CAN'T EVEN THINK ABOUT IT!
PLEASE ...

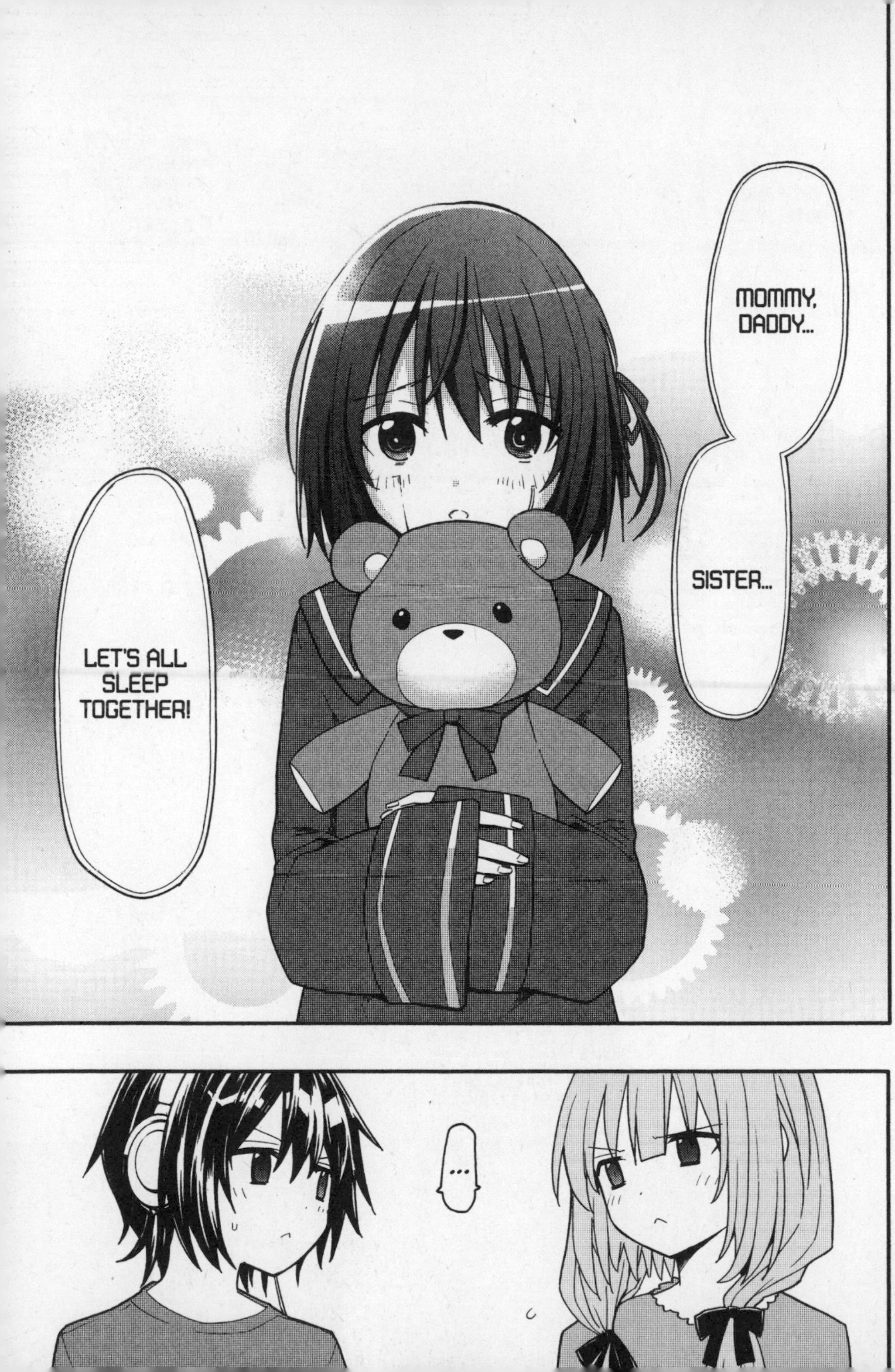
MOMMY, DADDY...
SISTER...
LET'S ALL SLEEP TOGETHER!
...

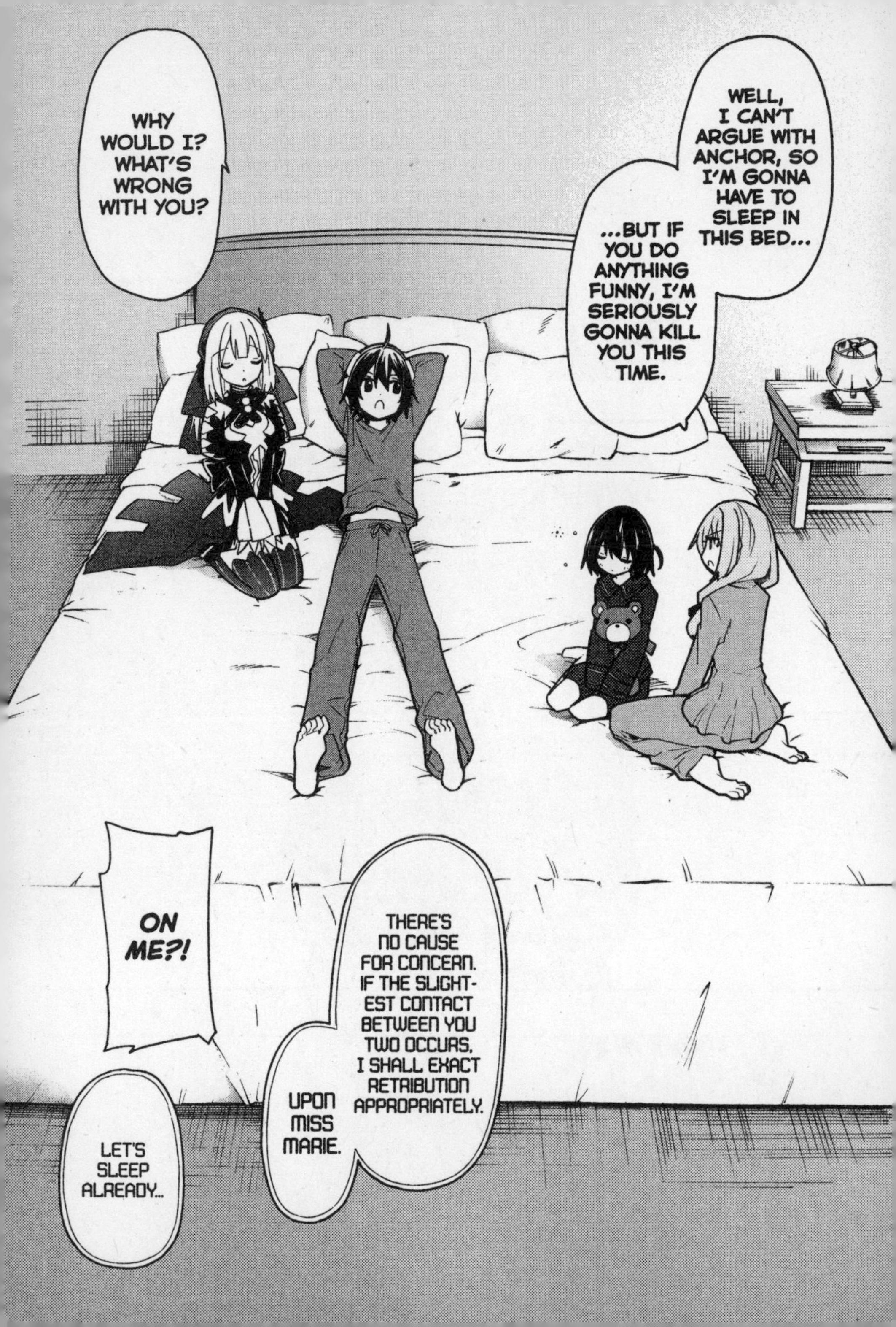
WELL, I CAN'T ARGUE WITH ANCHOR, SO I'M GONNA HAVE TO SLEEP IN THIS BED...
...BUT IF YOU DO ANYTHING FUNNY, I'M SERIOUSLY GONNA KILL YOU THIS TIME.
WHY WOULD I? WHAT'S WRONG WITH YOU?
THERE'S NO CAUSE FOR CONCERN. IF THE SLIGHT-EST CONTACT BETWEEN YOU TWO OCCURS, I SHALL EXACT RETRIBUTION APPROPRIATELY.
UPON MISS MARIE.
ON ME?!
LET'S SLEEP ALREADY...

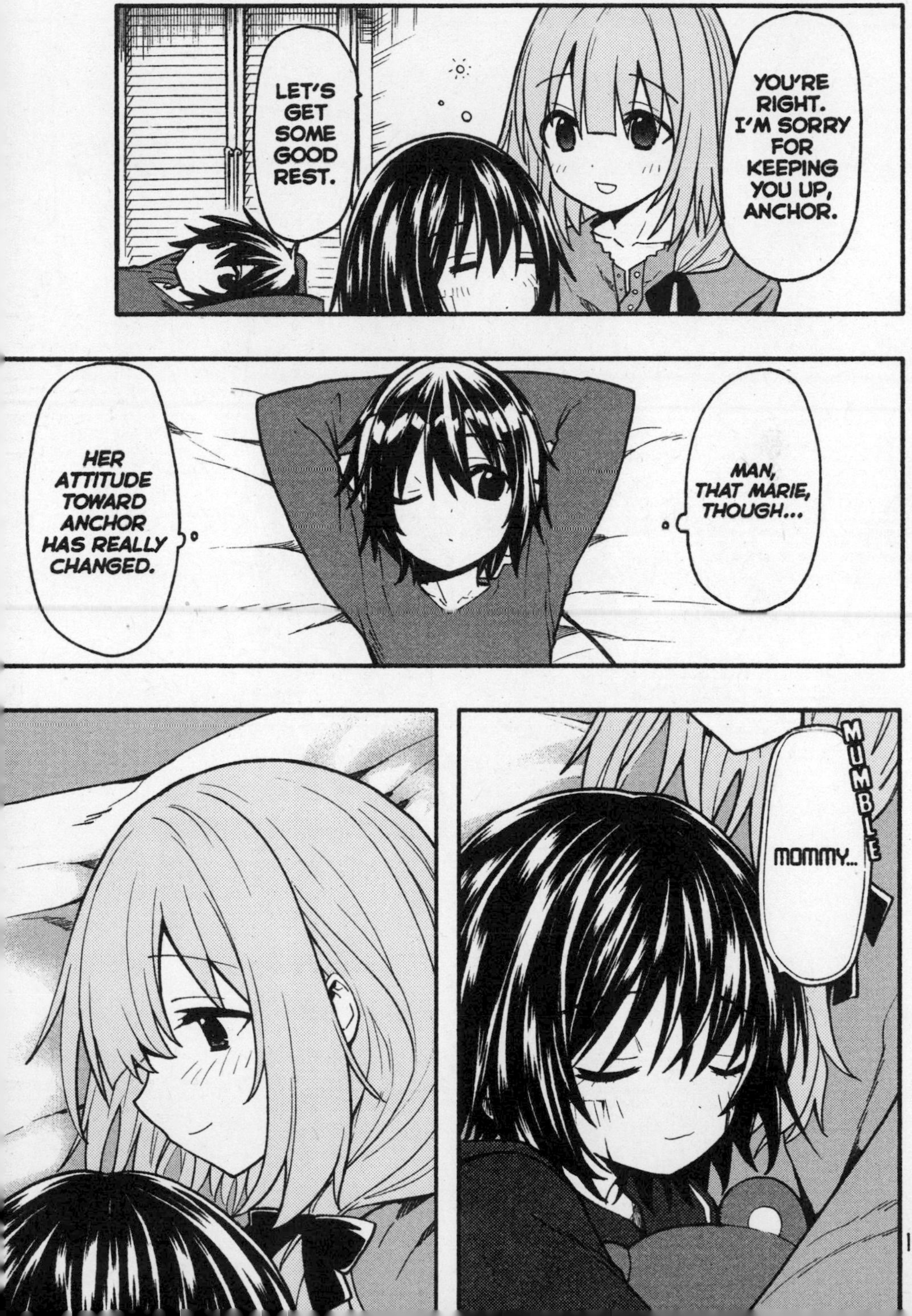
YOU'RE RIGHT. I'M SORRY FOR KEEPING YOU UP, ANCHOR.
LET'S GET SOME GOOD REST.
MAN, THAT MARIE, THOUGH...
HER ATTITUDE TOWARD ANCHOR HAS REALLY CHANGED.
MUMBLE
MOMMY...

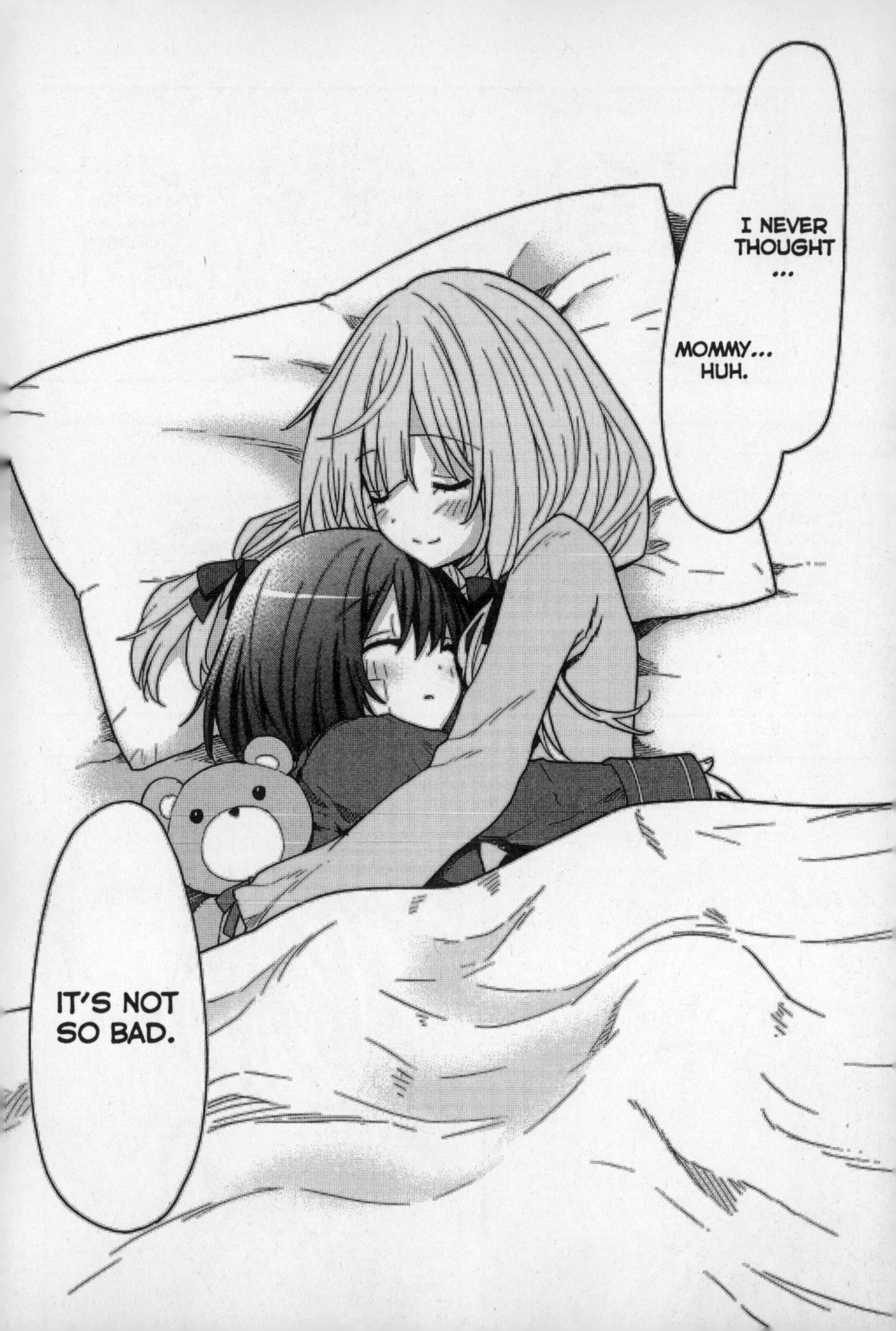
I NEVER THOUGHT ... MOMMY... HUH.
IT'S NOT SO BAD.

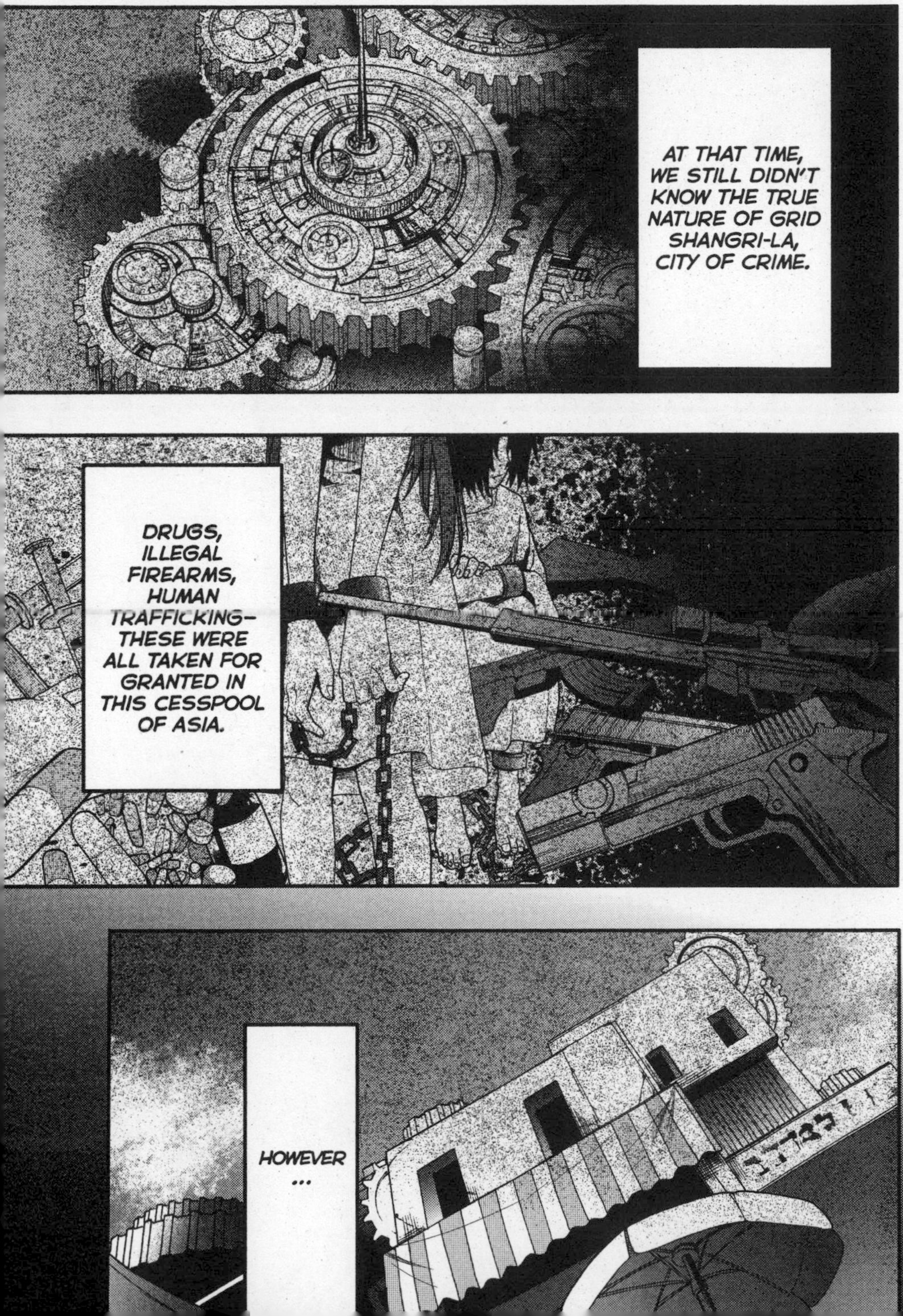
AT THAT TIME, WE STILL DIDN'T KNOW THE TRUE NATURE OF GRID SHANGRI-LA, CITY OF CRIME.
DRUGS, ILLEGAL FIREARMS, HUMAN TRAFFICKING—THESE WERE ALL TAKEN FOR GRANTED IN THIS CESSPOOL OF ASIA.
HOWEVER ...

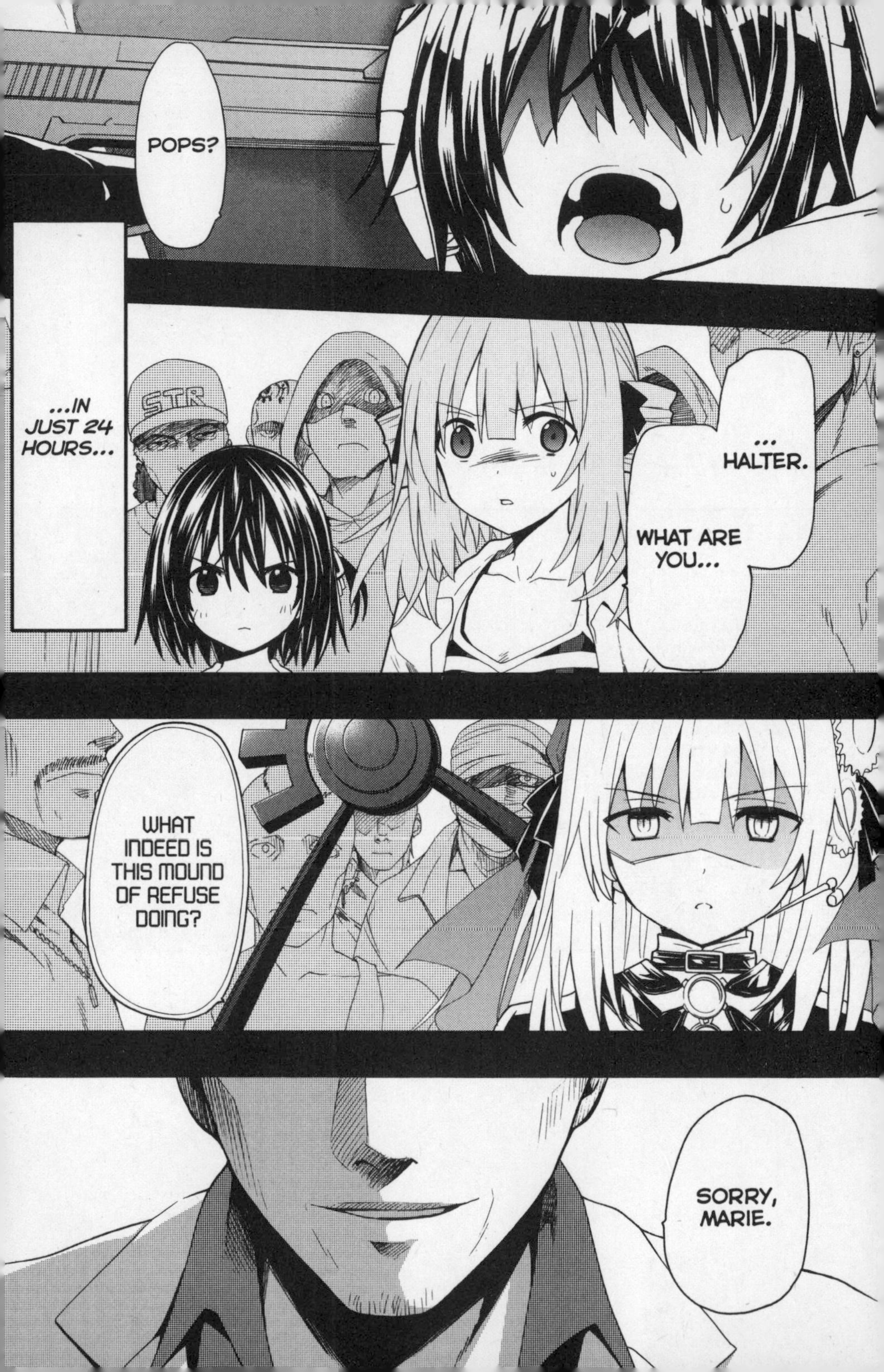
POPS?
... HALTER.
WHAT ARE YOU...
...IN JUST 24 HOURS...
WHAT INDEED IS THIS MOUND OF REFUSE DOING?
SORRY, MARIE.

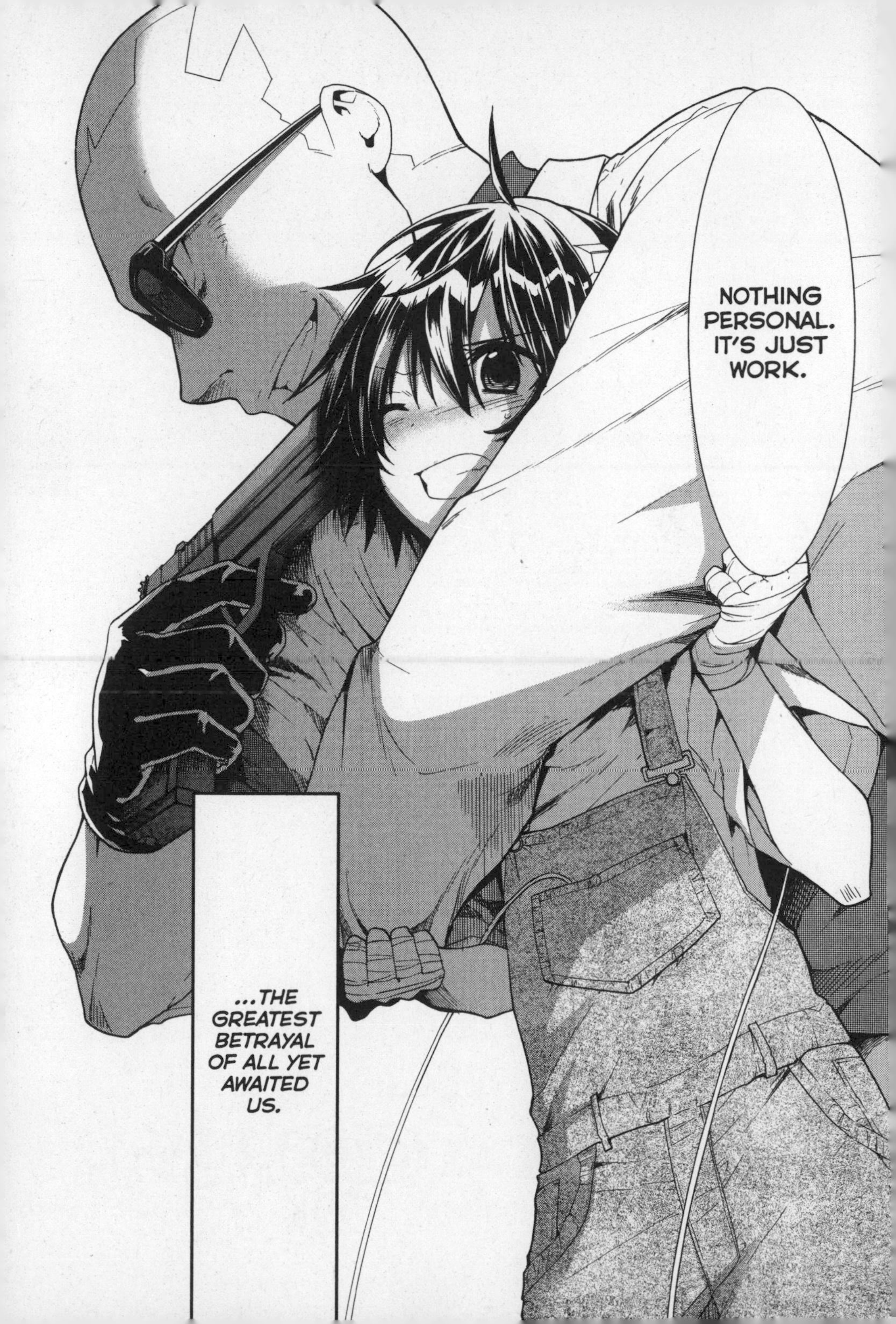
NOTHING PERSONAL. IT'S JUST WORK.
...THE GREATEST BETRAYAL OF ALL YET AWAITED US.

CLOCKWORK
PLANET

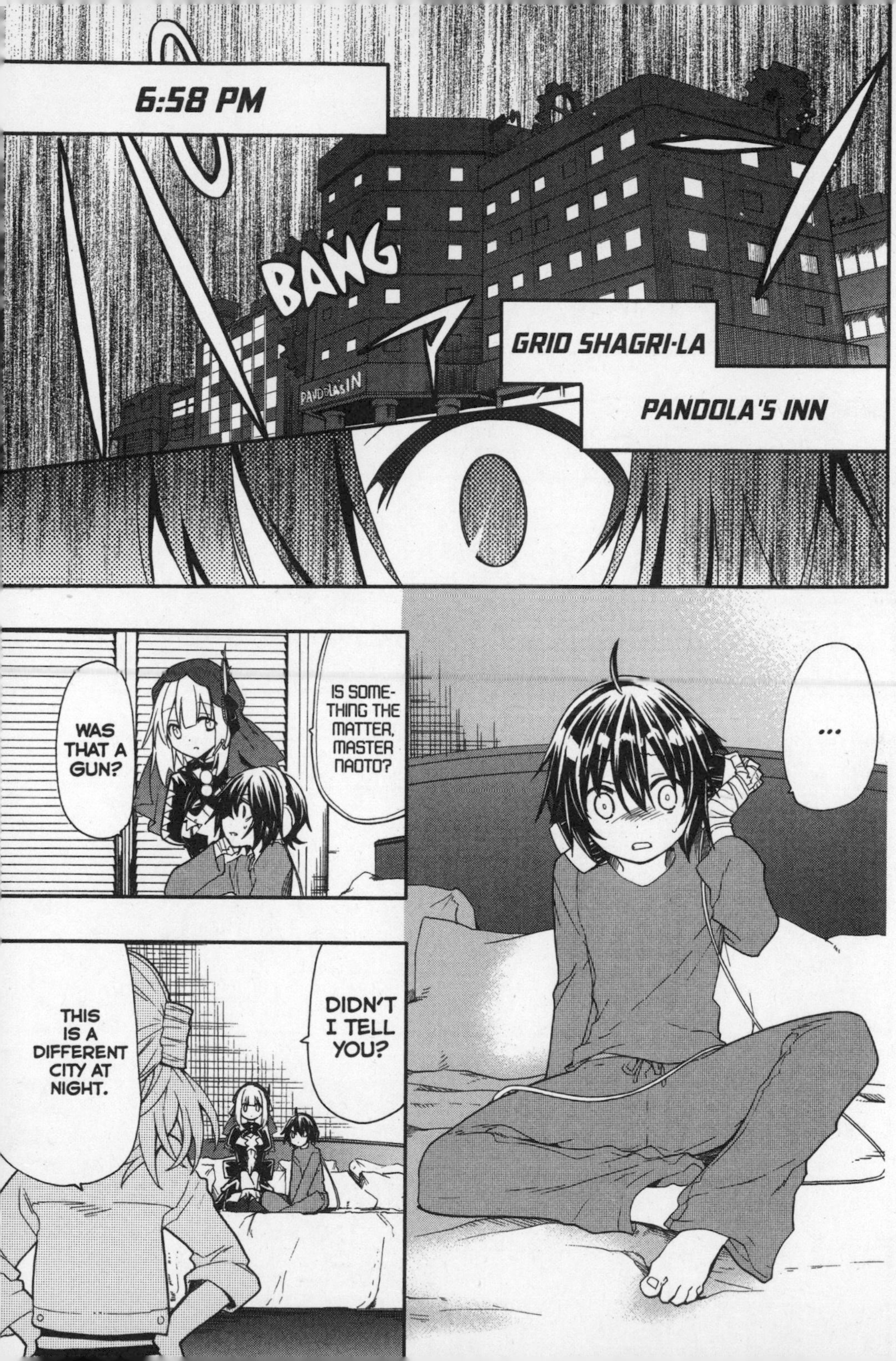
6:58 PM
BANG
GRID SHAGRI-LA
PANDOLA'S INN
...
IS SOMETHING THE MATTER, MASTER NAOTO?
WAS THAT A GUN?
DIDN'T I TELL YOU?
THIS IS A DIFFERENT CITY AT NIGHT.

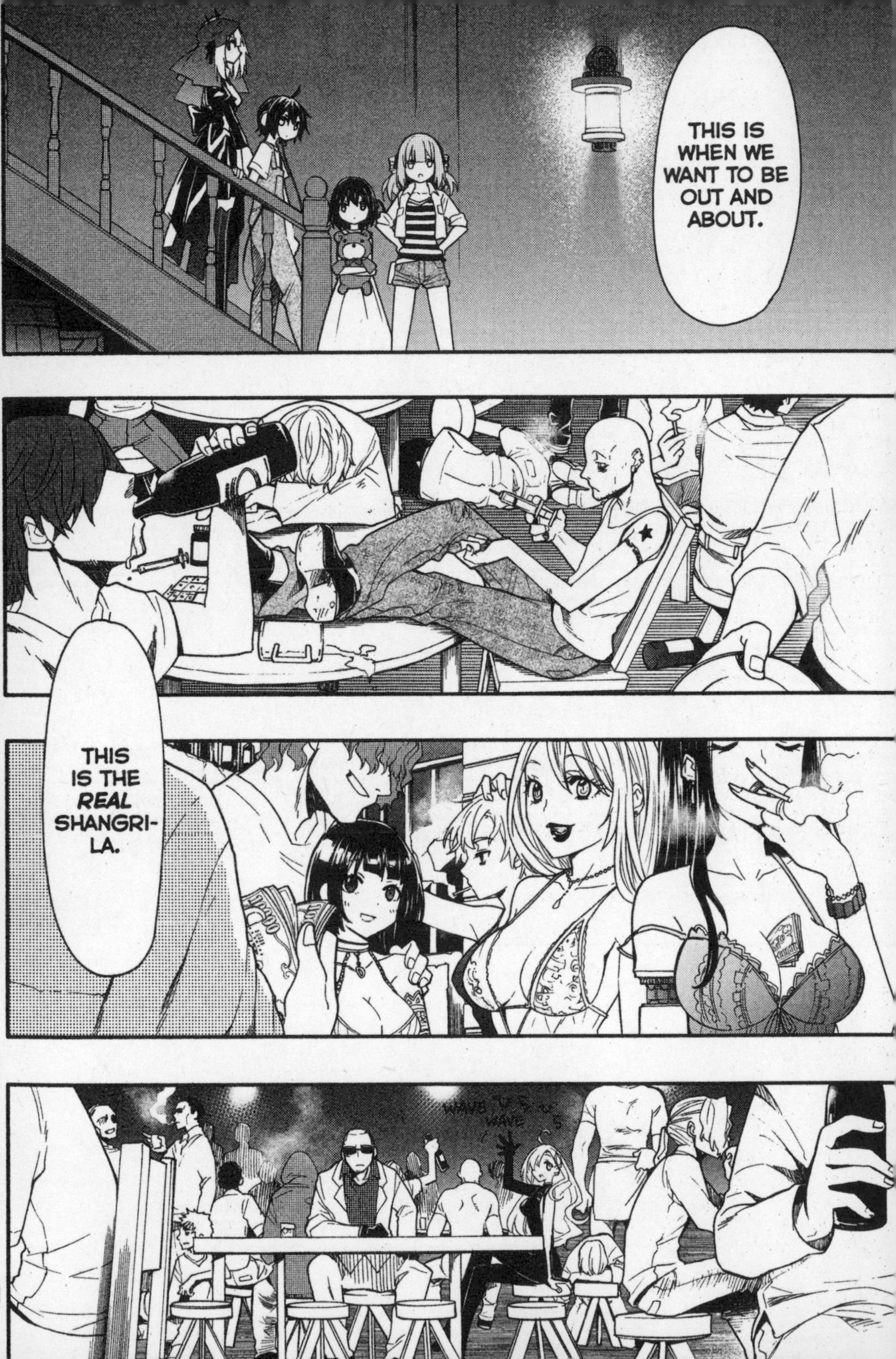
THIS IS WHEN WE WANT TO BE OUT AND ABOUT.
THIS IS THE *REAL* SHANGRI-LA.
WAVE
WAVE

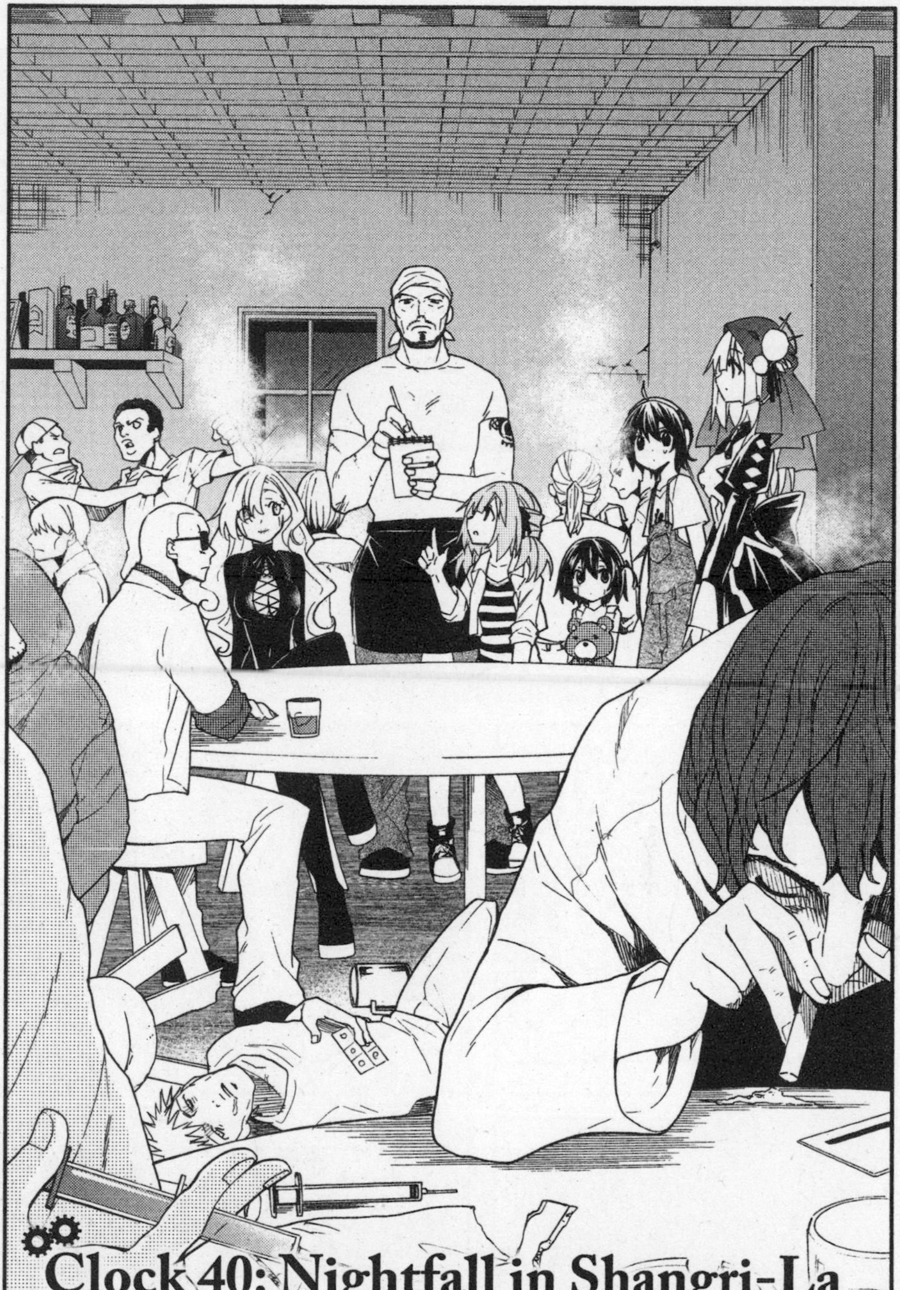

Clock 40: Nightfall in Shangri-La

SO.

HOW'S IT LOOKING REPAIRING ANCHOR?

WELL, I RAN THROUGH THE BASIC SERVICE...

BUT FRANKLY, IT'S GONNA BE TOUGH TO FIX HER.

THEN...

...WHAT DO WE...

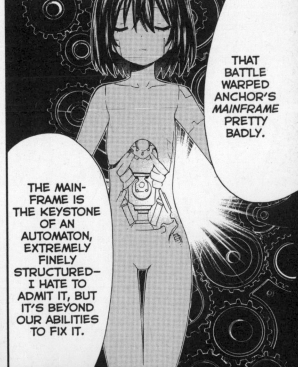

THAT BATTLE WARPED ANCHOR'S *MAINFRAME* PRETTY BADLY.

THE MAIN-FRAME IS THE KEYSTONE OF AN AUTOMATON, EXTREMELY FINELY STRUCTURED— I HATE TO ADMIT IT, BUT IT'S BEYOND OUR ABILITIES TO FIX IT.

DON'T YOU WORRY.

THERE'S THIS GUY...

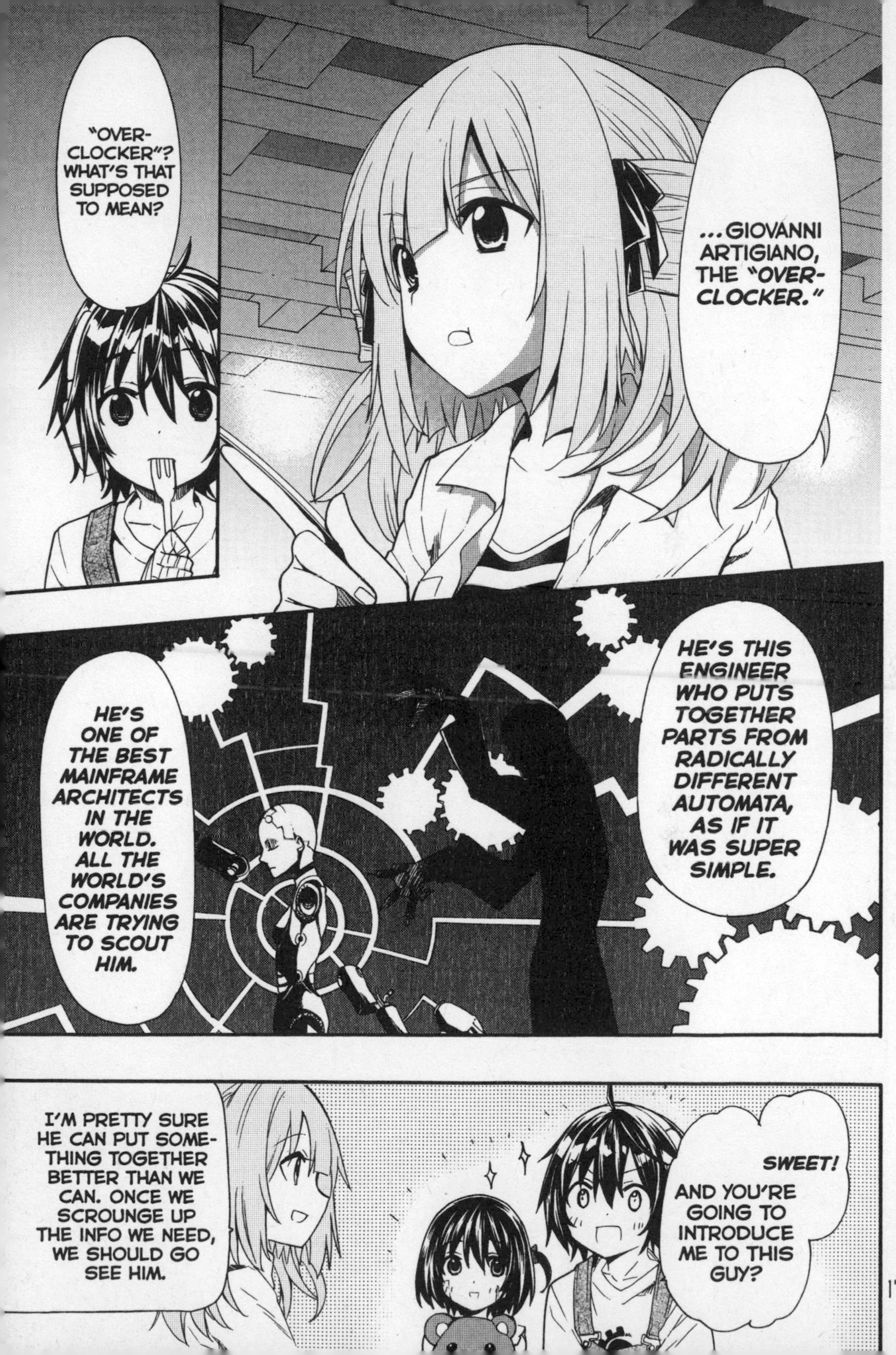
...GIOVANNI ARTIGIANO, THE "OVER-CLOCKER."
"OVER-CLOCKER"? WHAT'S THAT SUPPOSED TO MEAN?
HE'S THIS ENGINEER WHO PUTS TOGETHER PARTS FROM RADICALLY DIFFERENT AUTOMATA, AS IF IT WAS SUPER SIMPLE.
HE'S ONE OF THE BEST MAINFRAME ARCHITECTS IN THE WORLD. ALL THE WORLD'S COMPANIES ARE TRYING TO SCOUT HIM.
SWEET!
AND YOU'RE GOING TO INTRODUCE ME TO THIS GUY?
I'M PRETTY SURE HE CAN PUT SOMETHING TOGETHER BETTER THAN WE CAN. ONCE WE SCROUNGE UP THE INFO WE NEED, WE SHOULD GO SEE HIM.

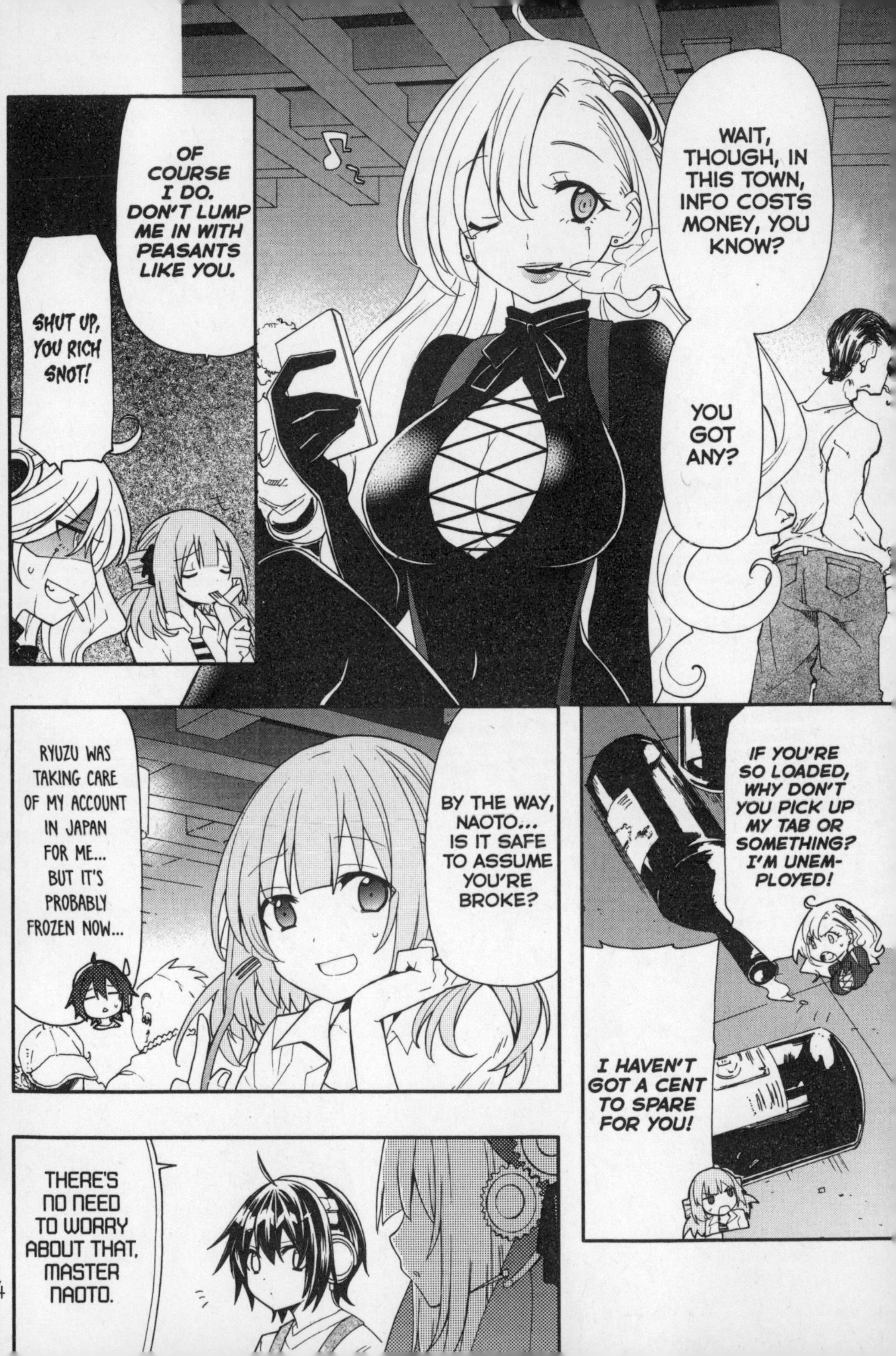
WAIT, THOUGH, IN THIS TOWN, INFO COSTS MONEY, YOU KNOW?
YOU GOT ANY?
OF COURSE I DO. DON'T LUMP ME IN WITH PEASANTS LIKE YOU.
SHUT UP, YOU RICH SNOT!
IF YOU'RE SO LOADED, WHY DON'T YOU PICK UP MY TAB OR SOMETHING? I'M UNEMPLOYED!
I HAVEN'T GOT A CENT TO SPARE FOR YOU!
BY THE WAY, NAOTO... IS IT SAFE TO ASSUME YOU'RE BROKE?
RYUZU WAS TAKING CARE OF MY ACCOUNT IN JAPAN FOR ME... BUT IT'S PROBABLY FROZEN NOW...
THERE'S NO NEED TO WORRY ABOUT THAT, MASTER NAOTO.

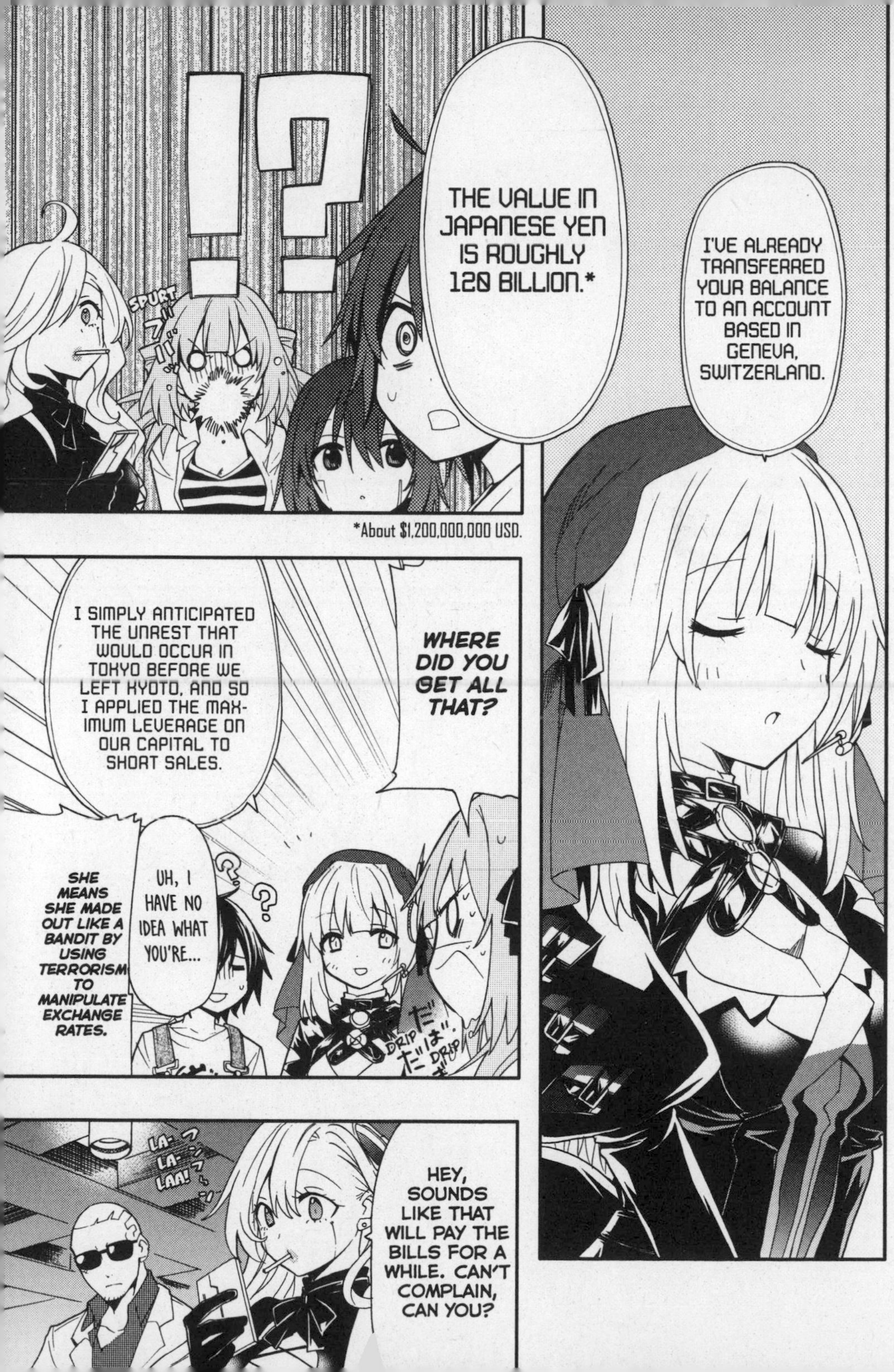
I'VE ALREADY TRANSFERRED YOUR BALANCE TO AN ACCOUNT BASED IN GENEVA, SWITZERLAND.
THE VALUE IN JAPANESE YEN IS ROUGHLY 120 BILLION.*
!?
SPURT
WHERE DID YOU GET ALL THAT?
I SIMPLY ANTICIPATED THE UNREST THAT WOULD OCCUR IN TOKYO BEFORE WE LEFT KYOTO, AND SO I APPLIED THE MAX-IMUM LEVERAGE ON OUR CAPITAL TO SHORT SALES.
UH, I HAVE NO IDEA WHAT YOU'RE...
SHE MEANS SHE MADE OUT LIKE A BANDIT BY USING TERRORISM TO MANIPULATE EXCHANGE RATES.
DRIP DRIP
HEY, SOUNDS LIKE THAT WILL PAY THE BILLS FOR A WHILE. CAN'T COMPLAIN, CAN YOU?
LA-LA-LAA!
*About $1,200,000,000 USD.

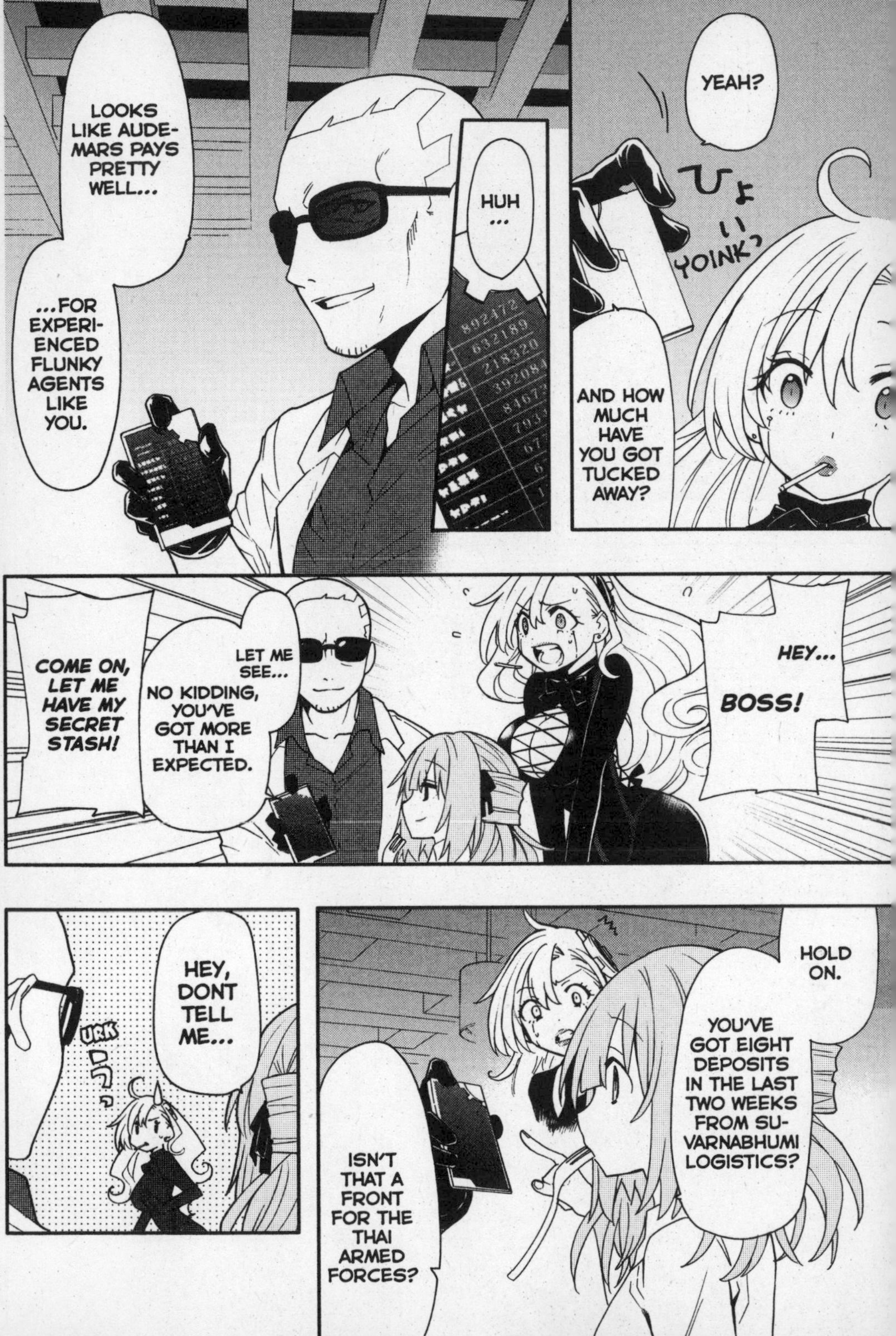
YEAH?
ひょい
YOINK
AND HOW MUCH HAVE YOU GOT TUCKED AWAY?
HUH...
LOOKS LIKE AUDE-MARS PAYS PRETTY WELL...
...FOR EXPERI-ENCED FLUNKY AGENTS LIKE YOU.
HEY...
BOSS!
LET ME SEE...
NO KIDDING, YOU'VE GOT MORE THAN I EXPECTED.
COME ON, LET ME HAVE MY SECRET STASH!
HOLD ON.
YOU'VE GOT EIGHT DEPOSITS IN THE LAST TWO WEEKS FROM SU-VARNABHUMI LOGISTICS?
ISN'T THAT A FRONT FOR THE THAI ARMED FORCES?
HEY, DONT TELL ME...
URK

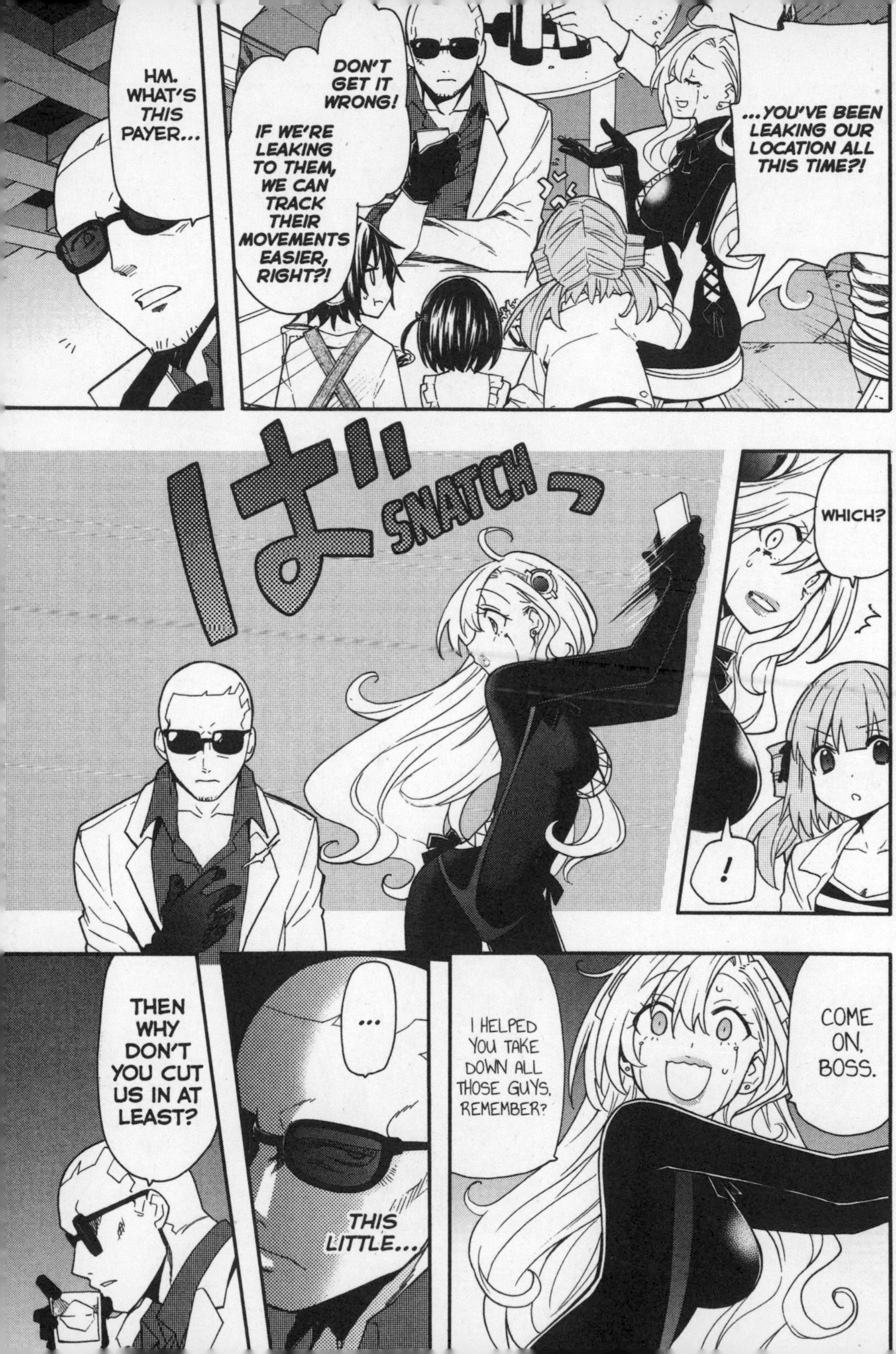
...YOU'VE BEEN LEAKING OUR LOCATION ALL THIS TIME?!
DON'T GET IT WRONG!
IF WE'RE LEAKING TO THEM, WE CAN TRACK THEIR MOVEMENTS EASIER, RIGHT?!
HM. WHAT'S THIS PAYER...
WHICH?
!
はっ
SNATCH
COME ON, BOSS.
I HELPED YOU TAKE DOWN ALL THOSE GUYS, REMEMBER?
...
THIS LITTLE...
THEN WHY DON'T YOU CUT US IN AT LEAST?

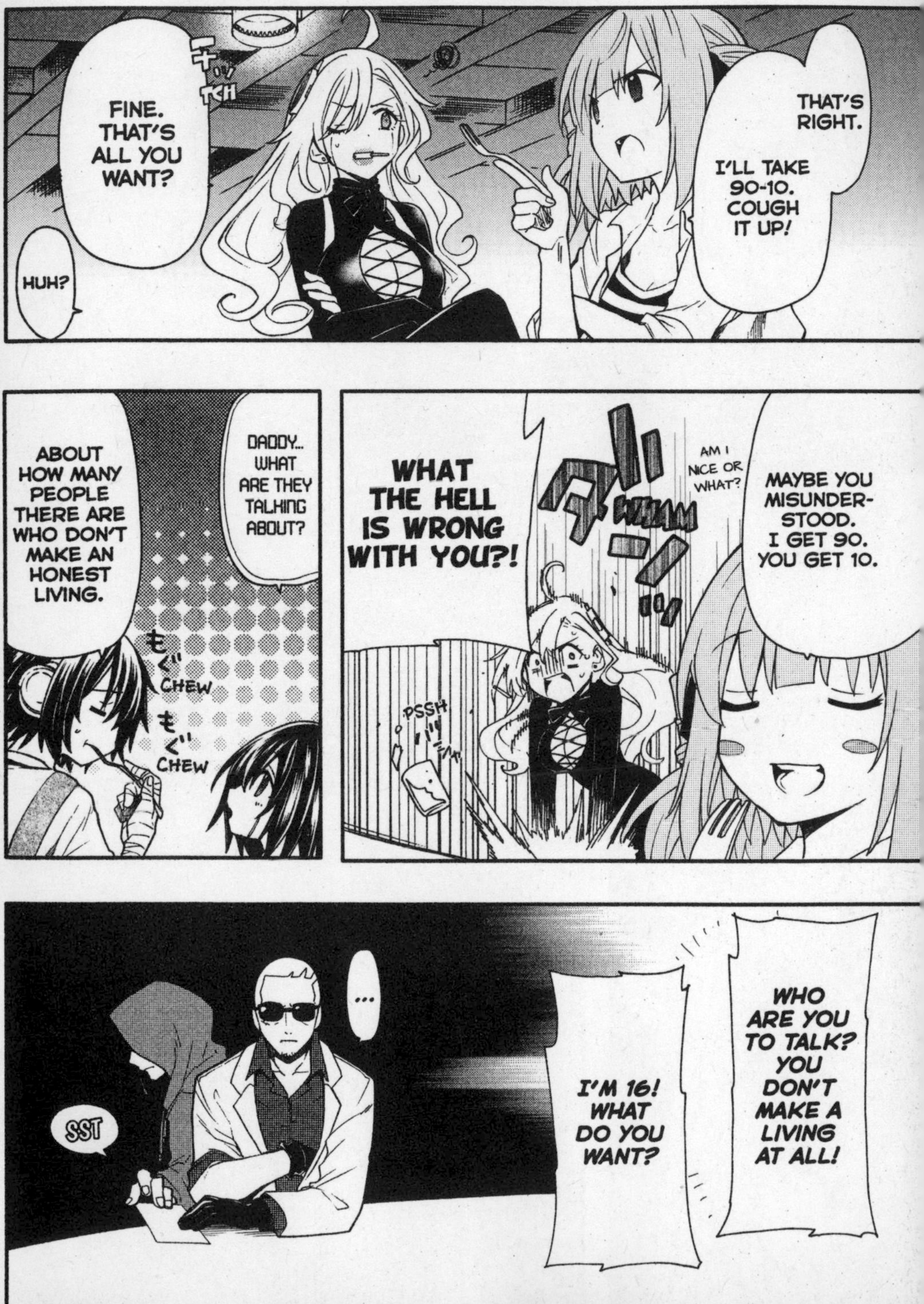
THAT'S RIGHT.
I'LL TAKE 90-10. COUGH IT UP!
TCH
FINE. THAT'S ALL YOU WANT?
HUH?
MAYBE YOU MISUNDERSTOOD. I GET 90. YOU GET 10.
AM I NICE OR WHAT?
WHAM
WHAT THE HELL IS WRONG WITH YOU?!
PSSH
DADDY... WHAT ARE THEY TALKING ABOUT?
ABOUT HOW MANY PEOPLE THERE ARE WHO DON'T MAKE AN HONEST LIVING.
CHEW
CHEW
WHO ARE YOU TO TALK? YOU DON'T MAKE A LIVING AT ALL!
I'M 16! WHAT DO YOU WANT?
...
SST

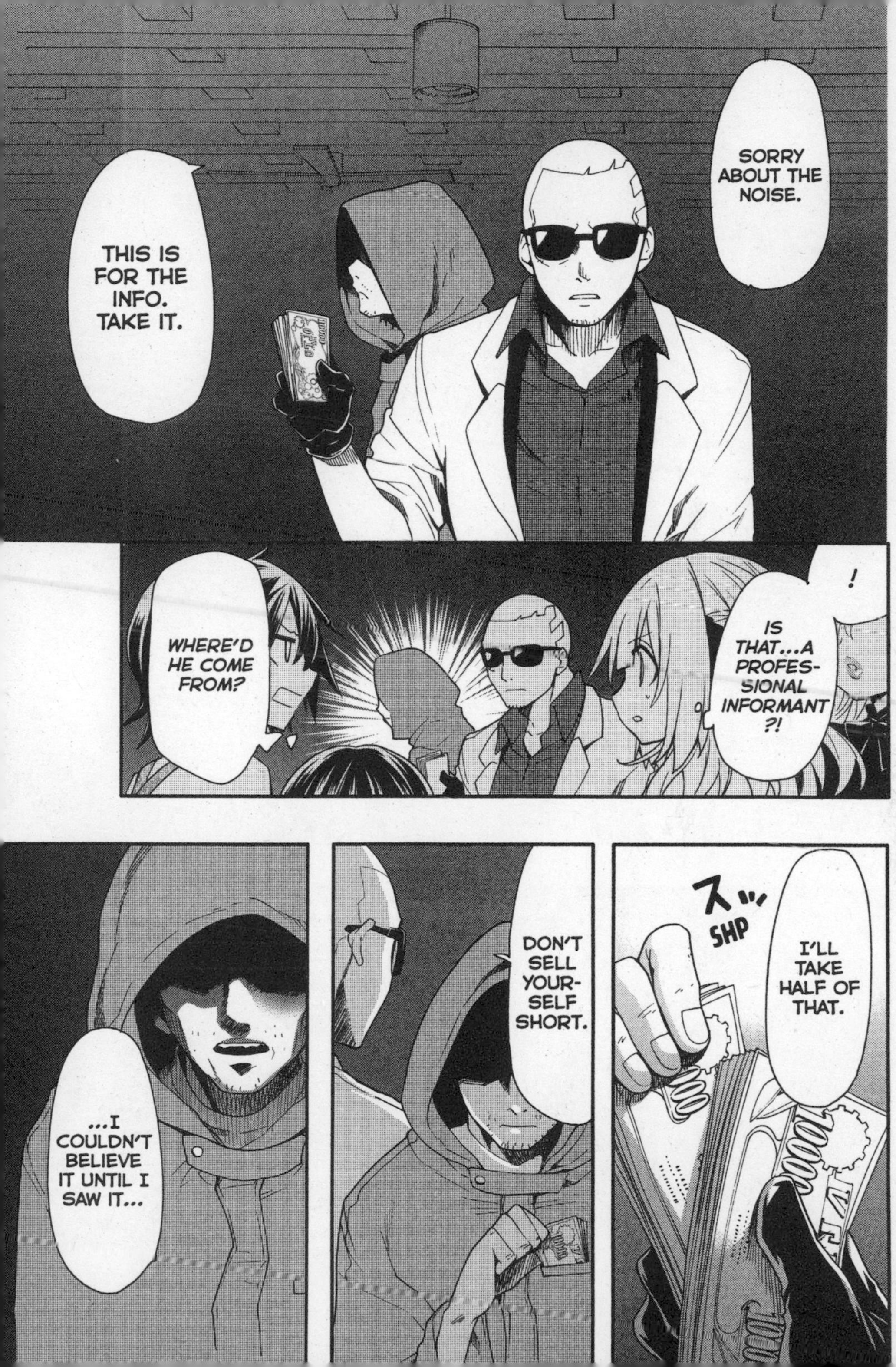
SORRY ABOUT THE NOISE.
THIS IS FOR THE INFO. TAKE IT.
!
IS THAT...A PROFES-SIONAL INFORMANT?!
WHERE'D HE COME FROM?
スッ
SHP
I'LL TAKE HALF OF THAT.
DON'T SELL YOUR-SELF SHORT.
...I COULDN'T BELIEVE IT UNTIL I SAW IT...

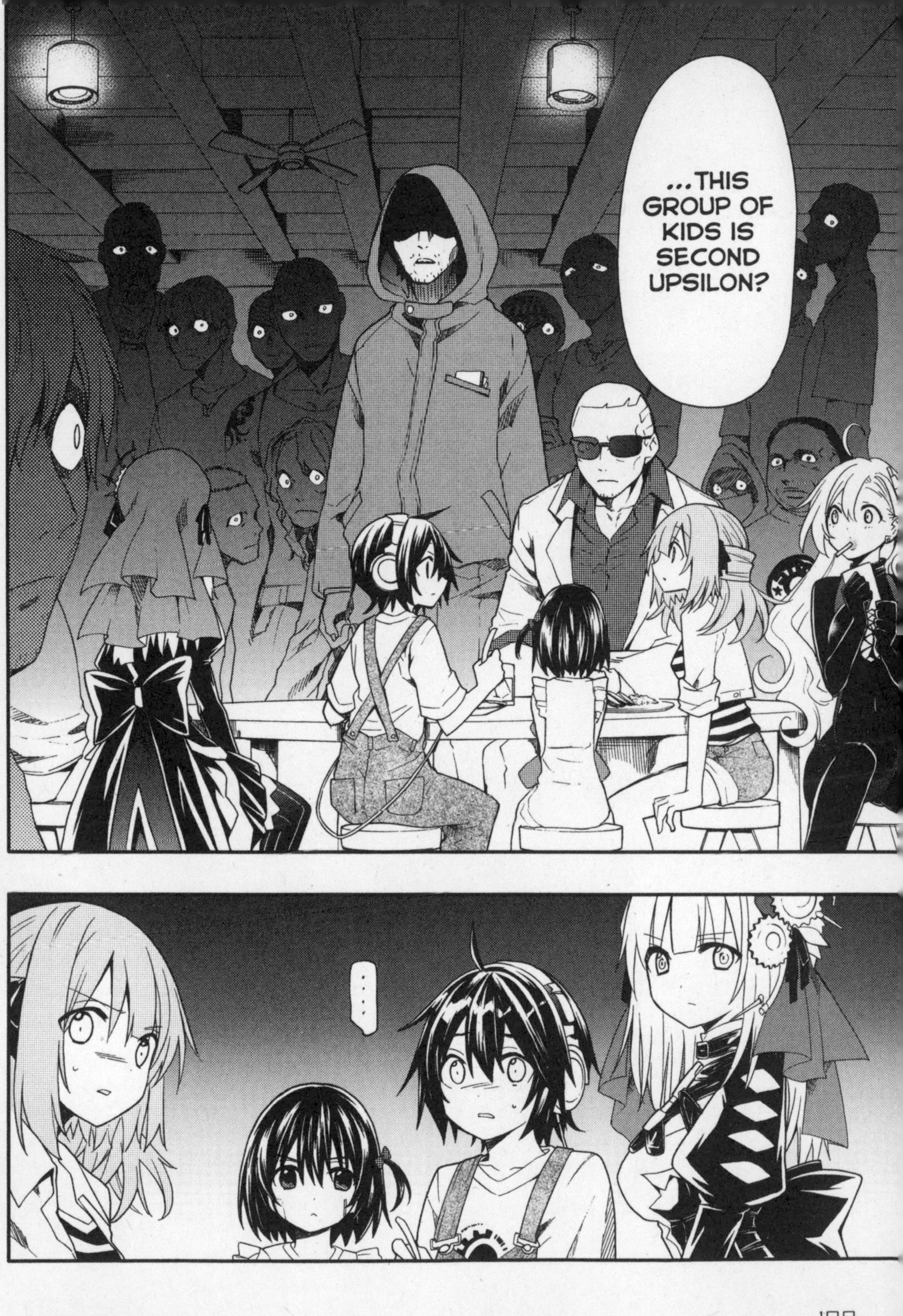
...THIS GROUP OF KIDS IS SECOND UPSILON?
....

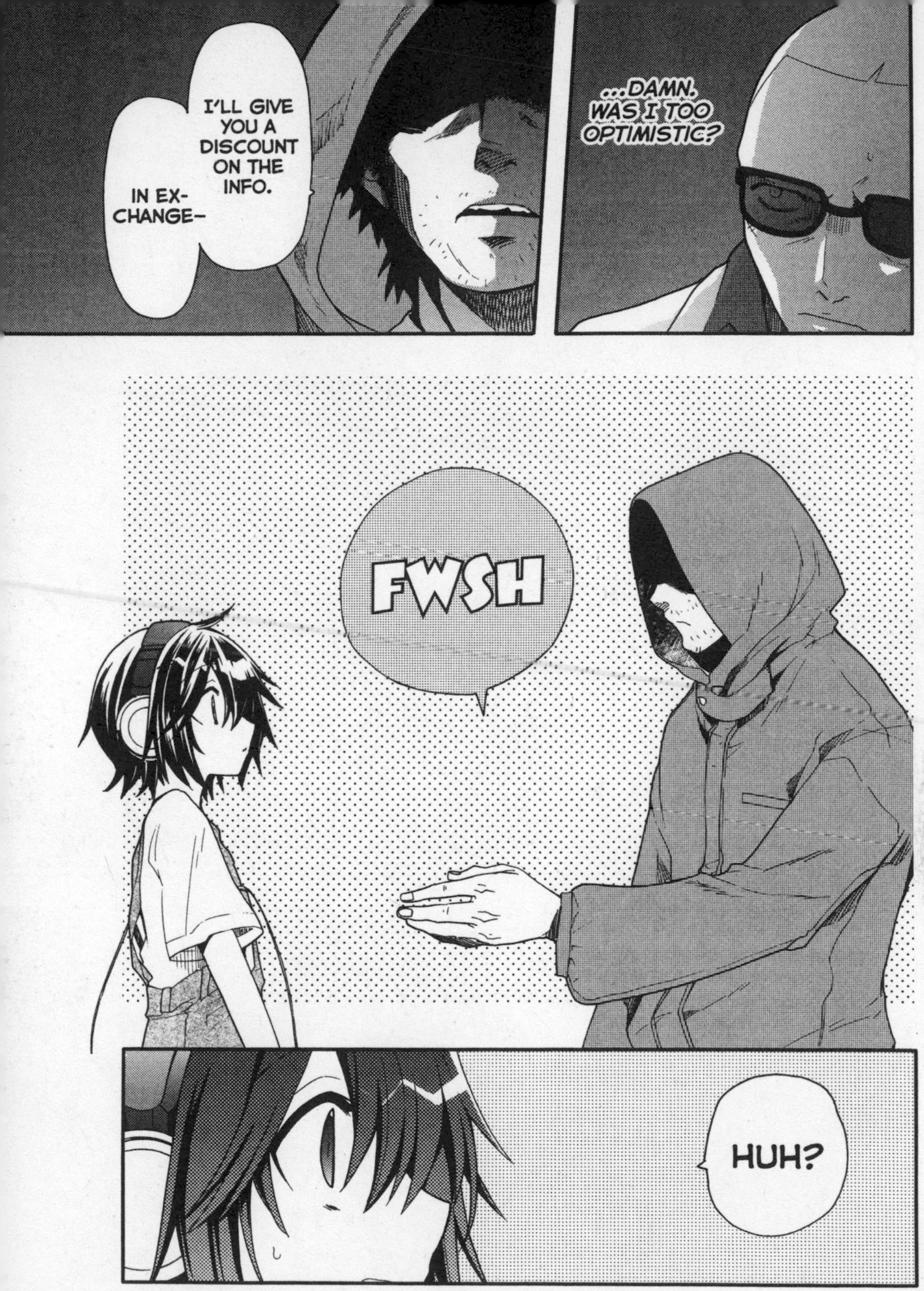
...DAMN. WAS I TOO OPTIMISTIC?
I'LL GIVE YOU A DISCOUNT ON THE INFO.
IN EX-CHANGE–
FWSH
HUH?

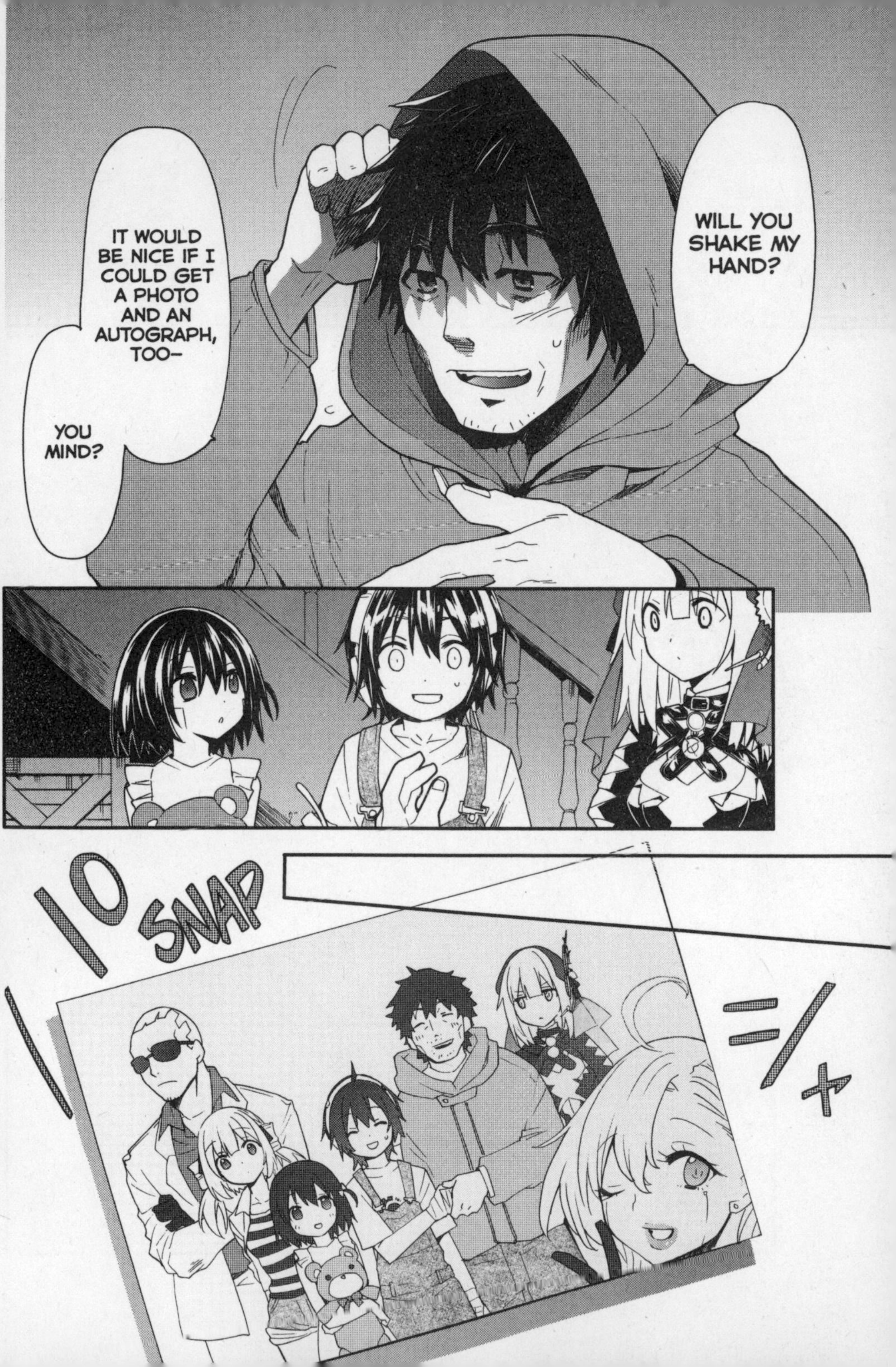
WILL YOU SHAKE MY HAND?
IT WOULD BE NICE IF I COULD GET A PHOTO AND AN AUTOGRAPH, TOO–
YOU MIND?
SNAP

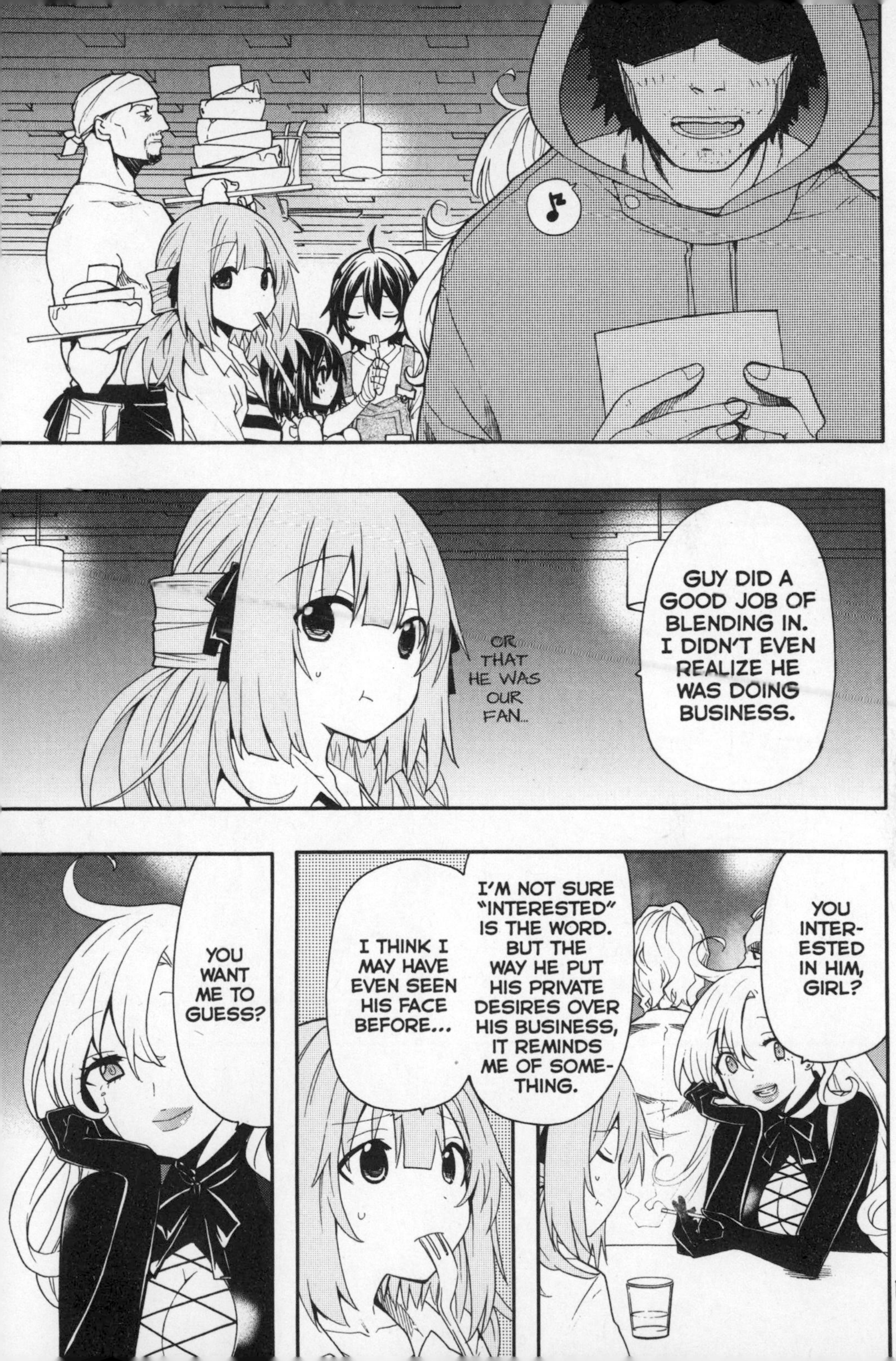
GUY DID A GOOD JOB OF BLENDING IN. I DIDN'T EVEN REALIZE HE WAS DOING BUSINESS.
OR THAT HE WAS OUR FAN..
YOU INTER-ESTED IN HIM, GIRL?
I'M NOT SURE "INTERESTED" IS THE WORD. BUT THE WAY HE PUT HIS PRIVATE DESIRES OVER HIS BUSINESS, IT REMINDS ME OF SOME-THING.
I THINK I MAY HAVE EVEN SEEN HIS FACE BEFORE...
YOU WANT ME TO GUESS?

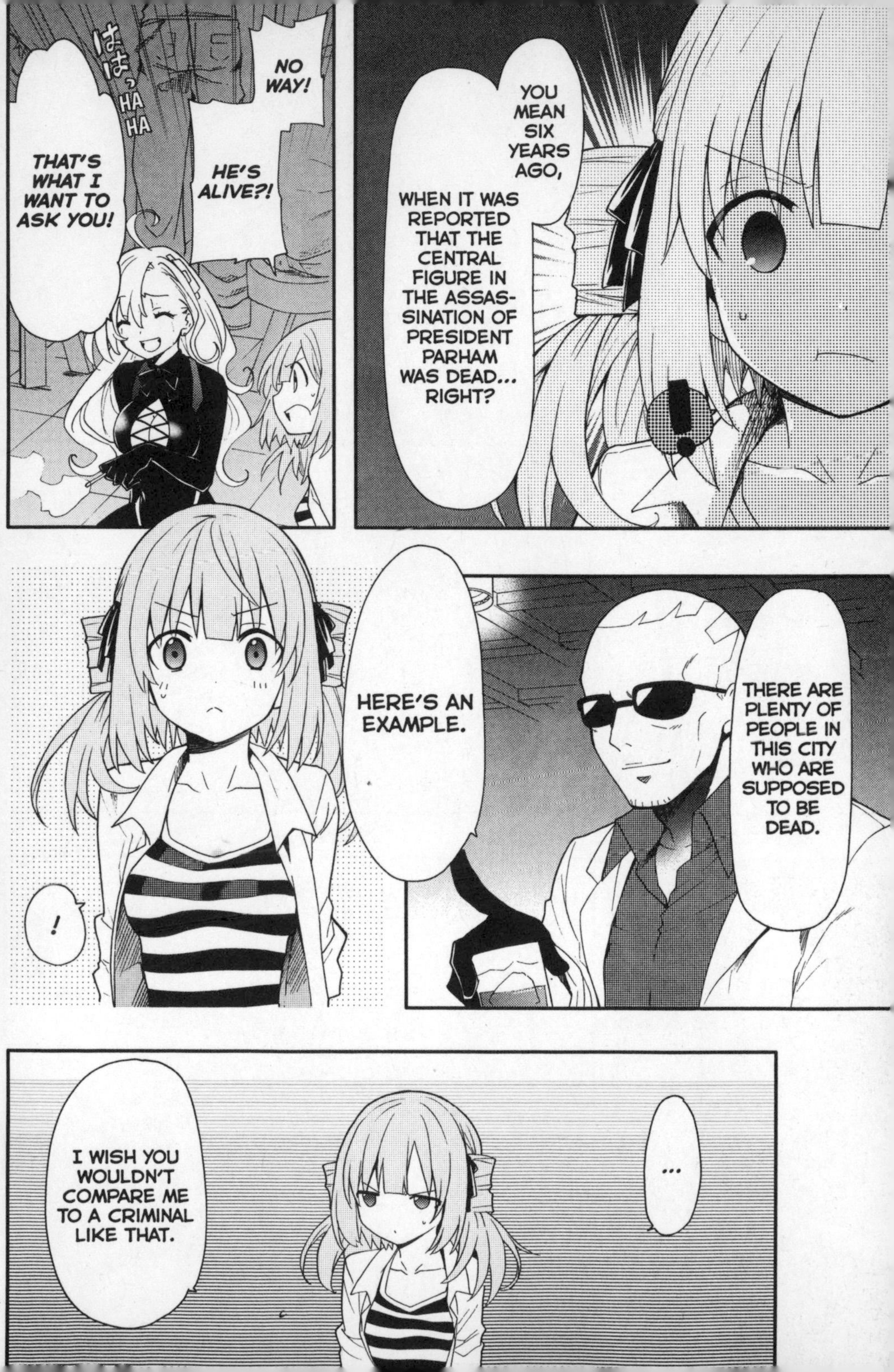
YOU MEAN SIX YEARS AGO,
WHEN IT WAS REPORTED THAT THE CENTRAL FIGURE IN THE ASSAS-SINATION OF PRESIDENT PARHAM WAS DEAD... RIGHT?
NO WAY!
HE'S ALIVE?!
はは HA HA
THAT'S WHAT I WANT TO ASK YOU!
THERE ARE PLENTY OF PEOPLE IN THIS CITY WHO ARE SUPPOSED TO BE DEAD.
HERE'S AN EXAMPLE.
!
...
I WISH YOU WOULDN'T COMPARE ME TO A CRIMINAL LIKE THAT.

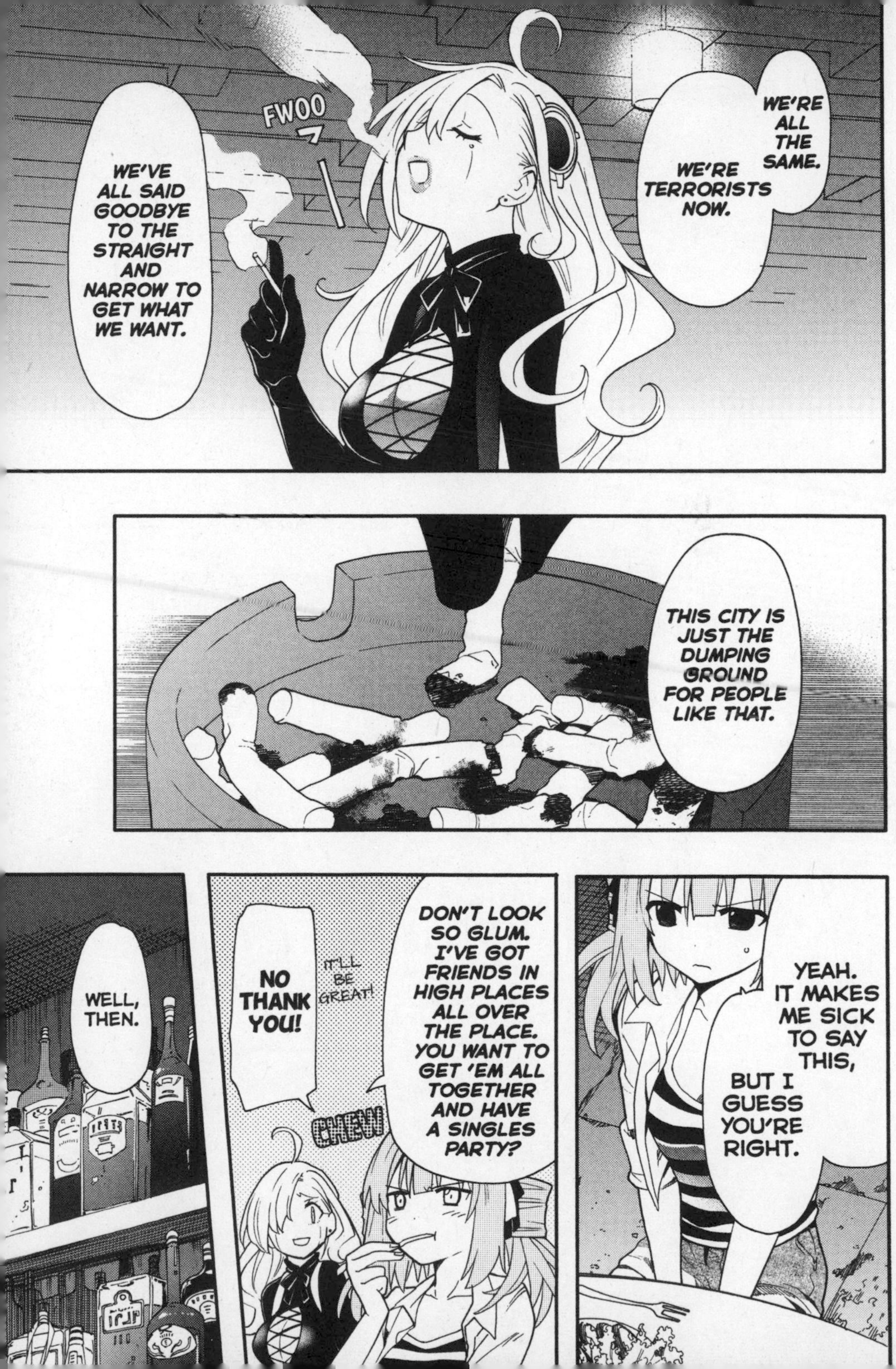
WE'RE ALL THE SAME.
WE'RE TERRORISTS NOW.
FWOO
WE'VE ALL SAID GOODBYE TO THE STRAIGHT AND NARROW TO GET WHAT WE WANT.
THIS CITY IS JUST THE DUMPING GROUND FOR PEOPLE LIKE THAT.
YEAH. IT MAKES ME SICK TO SAY THIS,
BUT I GUESS YOU'RE RIGHT.
DON'T LOOK SO GLUM. I'VE GOT FRIENDS IN HIGH PLACES ALL OVER THE PLACE. YOU WANT TO GET 'EM ALL TOGETHER AND HAVE A SINGLES PARTY?
CHEW
IT'LL BE GREAT!
NO THANK YOU!
WELL, THEN.

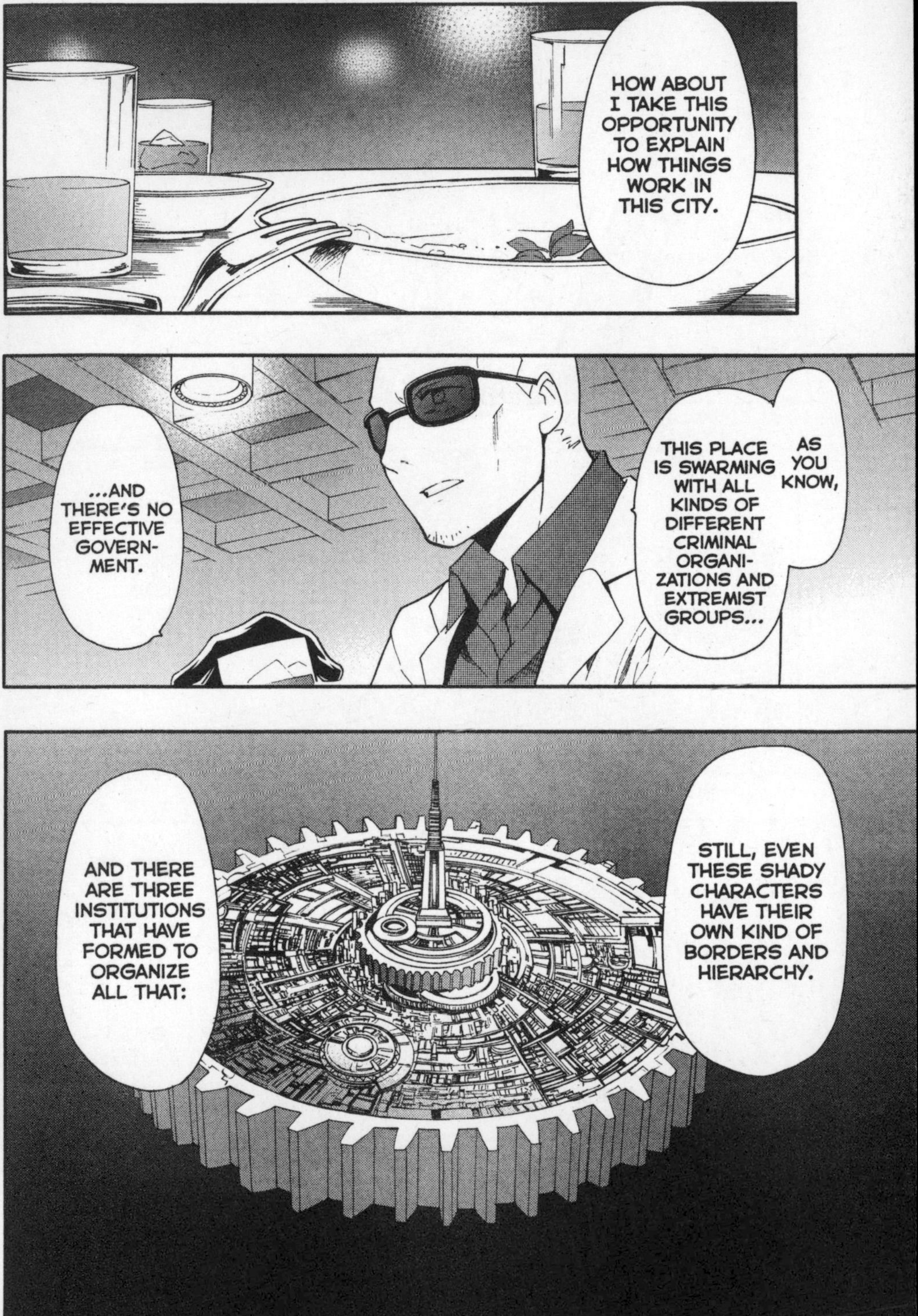
HOW ABOUT I TAKE THIS OPPORTUNITY TO EXPLAIN HOW THINGS WORK IN THIS CITY.
AS YOU KNOW,
THIS PLACE IS SWARMING WITH ALL KINDS OF DIFFERENT CRIMINAL ORGANI-ZATIONS AND EXTREMIST GROUPS...
...AND THERE'S NO EFFECTIVE GOVERN-MENT.
STILL, EVEN THESE SHADY CHARACTERS HAVE THEIR OWN KIND OF BORDERS AND HIERARCHY.
AND THERE ARE THREE INSTITUTIONS THAT HAVE FORMED TO ORGANIZE ALL THAT:

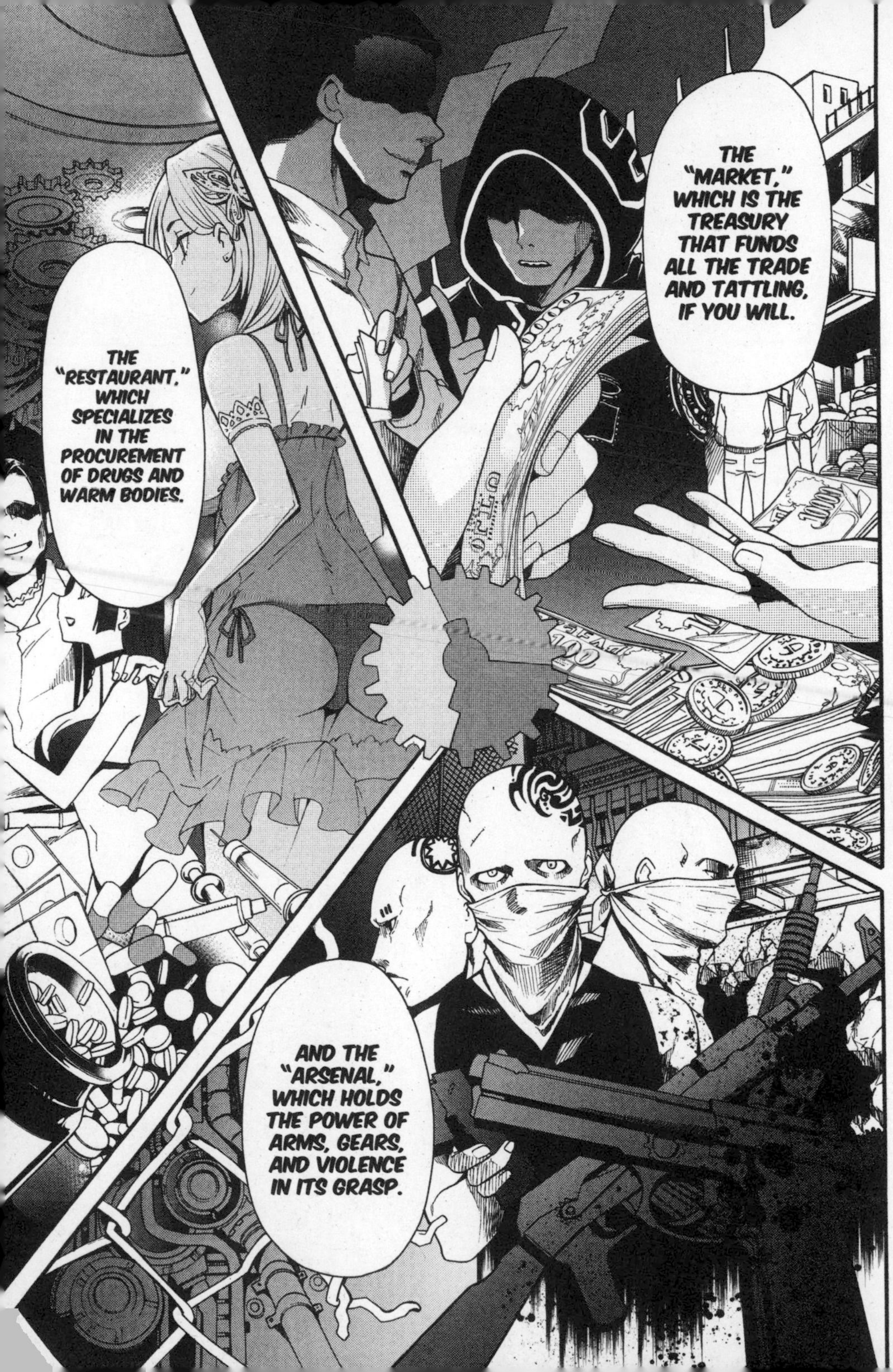
THE "MARKET," WHICH IS THE TREASURY THAT FUNDS ALL THE TRADE AND TATTLING, IF YOU WILL.
THE "RESTAURANT," WHICH SPECIALIZES IN THE PROCUREMENT OF DRUGS AND WARM BODIES.
AND THE "ARSENAL," WHICH HOLDS THE POWER OF ARMS, GEARS, AND VIOLENCE IN ITS GRASP.

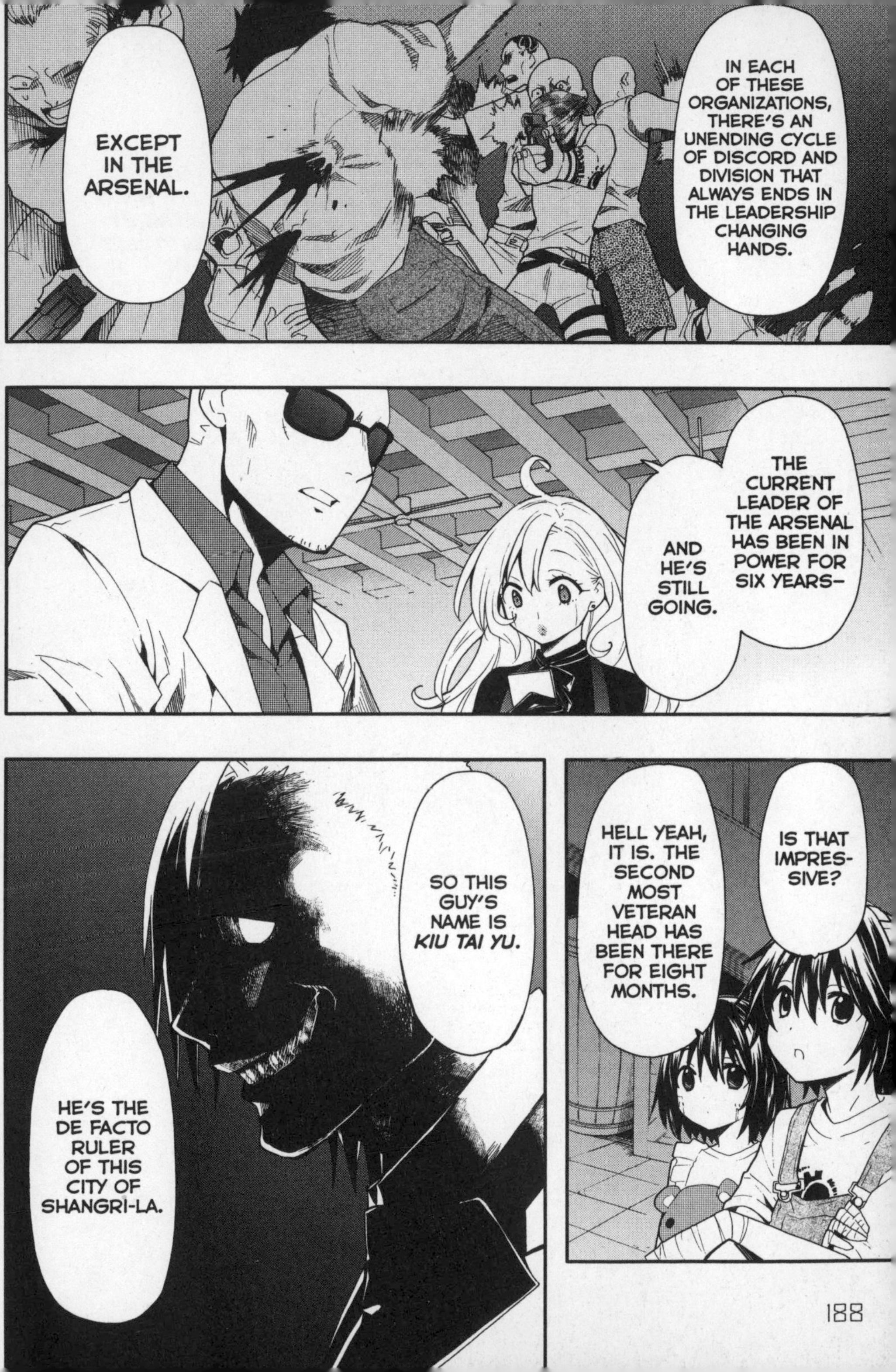
IN EACH OF THESE ORGANIZATIONS, THERE'S AN UNENDING CYCLE OF DISCORD AND DIVISION THAT ALWAYS ENDS IN THE LEADERSHIP CHANGING HANDS.
EXCEPT IN THE ARSENAL.
THE CURRENT LEADER OF THE ARSENAL HAS BEEN IN POWER FOR SIX YEARS–
AND HE'S STILL GOING.
IS THAT IMPRESSIVE?
HELL YEAH, IT IS. THE SECOND MOST VETERAN HEAD HAS BEEN THERE FOR EIGHT MONTHS.
SO THIS GUY'S NAME IS *KIU TAI YU*.
HE'S THE DE FACTO RULER OF THIS CITY OF SHANGRI-LA.

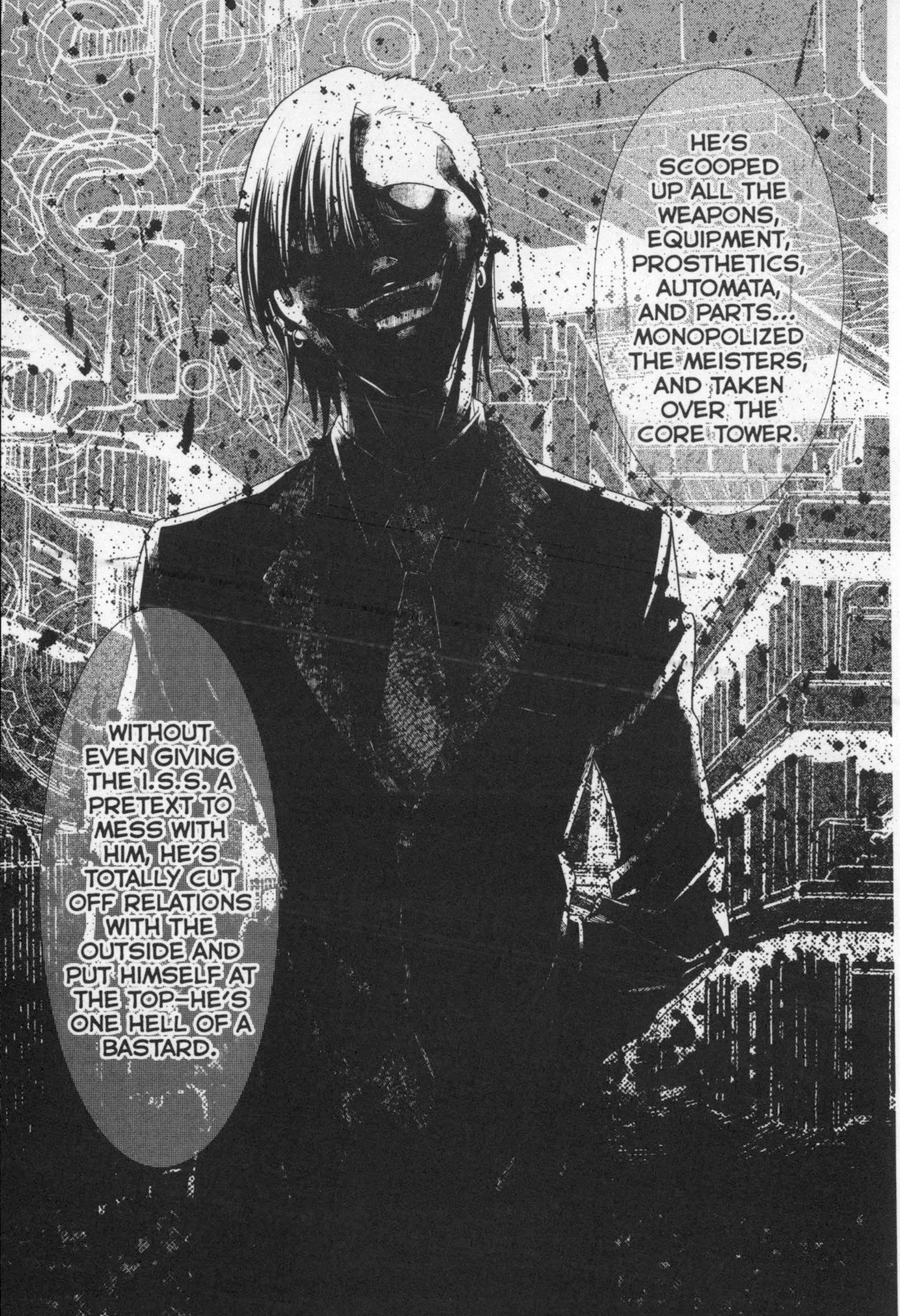
HE'S SCOOPED UP ALL THE WEAPONS, EQUIPMENT, PROSTHETICS, AUTOMATA, AND PARTS... MONOPOLIZED THE MEISTERS, AND TAKEN OVER THE CORE TOWER.
WITHOUT EVEN GIVING THE I.S.S. A PRETEXT TO MESS WITH HIM, HE'S TOTALLY CUT OFF RELATIONS WITH THE OUTSIDE AND PUT HIMSELF AT THE TOP—HE'S ONE HELL OF A BASTARD.

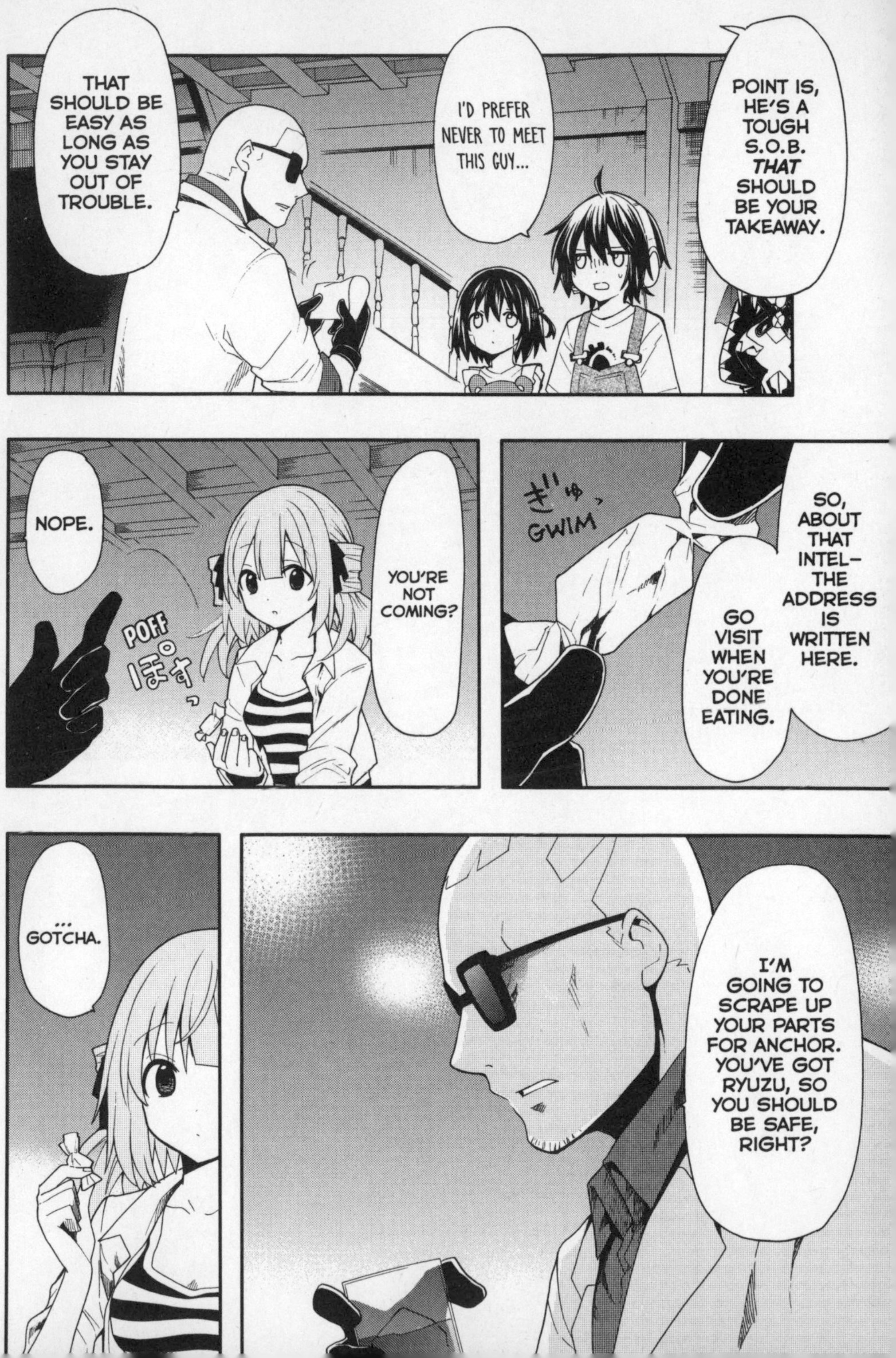
POINT IS, HE'S A TOUGH S.O.B. *THAT* SHOULD BE YOUR TAKEAWAY.
I'D PREFER NEVER TO MEET THIS GUY...
THAT SHOULD BE EASY AS LONG AS YOU STAY OUT OF TROUBLE.
SO, ABOUT THAT INTEL— THE ADDRESS IS WRITTEN HERE.
GO VISIT WHEN YOU'RE DONE EATING.
ぎゅっ
GWIM
YOU'RE NOT COMING?
NOPE.
ぽすっ
POFF
I'M GOING TO SCRAPE UP YOUR PARTS FOR ANCHOR. YOU'VE GOT RYUZU, SO YOU SHOULD BE SAFE, RIGHT?
...GOTCHA.

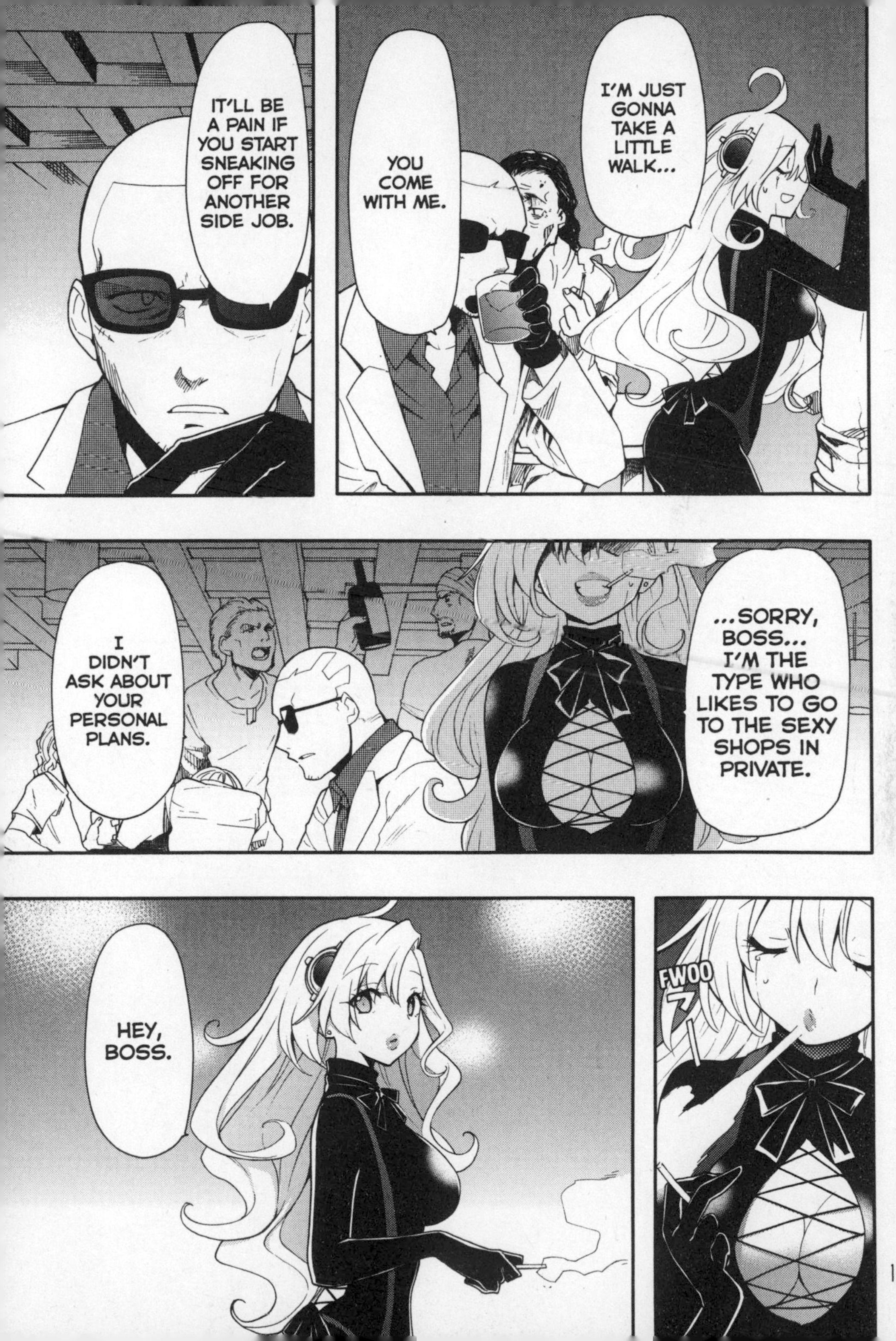
I'M JUST GONNA TAKE A LITTLE WALK...
YOU COME WITH ME.
IT'LL BE A PAIN IF YOU START SNEAKING OFF FOR ANOTHER SIDE JOB.
...SORRY, BOSS... I'M THE TYPE WHO LIKES TO GO TO THE SEXY SHOPS IN PRIVATE.
I DIDN'T ASK ABOUT YOUR PERSONAL PLANS.
FWOO
HEY, BOSS.

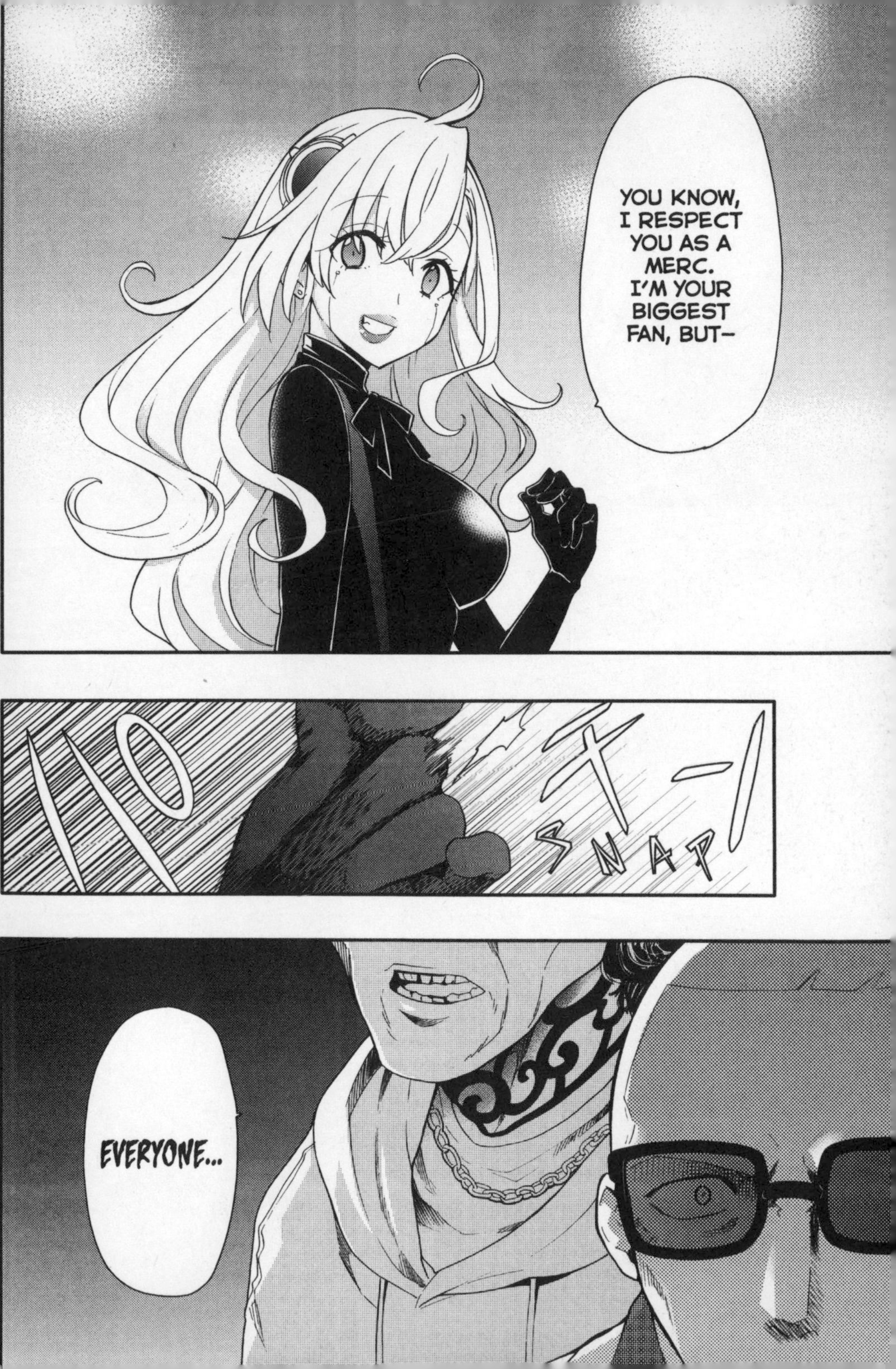
YOU KNOW, I RESPECT YOU AS A MERC. I'M YOUR BIGGEST FAN, BUT–
SNAP
EVERYONE...

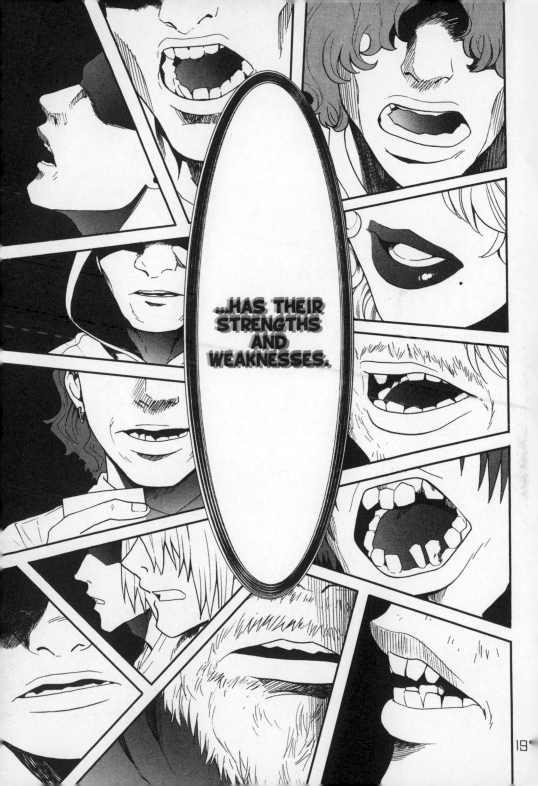

...HAS THEIR STRENGTHS AND WEAKNESSES.

19

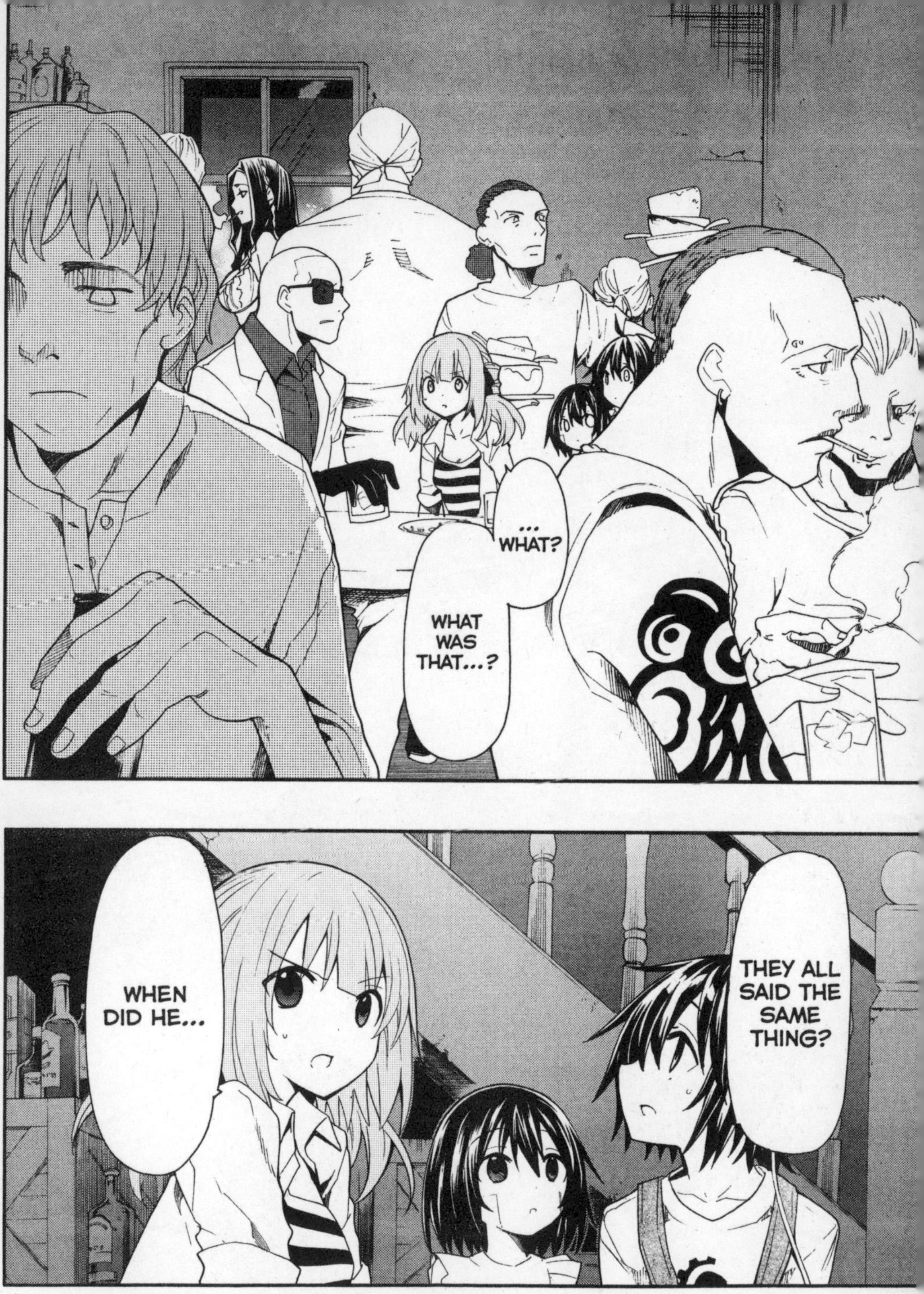
... WHAT?
WHAT WAS THAT...?
THEY ALL SAID THE SAME THING?
WHEN DID HE...

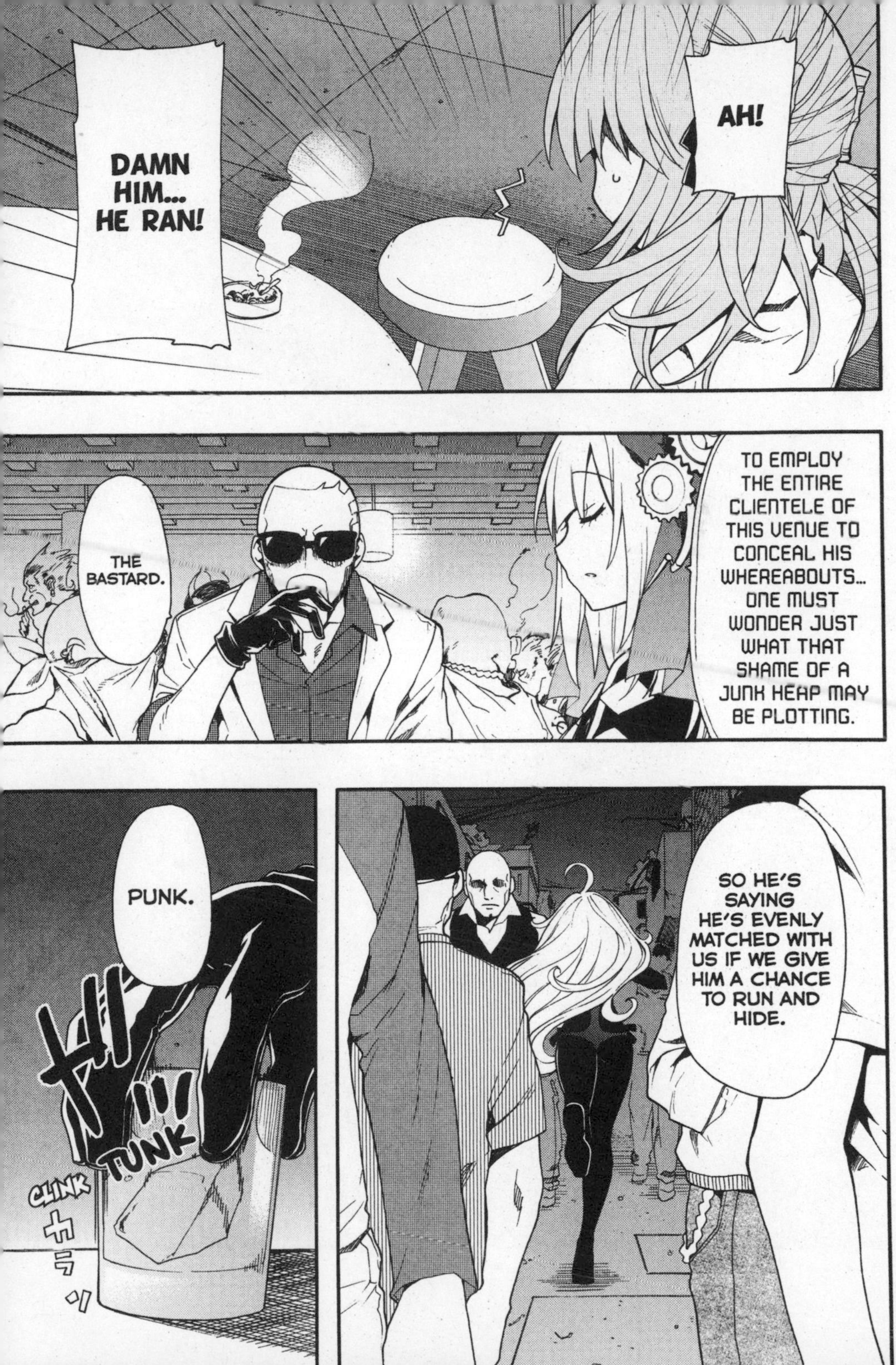
AH!
DAMN HIM... HE RAN!
TO EMPLOY THE ENTIRE CLIENTELE OF THIS VENUE TO CONCEAL HIS WHEREABOUTS... ONE MUST WONDER JUST WHAT THAT SHAME OF A JUNK HEAP MAY BE PLOTTING.
THE BASTARD.
SO HE'S SAYING HE'S EVENLY MATCHED WITH US IF WE GIVE HIM A CHANCE TO RUN AND HIDE.
PUNK.
TUNK
CLINK

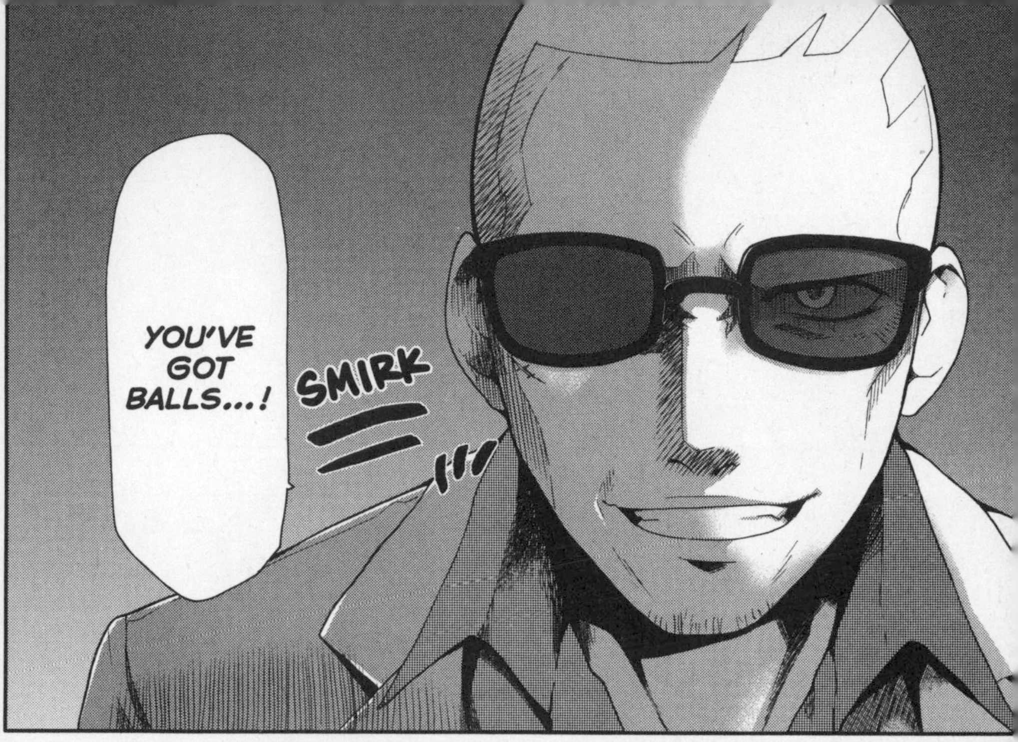
YOU'VE GOT BALLS...!
SMIRK

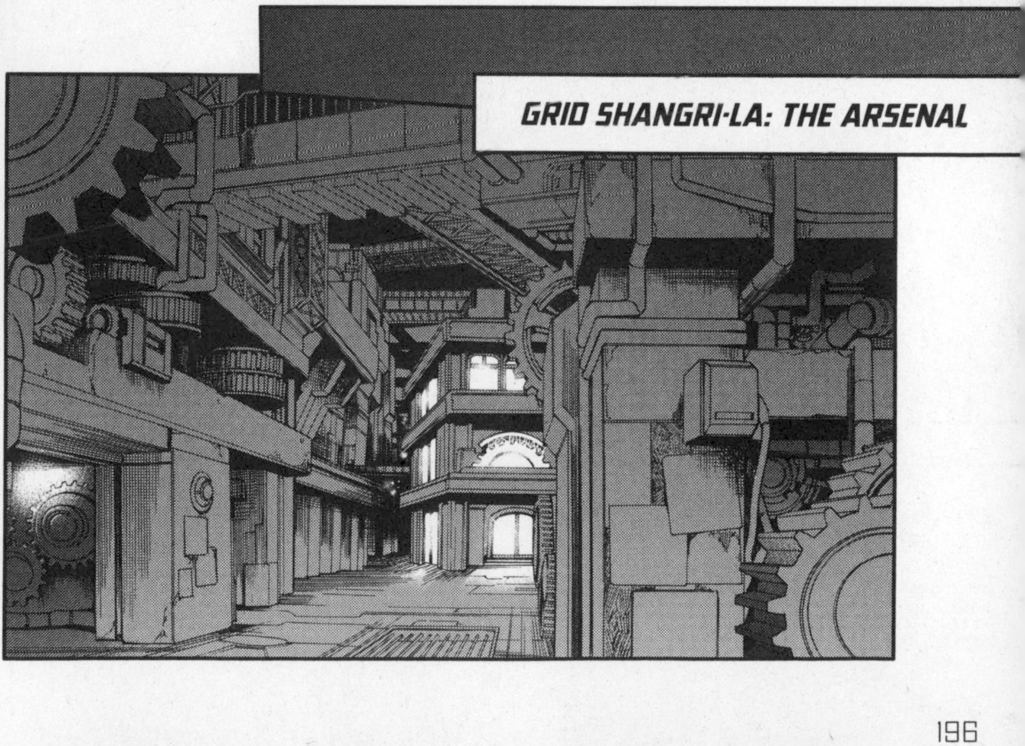
GRID SHANGRI-LA: THE ARSENAL

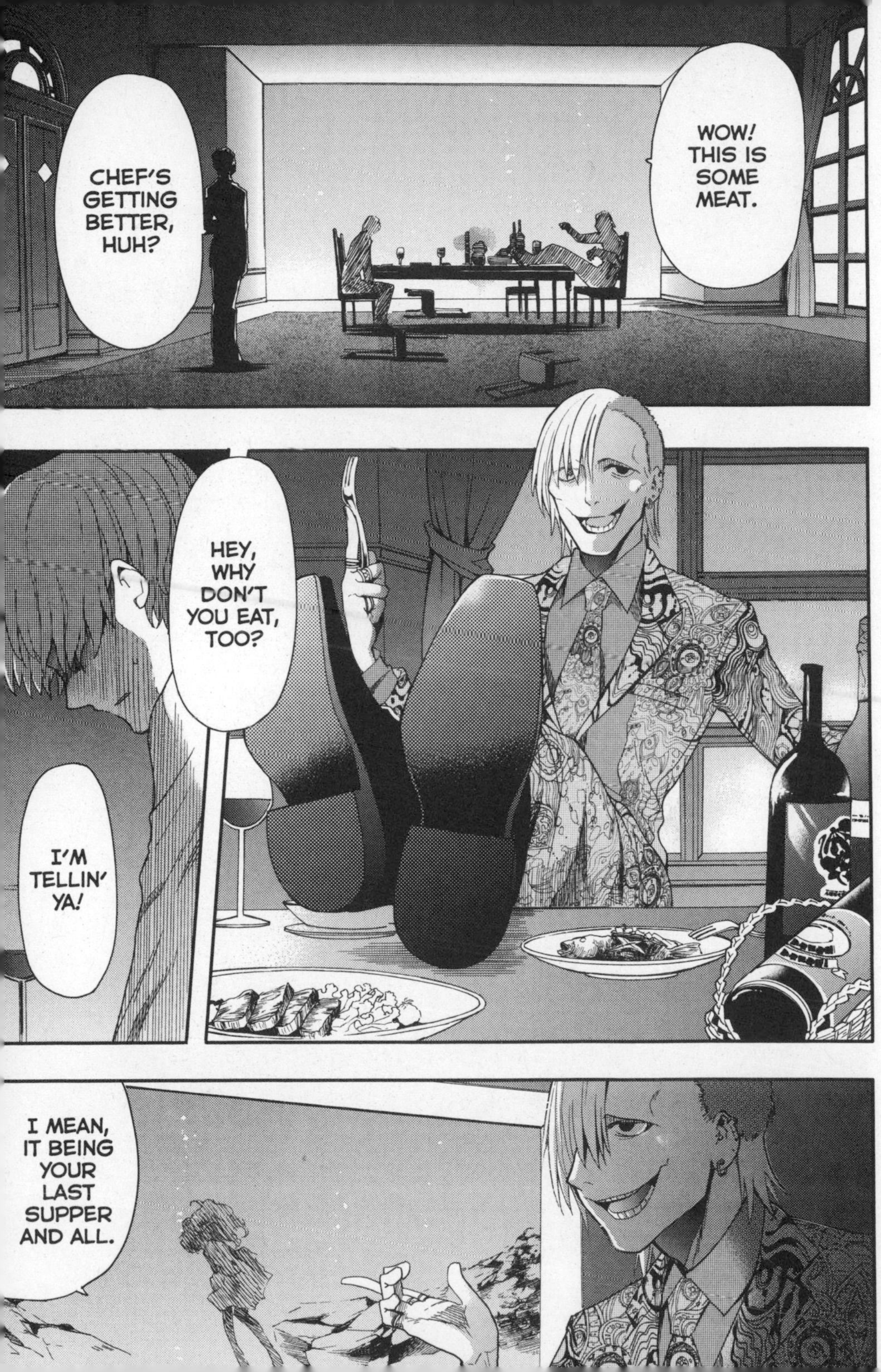
WOW! THIS IS SOME MEAT.
CHEF'S GETTING BETTER, HUH?
HEY, WHY DON'T YOU EAT, TOO?
I'M TELLIN' YA!
I MEAN, IT BEING YOUR LAST SUPPER AND ALL.

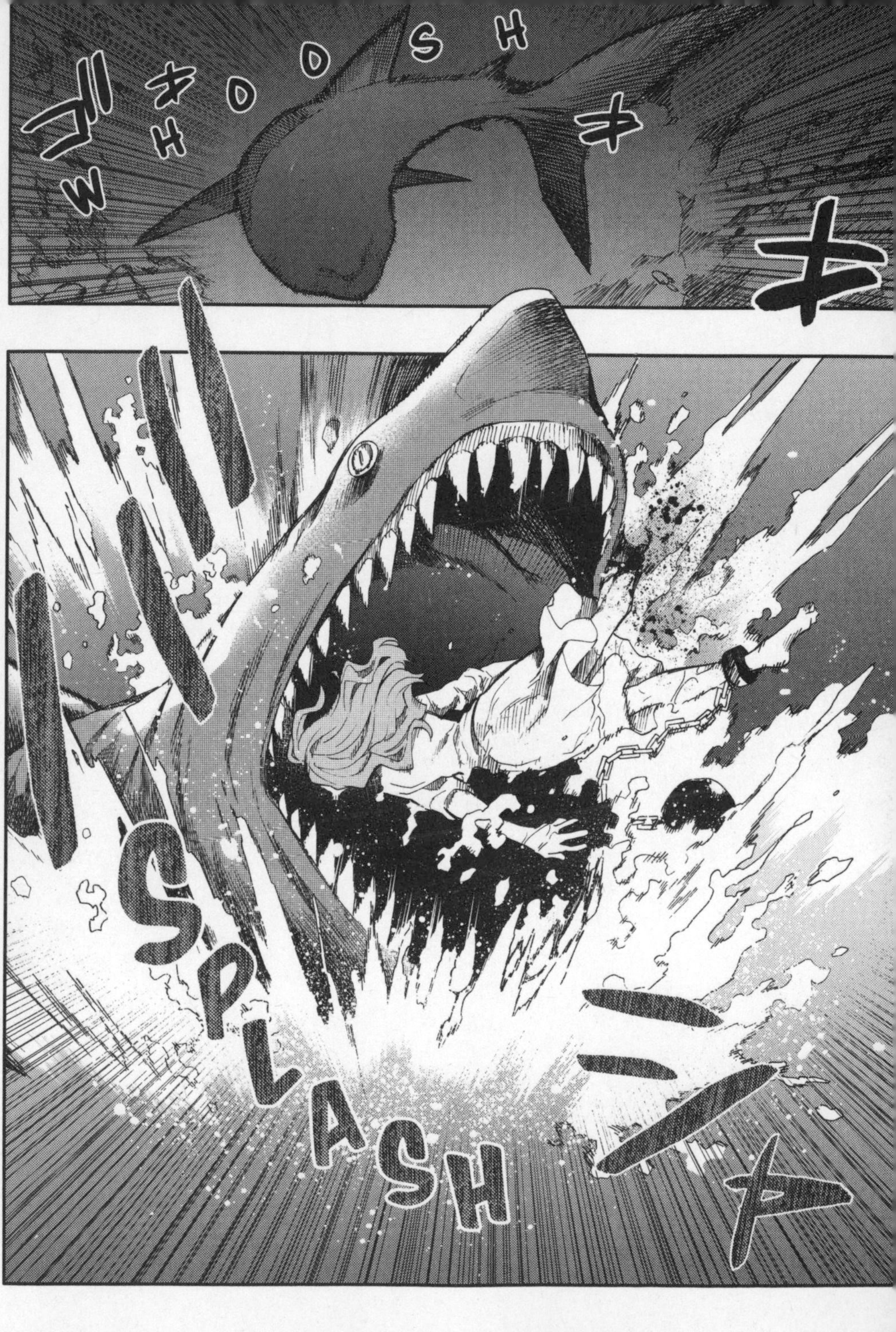
WHOOSH
SPLASH

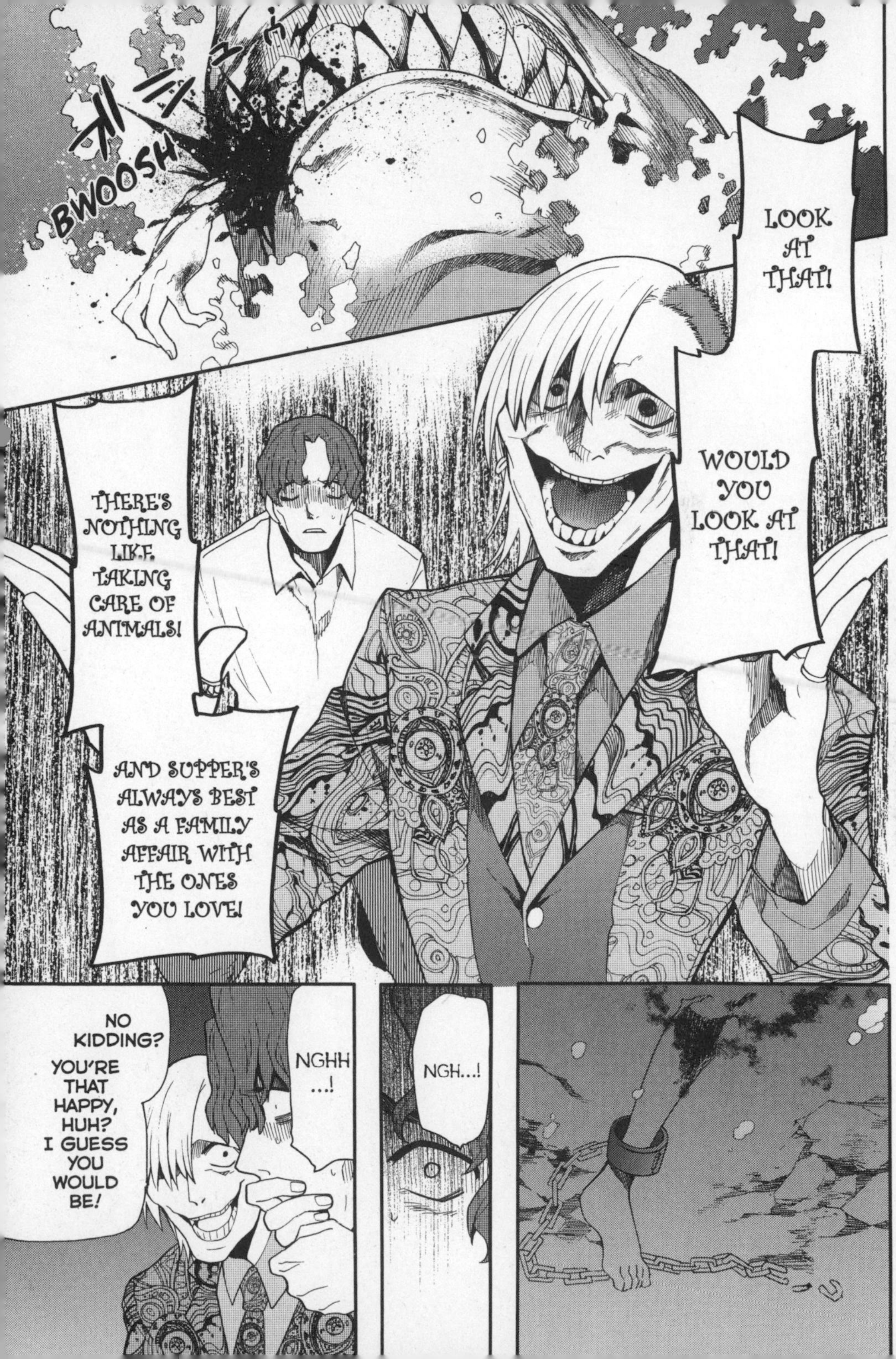
BWOOSH
LOOK AT THAT!
WOULD YOU LOOK AT THAT!
THERE'S NOTHING LIKE TAKING CARE OF ANIMALS!
AND SUPPER'S ALWAYS BEST AS A FAMILY AFFAIR WITH THE ONES YOU LOVE!
NGH...!
NGHH...!
NO KIDDING?
YOU'RE THAT HAPPY, HUH? I GUESS YOU WOULD BE!

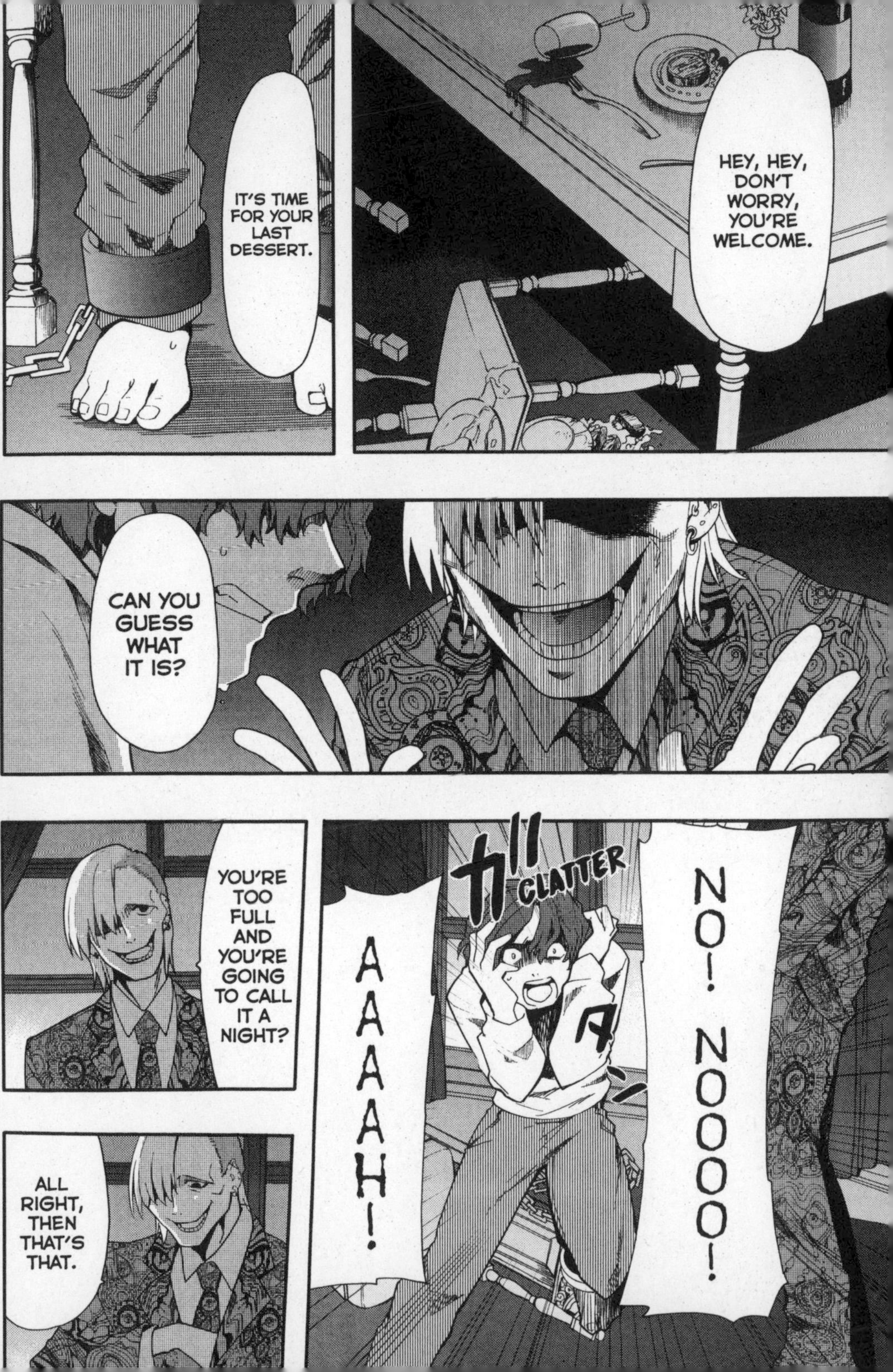
HEY, HEY, DON'T WORRY, YOU'RE WELCOME.
IT'S TIME FOR YOUR LAST DESSERT.
CAN YOU GUESS WHAT IT IS?
NO! NOOOO!
CLATTER
AAAAAH!
YOU'RE TOO FULL AND YOU'RE GOING TO CALL IT A NIGHT?
ALL RIGHT, THEN THAT'S THAT.

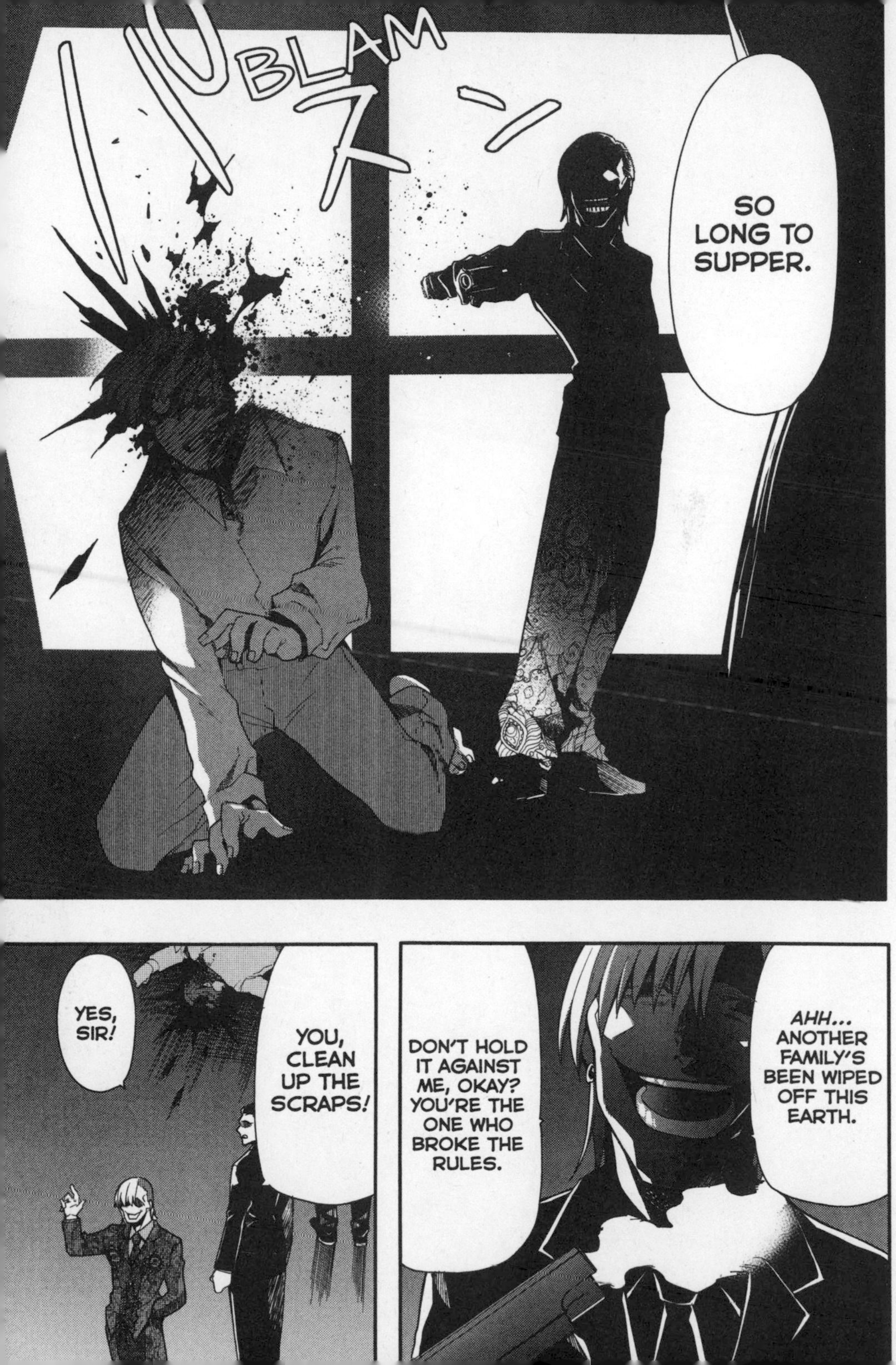
BLAM
SO LONG TO SUPPER.
AHH... ANOTHER FAMILY'S BEEN WIPED OFF THIS EARTH.
DON'T HOLD IT AGAINST ME, OKAY? YOU'RE THE ONE WHO BROKE THE RULES.
YOU, CLEAN UP THE SCRAPS!
YES, SIR!

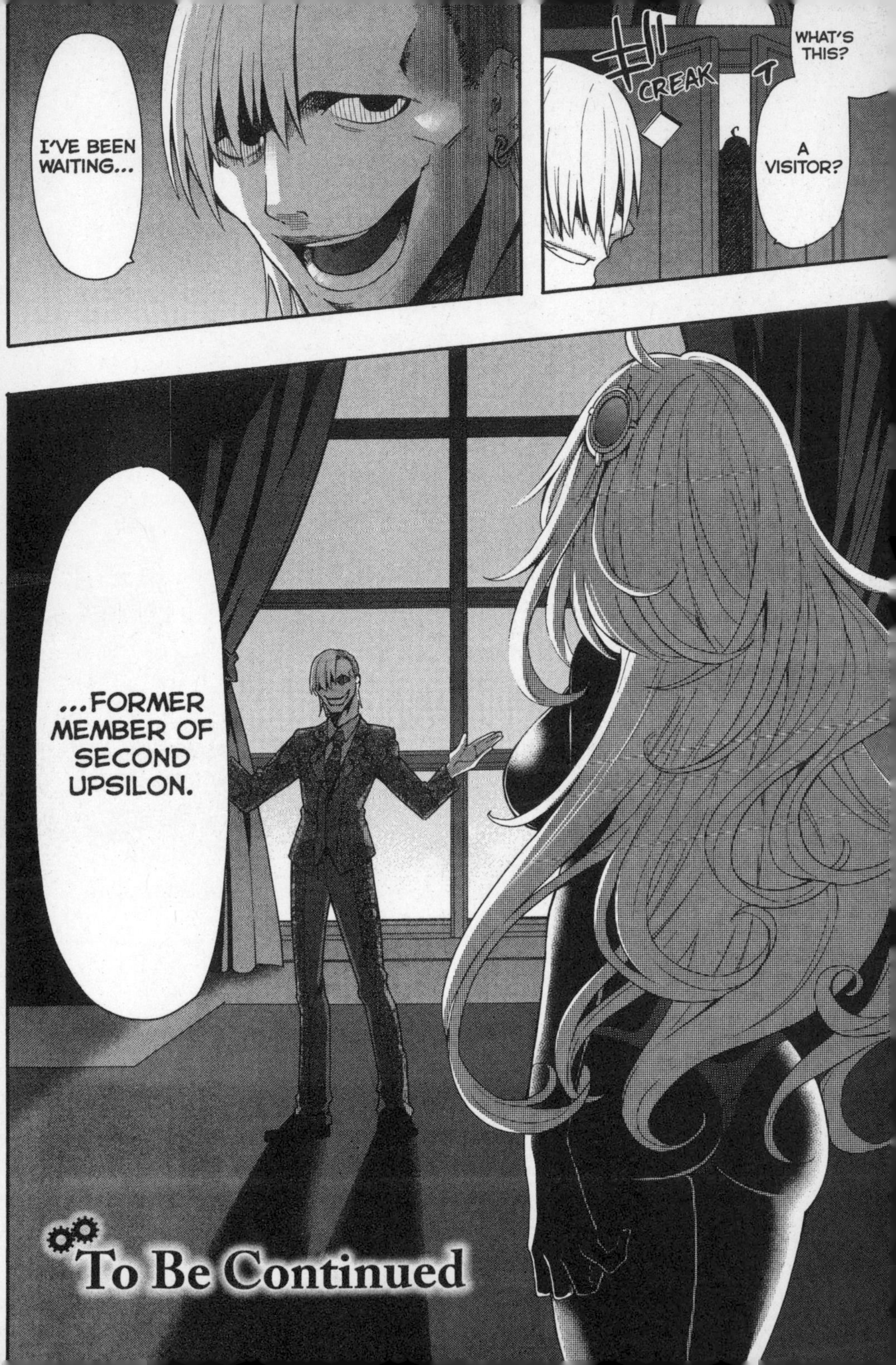
WHAT'S THIS?
CREAK
A VISITOR?
I'VE BEEN WAITING...
...FORMER MEMBER OF SECOND UPSILON.
To Be Continued

CLOCKWORK PLANET

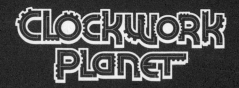

Yuu Kamiya & Tsubaki Himana

Afterword

: Ya know, lately, I've been thinking, and I've been reading philosophy again.

: Now you're not even bothering with the formalities at all... Oh hey, this is Tsubaki, called here to put my failure at life display as "something funny." So, Mr. Kamiya, what have you been thinking about?

: Yeah, I was thinking, post-medieval Western philosophy is more or less synonymous with German philosophy.

: Uh, hey, look. I'm not really that interested in this crap, so let's—

: And when you think about it, most of those German philosophers—Leibniz, Nietzsche, Schopenhauer, all those rs—they were all losers, leeches, outcasts, lifetime virgins, and forever alones.

: (*with great interest*) Yeah, and? Continue.

: So. Kant was single all his life and probably never got any—and this is what he had to say.

> Love is a matter of feeling, not of will or volition, and I cannot love because I will to do so, still less because I ought.
> —Immanuel Kant (1724–1804)

: See—basically, he's saying, "Love? If I could have, I would have, stupid." (*Gulps.*)

H: ...A forever alone (and possibly virgin) speaks on love... I sense darkness. (*Gulps.*)

K: Right? (*Gulps.*) And consider his major works: *Critique of Pure Reason*, *Critique of Practical ason*, *Critique of Judgment*. All the guy can do is critique. He says we can't trust anything, not r thoughts nor our judgment.

H: (*convinced*) So he's basically just a twisted old grump with darkness in his heart.

K: Right, so. Recently, I came into contact with a philosopher who said something very similar, ay?

H: Huh... You've met a curmudgeon of darkness worthy of being called the modern Kant?

K: Yes... And he said to me in earnest, "What is love? Could it be that what I want is not love, t servitude?" His name was Tsubaki Himana. I suspect he may have been German. (*A brilliant duction.*)

H: ...Hmm. That is indeed an intriguing hypothesis. If correct, it would historically justify my atus as a loser, an outcast, and a virgin who's forever alone, would it not?!

K: I will respectfully ignore the fact that you ignored the "leech" part. So what do you think?

H: The thing is, however—everyone in my family going back for generations, me, my parents, en the new bride, we're all Japanese...

K: Bride?

H: We had the wedding just a while ago.

H: For my little *brother*. Don't look at me like I've finally lost it.

K: Uh, oh! I—I see, your brother! Holy—I mean, congratulations, that's nice, isn't it?!

H: Yes...the third son. Who's about a decade younger than me. Who, unlike me, has charged ead in the path of life and gotten some like it's nothing. He went ahead and got married with etty much no problems at all. Therefore, as his kin in the first degree, I must regretfully infer at I am not German. (*A brilliant deduction.*)

K: ...Uh, well, what were you doing around then, big brother? Weren't you getting along with e staff of the anime that just concluded?

H: Don't they say solitude makes people stronger? Check it out, I'm getting stronger physically. y dumbbells listen to me. My muscles will never betray me.

K: Uh, uhh... Hey, hold on! A-as Kant also said—!

> I am alone; I am free; I am lord of myself.

H: ...I wonder, what is the role of the lord of a realm without people? I thought I was hitting it off so well with the staff hen the anime was being produced and when it was airing. Now my realm is empty except for my dumbbells. What should ch a lord do? (*A contemplation broader than that of love.*)

K: ...He should, maybe, find enlightenment? Shut himself away like Zarathustra or something? And then announce to the orld that "God is dead." In particular—maybe announce to the world the fifth volume of the light novels, which the manga as almost caught up to. (*A pressing reality.*)

H: ...Excuse me. What kind of lord has to meet deadlines? Am I truly free? (*Philosophy.*)

K: Well, with that! I hope to see you soon in the afterword of the fifth *Clockwork Planet* light novel!

H: I understand now. This must be absolute destiny [flagged]! (*Philosophy.*)

AFTERWORD

Every time, my editor asks me, "How are you going to draw this?" I answer, "I have no idea..." But I'm glad that I was somehow able to manage the "finished fantasy," Naoto's "lesson," and the "terminal maneuver." I'm so relieved...!

The one regret I have was that I tearfully had to cut the scene where Marie finally accepts AnchoR. Anyway, they'll have a lot more interaction in the Shangri-La arc, so look forward to it! Halter's going to figure in big, too!

-Special Thanks

<Staff> Rin Nekoya, Miho Miyanishi, Kiyo Nekota
<Editor> Hiroshi Ogasawara
<Designer> Ryo Hiiragi
　　　　　(I.S.W Designing)

KURO
2017.9.8

Translation Notes

CLICK CLOCK, pages 41-42
The original sound effect, *kachi kochi*, is the same as for *tick tock* but also applies to putting metal parts together. Outside of this work, *tick tock* is usually *kachi kachi*, but in *Clockwork Planet* the sound of clockwork is frequently represented as *kachi kochi*. In fact, it is the very first phrase of the first novel.

Absolute destiny [flagged], page 204
In the Japanese, Himana is flagged for saying the full title of "*zettai unmei mokushiroku*" (*Absolute Destiny: Apocalypse*), which is an original song by J.A. Seazer from the *Revolutionary Girl Utena* soundtrack.

CLOCKWORK PLANET

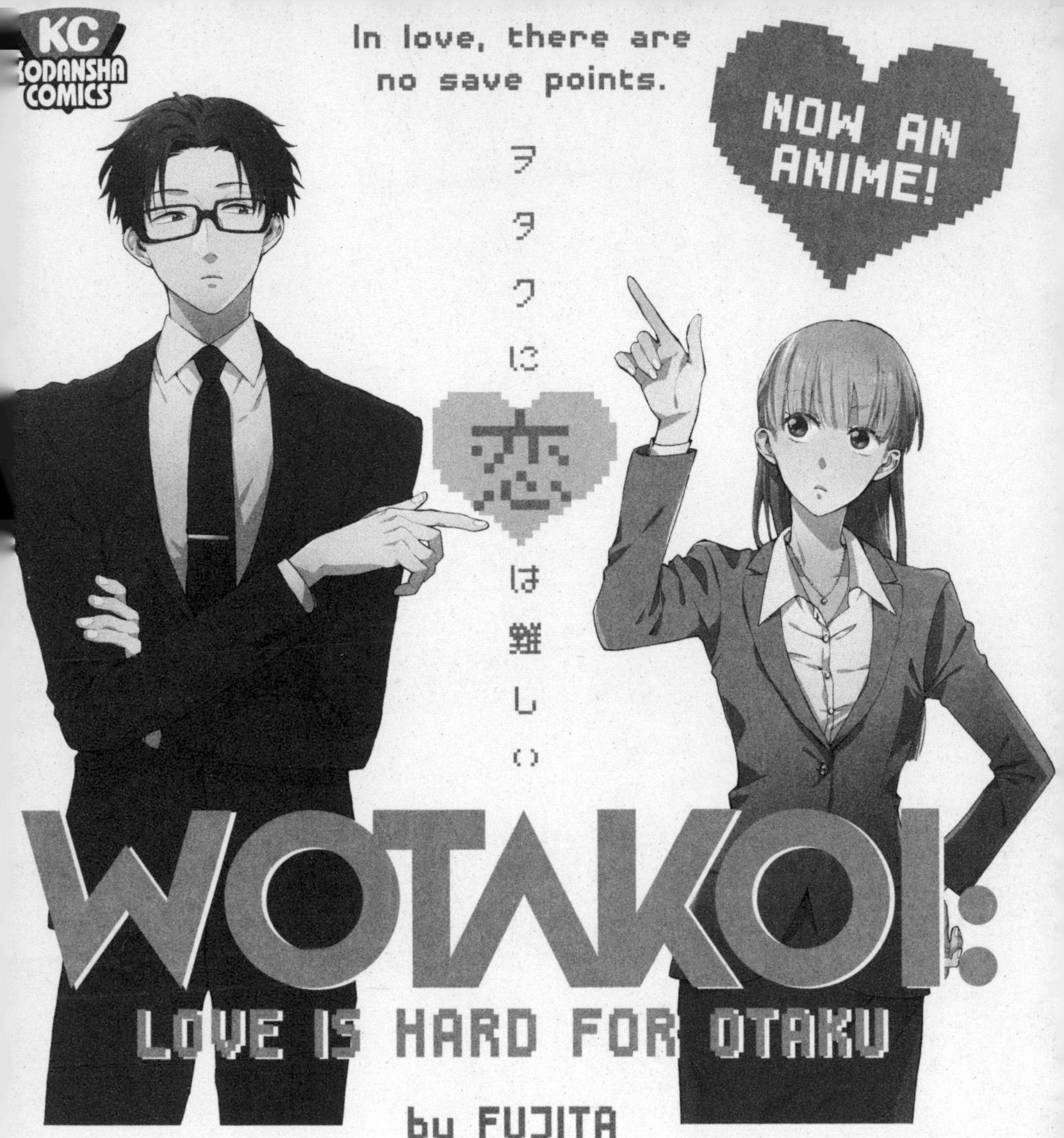
KC
KODANSHA COMICS
In love, there are no save points.
NOW AN ANIME!
ヲタクに恋は難しい
WOTAKOI:
LOVE IS HARD FOR OTAKU
by FUJITA

Narumi has had it rough: Every boyfriend she's had dumped her once they found out she was an otaku, so she's gone to great lengths to hide it. At her new job, she bumps into Hirotaka, her childhood friend and fellow otaku. When Hirotaka almost gets her secret outed at work, she comes up with a plan to keep him quiet. But he comes up with a counter-proposal: Why doesn't she just date him instead?

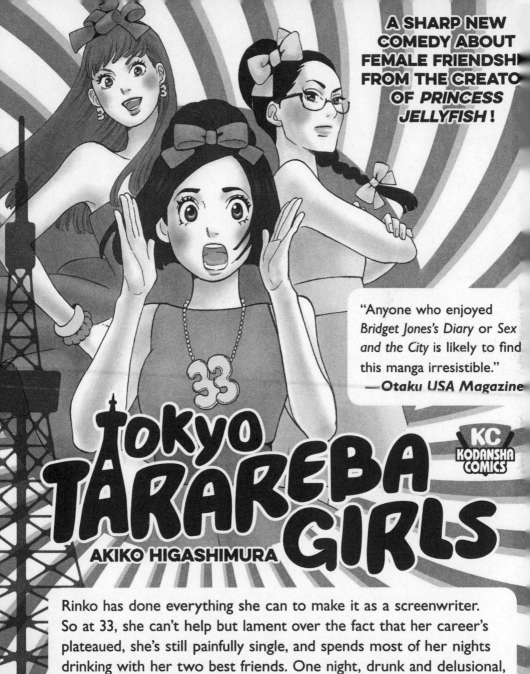

A SHARP NEW COMEDY ABOUT FEMALE FRIENDSHI[P] FROM THE CREATO[R] OF *PRINCESS JELLYFISH*!

"Anyone who enjoyed *Bridget Jones's Diary* or *Sex and the City* is likely to find this manga irresistible."
—*Otaku USA Magazine*

Tokyo TARAREBA GIRLS
AKIKO HIGASHIMURA

Rinko has done everything she can to make it as a screenwriter. So at 33, she can't help but lament over the fact that her career's plateaued, she's still painfully single, and spends most of her nights drinking with her two best friends. One night, drunk and delusional, Rinko swears to get married by the time the Tokyo Olympics roll around in 2020. But finding a man—or love—may be a cutthroat, dirty job for a romantic at heart!

ANIME COMING OUT SUMMER 2018!

Mikami's middle age hasn't gone as he planned: He never found a girlfriend, he got stuck in a dead-end job, and he was abruptly stabbed to death in the street at 37. So when he wakes up in a new world straight out of a fantasy RPG, he's disappointed, but not exactly surprised to find that he's facing down a dragon, not as a knight or a wizard, but as a blind slime monster. But there are chances for even a slime to become a hero...

"A fun adventure that ntasy readers will relate to and enjoy." —AiPT!

THAT TIME I GOT REINCARNATED AS A SLIME

Princess Jellyfish

Akiko Higashimura

ALSO AN ANIME!

Tsukimi Kurashita is fascinated with jellyfish. She's loved them from a young age and has carried that love with her to her new life in the big city of Tokyo. There, she resides in Amamizukan, a safe-haven for geek girls where no boys are allowed. One day, Tsukimi crosses paths with a beautiful and fashionable woman, but there's much more to this woman than her trendy clothes...!

ANIME COMING SUMMER 2018

The award-winning manga about what happens inside you!

"Far more entertaining than it ought to be... What kid doesn't want to think that every time they sneeze, a torpedo shoots out their nose?"

—Anime News Network

Strep throat! Hay fever! Influenza! The world is a dangerous place for a red blood cell just trying to get her deliveries finished. Fortunately, she's not alone. She's got a whole human body's worth of cells ready to help out! The mysterious white blood cell, the buff and brash killer T cell, the nerdy neuron, even the cute little platelets— everyone's got to come together if they want to keep you healthy!

Cells at Work!

はたらく細胞

By Akane Shimizu

KC

KODANSHA
COMICS

Japan's most powerful spirit medium delves into the ghost world's greatest mysteries!

Story by Kyo Shirodaira, famed author of mystery fiction and creator of *Spiral*, *Blast of Tempest*, and *The Record of a Fallen Vampire*.

Both touched by spirits called yôkai, Kotoko and Kurô have gained unique superhuman powers. But to gain her powers Kotoko has given up an eye and a leg, and Kurô's personal life is in shambles. So when Kotoko suggests they team up to deal with renegades from the spirit world, Kurô doesn't have many other choices, but Kotoko might just have a few ulterior motives...

IN/SPECTRE

STORY BY KYO SHIRODAIRA
ART BY CHASHIBA KATASE

A Kodansha Comics Trade Paperback Original
Clockwork Planet volume 8 copyright © 2017 Yuu Kamiya/Tsubaki Himana/Sino/Kuro
English translation copyright © 2018 Yuu Kamiya/Tsubaki Himana/Sino/Kuro
All rights reserved.

Published in the United States by Kodansha Comics, an imprint of
Kodansha USA Publishing, LLC, New York.

Publication rights for this English edition arranged through
Kodansha Ltd, Tokyo.

First published in Japan in 2017 by Kodansha Ltd., Tokyo

ISBN 978-1-63236-620-7

Printed in the United States of America.

www.kodanshacomics.com

9 8 7 6 5 4 3 2 1
Translation: Daniel Komen
Lettering: David Yoo
Editing: Haruko Hashimoto
Kodansha Comics edition cover design by Phil Balsman